Video Game Design FOUNDATIONS

D. Michael Ploor, MBA
National Board Certified Teacher
STEM Curriculum Integration Specialist
School District of Hillsborough County
Tampa, Florida

Publisher
The Goodheart-Willcox Company, Inc.
Tinley Park, Illinois
www.g-w.com

Introduction

*V*ideo Game Design Foundations provides students with a complete understanding of the technological and creative aspects of video game design in an easy-to-follow format. This "turnkey" curriculum is the complete guide to immersion in the field, from beginning each game build project through completion, integration, and marketing. Simulated design teams will have the opportunity to learn all aspects of team building, including the creative, business, and technological components required to launch a new video game system.

Students will participate in a simulation of a real video game design team, seeing each project from origination to fruition. This provides a valuable lesson in team building that can be applied to any other aspect of the technology and engineering industries in real-life future careers.

Pivotal to the success of any employee is the application of soft skills and the ability to work on teams. Creative lessons take the students through a series of self-improvement lessons relevant to the workforce of today. Through self-assessment and critical analysis, students will be better able to evaluate themselves and others.

In addition to training in soft skill, students will develop mastery in the hard skills of art, science, and technology needed to design video games. In the end, students will be technically proficient and will demonstrate learning by constructing an original game build.

Video Game Design Foundations presents content in ten chapters, with each chapter acting as a building block that supports the next skill learned. This allows students to learn the objective of each lesson, practice the corresponding skill, and lay the foundation on which to acquire the next skill set.

You are encouraged to study *Video Game Design Foundations* to expand your understanding of the role technology plays in modern society and the future of high-quality jobs. Applying the key lessons, skills, and content of this curriculum will provide great insight into a growing technological society and provide a solid foundation demanded for success in the future world of technology.

The textbook provides the theory of video game design. It aligns with the International Game Developers Association (IGDA) recommended educational framework. Beginning with discussions on teamwork, the student learns about gaming, computerized gaming, and the evolution of gaming. Students then learn about artistic aspects of perspective, design, and animation. The technical aspects of collision theory and programming logic are discussed, followed by explanations of the hardware of video games. The text concludes with explanations of the global economy and supply chains.

STEM

Science, technology, engineering, and mathematics (STEM) is the foundation on which our 21st century society builds and maintains economic growth. This curriculum integrates the *rigor* and *relevance* of STEM into fun and exciting classroom lessons. Taking rigor from each of the core areas of study and placing it in the context of video game design allows students to recognize the relevance of study. Students will gain experience in the skills needed for most of the new jobs projected over the next two decades.

Through application and integration of all core areas of language arts, science, mathematics, and social sciences, students become engaged in learning through doing. Application and synthesis levels of learning are maintained for a truly unique student experience. Through this meaningful engagement in learning, students become better in all core subject areas and the foundations of technology as presented in this text.

About the Author

D. Michael Ploor is the author of three textbooks on the subject of video game design: *Introduction to Video Game Design, Video Game Design Foundations,* and *Video Game Design Composition.* He is a National Board Certified Teacher in Career and Technical Education and holds an MBA degree from the University of South Florida. He maintains professional teaching credentials in Business Education (6–12) and Education Media Specialist (K–12). He is currently employed by the School District of Hillsborough County in Tampa, Florida, where he has been teaching video game design at the high school and middle school levels since 2001.

Mr. Ploor developed STEM curriculum while serving as the lead teacher in the Career Academy of Computer Game Design at Middleton Magnet STEM High School. Mr. Ploor has applied his skills as a STEM Curriculum Integration Specialist in designing innovative curriculum and by collaborating to construct the state standards for video game design in several states. He has also been instrumental in authoring competitive events for Career and Technical Student Organizations such as the Future Business Leaders of America (FBLA) and Phi Beta Lambda (PBL). He continues to work closely with many game design studios, producers, and software developers to align educational objectives to workplace-ready skills. In addition to publishing textbooks and lessons, Mr. Ploor provides professional development as a frequent presenter at regional and national conferences to promote STEM education and video game design curriculum for the high school and middle school levels.

Reviewers

The author and publisher would like to thank the following individuals for their review of the materials in this teaching package.

Henrietta I. Ortiz
Teacher
Sheridan Technical Center
Hollywood, Florida

John Wagner
Teacher
North Country Career Center
Newport, Vermont

Brief Contents

Expanded Table of Contents

Chapter 5

Chapter 6

Game Systems, Personal Computers, and Hardware **204**

Chapter 7

Play and Game Culture **240**

Chapter 8

Reverse Engineering and Professional Reviews 272

Chapter 9

Large-Scale Design Process 300

Chapter 10

Content Connected

Formative Assessment

Review Your Knowledge

These questions provide an opportunity to measure your knowledge of the content presented in the chapter. Included are vocabulary questions.

Apply Your STEM Knowledge

This section challenges you to apply the knowledge you have gained in the chapter and previous chapters to cross-curricular activities.

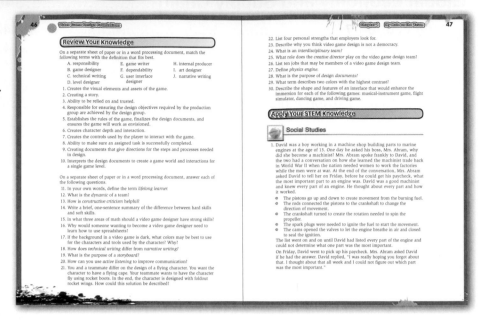

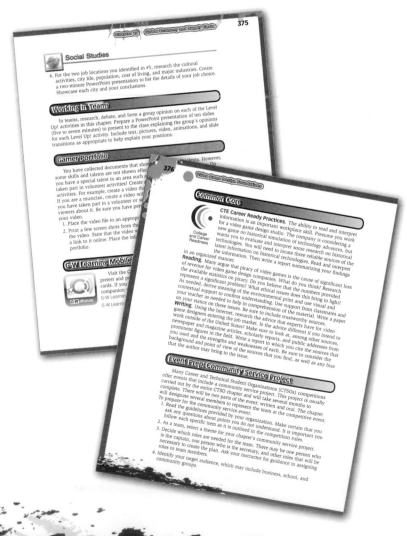

End-of-Chapter Activities

Working in Teams

These activities require you to work collaboratively with a team to apply skills and knowledge in the content presented in the chapter.

Gamer Portfolio

An important part of searching for a job in the video game design field is having a portfolio of your work to show to employers or for college admissions. The Gamer Portfolio feature guides you through starting to build a portfolio.

Common Core

These activities provide real-world literacy skills in the areas of reading, writing, speaking, listening, and career and technical education to help prepare you for life beyond high school.

Event Prep

The Event Prep features provide guidance for preparing for Career and Technical Student Organization (CTSO) competitions.

Features Spotlighted

Reading Prep

A Reading Prep feature opens each chapter to engage you in the content to be presented in the chapter. These features are called out by the College and Career Readiness icon.

College and Career Readiness

Reading Prep. In preparation for reading the chapter, read a newspaper or magazine article on the latest development in game design or on a recently released game system. Summarize the information. As you read, keep in mind the author's main points and conclusions.

Green Gamer

The Green Gamer features share tips on how a gamer or video game design studio can engage in best practices for the environment.

Green Gamer

Saving money is at the top of the list for many schools as well as consumers. Up to 25 percent of energy costs can be saved by simply turning off equipment when not in use. Turn off all computers and game consoles each evening to save energy. Make sure the lights are off whenever you leave a room or if there is enough natural light to brighten the room.

Ethical Gamer

The Ethical Gamer features provide information related to ethic issues facing gamers and video game design studios.

Ethical Gamer

Most schools establish a set of ethics that outlines acceptable behavior when interacting with other students and school personnel. As a student, it is important to know the code of ethics for your school so you can behave in a correct manner.

Cheat Code

Cheat Codes provide vocabulary definitions for terms not defined in the context of the reading materials.

CHEAT CODE: BALANCE

Your life should have balance in the activities you do. There should be a mix of physical activities, mental activities, and entertainment/relaxation activities. Spending too much time on one type of activity means the other types are being neglected.

Level Up!

The Level Up! features provide an opportunity to think about the material just presented and to engage in an activity at the point of learning.

Think about a task that you are really good at performing. It might be shooting a basketball, doing a math problem, or anything else. Chances are you were not a superstar on your first attempt at doing this task. How did practice make you better?

Software Design Guide

The available software design guide (SDG) provides the hands-on application of the theory presented in the textbook. The SDG should be considered an integral part of the curriculum. It is where you take the theory learned in the textbook and use that knowledge to build video games. Working in simulated design teams, you will experience all aspects of video game design, from the planning stages, through the design and programming, and concluding with a capstone project.

Each chapter in the SDG is correlated to the textbook chapter. There are several activities for each chapter. Many of the activities are scripted game builds. These types of activities conclude with review questions. The last chapter in the SDG is a capstone project that requires you to apply all of the knowledge you acquired in the textbook and SDG.

Learning objectives for each chapter.

Chapter 5
Collision Theory and Logic

Objectives

After completing this chapter, you will be able to:
- Use computer tools to create programming and artwork for a video game.
- Create a playable game using a game engine.
- Create animated objects.
- Debug a video game build.
- Engage in constructive criticism.
- Explain different user interface designs for avatar movement.

You Must Find: KEY

Daily bellwork to start each class period.

Bellwork

Day	Date	Activity
1		Complete the anticip chapter.
2		A computer progr cause-and-effect than action-reac in programming statement?
3		Which logic o condition is f
4		Write a log state how chicken v
5		Describe a coyot does n
6		Which hold the
7		W F t
8		
9		
10		

Figure 1

Learning objective for lesson. Provides an overview of the situation for the lesson. Step-by-step instructions for the game build in the lesson.

Name: _____
Date: _____
Class: _____

Activity 5-1
Logic and Collision in Practice

Objective

Students will use a game engine to create a playable video game. Students will be able to apply logic and collisio

Situation

You are a ne game engine tecl provided to buil a plane while av

How to Be

Launch The doing this, if nee

Setting the E
1. Click the N
2. Double-clic

New

Name: _____
Date: _____
Class: _____

Anticipation Guide

Before Reading the Chapter

Read each statement in the table below. In the column titled Before Reading, writ if you agree with the statement or F if you disagree with the statement.

After Reading the Chapter

Re-read each statement in the table below. In the column titled After Reading, writ if you agree with the statement or F if you disagree with the statement. Be prepared to justify your answers in a class discussion.

Before Reading	Statement	After Reading
	Collision theory is the rules concerning how objects react in games when they touch each other.	
	A major component of logic is the "because" statement.	
	Most logic in games can be expressed as a cause-and-effect relationship.	
	Programmers refer to a path where a folder is located as a program tree.	
	It is not possible to combine logic statements. Each condition must be individually programmed!	
	The Games Factory 2 is an object-based programming product.	

Anticipation guide for each chapter tracks learning progress from before the lesson to after completion of the lesson.

Technology Applied

Technology is an important part of your world. So, it should be part of your everyday learning. In this text and the available software design guide, you will find the following.

- A pretest and posttest are provided for each textbook chapter for self-assessment. These can be accessed by scanning the QR code to visit the mobile site or you can visit the companion website to take the test.
- Data files needed for the game builds in the software design guide are provided on the companion website.
- Samples of the completed game builds in the software design guide are provided on the companion website.

G-W Learning Companion Website

www.g-wlearning.com

The G-W Learning companion website for *Video Game Design Foundations* is a study reference that contains matching vocabulary games, e-flash cards, and interactive quizzes. Also included are data files for the game builds in the software design guide, as well as sample game builds.

G-W Learning companion website:

www.g-wlearning.com

G-W Learning Mobile Site

The G-W Learning mobile site* is a study reference to use when you are on the go. The mobile site is easy to read, easy to use, and fine-tuned for quick access.

For *Video Game Design Foundations,* the G-W Learning mobile site contains chapter pretests and posttests and e-flash card vocabulary practices. If you do not have a smartphone, these same features can be accessed using an Internet browser to visit the G-W Learning companion website.

G-W Learning mobile website:

www.m.g-wlearning.com

Scan now!

Goodheart-Willcox QR Codes

This Goodheart-Willcox product contains QR codes*, or quick response codes. These codes can be scanned with a smartphone bar code reader to access information or online features. For more information on using QR codes and a recommended QR reader, visit the G-W Learning companion website at www.g-wlearning.com.

Scan now!

*An Internet connection is required to access the QR code destinations. Data-transfer rates may apply. Check with your Internet service provider for information on your data-transfer rates.

Objectives

After completing this chapter, you will be able to:

- Define the roles and responsibilities of team members on a video game design team.
- Describe the effects of group dynamics and the importance of team building for a video game design team.
- Discuss methods of communication and scheduling for video game design teams.
- Explain the relationship between development schedule and budget constraints in video game design.

Chapter 1
My Role on the Team

A video game team is made up of many different people with unique skills and abilities that make the entire team stronger. All modern video games are developed by teams of individuals each of whom is a specialist in performing one part of the game build. This chapter explores the individual strengths and weaknesses of video game design team members, the hard skills and soft skills needed for a design team member, and a description of the roles and responsibilities of a design team.

Check Your Video Game IQ

Before you begin this chapter, see what you already know about video game design by taking the chapter pretest.

www.m.g-wlearning.com

www.g-wlearning.com

College and Career Readiness

Reading Prep. Review the table of contents for this text. Summarize the development of the content that is being presented from simple to complex ideas.

- Use listening, speaking, telecommunication, and nonverbal skills to effectively communicate with supervisors, coworkers, and customers.
- Create written communication appropriate for the video game development industry.
- Define terminology appropriate for the video game development industry.
- Engage in constructive criticism.
- Demonstrate personal and interpersonal skills appropriate for the workplace.
- Solve problems by collaborating with others.
- Identify personal strengths and weaknesses related to learning and work environments.
- Describe job requirements for a variety of occupations within the game development industry.

A **video game** is an electronic game that creates an artificial game environment on a video screen, as shown in **Figure 1-1.** A **video game designer** is a person involved in creating a video game. The successful video game designer needs to be able to do many different things. Additionally, the designer must interact well with others to get these things done. When you work as a video game designer, you will be part of a team. This requires you to not only have all of the skills needed to actually design the game, but also the skills needed to communicate and get along with your team. In that sense, a game designer is the ultimate "team player."

The video game designer needs a set of physical and mental skills to complete the tasks demanded by their employer and the game being developed. To obtain these skills, you may need to take classes and workshops to properly develop skills for areas in which you are not very strong. Taking classes and workshops to keep technology and employability skills fresh makes the designer a lifelong learner.

There is no end in sight for new technology. As ideas for new technology become reality, a designer will have to acquire a working knowledge of how to use the technology in building game worlds. Be prepared to update your skills in any technology and especially in game design. Reading technical manuals and trade magazines can help you stay in touch with new technologies.

Figure 1-1.   A modern video game has detailed graphics and realistic images. Notice how *EA Sports F1 2001* uses shadows for a better visual effect. A complex simulated environment of a racetrack was created for the game.

Qualities of a Game Designer and Team

Working in the **virtual world** of game design almost gives you the idea the perfect designer could be built. If it were possible to assemble all of the attributes of imagination, technology skills, mathematics, linguistics, artistry, knowledge, and communication into a single person, perhaps designers would not need to work in teams. But, the essential *dynamic* of a team is how the strengths and weaknesses of each member work together to create a better product. This dynamic makes a team better than a single, superhuman designer.

CHEAT CODE: VIRTUAL WORLD

A virtual world is the imaginary world created by computers. This imaginary place allows for both realistic and unrealistic events and characters. The designer determines how realistic the virtual world is that they create.

Each team member excels at certain things, but is not as good doing other things, as illustrated in **Figure 1-2.** For example, one team member may be very artistic, but lacks an understanding of programming. On the other hand, another team member may be a topnotch programmer, but is weaker in the artistic area. If a team is to meet its objective, other members of the team will have to help in the areas where one individual may not have fully developed skills. In doing so, team members must be respectful of everybody on the team. *Constructive criticism* can help move a project forward by providing positive reinforcement and offering possible improvements or solutions. Negative criticism leads to bad feelings and does not help the person or team.

Teams are designed with the strengths and weaknesses of people in mind, as seen in **Figure 1-3.** Someone who is great at creating artistic backgrounds may not be very good at building logic statements. Would this person need to be on the team? Of course, because the team needs a great artist.

Goodheart-Willcox Publisher

Figure 1-2.

People on design teams may look very different from you, but they are all needed to get the job done.

Figure 1-3.

Just like an athlete, you need to know what you are capable of doing well. Determining your strengths and weaknesses will prepare you for working well on a team. When you find you cannot do something, get help or, if needed, training. This will make you more valuable in the future.

Comstock

To overcome the weakness in writing logic statements, the team just needs to find someone with great logic skills. Together, the team is a better group because each team member is allowed to excel in their best area. You are not going to be the best at every aspect of design. The trick is to balance the design team to build up strengths and overcome some weaknesses.

Once you have your team built, you will need some means of effective communication to keep it working properly and to avoid conflict. Good communication skills will help keep the team on track and focused on the goal: the creation of a quality game. The next sections discuss some attributes of an individual game designer.

If you take a broader look at these skills, they are also the attributes of an effective design team.

1.1

Think about a time when you were on a team and you felt you were best to lead a certain task. While being respectful of others on your team, how could you have communicated that you had the strengths needed to do the job?

Hard Skills

Hard skills are the technical requirements for a job. Most hard skills can be obtained through training and research. On the opposite side are soft skills. Soft skills are social graces, attitudes, and behaviors employers want. These are discussed later in this chapter. Together hard skills and soft skills make up the character of the employee.

CHEAT CODE: HARD SKILLS

Many hard skills you will learn in high school or college. Skills in areas such as math, reading, writing, computer programming, art or graphics design, keyboarding, and so on, require training and practice to become an expert. Design teams expect you to have a portfolio to display these hard skills to show during your interview.

CASE STUDY

Sonic Heroes and Teamwork

Released in 2003 and 2004, *Sonic Heroes* introduced a new gameplay format that focused on teamwork. Instead of the standard mentality of a one-person army, this game focused on using a team with each member having unique strengths and weaknesses. Regardless if you chose team Sonic, Dark, Rose or Chaotix, your team consisted of characters with strength in either speed, flight, or power.

If you look at team Sonic and examine the strengths of the team members, you find Sonic has speed, Tails has flight, and Knuckles has power. During gameplay, the player must switch the lead character on the team to overcome certain obstacles and allow the rest of the team to follow. By forcing the player to determine which team member is best suited for each task, gameplay is enhanced. The player must use the strengths of all team members to achieve the goal of defeating Doctor Eggman.

When working on a design team or a cooperative team in your class, you will have to use the strengths of your team members to overcome obstacles. Each team member will have to take the lead in their area of strength. In this way, your differences are your strengths. Mixing your team with members who have different abilities and letting them each lead when their strengths are best suited for the situation will help everyone achieve the common goal of finishing the game.

Goodheart-Willcox Publisher

Sonic Heroes requires teamwork to complete the set goal.

Goodheart-Willcox Publisher

The player must use the strengths of each team member to achieve the goal of defeating Doctor Eggman.

Goodheart-Willcox Publisher

A team should have a good mix of skills and abilities.

CHEAT CODE: GAME WORLD

The game world is the setting in which gameplay takes place. In many cases, this is an imaginary place with make-believe rules where unique and original characters interact. In other cases, the game world may be based on a real place where actual laws of physics apply. A baseball game would be set in a stadium, but another game may seek to realistically recreate a World War II battlefield.

Imagination

Imagination is the act of creating a picture in your mind of something that does not exist or is not where you can see, hear, smell, or touch it. A game designer must be able to use imagination to create original settings, characters, and stories for the **game world**. To create this game world, you must first imagine the parts of the game.

Technology Competence

Technology competence, as related to video game design, is the ability to understand and use the newest computer/game platforms and programming/scripting languages. This skill is essential for video game design. Having a good level of competence in various technologies allows the designer to understand what can and cannot be done.

CHEAT CODE: RPG

A role-playing game, known simply as an RPG, is an action game in which the player takes on the role of a hero. The central premise of an RPG is for the player to gain strength and experience through quests, battles, and challenges.

For example, a designer might envision a game world for an **RPG** where the game player speaks into a microphone to communicate with the characters in the game or a game where the player must identify smell. These are great ideas and awesome immersion strategies, but they are not realistic goals based on current technology.

Immersion strategies are ideas that will connect the player to the action in the imaginary game world. Realistic graphics, storyline, plot, interesting characters, and player actions are all great immersion strategies used by designers with today's technology.

The designer may not need to have the technical skills to develop new technologies, but must understand the limits of current technology, as shown in **Figure 1-4.** Having said this, a designer must also attempt to push technology to the limits and beyond. Without attempts to do more than has been done before, we would all still be playing tic-tac-toe on scratch paper.

Analytical/Logical Competence

It takes a good grasp of basic logic to convert an idea into a program line in a **game engine**, like that shown in **Figure 1-5.**

CHEAT CODE: GAME ENGINE

A game engine is a computer software program that simplifies the design process converting the game's simple commands into complex computer code.

More than just scripting, a video game designer must be able to analyze what strengths and weaknesses will work on each character or character class. Creating a logical structure of initial strength and a means of gaining strength and skill will help build a better game structure.

A video game designer needs to analyze how the player will navigate obstacles. The designer also needs to establish structures so the player will have the power or skill to defeat stronger obstacles or challenges as the game progresses.

○ When will the player "level up?"
○ What is the reward for the completion of a task?
○ What tools or weapons will be needed for the quest?

These types of questions help the designer analyze the game and logically construct a functioning game.

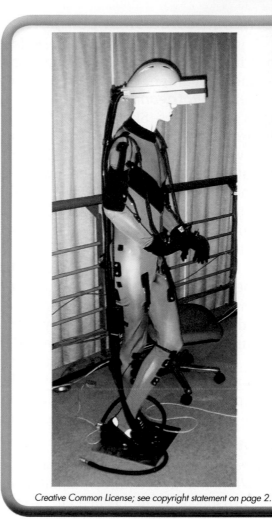

Figure 1-4.

Keeping up to date on the newest technology, like the virtual reality data suit shown here, is critical to designing the newest forms of video game entertainment.

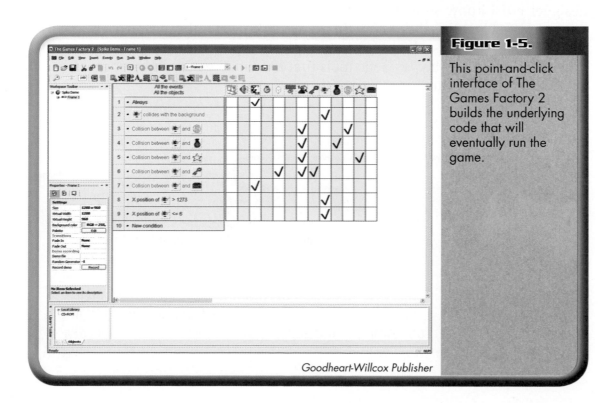

Figure 1-5.

This point-and-click interface of The Games Factory 2 builds the underlying code that will eventually run the game.

Mathematics/Science Competence

If you do not have good math skills, you are well behind the competition when it comes to applicants looking for the best jobs in video game design. Designers need to have both basic math and higher-level math skills including **geometry** and **trigonometry,** which are fields of math dealing with shapes, angles, and curves. Skill in **probability,** which is math dealing with random numbers and possible outcomes, is also a necessity.

A working knowledge of physics and the mathematical formulas needed to simulate the real world is often a requirement. **Physics** is the science of matter and energy: how things like gravity or the path of an object in motion work in the real world. In the game world, characters and objects interact with their surroundings. A video game designer can use physics to help determine how this interaction occurs.

In addition to math and science skills, employers expect video game designers to have a basic understanding and working knowledge of mathematical computer applications, such as spreadsheets. **Spreadsheets** show data in tables or charts. They are useful tools for creating project budgets. Working with budgets and keeping budget records are also very important in design. Costs and expenses need to be recovered through selling the game. When more time is spent on a project than planned for, the cost of the project goes up. Going **over budget,** or spending more money than has been allocated for the project, is very bad management.

Aesthetic Competence

Aesthetic competence is the ability to determine what is pleasing to the eye. While it is not required that all video game designers be expert artists, some artistic skills are needed. To produce character sketches, backgrounds, and game objects that are both visually appealing and properly scaled, a designer must know some basic art skills. These skills are required, for example, to select the appropriate background between those shown in **Figure 1-6.** Size and scale, proportions, colors, appropriate sounds, and sound levels are all part of the aesthetic tools that the video game designer must evaluate during production.

Green Gamer

When you go to the store to buy a video game or other items, consider bringing along a reusable bag. Reusable bags save thousands of pounds of landfill waste every year. While there are different schools of thought on this topic, it is generally accepted that plastic bags take nearly 1,000 years to degrade. Additionally, discarded plastic bags can pose threats to wildlife and contaminate the soil.

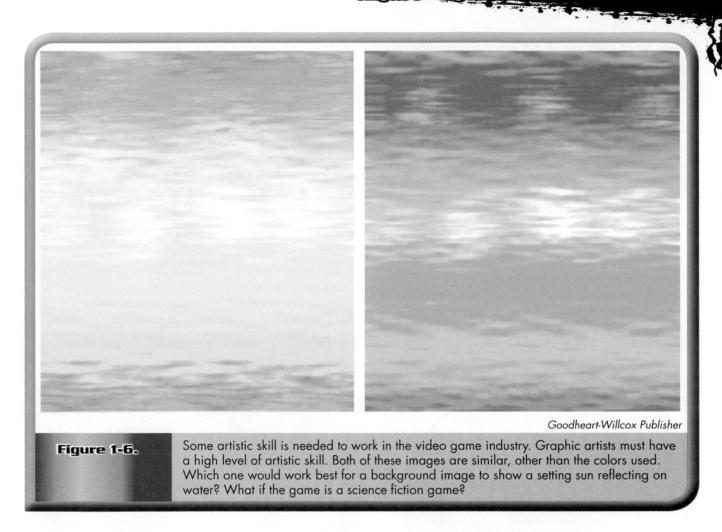

Goodheart-Willcox Publisher

Figure 1-6. Some artistic skill is needed to work in the video game industry. Graphic artists must have a high level of artistic skill. Both of these images are similar, other than the colors used. Which one would work best for a background image to show a setting sun reflecting on water? What if the game is a science fiction game?

A simple example of aesthetic competence might be to know what color of ball shows up best on a dark blue background. Imagine if your choices are a black ball or an orange ball. The orange ball is a contrasting color to blue and would show up better. The black ball might not be seen on a dark blue background.

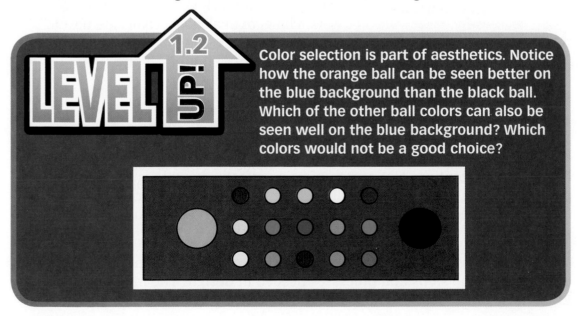

LEVEL UP! 1.2

Color selection is part of aesthetics. Notice how the orange ball can be seen better on the blue background than the black ball. Which of the other ball colors can also be seen well on the blue background? Which colors would not be a good choice?

CASE STUDY

The Color Wheel

The three primary colors are red, blue, and yellow. These three colors are mixed to create all other colors. A device called a color wheel is used to select colors that work well together. The three secondary colors are green, orange, and purple. These colors are made by mixing the two adjoining primary colors, such as yellow and red to make orange. The tertiary color wheel shown here contains the three primary colors, three secondary colors, and six tertiary colors. An infinite number of mixes means millions of different color combinations can be created.

Printers use a slight variation of the three primary colors. They use cyan, magenta, and yellow, along with a key color (CMYK), to blend all colors. Video equipment, such as computer displays and televisions, uses another variation of the three primary colors. This equipment uses red, green, and blue (RGB) color values to make all colors. RGB mixing can produce 16,581,375 color combinations at 24-bit color depth. Notice the color wheel from the software 3ds Max shown here.

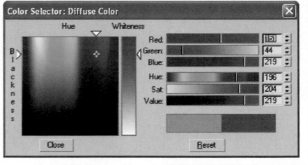

Goodheart-Willcox Publisher

Computer display uses a variation of the three primary colors, known as RGB.

Goodheart-Willcox Publisher

A tertiary color wheel shows the primary, secondary, and tertiary colors.

Two basic principles of color are used to create a pleasing image. These principles involve the position of colors on the color wheel. Matching, or analogous, colors are next to each other. Opposing, or complementary, colors are across from each other.

Communication Competence

The ability to write and speak well is important for any job. Video game design is no exception. Not communicating effectively will result in a poor product and may lead to hurt feelings. The next sections describe the areas of emphasis needed for video game designers to properly communicate.

Writing Skills

Technical writing is creating documents in a precise manner that give directions for the steps and processes needed in design. The instruction manual for a video game is an example of technical writing, as are letters and memos.

A character or object should be created with matching colors to create maximum harmony for that design. Use of matching colors helps the entire object appear unified and not a mixture of many pieces. Contrast indicates how well one color looks against another. To create maximum contrast, use complementary colors directly opposite of each other on a color wheel. Contrasting colors need not be exactly opposite. But, the closer they are to opposite, the higher the contrast.

Look at the blue and purple boxes shown here. The color in the small boxes is the same. Notice how the small box is easier to see in the large purple box. In this example, the blue box is a dominant color due to the large size when compared to the small box. Your eyes tend to focus on the contrasting color elements of the subordinate color in the small box.

Now, look at the blue and purple boxes with light-colored circles. All balls are the same size and color. The ball to the far left is the most obvious and easiest to see. The ball to the far right is the least obvious and hardest to see. Notice how the ball on the far right almost disappears as it gets farther away from the darker blue background.

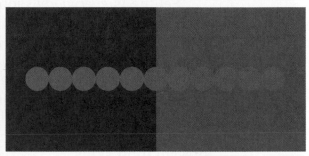

Goodheart-Willcox Publisher

The ball on the far left is easiest to see, while the ball on the far right is hardest to see.

Goodheart-Willcox Publisher

Notice how color choice has a dramatic impact on how you see the small rectangle.

The ability to create these types of documents is an essential skill for the video game designer.

Narrative writing is creating a story. Examples of these types of documents include **storyboards** and the part of the game manual that describes the game world. Narrative writing includes the scripting for the story of the game

CHEAT CODE: STORYBOARD

A storyboard is a graphical plan of action. It includes a simple drawing of a scene and a quick detail about the action. A storyboard is like a cartoon strip of what you are going to create.

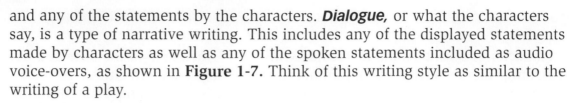

and any of the statements by the characters. *Dialogue,* or what the characters say, is a type of narrative writing. This includes any of the displayed statements made by characters as well as any of the spoken statements included as audio voice-overs, as shown in **Figure 1-7.** Think of this writing style as similar to the writing of a play.

Presentation Skills

Public speaking skills are a must for game designers. You will have to pitch your ideas to your team, management, and investors. You must be comfortable with speaking in front of others. You need to know how to get your point across in a brief summary format that gains interest in your ideas and excitement for the product.

Selling is *everybody's* job. Without sales, there is no money to pay anyone. That does not mean you will be expected to stand on the corner exchanging games for cash. It does mean that you will be asked to present your ideas and stand behind your final product. If you designed it and it is your vision on screen, you had better be able to talk about it and convince others that your ideas are the best for this project. Whether it is selling your ideas to your team, selling your game concept to management, or a more formal presentation at a convention, you need good speaking and presentation skills.

Listening Skills

Listening skills are some of the most important communication skills. Before you can effectively communicate, you need to understand the points and opinions others present to you. If you are close minded and do not actively listen to the concerns and comments of others, you will miss the point and do things all wrong. Pay attention, because your job depends on it.

- When you are listening to others, take notes. It is not impolite to bring a pad and pencil to a meeting. Write down the important points.
- Ask questions. When there is something you did not quite "get," ask someone to clarify the point. Do not be afraid to get clarification.

Figure 1-7.

Many video games include dialogue. This must be written by somebody involved in the design of the game.

Eric Sparrow :
Hey! Help me out here...
Press X to continue.

Goodheart-Willcox Publisher

- Listen carefully because if you do not do the job correctly, you will have to do it again or look for a new job.
- When you speak with someone, try to summarize their points when speaking with them. This **active listening skill** is very important to your understanding of the discussion and also allows the other person to know that you "get" what they are trying to say.

An example of active listening may be a statement like:

> "Let me see if I understand you correctly; you want the character to be able to fly many different airships and have the ability to jump from one to the other when they get close."

This statement may have summarized a ten-minute presentation into a single sentence for clarification.

Compromise

Learning and accepting that you will likely never get exactly what you want is critical to success in designing a video game. Your vision of a video game may need many items changed, modified, or even deleted. Sometimes it is just too difficult to complete, too expensive to implement, will take too long to complete, or is outside of the team's vision. You *will* work on a team in the video game design field, as shown in **Figure 1-8.**

You need to understand and respect the opinions of others, just as they must be willing to understand and respect your opinions. Without this respect, nothing would get done because of all of the arguing. You need to be willing to allow certain changes in exchange for some of your ideas. This solution is called a **compromise,** where everybody gets some of what they want, but not necessarily all of what they want.

Figure 1-8.

This design team is working on a problem. Teamwork is important in all businesses and this is true of video game design as well.

Shutterstock.com

CHEAT CODE: CINEMATIC CUT SCENE

A cinematic cut scene is a movie-like segment of a game that does not require the player to interact with any game element. A cut scene is often placed between levels. It can be used to give the player a break, provide a visual reward to the player, or give a visual summation of what just happened or what is in store for the player.

An example of a compromise might be in your character. You want a tall character, but the background designers want a short background frame to save on computer memory. You might both compromise to include some changes to your character so it will fit the background and the game plays correctly. In exchange, you might get to include a **cinematic cut scene** with your character in full detail. Look for a decision where both parties win. This is called a *win-win solution.*

LEVEL 1.3 UP!

Think about a time when you had a disagreement with your parents, a teacher, or a friend. Could you have made a compromise to get a win-win situation? Describe how you could have compromised.

Background Information and Research

Essential to game designers is the ability to conduct **research.** Finding out what is current in publishing, gaming, art, technology, and so on, is one of the most important elements to a current and successful game. This does not mean that you just use the Internet. Research might mean going to stores, surveying game players, going to trade shows, creating an interactive blog, and networking with other game designers and computer engineers to find out what might be in development for three to five years from now. Getting information on what others are doing will give you an edge to getting involved in more projects and more high-end game builds.

Some of these research skills play an important role in marketing and finding a target audience. Although, you may need to use these skills in other ways. If you are designing a video game with ninja characters, maybe you will have to research the history, geography, and culture of Japan at that time. Using symbols and artifacts that have meaning to that time period or culture will help bring a realistic feel to the game. Additionally, if you design a space-based game, you may need to find out information on the planets, gravity, and momentum to program events to work in space. For example, you might do some research on new discoveries in space and use names of real planets, stars, and galaxies in your game, as shown in **Figure 1-9.** With a little research you could find out if there is a real planet where scientists think life might be found. Using some imagination, you could create a concept based on that information.

You need to be able to continue to learn and research needed information to stay on top as a game designer. New ideas are needed. Your job will be to find out what they are and how they work.

Figure 1-9.

A researcher might take a quick trip to the NASA website and find inspiration like this artistic rendering of Epsilon Eridani images taken from the Spitzer space telescope. Three-dimensional models, textures, and many other game development tools are available at no charge from NASA for game and simulation designers.

NASA

Soft Skills/Workplace Skills

Just as important as the technical skills and competencies discussed above (hard skills) are the soft skills needed to be a good employee. *Soft skills* are personal qualities and behaviors that help create better personal and interpersonal skills. Each of these skills is more of a character trait or habit than a learned skill. If you were building a virtual employee, you would want to give them lots of "strength points" in the following areas.

- *Responsibility* is the ability to bring an assigned task to a successful conclusion.
- *Dependability* is the ability to be relied on and trusted.
- *Punctuality* is being on time and prepared.
- *Positive attitude* is an outlook on a situation that emphasizes an upbeat outcome.
- *Initiative* is forward thinking and taking on additional responsibilities without having to wait for someone to tell you to do it.
- *Respect for self* is a belief that you are important and treating yourself as important.
- *Respect for others* is a belief that the opinions and beliefs of others are important.
- *Professional dress* is clothing appropriate for the workplace or event.

Some of the most important skills needed to be successful on a team are not those found in a textbook or college course. They are the simple, everyday soft skills needed to treat people with respect and effectively communicate. Regardless of your strengths in hard skills, if you cannot work on a team, you will not be working in this field for very long. The games are too complex for a single person to complete in their lifetime. Now is the time to practice getting along with people and gain strength in soft skills.

Video game design studios are often fun and exciting places to work with benefits hard to find in other employment opportunities. Included in the soft skill set was the professional dress. While it is commonplace for a design studio to allow tee shirts and flip-flops to help the employees feel comfortable and relaxed, it is important to remember there are times when a more professional dress is required. The professional dress requirement may change with your responsibilities. When at the studio, casual dress may be the norm. However, at a client meeting or convention presentation, more formal attire will be required.

As with most of the attributes of a game designer, there is a range between a *strength* and a *weakness*. Each job title has a specific requirement for just how strong an employee must be in that area. Those who aspire to become a creative director or other high-ranking manager will need high strength in all of the soft skill areas as well as high strength in their specific area of expertise (hard skill). The next section takes a look at some of the jobs available on a design team and what skills are most important for each.

I Am a Team Player

A video game design team is essential to designing today's large games. The video game design industry is not standardized or held to the structure of the job titles listed in this book. However, this section attempts to give some structure to the roles needed for video game development.

www.g-wlearning.com

Level up
your know-how with Animated Review 1-1.

Most video game design companies assign jobs and responsibilities based on experience, skill, and the needs of a game design project. Teams might be very flexible. A skilled employee might function as a specialist on several teams at the same time due to the limited availability of that person's special skill set. A **specialist** is someone with strong attributes in a certain area. These attributes are often unique strengths that required special training to achieve. As discussed in the previous section, teams function best when strengths and weaknesses are balanced. This balancing is the main driving force for role assignment. Individuals with the greatest number of strengths will typically have more opportunities to work on and lead more teams.

By dividing the responsibilities that come with a large video game project, the project becomes more manageable and easier to build. A large team may have one or more of each of the team members discussed in this section.

A common misconception about the game design team is that all people have equal say in the design process. This is not true. Game design is *not* a democracy with everyone voting on what might be the best option.

Ethical Gamer
Social media is commonly used by students for a variety of purposes. Use good judgment and represent yourself in a respectable manner. It is unethical to misrepresent yourself on social media.

Everyone has a supervisor and that supervisor has the final word on any element of the game. This results in a team **hierarchy** such as the one shown in **Figure 1-10.** This is similar to how your school works. You have teachers to report to and ask questions of. The teacher is like your supervisor. A problem you report to your teacher (supervisor) will be taken to the next administrator for a decision if needed. Otherwise, all the students would ask the principal every question. If you want to see changes, you have to convince your superiors that your idea is a better way. Work on communication and compromise to get that done.

CHEAT CODE: HIERARCHY

Design companies are organized in a hierarchy to streamline decision-making. Just like in the military, job titles show the rank of the employee. In the army, you might hold rank as a private or a general. On the design team you might hold job title as a level designer or a lead designer. Each person reports to a boss with higher authority.

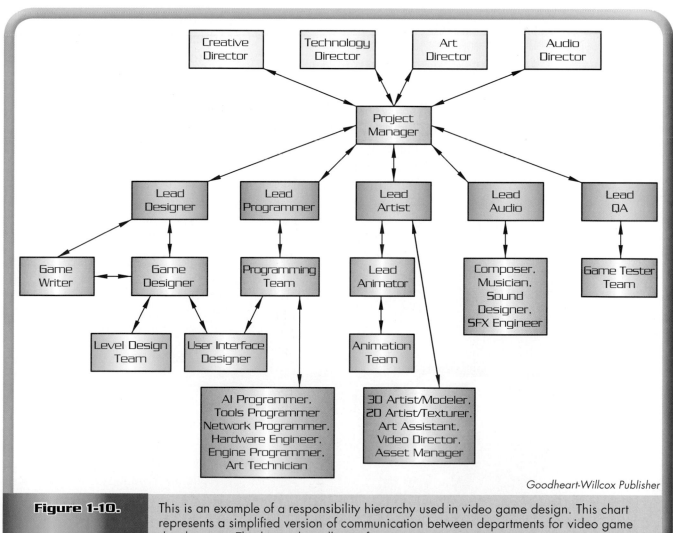

Goodheart-Willcox Publisher

Figure 1-10. This is an example of a responsibility hierarchy used in video game design. This chart represents a simplified version of communication between departments for video game development. This hierarchy will vary from company to company.

Of course, the team has a say in the building of the game. Many game studios use **scrum methodology.** Scrum is a rugby term used to describe how the teams line up to get the ball. They interlock to form one big wall of players acting as a single unit, as shown in **Figure 1-11.** In video game design, this scrum is composed of all members of an interdisciplinary team. An **interdisciplinary team** is one composed of members with different skills—designers, programmers, artists, sound designers, quality assurance—assigned to a single project. These teammates work together and share ideas to get the final product completed. They ask for help from the project leads, specialists, creative director, and **internal producer (IP)** when needed. The management of the team falls to the project lead. The IP is assigned a game to oversee. The job of the IP is to make sure the project is on time and meets the needs of the **outside producer (OP).** All of these people work together with a single goal of completing the game.

CHEAT CODE: PRODUCER

The publisher is responsible for the marketing and selling of a video game. The internal producer (IP) works with the design team to include features that will make the game sell. The IP sets the design timeline and makes sure the design team keeps true to the original concept of the game. The outside producer (OP) is in charge of making the game discs and all packaging. The OP also sets up promotions and advertising to get people to buy the game after it is ready to sell.

Creative Director

In a large project, a **creative director** will be assigned to set the vision and direction the team will take in completing the game. This person may be responsible for selecting the personnel and assigning job roles for each person or team used to build a game. Additionally, most communication between the company management and the design team will be done through the creative director.

Figure 1-11.

Shown here is a rugby scrum. Notice how all of the players interlock to form a single working group.

PhotoStock10/Shutterstock.com

Most marketing functions to promote the game and present the progress of the game development will be performed by the creative director. The creative director also communicates with the other director-level managers within the company to monitor progress and set the creative vision of the projects. In most companies, a creative director will oversee many game projects at the same time.

Project Manager

The **project manager** is responsible for coordinating all of the lead managers and ensuring that all project components are on task and well-managed. This role may be a stand-alone position on a large **game build,** but is more typically assigned to the lead designer or other leader in smaller

CHEAT CODE: GAME BUILD

More than just game design, a game build incorporates design, programming, art, sound, testing, marketing, prototyping, and more. A game build includes all of the effort needed to construct a game from concept to finished product.

game builds. A project manager will only manage a single project at a time.

One of the most important roles of the project manager is the setting of the production schedule and tracking that all jobs are completed on time and on budget. A useful tool in the management of any project is a Gantt chart. A **Gantt chart** helps display the tasks needed by each department along a timeline for completion, as shown in **Figure 1-12.** Many software products are available to help project managers track their progress using a Gantt chart.

Lead Designer

A **lead designer** reports to the creative director and acts as the day-to-day leader of the team. This person is responsible for the overall function of the design team, project completion, budgeting, final build decisions, and coherent flow from level to level. This includes following the vision of the game and

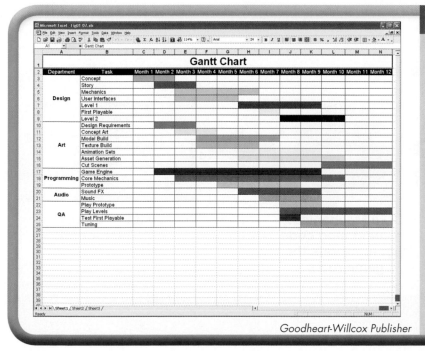

Figure 1-12.

This is a sample Gantt chart displaying some common tasks of a video game design team. The colored bars are used to represent when tasks are to begin and end to meet the deadline of production. Equally important is the view in each column that shows which tasks will be occurring at the same time.

Goodheart-Willcox Publisher

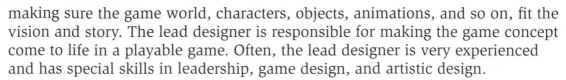
making sure the game world, characters, objects, animations, and so on, fit the vision and story. The lead designer is responsible for making the game concept come to life in a playable game. Often, the lead designer is very experienced and has special skills in leadership, game design, and artistic design.

Game Designer

The **game designer** reports directly to the lead designer and lead programmer. This person is responsible for establishing the rules of the game, finalizing the design documents, and ensuring the game will be assembled and working as imagined. In other words, this job is the one that makes sure the game works according to the vision. This vision will include the overall view of the complete game world and how the player will progress from one level to another to tell the story of the game.

CHEAT CODE: PHYSICS ENGINE

Sometimes the programming of the core mechanics might include creating a physics engine. The physics engine uses mathematical formulas to create rules for movements, like gravity, speed, flight, the traveling path of a projectile, bouncing, explosions, and other game movements.

The game designer has the skills to perform most of the duties needed in the game build. Most important to this position is the ability to program the core mechanics of the game. The **core mechanics** are the programming rules that determine how the game works, as illustrated in **Figure 1-13.**

The core mechanics establishes the game rules or **physics engine,** such as that the characters can walk on grass and will sink on water or open spaces. Another rule might be that a player can pass through a cloud, but cannot pass through a tree, door, or wall. Each of these rules needs to be programmed into the game. Without good rules in the core mechanics, players think a game has a **glitch,** which is a programming error.

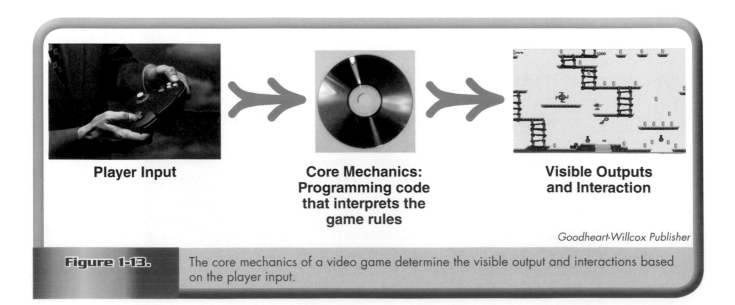

Player Input

Core Mechanics: Programming code that interprets the game rules

Visible Outputs and Interaction

Goodheart-Willcox Publisher

Figure 1-13. The core mechanics of a video game determine the visible output and interactions based on the player input.

Level Designer

As you may have guessed, a *level designer* is responsible for creating the game world and game functions for a single level. In a multilevel game, it would be reasonable to have several level designers who report to the game designer. Each level designer is responsible for implementing the designs from the **design documents** into working game levels. This job also requires great communication skills as the ability to construct a level will take input from the user interface designers, game writers, art designers, and audio engineers.

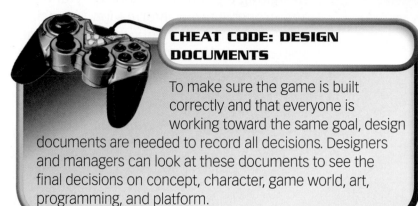

CHEAT CODE: DESIGN DOCUMENTS

To make sure the game is built correctly and that everyone is working toward the same goal, design documents are needed to record all decisions. Designers and managers can look at these documents to see the final decisions on concept, character, game world, art, programming, and platform.

The level designer brings all of the parts, objects, backgrounds, characters, and actions together. Using the rules of the core mechanics, each part on the level must be programmed to perform properly. A level designer will take the characters designed by the art department and program how they move on the screen and interact with the player. Everything from the game level map, background objects, characters, animation sequences, and displays must be programmed according to the game rules. The ultimate goal of a level designer is to design and program a part of the game so the player can input control to the game without incurring a glitch. Most of the hands-on programming is done by the level designer.

User Interface Designer

A *user interface (UI)* is basically the controls that the player uses to move and interact with the game. Thus, the *user interface designer* is responsible for creating these controls. In the early days of video game design, there was really little need for this specialist position. Most games used a standard controller or joystick. But in today's huge games with multiplayer and online gameplay, the job of making all the players function properly and connect to the game world is a full-time job.

Added recently to this role is the use of game-specific controllers, like the guitar shown in **Figure 1-14.**

Figure 1-14.

The games *Guitar Hero* and *Rock Band* use game-specific controllers. Here, a guitar controller is being used.

Goodheart-Willcox Publisher

Designing a guitar for *Guitar Hero* and instruments for *Rock Band* that function and properly input information for each player is a major component of the game. Additionally, motion-based controllers like those on the Nintendo Wii system can take teams of user interface designers to get these games to function as imagined.

The major role of the user interface designer is to help the player connect to and become immersed in the game world. This job is even more important as the ultimate goal of any game is to increase **immersion,** which is the feeling of being part of the game world. Realistic UI designs that bring the player closer to being in a true virtual reality game world means the user interface designer must be able to use the most advanced technology to make the game interaction as realistic and **ergonomic** as possible.

CHEAT CODE: ERGONOMICS

A formal definition of ergonomics is the study of how the body works and how humans interact with tools and environments. Game designers simplify this definition to mean how comfortable players are while performing tasks without injury. In gaming, ergonomics typically focuses on how the controller is designed and how the player can use the controller without much training. If a controller is complex, hard to understand, or uncomfortable to use, players will quit playing. This would be a failure of the user interface designer and an unsuccessful game.

The user interface designer works closely with both the creative director and lead director when designing a new user interface control. Later in the design process, this person will work more closely with the game designer to program the controller into the core mechanics.

Using a standard controller does not eliminate the need for a user interface designer. Some typical UI problems using a standard controller might include being able to press a jump or shoot button while moving. Having to press too many buttons at the same time or buttons that are far apart will make the game too hard to play, destroy the immersion, and frustrate the player.

LEVEL UP! 1.4

To make the game experience as realistic as possible, user interface designers are making more-realistic controls. Think about your favorite game. What changes to the user interface would you make?

CASE STUDY

NASA Flight Simulators

Flight simulators are popular video games. The controls simulate a complete reality. The game even gives the sensation of movement, of rising and falling, based on user input and the surrounding virtual environment.

One of the most advanced flight simulators is the Vertical Motion Flight Simulator at NASA. This simulator allows for the most realistic flight simulation experience. To accomplish this, it uses a cabin mounted on a hydraulic platform to create real movement. In addition to the shifting movement from the hydraulic platform, this simulator actually moves up and down as much as 60 feet and front to back as much as 40 feet for extremely realistic simulation of movement. Pilots of the space shuttle train using this simulator.

For the pilots training on this simulator, the feeling of movement in the cabin realistically represents almost any feeling of actual flight. To make the simulation truly realistic, three additional elements are needed to complete the overall experience. Out-the-window graphics, flight instruments, and flight controls are programmed to interact with the movement of the cabin.

Out-the-window graphics uses multiple video screens to simulate the view from each window. Complete with high-definition video, it can be difficult to tell the difference between the simulation and the real view outside of the actual space shuttle window. This helps pilots experience conditions they will actually see in the real world.

Flight instruments are exact copies of those the pilot would see in the real world. These are in the same location as in the space shuttle. They also function in the same way as the real instruments.

NASA and the Ames Research Center

The cabin is mounted on a hydraulic platform. The cabin can be removed and replaced with a different cabin to change from a space shuttle simulator to a jet fighter simulator. Four different cabins/cockpits have been designed for this simulator.

NASA and the Ames Research Center

This is a cockpit view with multiple screens to simulate an out-the-window view.

(Continued)

CASE STUDY (Continued)

NASA and the Ames Research Center

Some control screens use a heads-up display to overlay information directly on the viewing screen. This feature, also used in video games, allows the user to see the information without looking away from the screen.

NASA and the Ames Research Center

These are the joystick and foot pedals used in this simulator cabin.

The last piece of the puzzle to make this simulator the most realistic possible is the use of flight controls. The flight controls are identical to those used on the actual vehicle. The user interface designer had to incorporate real controls into this "video game" to make the simulator a true representation of what the pilot will experience in the real world.

In addition to the controls, the user interface design team had to program features of the heads-up display (HUD), instrument readouts, the hydraulic movements of the cabin, and movement of the base platform to create the complete user experience. Together these control systems create the ultimate 3D adventure.

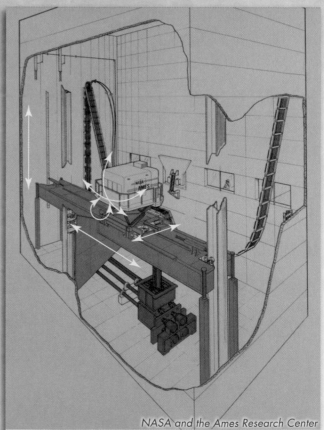

NASA and the Ames Research Center

This drawing shows the movements possible for the cabin. Yellow arrows show the tilting movements of the hydraulic platform. They show the movement of the motion platform in real three-dimensional space.

Game Writer

Game writers are the dramatic writers for the team. These writers are responsible for creating character depth and interaction. For character depth, a writer might create a **backstory,** or history, of how and why this character came to be. A game introduction also provides dramatic information for the player to understand the imaginary world that the game is trying to create.

Along with the historical and storyline writing, the game writers have to add dialogue. This may be in either written or verbal form. Dialogue allows interaction between the player and the other characters within the game world. Many other types of story-based dialogue and dramatic writing take place within a game or a cut scene.

This job requires skills beyond simple writing skills. It takes a person who is a good dramatic writer, savvy with technology, and an excellent communicator. Everyone on the team will be begging for cut scenes and interactive dialogue to make their levels and characters come to life. A game writer must make some compromises as a daily part of work to make the level designers and game designer happy.

The hardest part of the game writer's job is to keep all of the aspects of character and dialogue moving the story forward. From the opening scene to the final obstacle, the game must be written to properly flow from start to finish. Without good writing and dialogue to tell the player what they are expected to do, a game will fail. For this reason, the game writer will ultimately report directly to the lead designer.

Art Designer/Lead Artist

The **art designer,** sometimes called the **lead artist,** creates the visual elements of the game. These visual elements will be either two dimensional (2D) or three dimensional (3D). The difference between 2D and 3D can be seen as a real life example of a sheet of paper. A flat sheet of paper is a 2D object that has only height and width. If you take that same sheet of paper and ball it up, it becomes a 3D object with height, width, and depth. Often, an art designer will work on several teams at the same time. Since their work on the project is vital to the success of the game and its vision, art designers report directly to the lead designer or creative director.

The visual elements of a game are called assets. An **asset** is an object, character, or background that can be inserted into a game. A two-dimensional (2D) asset is called a **sprite.** A three-dimensional (3D) asset is called a **model.** Examples of each are shown in **Figure 1-15.** Depending on the need for each game, an asset may be animated with multiple poses, like a walking character, or a static (nonmoving) object, like a fire hydrant. It is the job of the art director and the team of artists to produce each asset for the design team to program into the working game.

Every character, building, movement, object, backdrop, and everything else seen on screen must be created and designed to properly function. A level designer might want a 3D tree model in the level. The art designer has to create a tree that will fit with the theme and style of the level. Imagine a creepy scene with a scary house and then a bright, cheery peach tree in front of the house.

Goodheart-Willcox Publisher

Figure 1-15.   A—Two-dimensional game assets are known as sprites.
B—Three-dimensional game assets are known as models.

This tree does not fit the theme and feel of the scene. Instead, a dying tree with scraggly branches and broken limbs might work better in the scene. Each visual element of the game must match the others and function within the level. To create these visual elements, developing and editing tools are used similar to those shown in **Figure 1-16.**

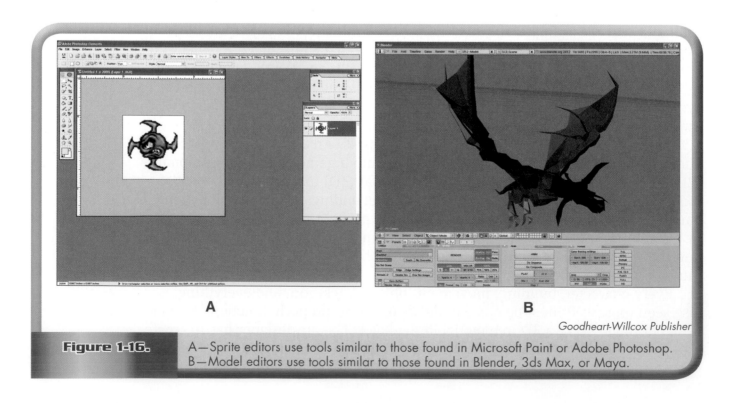

Goodheart-Willcox Publisher

Figure 1-16.   A—Sprite editors use tools similar to those found in Microsoft Paint or Adobe Photoshop.
B—Model editors use tools similar to those found in Blender, 3ds Max, or Maya.

The art designer might start work with a basic sketch of a character. Then, all of the features of the character are built based on the sketch. This process may take a lot of patience. The lead designer may request several changes on each design until it looks exactly right. Characters might be the most important and most difficult features to design. A character might be made up of a hundred moving parts with tools and movements that change during gameplay.

Art designers have one of the most significant and important jobs in creating a successful video game. This usually requires a team of artists working together to get all of the assets designed for a single video game. With video game trends leaning toward high-definition graphics and realistic movements, skilled art designers are usually in high demand.

Audio Engineer

The job of the **audio engineer** is to create all of the sounds that add depth to the game. Every noise and sound needs to be created by the audio engineer using tools like the one shown in **Figure 1-17.** This includes:

○ **Active sounds,** like that of a door creaking as it is opened.
○ **Background music** needed to set the mood of the level.
○ **Voice-overs** used in dialogue and narrations.
○ **Ambient sounds,** like the buzzing of a bee or leaves rustling in the wind.

Just like the art designer, the audio engineer might be working on several projects at the same time. The project manager and game designer are in constant communication with the audio engineer to make sure the sounds match the vision and mood of the game they are creating.

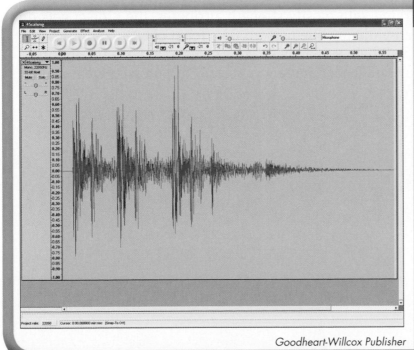

Figure 1-17.

A sound engineer will use sound mixing and editing software, similar to Audacity shown here, to add sound tracks and create needed sounds for the game. Audacity is a useful freeware program used by many beginners and students.

Goodheart-Willcox Publisher

Quality Assurance Tester/Game Tester

The *quality assurance (QA) tester,* or *game tester,* is the person that actually gets paid to play video games. This is usually an entry-level position in a video game design studio. A game tester will play games and levels over and over again to test every part of the game for proper operation.

CHEAT CODE: CHEAT CODE

To make the job of the QA team easier, programmers put in codes to allow the testers the ability to have unlimited lives, unlimited cash, jump to levels, and other features. This prevents the game tester from having to start over after running into the first obstacle tested. Cheat codes are usually not removed after the game is published and these codes are eventually leaked to the public. It is typically not the purpose of the video game design team to allow the player to cheat their way past an obstacle, but these hidden codes are needed to allow proper testing.

When the game passes all of the quality assurance tests, it is free of bugs. **Cheat codes** are built into the game for the QA team to help them navigate through the game. A game tester might have to spend the day running into every obstacle in a game or doing things to try to make the game crash. The objective here is to make sure each object reacts as it should. This is a different objective than the game player. A game player, such as yourself, wants to beat the game and assumes everything works properly.

A QA job requires a very good game player with some programming knowledge. The game tester needs to be able to navigate the game, give input to the designers on glitches discovered, and tell the user interface designer how the controls work. This means a lot of communication.

Each member of the QA team plays a specialist's role in creating their part of the game. Together their strengths build on each other through the division of labor. With **division of labor,** each person does the job they can do best. With each person working with mostly strength attributes, the project gets done quicker and better than with any one person. Be a team player, communicate well, and listen. This will help you achieve your goals and move up within a company to become a team leader and an important reason why great games continue to be made.

Chapter Summary

- Video game design team members are individuals who have a specific set of physical and mental skills that allow them to complete the tasks demanded by the game being developed.
- The group dynamic is the way in which the strengths and weaknesses of each team member work together to create a balanced team.
- Good communication skills, both written and verbal, will help keep the team on track and focused on the goal: the creation of a quality game.
- The project manager is responsible for setting the production schedule and tracking all jobs to make sure they are completed on time and on budget.
- Effective listening, speaking, telecommunication, and nonverbal communication skills are necessary to effectively communicate with supervisors, coworkers, and customers.
- Written communication for the video game development industry includes technical writing, narrative writing, dialogues, backstories, and storyboards.
- Video game designers need to be well-versed in the terminology of the video game industry.
- Constructive criticism provides someone with suggestions for possible improvements or solutions in a positive manner.
- Soft skills are more of a character trait or habit than a learned skill and include: responsibility, dependability, punctuality, positive attitude, initiative, respect for self, respect for others, and professional dress.
- A good approach to solving many problems is to collaborate with others.
- Taking classes and workshops to keep technology and employability skills fresh makes the designer a lifelong learner.
- Some of the possible positions within the game development industry include: creative director, project manager, lead designer, game designer, level designer, user interface designer, game writer, art designer, audio engineer, and quality assurance tester.

Check Your Video Game IQ

Now that you have finished this chapter, see what you know about video game design by taking the chapter posttest.

www.m.g-wlearning.com

www.g-wlearning.com

Review Your Knowledge

On a separate sheet of paper or in a word processing document, match the following terms with the definition that fits best.

A. responsibility
B. game designer
C. technical writing
D. level designer
E. game writer
F. dependability
G. user interface designer
H. internal producer
I. art designer
J. narrative writing

1. Creates the visual elements and assets of the game.
2. Creating a story.
3. Ability to be relied on and trusted.
4. Responsible for ensuring the design objectives required by the production group are achieved by the design group.
5. Establishes the rules of the game, finalizes the design documents, and ensures the game will work as envisioned.
6. Creates character depth and interaction.
7. Creates the controls used by the player to interact with the game.
8. Ability to make sure an assigned task is successfully completed.
9. Creating documents that give directions for the steps and processes needed in design.
10. Interprets the design documents to create a game world and interactions for a single game level.

On a separate sheet of paper or in a word processing document, answer each of the following questions.

11. In your own words, define the term *lifelong learner*.
12. What is the *dynamic* of a team?
13. How is *constructive criticism* helpful?
14. Write a brief, one-sentence summary of the difference between hard skills and soft skills.
15. In what three areas of math should a video game designer have strong skills?
16. Why would someone wanting to become a video game designer need to learn how to use spreadsheets?
17. If the background in a video game is dark, what colors may be best to use for the characters and tools used by the character? Why?
18. How does *technical writing* differ from *narrative writing?*
19. What is the purpose of a *storyboard?*
20. How can you use *active listening* to improve communication?
21. You and a teammate differ on the design of a flying character. You want the character to have a flying cape. Your teammate wants to have the character fly using rocket boots. In the end, the character is designed with foldout rocket wings. How could this solution be described?

22. List four personal strengths that employers look for.

23. Describe why you think video game design is not a democracy.

24. What is an *interdisciplinary team?*

25. What role does the *creative director* play on the video game design team?

26. List ten jobs that may be members of a video game design team.

27. Define *physics engine.*

28. What is the purpose of *design documents?*

29. What term describes two colors with the highest contrast?

30. Describe the shape and features of an interface that would enhance the immersion for each of the following games: musical-instrument game, flight simulator, dancing game, and driving game.

Apply Your STEM Knowledge

 ## Social Studies

1. David was a boy working in a machine shop building parts to marine engines at the age of 13. One day he asked his boss, Mrs. Abram, why did she become a machinist? Mrs. Abram spoke frankly to David, and the two had a conversation on how she learned the machinist trade back in World War II when the nation needed women to work the factories while the men were at war. At the end of the conversation, Mrs. Abram asked David to tell her on Friday, before he could get his paycheck, what the most important part to an engine was. David was a good machinist and knew every part of an engine. He thought about every part and how it worked.

   - The pistons go up and down to create movement from the burning fuel.
   - The rods connected the pistons to the crankshaft to change the direction of movement.
   - The crankshaft turned to create the rotation needed to spin the propeller.
   - The spark plugs were needed to ignite the fuel to start the movement.
   - The cams opened the valves to let the engine breathe in air and closed to seal the ignition.

   The list went on and on until David had listed every part of the engine and could not determine what one part was the most important.

   On Friday, David went to pick up his paycheck. Mrs. Abram asked David if he had the answer. David replied, "I was really hoping you forgot about that. I thought about that all week and I could not figure out which part was the most important."

Ford

Mrs. Abram reached in her desk and took out David's paycheck. She said, "The answer is, the part that is broken." She handed David his paycheck and stated, "When any one part is broken, all of the others won't work."

David thought about the parts of the engine again and how if any one part was missing, the entire system would not work. He thanked Mrs. Abram and left.

David is now the Vice President of International Ship Repair. He tells this story to keep the memory of his friend and mentor, Mrs. Abram, alive.

A. Apply the "most important part of an engine" story to a video game design team. Explain how the teammates work together and which part is the most important part.

B. Research and list three modern-day jobs that you feel are male dominant. List another three modern-day jobs that you feel are female dominant.

 ## Language Arts

2. A Gantt chart is shown in **Figure 1-12.** Use spreadsheet software, such as Microsoft Excel, to create a Gantt chart showing all of the classes you intend to take before you graduate. Use a timeline in months or semesters and organize your classes by subject (department) and course (task). Using a word processor, such as Microsoft Word, write a one-page memo to your instructor describing what you wish to achieve by taking the courses you have outlined.

Mathematics

3. Two-dimensional figures have only height and width. Look at the 2D bear figure below on a grid map.

   A. How many units tall is the bear?
   B. How many units wide is the bear?
   C. What would the height of the bear be if it is reduced to 1/3 of its current value?
   D. To keep the bear proportional (same scale for height and width), what would the width of the reduced figure be?

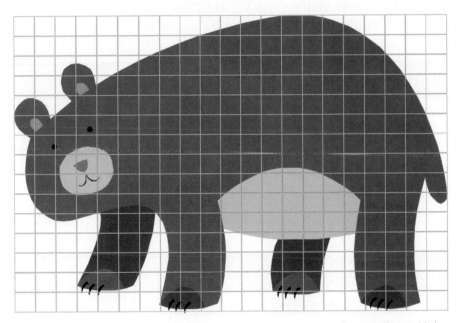

Goodheart-Willcox Publisher

 ## Language Arts

4. Form into groups of two or three. Research, debate, and form a group opinion on each of the Level Up! activities in this chapter. Prepare a PowerPoint presentation of ten slides (five to seven minutes) to present to the class explaining the group's opinions for each Level Up! activity. Include text, pictures, video, animations, and slide transitions as appropriate to help explain your positions.

Working in Teams

This chapter discusses hard and soft skills. Working with a team, make a list of hard and soft skills members of the team have. Discuss the team's skill set. Are any skills missing?

Gamer Portfolio

A portfolio is a selection of materials that you collect and organize to show your qualifications, skills, and talents. When you apply for a job, community service, or college, you will need a portfolio to showcase your qualifications for the opportunity for which you are applying. There are two types of portfolios that are commonly used: print portfolio and electronic portfolio (e-portfolio). An e-portfolio is also known as a digital portfolio.

1. Use the Internet to search for print *portfolio* and *e-portfolio.* Summarize each type and create an overview of how to create each one.

2. You will be creating a portfolio in this class. Which portfolio type would you prefer to create? Write several paragraphs describing the type of portfolio you would prefer and why.

G-W Learning Mobile Site

Visit the G-W Learning mobile site to complete the chapter pretest and posttest and to practice vocabulary using e-flash cards. If you do not have a smartphone, visit the G-W Learning companion website to access these features.

G-W Learning mobile site: www.m.g-wlearning.com

G-W Learning companion website: www.g-wlearning.com

Common Core

College and Career Readiness

CTE Career Ready Practices. Create a one-act play for two persons that depicts a positive interaction between two students or coworkers. Be sure to include notes to the actors about body language and facial expressions. Do the same to illustrate a negative interaction on the same topic. What is the essential difference between the two plays/interactions? How does the way you say something influence whether it will be received negatively or positively?

Reading. Read a magazine, newspaper, or online article about the impact of technology on video game design. Determine the central ideas of the article and review the conclusions made by the author. As needed, derive meaning of the environmental print and use visual and contextual support to confirm understanding. Use support from classmates and your teacher as needed to help in comprehension of the material. Provide an accurate summary of your reading that incorporates both what the author said as well as your understanding of how technology impacts video game design.

Writing. Conduct a short research project to answer the question, "What was the first video game?" Using information from multiple sources, write a report on your response to this question.

Event Prep: Student Organizations

Professional student organizations are valuable assets to any educational program. These organizations support student learning and application of skills learned to real-world situations. Also, participation in career and technology education student organizations can promote lifelong responsibility for community service and professional development. There are a variety of organizations from which to select, depending on the goals of your educational programs. To prepare for any competitive event:

1. Contact the organization before the next competition. This gives you time to review and decide which competitive events are correct for you or your team.

2. Closely read all guidelines. These rules and regulations must be strictly adhered to or disqualification can occur.

3. Competitive events may be written, oral, or a combination of both.

4. Communication plays a role in all competitive events, so read which communication skills are covered for the event you select. Research and preparation are important keys to successful competition.

5. Go to the website of your organization for specific information for the events. Visit the site often as information may change.

6. Select one or two events that are of interest to you. Print the information for the events and discuss your interest with your instructor.

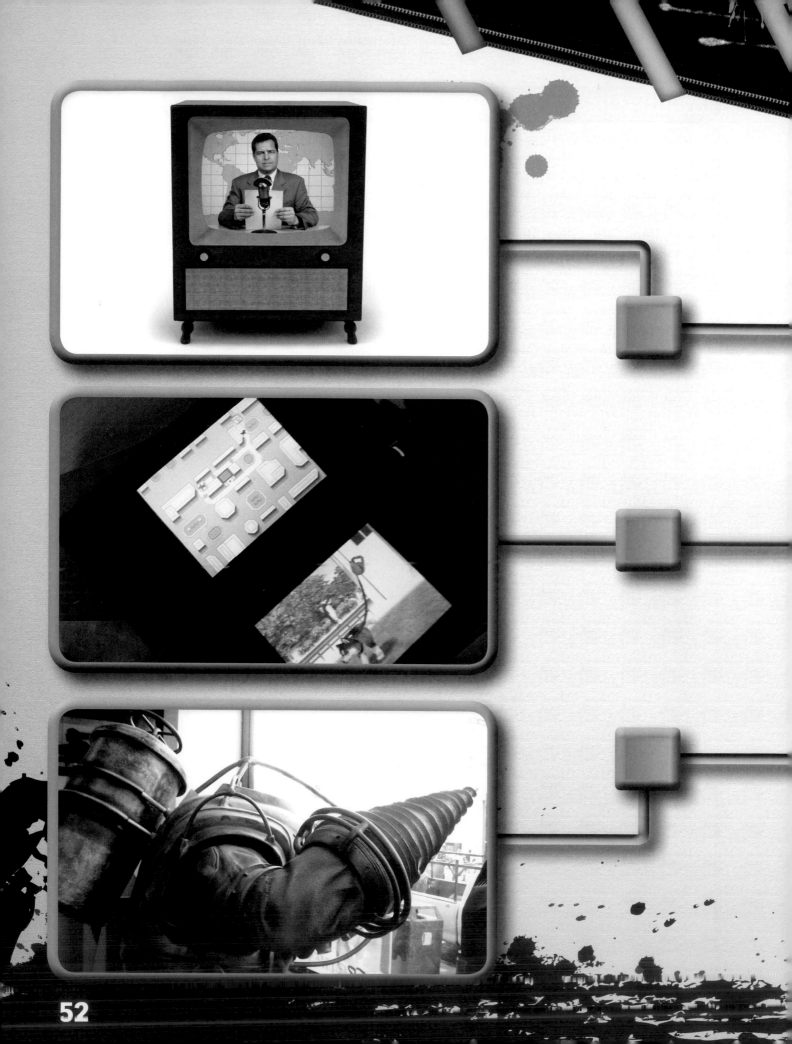

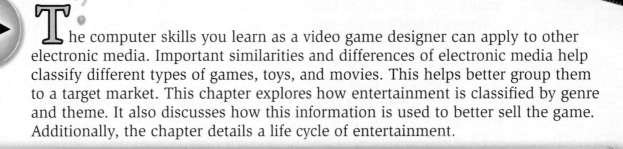

Chapter 2
Computerized Entertainment and Classification

The computer skills you learn as a video game designer can apply to other electronic media. Important similarities and differences of electronic media help classify different types of games, toys, and movies. This helps better group them to a target market. This chapter explores how entertainment is classified by genre and theme. It also discusses how this information is used to better sell the game. Additionally, the chapter details a life cycle of entertainment.

Check Your Video Game IQ

Before you begin this chapter, see what you already know about video game design by taking the chapter pretest.

www.m.g-wlearning.com

www.g-wlearning.com

Reading Prep. Before reading, observe the objectives for this chapter. As you read, focus on how the chapter is structured. Summarize the structure of the chapter. Does this structure make points clear, convincing, and engaging?

College and Career Readiness

Objectives

After completing this chapter, you will be able to:

- Describe different gaming genres.
- Define video game terms related to various gaming genres.
- Discuss the history of radio, movies, television, art, and theater.
- Classify different computerized entertainment media.
- Categorize different games and toys into appropriate genre and themes.
- Describe the life cycle of media from experimental to mainstream.
- Discuss the use and importance of genre classification in game marketing.
- Identify the unique selling points of various games.
- Explain the importance of target marketing as related to the total marketing effort.

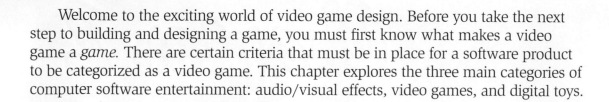
Welcome to the exciting world of video game design. Before you take the next step to building and designing a game, you must first know what makes a video game a *game*. There are certain criteria that must be in place for a software product to be categorized as a video game. This chapter explores the three main categories of computer software entertainment: audio/visual effects, video games, and digital toys.

Audio/Visual Effects

By definition, **audio** means something you hear and **visual** means something you see. Together, **audio/visual effects** are any entertainment that can be seen or heard. When referring to this category of products, most people would refer to them as simply "media." Some items that fall into this design category might include screen savers, movies, cut scenes, and presentations. For these media, there is no user interface to control the action. This entertainment is simply enjoyed. Sit back, relax, and enjoy the show.

Audio/visual effects have taken a long time to get to the advanced, computer-generated presentations of today. Throughout the history of media and entertainment, there have been examples of media that seemed to do what was normal or expected. There are also examples that went counter to the establishment and represented a change. The former is called mainstream media and the latter is called experimental media. The **mainstream media** is popular at the time, accepted by most people, and generally a part of everyday life. The experimental media is just the opposite. This is typically not popular with most people. **Experimental media** is liked by a small group of people who embrace the message. In some cases, they may create an almost cult-like following. Often, experimental media makes use of a new technology that threatens the status quo of the established mainstream media. Throughout history, experimental media was often feared by the establishment.

Everyone would agree these are all audio/visual effects or media: art, theater, radio, movies, and television. History would call each item experimental *and* mainstream. It only depends on the time frame at which you are looking. Often, especially when referring to technology, something begins as experimental, becomes mainstream, and then ends up **obsolete.** The next sections take a look back through history to get a better perspective.

Pushing media along this time line of experimental use to obsolescence is typically some type of improvement in technology. As shown with the computer storage example in **Figure 2-1,** the new technology of optical storage used in a CD replaced the magnetic storage of a floppy disk. Today, the new

CHEAT CODE: OBSOLETE

An item becomes obsolete when it no longer performs a valuable task. Typically, something that is obsolete has been replaced by a better or more efficient technology. If you look at the example of computer storage, a floppy disk became obsolete when computer files started becoming larger than a single disk could hold. A CD-ROM can store the same amount of information as about 450 floppy disks. A DVD-ROM can store about seven CD-ROMs worth of information and flash drives even more.

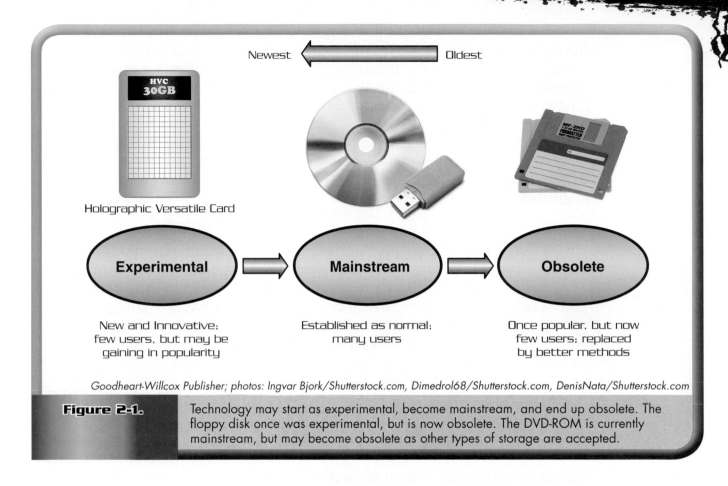

Newest ← Oldest

HVC 30GB

Holographic Versatile Card

Experimental → Mainstream → Obsolete

New and Innovative; few users, but may be gaining in popularity

Established as normal; many users

Once popular, but now few users; replaced by better methods

Goodheart-Willcox Publisher; photos: Ingvar Bjork/Shutterstock.com, Dimedrol68/Shutterstock.com, DenisNata/Shutterstock.com

Figure 2-1. Technology may start as experimental, become mainstream, and end up obsolete. The floppy disk once was experimental, but is now obsolete. The DVD-ROM is currently mainstream, but may become obsolete as other types of storage are accepted.

flash memory storage is replacing CD and DVD optical storage. Computer-generated media has advanced with the larger storage capacity of each experimental storage **medium**. Better graphics, faster play, and more features are added when the technology permits it. The next sections take a look back through history to get a better perspective on how technology has been linked to media experimentation and eventual obsolescence.

CHEAT CODE: MEDIUM

Entertainment media is often constructed on or stored in a medium. Here, the term *medium* describes the physical object on which information is stored. This can take the shape of a film strip, DVD, computer hard drive, or even the canvas of a painting. Where confusion takes place is that the plural form of the word *medium* is *media*. Where a single DVD is a storage medium, a stack of ten DVDs is termed DVD storage media. This dual meaning of the word media describes both the physical medium of DVD storage and the entertainment media stored on the DVD.

Ancient Times

In ancient times, art was the mainstream media of the day. Brilliant painting, sculptures, architecture, songs, and frescos were produced for the enjoyment and entertainment of the people. An art historian might point out that the great works of art from ancient Greek and Roman civilizations were the mainstream statues and paintings of their time.

The ancient Greek civilization began using the experimental media of theater, as shown in **Figure 2-2.** *Theater* involved a performance using actors to tell a story. Art was still mainstream and continued to be that way for centuries. Initially, theater was thought to be a fanciful activity and had little following. The comedies and tragedies written by the Greeks were often quirky and silly, as viewed by today's standards.

As time passed, theater began to gain greater acceptance. By the time of the ancient Romans, large theaters were being built to display theatrical performances. The Romans embraced theater and made it part of the mainstream media of their day.

CHEAT CODE: MOVIE

Movie is a slang term for a motion picture. This term derives from the idea that the picture was moving (in motion). Later, when sound was added, the motion pictures were termed "talkies" to indicate that sound and speech were included. Regardless of storage medium used, the movie itself is the moving action captured and not the medium of film, video, or DVD.

Last Century

Another big step in experimental media came with the invention of the *motion picture,* which used equipment like that shown in **Figure 2-3.** Today, these are called **movies,** whether delivered on film, video, or DVD. For the first time, people could see past events in motion. Before this, people could only see a still image—a photograph—of something. Early motion pictures had no sound and were short films showing fairly average scenes, like a person dancing, a baseball player hitting a ball, or children playing.

Eventually, motion pictures began to gain acceptance. After sound began to be integrated into the motion picture, people quickly accepted this media. Motion pictures began to replace live performances in theaters. The experimental media started to make its move toward becoming mainstream media.

Figure 2-2.

Theater was once the main form of entertainment. Ancient Greeks and Romans built amphitheaters and coliseums for plays and other forms of entertainment. Now, many people still enjoy theater, but other media, such as movies and television, have become the main sources of mainstream entertainment.

Shutterstock.com

Radio began as experimental media created by individuals who wanted to talk to each other over distances. Amateur radio operators built devices in their basements and connected them to huge antennas to transmit their voices. As the cost of technology for radio dropped, more people had access to the technology. This helped move radio from experimental media to mainstream media.

Unlike the radio broadcasts of today, early radio broadcast included scheduled shows and programming. This was much like television programming today, but without the picture. Voice actors would perform plays and programs just by speaking and using sound props. For example, tapping halved coconuts on a table sounded like a horse walking. Soon radio became mainstream media of the day. Eventually, people would gather around the family's radio to listen to voice drama. **Figure 2-4** shows an example of an early radio.

Even with radio as a mainstream media, there were radio broadcasts considered experimental. In the early days of rock and roll, people feared the jazzy sounds and controversial lyrics. Many people feared the message sent out to the children of the day. In some cases, they burned rock-and-roll records and forbade their children from listening to the music. As time passed, even rock and roll became mainstream. Today it is very popular and usually just called "rock."

Figure 2-3.

Motion pictures on film were once so common that most schools had several film projectors to show movies in classrooms. Now, these projectors are considered relics because the mainstream delivery method for movies is DVDs. Current experimental media for movies includes video taken with a cell phone.

Shutterstock.com

Figure 2-4.

Unlike today's MP3 players, which fit into your pocket, the early radios were huge pieces of furniture.

Shutterstock.com

Green Gamer

Avoid chemical cleaners when removing the smudge marks from an LCD or TV screen or a computer monitor. Look for environmentally friendly cleaners that will not harm equipment to protect your investment as well as the environment.

Figure 2-5.

Imagine watching television without color. That's right! Your grandparents, and maybe even your parents, may have watched most of their television on a black and white set. Today, you can watch color video on your cell phone.

Next up was experimental media that broadcast both sound and images. The **television** began to show up in homes in the late 1940s. Broadcasting was limited to one or two programs per day. The rest of the day it was just static and test patterns. Shows were in black and white, not color, as seen in **Figure 2-5.** As television stations began to provide more and more programming, radio stations switched from theatrical programming to music formats. In the early 1950s, television was rapidly becoming the preferred media of the day. By the mid 1950s, over half of the households in America had one TV set. In other words, television had moved from experimental media to mainstream media. Today, most homes in the United States have three or more televisions.

Current Times

In the present day, television is still mainstream, but several other important media have been developed. There has also been a move from audio/visual effects entertainment to interactive entertainment media. Interactive entertainment media, such as video games, incorporates audio and visual effects.

One of the new technologies developed over the past few decades is computers, like the one shown in **Figure 2-6.** In the early days of computers,

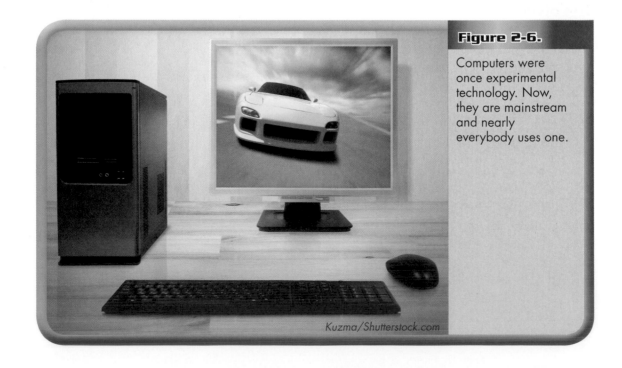

Figure 2-6.

Computers were once experimental technology. Now, they are mainstream and nearly everybody uses one.

few people were using this experimental technology. Most people thought only these few would ever use a computer. Today, the computer is mainstream and everywhere in everyday life. Computer entertainment media is now plentiful and takes on many forms. Movies, games, books, magazines, museum art, and many other media are readily available in computerized format. It would be nearly impossible to go an entire day without experiencing something not affected by computers.

With the mainstreaming of computers, new media were invented for delivery on a computer. One such media is the Internet. As recently as 20 years ago, many people had never used the Internet. At that time, the Internet was experimental media, just a curiosity for a few computer enthusiasts. Today, the Internet is mainstream and used by nearly every student. It can be accessed by desktop computers, laptop computers, cell phones, and other electronic devices.

Advancement Summary

Most technological advancements have followed the experimental–mainstream–obsolete model, as illustrated in **Figure 2-7.** Think about the telephone and cell phone. Many people no longer have a traditional "land line" telephone, instead they are using a cell phone for all voice communication over distances. In music, cassette tapes never fully replaced records, but compact discs (CDs) completely replaced both cassette tapes and records. Now, downloaded MP3 files used on MP3 players are threatening to make CDs obsolete. The next chapter looks at video games and how they replaced earlier formats of entertainment, moving from experimental to mainstream.

The audio/visual effects used today are created with highly advanced computer software products. Digital images and computer-generated (CG) characters are used in movies. Often, these characters are hard to distinguish from real objects and people. Today's audio/visual effects were refined through the process of obsolescence. This process has led to high-quality effects. Next time you watch a movie or television show, see if you can find a computer-generated audio or visual effect.

www.g-wlearning.com

Level up
your know-how
with Animated
Review 2-1.

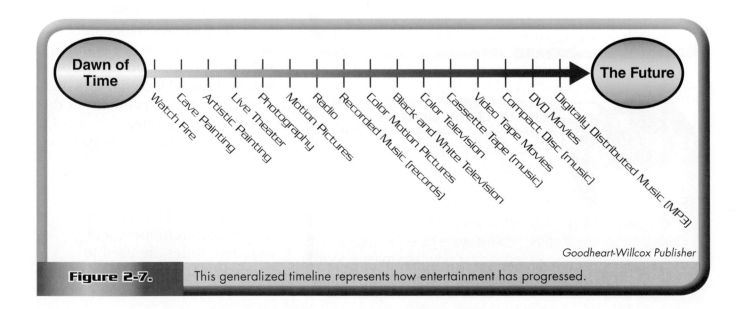

Goodheart-Willcox Publisher

Figure 2-7.   This generalized timeline represents how entertainment has progressed.

Technology changes rapidly. Things that were popular just a few years ago are now obsolete and unused. Think about some electronic devices you had when you were a kid that have been replaced by a new technology. What do you think caused each device to become obsolete?

Video Games

From almost the beginning of computers, designers developed games that used computer software. A video game is an electronic software product that has all of the elements of a game. It is played by combining a computer-generated game environment with a graphic display and a user interface.

Figure 2-8.

A game consists of rules, a game environment, and victory conditions.

Rules

Victory Condition

A Game

Game Environment

Goodheart-Willcox Publisher

Game Definition

The first part of the definition of a video game requires that it have all of the elements of a game. A *game* is defined as:

- an activity organized by rules;
- with an objective, goal, or victory condition; and
- in a game environment that enables play or pretending.

Figure 2-8 illustrates these three components of a game.

Later, you will compare and contrast different electronic software products. In doing so, you will see why digital toys and audio/visual effects do not fit the definition of a game.

The **rules** of a video game determine what *can* happen in the game world. This is more than just a list of instructions that tell the player what is permitted, prohibited, and required. Rules are used to create the challenges, goals, and victory conditions of the game.

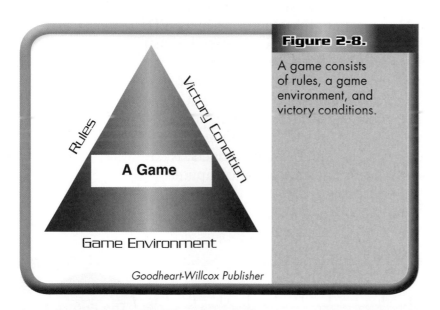

CHEAT CODE: RULES

The computer controlling a video game makes certain that the player cannot cheat the rules. Players of board games and card games have found ways to go undetected when cheating. Computers take the burden off of the other players for enforcing these rules and eliminating cheating. However, many video games contain cheat codes, as discussed in Chapter 1.

The **victory conditions** outline what is required to successfully complete or win the game. For example, in chess, the victory condition is to checkmate your opponent.

In the game world, the designer establishes rules for pretending. Real-world properties need not be included. A game world can include many situations that could never occur in the real world. Some examples of this might include loss of gravity, fantasy characters, ability to pass through walls, or whatever the game designers can imagine and program. One of the most common rules that exists in the game world is that amulets or tokens can provide special powers. Additionally, rules define play such as requiring a player to obtain a key to open a treasure chest. Together, all of the rules make the game work and keep the player moving toward the goal and victory condition.

Gameplay

Now that the victory condition, game environment, and rules are defined, something needs to bond it all together to make a game. **Gameplay** is what the player experiences during the game as a result of the core mechanics and structure of the game. This includes the set of challenges and obstacles the player must interact with in the game world. It also includes the actions a player can take to avoid and overcome those challenges or obstacles. Gameplay is nothing short of everything the player does and how the game makes it happen. It is the total experience that incorporates these gameplay subsystems:

○ how the user interface controls move the player's character
○ how the obstacles move to hinder the player
○ the way the player needs to overcome an obstacle
○ how the player successfully completes the game

In today's video games, gameplay can exist in multiple **gameplay modes,** such as: multiplayer mode, advanced mode, easy mode, quest mode, and online play mode. Choosing a different character with different skills may also change the gameplay mode. Anything that can change the way the game plays or how the challenges are presented is considered a different gameplay mode.

Ethical Gamer

Using age, gender, race, disability, or ethnicity as a way to describe others is unethical and sometimes illegal. Use bias-free language in all of your communication, whether verbal or printed, to show respect for those with whom you come in contact.

CASE STUDY

Invaders

In the classic video game *Space Invaders,* the player must overcome the challenge of aliens marching closer to Earth. The victory condition is destroying the alien force.

Creative Common License; see copyright statement on page 2.

In the classic game *Space Invaders,* the goal is to destroy all aliens before they reach Earth. As the game progresses, the challenge of doing so increases.

The gameplay allows the player to move left or right, hide behind barricades, and fire one shot at a time to destroy the alien invaders. The player has a left/right joystick and a fire button to control the gameplay for the player.

The character design, backgrounds, speed, direction, levels, and other aspects of the obstacles and challenges are controlled by the gameplay rules. The gameplay allows one player at a time to move and interact with the challenges and obstacles as they move toward the victory condition. Simultaneously, the rules control the limits of the gameplay by allowing only one fire at a time and the use of a single type of fire. There are no other weapons available and the player cannot change the weapon or rate of fire. The gameplay is the total experience and challenge of destroying the aliens with limited firepower.

Victory Condition	Game Environment	Basic Rules	Gameplay
Destroyed all aliens	Single screen Aliens in rows Four barricades Player at bottom	Aliens descend one space when they reach screen edge Aliens fire down toward Earth Aliens speed increases as number of aliens decreases Aliens rate of fire increases as number of aliens decreases Aliens move right at start Aliens reverse direction at screen edge Alien destroyed if hit by player fire Player moves right or left only at bottom Player losses a life if hit by alien fire Player awarded points for destroying an alien Player can fire by pressing fire button Player cannot fire again until shot leaves screen or hits an alien Game ends when player losses all lives Game ends if aliens reach Earth	Single mode: player as defender Single player Multiplayer, turn based Reset obstacles after each level Increase aliens speed on each level Increase aliens rate of fire on each level Display lives remaining Display score Record high scores

This chart shows the victory condition, game environment, basic rules, and gameplay for the classic video game *Space Invaders.*

Graphic Display

The second part of the definition of a video game requires the use of a graphic display generated by a computer. The display may be shown on a television, computer monitor, or handheld device (such as a GameBoy or cell phone). The *computer-generated graphic display* is an important element to the definition of a video game.

Take the example of a modern pinball machine, like that shown in **Figure 2-9.** The components, scoring, and mechanical devices are all controlled by a computer inside of the machine. The machine has a user interface, including flippers and a plunger to redirect the ball. These aspects easily fit the criteria for an *electronic* game. However, the pinball machine is not a *video* game because it does not have a computer-generated display or video that presents the game environment. It may have some

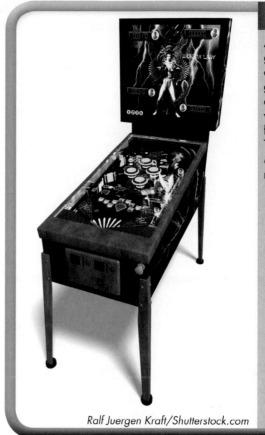

A modern pinball game is computer controlled, but the game environment is a mechanical board with mechanical flippers and obstacles. Therefore, it is an *electronic* game, but is not a *video* game.

Ralf Juergen Kraft/Shutterstock.com

video features to display the scores and animated scenes to enhance gameplay. The game environment, however, is a mechanical board with mechanical obstacles, *not* a video projection. For a pinball game to be a video game, the game environment must occur within the video display. Several pinball games have been created as video games. A virtual ball bounces on a video screen. The ball movement is controlled by virtual flippers and virtual obstacles. Since the game environment appears on a computer-generated video display, it qualifies as a video game.

LEVEL UP! 2.2

Think about a recent trip to a video arcade. Other than a pinball machine, what games did you see that were computer controlled, but not *video* games? Think about how each game functions and what feature of a video game was lacking? Is each game better as it is or should it be made into a video game? Why?

User Interface

The last requirement for a video game is that the movements of the player and obstacles are controlled through a user interface. The user interface is any device used to input information from the player into the computer running the video game. The most common of these are the game controller, keyboard, and mouse. Whatever the form of the user interface, this is how the player "enters" the game environment.

CHEAT CODE: VIRTUAL REALITY

Today there are virtual reality interfaces that use no controllers. Kinect for the Microsoft Xbox 360 system is one such virtual reality interface. The system scans your body and inputs the movements of your entire body inside the game without anything attached to you. You can interact with the game environment as if you were really there.

New games have very sophisticated user interface devices, including wireless, motion-based controllers. You may have played games where the player swings a bat-style controller. The swing you take is input into the game as the swing of your character's bat in a baseball game. Other games might use a dance pad, guitar, or other game-specific user interface. Some **virtual reality** games have very complex user interface devices that can almost perfectly integrate the real world with the game world.

Types of Games (Genre and Themes)

A game *genre* is a type or major category of game. Some common genres are illustrated in **Figure 2-10.** Most video games can be categorized into at least one genre:

○ action: focus on the player moving to build skill and game difficulty
○ board/card/quiz: adapted from existing board games, card games, or quiz show games
○ educational: purposely built to train or educate the player
○ fighting: use character animations to perform a physical hand-to-hand battle
○ music/party: use songs and rhythm as the main feature
○ puzzle: require solving a spatial puzzle
○ role playing: focus on fantasy role playing whereby the player's avatar performs quests and battles to build skill points and increase power levels
○ shooter: main feature is launching an object towards characters or objects
○ simulation: seek to emulate real-world situations and activities
○ sports: derived from physical sporting games
○ strategy: require thought and planning to beat the opponent or computer
○ toy: lacks interactivity, rules, or objectives

Many games can be placed into more than one genre. A single game may use elements of several genres to create an original story and gameplay.

Each genre may be subdivided into subcategories, or *themes,* to group games with similar characteristics. The easiest way to understand game themes is in the sports genre. "Sports" is a big umbrella that covers all types of sports. Below the genre of sports are themes that separate each game by the individual sport. Here, football games are grouped away from other themes, like soccer and basketball. Each sport gets its own theme. Most other genres have multiple themes, as well.

Video Game Genres and Themes

Action
Adventure
Bat and Ball
Crime
Flight
Horror
Platform
Tactical

Board Games, Card Games, and Game (Quiz) Show

Educational/ Edutainment

Fighting
Martial arts
Other

Music and Party
Dance
Music
Party
Singing

Puzzle
Guessing game
Logic puzzle
Mechanical puzzle
Transport puzzle
Word puzzle

Role Playing (RPG)
Single/ multiplayer
Massive multiplayer

Shooter
First person
Side scrolling (shoot 'em)
Third person

Simulation
A-life
Flight
Sim
Tycoon

Sports
Baseball
Basketball
Bowling
Fishing
Football
Golf
Hockey
Hunting
Racing
Skateboarding
Snowboarding
Soccer
Tennis
Wrestling

Strategy
Turn based

Toys
AI pets
Screen savers

Figure 2-10. This shows some typical genres and themes for video games.

Goodheart-Willcox Publisher

Digital Toy

Unlike a video game, a ***digital toy*** does *not* meet the criteria of a game. It does not have a structured set of rules on how to play with it correctly or it has no objective or gameplay goal. A digital pet might be an example of a digital toy, like that shown in **Figure 2-11.** The user interface may allow the owner of a digital pet to scratch or pet the animal, feed it, and even throw it a stick to chase. These actions are all entertaining, but do not really establish a meaningful gameplay goal, as there are no real challenges or purpose for playing. Most notably absent is the lack of a set of rules to define a victory condition.

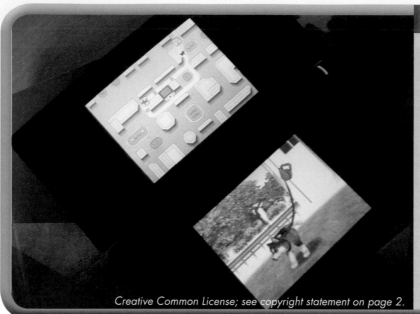

Figure 2-11.

An electronic pet is a toy, not a game. It has no set victory condition; therefore it is not a game.

Some digital toys try to incorporate some gameplay goals, such as training a dog to sit, stay, or rollover. Some of these digital toys have even evolved into simple games where the pet can grow into something else with greater power or ability. Players can then test their pet against other players and establish a game world with gameplay features. But, for the most part, the interactions between the player and toy are simply there for enjoyment. There are no points, levels, or mission objectives. In the hierarchy of games, digital toys are still included by most designers. More and more frequently, digital toys are incorporating more aspects of gameplay. Some digital toys are bridging the gap and blurring the line between what is a digital toy and what is a simple game platform.

Marketing Your Video Game

Different people like different things and similar people like similar things. This is the most important statement in marketing. The goal of marketing is to find a group of potential buyers that share similar interests aligned with your video game.

Genre-Based Marketing

Before you begin designing a video game, you will need to know the genre and theme under which you will be marketing it. Each game theme has a set of loyal followers, or **current customers,** who prefer those types of games. People who currently purchase a particular type of game are likely to purchase other games of that same genre/theme.

When looking at who might be willing and able to buy your game, start with the entire population in the area where you are going to sell the game. This might be the United States, North America, Europe, and so on. The entire population is a very large group that includes people who might buy your game, some who will buy it, and others who will not buy it. Your goal in looking at this population is to identify one or more target markets for your game.

A *target market* is the segment of the population on which you will focus your attention and resources to attract as buyers. **Figure 2-12** shows how a general population can be refined to a target market. The target market should be a group of potential customers who would likely purchase a game of a certain genre/theme. A *potential customer* is anyone who is willing and able to buy your product. A group of potential customers is typically made up of new customers, current customers, and anyone else willing and able to buy the product. You may have many different target markets for your game. Different advertising and promotions may be produced to attract each targeted group.

To fully understand how these marketing items might figure into your game design and selling, take a look at the following example. The target market for a basketball-themed game includes all of the people who currently play *NBA Live, NCAA Basketball, NBA 2K13, Backyard Basketball,* and all other versions of basketball games currently available. You should choose a target market that includes people in your population that are significantly likely to purchase a basketball-themed game based on **demographic segmentation**. Certain demographic information, such as age, income, and gender, can help determine the most likely potential buyers.

CHEAT CODE: DEMOGRAPHIC SEGMENTATION

Demographic segmentation refers to the use of characteristics such as age, income, and gender to segment or separate a population. This separation process groups people with similarities to each other. If a demographic segment is large enough, it may become a target market. A population of pet owners may be segmented by the type of pet and the age of the owner. Here, dog owners over the age of 55 may become a demographically segmented target market for a company selling a dog-walking service.

To find the demographic segmentation for basketball-themed games, marketing teams survey current owners of basketball games to determine the personal characteristics, or demographics, of the buyers. In this example, in a large population, the surveyed buyers were found to be males, age 16 to 24,

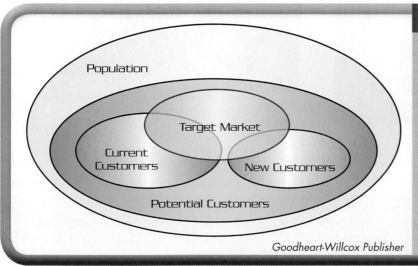

Population

Target Market

Current Customers

New Customers

Potential Customers

Figure 2-12.

This Venn diagram (a diagram with overlapping ellipses) shows how a group of potential customers is smaller than the entire population. A marketing campaign should target the potential customers, not the rest of the population who will not or cannot buy the game.

Goodheart-Willcox Publisher

with incomes of between $25,000 and $39,000 per year (for those who reported an income). Based on this survey information, all males fitting these criteria would likely be interested in basketball-themed games. Therefore, as potential customers, they are part of the target market. Target markets will vary with the product, as shown in **Figure 2-13.**

Think about using demographic segmentation and target marketing. Why would a dog-walking service want to segment the pet owners of dogs from all other pets available? Why do you think they would select the demographic of over age 55 as a target market? Do you think demographic segmentation is fair or discriminating? Why?

Marketing Tools

Once you find your target market, you need to select marketing tools to attract buyers to your product. *Marketing tools* are any device or action that draws attention to your product. Examples of marketing tools include:

- television commercials;
- e-mail blasts (targeted mass e-mails, *not* spam);
- product website;

Goodheart-Willcox Publisher

Figure 2-13. The target market for each of these games is very different. One of these games is designed for children under the age of 10, while the other game is designed for players over the age of 17.

- free trials or demos;
- marketing brochures;
- game packaging;
- billboards;
- computer screen savers;
- demonstrations; and
- booths at trade shows.

The list could go on and on. Anything a company does to encourage buyers or publicize the product is a marketing tool, such as that shown in **Figure 2-14.**

Why is a genre so important? From a marketing perspective, the genre is critical in determining if there are enough people willing and able to purchase your product. Knowing what your competition is currently selling in a given genre/theme and how your game will be different are likely the most important aspects of commercial success.

Unique Selling Point

Each product must have a ***unique selling point (USP)*** that is significant enough for people to tell one competing game apart from another. The unique selling point is simply what your product offers that other products do not. A USP for *NCAA Basketball* over *NBA 2K13* is that *NCAA Basketball* features college basketball teams. On the flip side, the USP of *NBA 2K13* over *NCAA Basketball* is it features professional basketball teams. A critical feature of each game is incorporated in their USP. A person who loves college basketball and cannot live without watching their favorite team, may prefer the NCAA game over the NBA version. Both games have similar gameplay, but each has a USP of available teams, characteristics of individual players, their gameplay abilities, and attributes. This allows for multiple products for sale in the same theme. The USP can also become an important marketing tool, as shown in **Figure 2-15.**

Figure 2-14.

Use of point-of-purchase displays can help guide customers to your game. This is a full-size character of Big Daddy from *Bioshock*. Does this cool display make you want to see more *Bioshock* characters or find out what Big Daddy does? Does it make you want to walk into the gaming store and take a look around?

Figure 2-15.

The Mario franchise represents a great USP for Nintendo. Marketing displays such as this inflatable Mario character promote the USP.

With your USP, you can also help target potential customers. If you were designing a college basketball video game, you might have a display on college campuses. You may even have a kiosk set up during home basketball games for students to play your game. Imagine having fans play a video game at your kiosk between the same two teams that will be playing the actual basketball game. This would generate in these fans a lot of interest for your video game. The fact they are attending a college basketball game likely means they will be interested in the teams featured in your video game. Having a video game based on professional basketball at the kiosk may not generate as much interest because the USP of that game is not college basketball.

Think about one of your favorite games. What USP made you purchase that game over other games in the same genre/theme?

Marketing Effort

Marketing effort is the time, energy, and expense undertaken to promote your product. The marketing effort needed to gain interest in a large group of people with a lot of differences is huge. On the other hand, the marketing effort needed to gain interest in a group of people that are similar is smaller.

Take the example of a college basketball video game presented earlier. If you were to run the same demonstration kiosk at a professional football game, you might have fewer people interested. This is because a fan at a professional football game is likely different from a fan at a college basketball game. While there will likely be some people who are fans of both sports, your marketing effort to get the same number of people interested in your product would be higher at the professional football game. This audience is dissimilar from an audience at a college basketball game.

Target marketing and genre recognition are very important. Do not waste time and money trying to sell a video game about fashion design at a football game. Target your marketing effort. Think about your game and how you will promote it before, during, and after the design stage.

Chapter Summary

- A game genre is a type or major category of game and can include action, role playing, education, simulation, and sports.
- Gaming genres may be subdivided into themes to group games with similar characteristics.
- Theater was once the mainstream entertainment, but it was replaced by other media such as radio, movies, and television.
- Computerized entertainment media generally falls into the categories of a video game or a digital toy.
- A video game in which a user plays soccer would fall into the genre or "sports" and the theme of "soccer" while a game in which the user cares for a cat would be classified a digital toy.
- Most technological advancements, including media, have followed the experimental to mainstream to obsolete life cycle.
- Each game genre and theme has a set of current customers who are likely to purchase other games in the same genre/theme.
- A unique selling point is what a given product offers that other products do not.
- Marketing effort is the time, energy, and expense undertaken to promote a product and should be directed to the target market in order to get the most benefit for the effort expended.

Check Your Video Game IQ

Now that you have finished this chapter, see what you know about video game design by taking the chapter posttest.

www.m.g-wlearning.com

www.g-wlearning.com

Review Your Knowledge

On a separate sheet of paper or in a word processing document, match the following terms with the definition that fits best.

A. marketing tools
B. potential customer
C. virtual reality
D. target market
E. theater
F. unique selling point
G. motion picture
H. demographic segmentation
I. marketing effort
J. gameplay mode

1. Complex user interface that reads body motion and displays it in the game world.

2. Anyone willing and able to buy your product.

3. Special feature one product offers that other similar products do not possess.

4. Segment of the population determined to be the most likely potential customers.

5. Time, energy, and expense undertaken to promote a product.

6. Different game segments that change the way the game plays or how the challenges are presented.

7. Movie delivered on film, video, or DVD.

8. Any device or action that draws attention to a product.

9. Performance by actors to tell a story.

10. Use of characteristics such as age, income, and gender to segment a population.

On a separate sheet of paper or in a word processing document, answer each of the following questions.

11. Define *audio/visual effect*.

12. What is *mainstream media*?

13. Describe the process by which an experimental media becomes mainstream.

14. What is a *video game?*

15. List the three criteria for an activity to be classified as a game.

16. _____ are used to create the challenges, goals, and victory conditions of the game.

17. List three things that can exist in the game world that do not occur in the real world.

18. The term used to describe what the player experiences during the game as a result of the core mechanics and structure of the game is _____.

19. What is the *user interface?*

20. How is a genre different from a theme?

21. Explain why a digital toy is not a video game.

22. Who should be in the *target market* for your video game?

23. List five possible marketing tools for a video game.

24. What is the *marketing effort?*

25. List four gameplay subsystems.

Apply Your STEM Knowledge

Some things in life prove the statement, "truth is stranger than fiction." This is never truer than the reality of the platypus. A platypus is an interesting animal that lives in Australia. It might easily be described as a sort of Frankenstein's Monster of creation. It seems to have been assembled with random parts from other creatures that exist all over the planet. It has fur like a rabbit, a tail like a beaver, a beak like a duck, feet like an otter, lays eggs like a chicken, and has a sharp, poisonous barb called a spur on its hind foot like the thorn on a cactus. Until its discovery, most animals fit neatly into the classification system you learned about in science class: Kingdom, Phylum, Class, Order, Family, Genus, and Species. However, the platypus is a unique animal that does not neatly fit into the classification system.

Shutterstock.com

 ## Social Studies

1. In addition to the platypus, Australia has many creatures that are unique when compared to animals in other parts of the world.

   A. Research Australia and list ten interesting animals and their unique characteristics.

   B. Locate Australia on a map or globe. Explain how Australia's location might allow for the unique adaptations found in its wildlife population.

Science

2. Video game designers may use features from many different animals to create characters, like a person with wings. These parts add style to the character and also give it special powers, such as the ability to fly. If you were a video game designer faced with a character that looked like a platypus, what special strength abilities would you give it? Create a table listing the special body part or physical ability in one column and its special strength in a second column. Include a chart title and column headings.

Platypus Character Attributes and Strengths	
Part	Strength

Goodheart-Willcox Publisher

 Science

3. Locate pictures of a platypus or draw an original platypus game character. Import the picture into Microsoft PowerPoint. Draw arrows to text boxes to identify the physical attributes and list the special strength abilities of that part.

Super Spur: activates spur attack

Example

Goodheart-Willcox Publisher

Language Arts

4. Write five game rules to define the use of the strengths of your platypus character from activity 2. Example: Super Spur causes enemies to fall asleep for ten seconds.

Mathematics

5. The marketing department is looking at selling a new basketball game. It has completed a survey to determine the percentages of the population willing and able to purchase the new game. Their findings are shown in the second column of the table below. Assume the overall population will purchase in trends similar to the survey group. With a total population of 1,000,000 people, determine the total number of people who are potential customers, current customers, and new customers. Then, determine the size of the target market for the basketball game. On a separate sheet of paper, calculate the total number of people for A through D.

Research Information Summary		
Market Segment	**Survey Percentages**	**Total People**
Population size		1,000,000
Potential customers	25% of the population	A
Current customers	6% of the population	B
New customers	11% of the population	C
Target market	20% of the current and new customers	D

Goodheart-Willcox Publisher

Working in Teams

In teams, research, debate, and form a group opinion on each of the Level Up! activities in this chapter. Prepare a PowerPoint presentation of ten slides (five to seven minutes) to present to the class explaining the group's opinions for each Level Up! activity. Include text, pictures, video, animations, and slide transitions as appropriate to help explain your positions.

Gamer Portfolio

It is helpful to have a checklist of components that should be included in your portfolio. Your instructor may provide a checklist. If not, create a checklist that works best for you. Before you begin collecting information for your portfolio, write an objective related to creating the portfolio. The objective should contain enough details so that you can easily judge when it is accomplished. Creating a clear objective is a good starting point for beginning work on your portfolio.

1. Create a checklist to use as an ongoing reference as you create your portfolio throughout this class.

2. Decide on the purpose of the portfolio you are creating—temporary or short-term employment, career, or college application.

3. Do research on the Internet to find articles about writing objectives. Also, look for articles that contain sample objectives for creating a portfolio.

4. Write an objective for creating your portfolio that will be used in applying for a job or to a college. Include statements for both a print portfolio and an e-portfolio.

G-W Learning Mobile Site

Visit the G-W Learning mobile site to complete the chapter pretest and posttest and to practice vocabulary using e-flash cards. If you do not have a smartphone, visit the G-W Learning companion website to access these features.

G-W Learning mobile site: www.m.g-wlearning.com

G-W Learning companion website: www.g-wlearning.com

Common Core

College and Career Readiness

CTE Career Ready Practices. Go online and search for "desirable workplace skills." Pick five from the list. Beside each of the five you selected, indicate an academic skill that directly relates to the workplace skill.

Writing. Conduct research on how much money is spent annually on video game purchases. Write an informative report consisting of several paragraphs to describe your findings and the implications this may have for the video game design industry.

Speaking and Listening. Research the demographics of the largest groups of purchasers of video games. Ask questions of people who are in these groups. Compile information about these groups including their age range, average income range, and whether they are male or female. Use this information to create demographic segmentation for a hypothetical video game. Using various elements (visual displays, written handouts, technological displays), present your hypothetical game and its target market to the class. Explain why you chose the demographic segment you did.

Event Prep: Prejudged Computer Game

Creating a computer game is a competitive event that may be offered by your Career and Technical Student Organization (CTSO). This may be an individual or team event. There may be two parts to this event: the prejudged program and the performance portion. The event calls for the development of a computer game as outlined by the organization. The topic will be detailed on the organization's website. Students are given an opportunity to create a game that shows creativity, programming skills, and meets the definition of a video game. To prepare for creating a game:

1. Read the guidelines provided by your organization. Visit the organization's website early in the school year so you will have plenty of time to create your game. Make certain that you ask any questions about points that you do not understand immediately after you review the guidelines.

2. Create a checklist of the guidelines for the event.

3. There will be specific directions given as to the topic how the game should be created and presented to the judges. The prejudged portion of game creation will be submitted before the competition. Read the submission rules for the date, number of copies, and so on. These rules must be followed in order to qualify for the event.

4. The organization may specify a programming language or game engine to use or leave it to the participant's choice. Make certain you are clear on what can be used before beginning the process.

5. Creating a game can take a lot of time to properly prepare; therefore, it is important to start early. Set a deadline so that you can create the game at a comfortable pace.

6. After you create your first playable level, ask your teacher to review it and give you feedback.

7. Once you have the final iteration of your game, review the checklist. Make sure you have addressed all requirements. You will be penalized if a direction is not followed exactly.

Objectives

After completing this chapter, you will be able to:

- Discuss non-electronic games throughout history.
- Place electronic games on a time line of development.
- Describe significant trends in game development over the past twenty years.
- Project possible developments in new generations of video games.
- Explain how play has been important in developing societies and cultures.
- Explain how play helps children and adults gain knowledge.

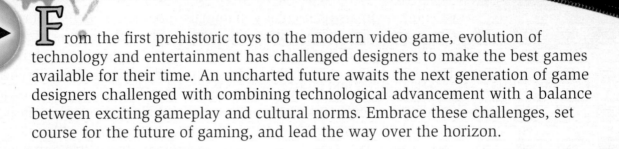

Chapter 3
Evolution of the Game

From the first prehistoric toys to the modern video game, evolution of technology and entertainment has challenged designers to make the best games available for their time. An uncharted future awaits the next generation of game designers challenged with combining technological advancement with a balance between exciting gameplay and cultural norms. Embrace these challenges, set course for the future of gaming, and lead the way over the horizon.

Check Your Video Game IQ

Before you begin this chapter, see what you already know about video game design by taking the chapter pretest.

www.m.g-wlearning.com

www.g-wlearning.com

College and Career Readiness

Reading Prep. In preparation for reading the chapter, read a newspaper or magazine article on the latest development in game design or on a recently released game system. Summarize the information. As you read, keep in mind the author's main points and conclusions.

- Discuss how violence in video games affects children and adults.
- Discuss how video games affect behavior, cognitive development, and motor skills.
- Describe how video game content is regulated.
- Use terminology appropriate for communication in the video game industry.
- Define terminology used by gamers and online gaming communities.
- Explain player immersion.
- Describe what factors result in player immersion.
- Identify factors in current games that result in player immersion.

One of the unique characteristics of human beings is their ability to design and use tools. At the dawn of humanity, early humans were adapting objects from their environment into the primitive tools needed to save labor when performing tasks. Conceivably, this was occurring before the first spoken word. As the adults sought out useful objects for survival, maybe a sharp stone or pointed stick to help prepare or catch food, the children sought out the entertainment that every juvenile uses to build physical dexterity, like that shown in **Figure 3-1**. *Physical dexterity* is skill or ability at performing physical tasks.

Early Play

Most young animals (particularly mammals) use tactics such as play fighting with siblings, chasing tails, and playful hunting. Each of these entertaining events helps build hunting skills and physical coordination. **Coordination** is how well your hands, feet, eyes, and so on, work together to complete a task. Imagine the playful kitten pouncing on a leaf blowing in the wind or the clumsy puppy trying to catch the tail of a littermate. Each action builds survival skills through play. Early humans certainly found the same skill building important. Development of hand-eye coordination, muscle memory, brain-extremity pathways, and motor skills are a few benefits of play.

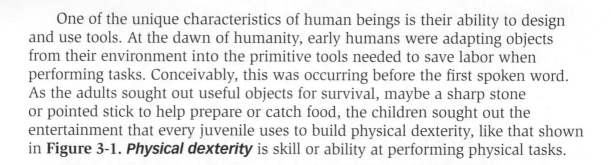

Figure 3-1.

Early humans needed to build strength and agility to survive. Children did this by playing with toys. Toys and games are still used today to build strong bodies.

Shutterstock.com

When you are able to see something and reach out and grab it, you are developing *hand-eye coordination.* Catching a ball requires hand-eye coordination to move your hand to the place the ball will be moments before the ball actually gets there. Practicing by playing catch teaches you how to get better at catching and how a ball travels. Eventually, when you see the ball moving, you can anticipate where it is traveling and move your hand to a place in the path of the ball.

Muscle memory is how the muscles in the body remember how to react. A great example of muscle memory is penmanship. Penmanship is the drawing of letters. When you were a child, you practiced penmanship to teach your hand muscles how to move a pencil to form each letter. Now when you think "A", your fingers remember how to properly move to draw an A. Typing is another good example of muscle memory.

Brain-extremity pathways are the connections from the brain to movement points throughout your body. When you were learning to walk, your brain had to send many signals to reach the correct muscle in your body. Eventually, your brain learned which path led to your leg muscles and created a pathway. The nerves along that path all work together to send the signal from the brain to the legs. Each nerve along that path has many branching dendrites, illustrated in **Figure 3-2,** through which the signal can enter and exit the nerve cell. If the signal to walk exits out of the wrong dendrite, you would miss a step, trip, and fall. Any nerve that did not send the signal along the correct pathway would stop the movement.

Motor skills put most of the other skills together to make the movement look smooth. This includes things like balancing or highly refined movements. The entire body is involved when someone is swimming. The arm movement, leg movement, breathing, head turning, and balance are all coordinated motor skills to make a person efficiently

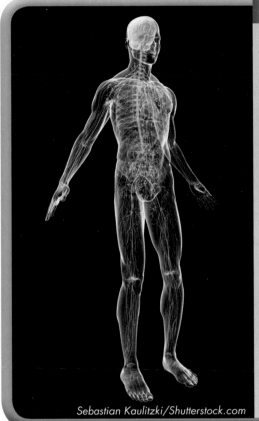

Figure 3-2.

Shown is a rendering of the human nervous system. The brain and spinal cord send electrical signals along nerves to your muscles. Repeated use of the same neural (brain-extremity) pathway creates muscle memory.

Sebastian Kaulitzki/Shutterstock.com

move in the water. Complicated body movements, like those used during swimming, involving large muscles are gross motor skills. Delicate movements, like cursive writing or threading a needle, that require very precise and small movements are called fine motor skills. All of these skills are developed through repeating the same movements over and over again. This practice makes you better at each physical activity.

As children, early humans probably kicked a stone, kicked it again, and again. It is conceivable that this simple stone quickly evolved into the first toy, perhaps something like those shown in **Figure 3-3.** Not yet a game with

Figure 3-3. Tools and toys like these were used by early humans for training and survival.

CHEAT CODE: REFLEX

A reflex is a quick, involuntary movement. The reflex action of getting hit in the knee is to kick your leg. This action is not processed by the brain, but it is interpreted on the spinal cord. This shortens the path the signal takes and the reaction is much faster. Repeated practicing can train your body to react on reflex and perform faster. A professional hockey goalie can react much faster than you to a puck flying 100 mph because of practice-induced reflexes.

the structure of rules and a victory condition, but certainly entertaining. Not long after, someone probably picked up a stick to hit the stone and developed another toy. As play continued, hand-eye coordination increased, reaction times decreased, and **reflexes** grew quicker. Early humans began to socialize with these toys. *Socializing* is interacting in a group environment. Eventually, communication between humans advanced enough to establish rules for how to use toys.

Early craftsmen began shaping the natural objects around them to fashion toys designed for a specific use. An early toy was the yo-yo, shown in **Figure 3-4.** Several examples of this simple toy carved out of marble have been uncovered in ancient civilizations. Attaching a string or strip of leather to the center of a rock can amuse a child, but it was still not a *game*. A game is:

- an activity organized by rules;
- with an objective, goal, or victory condition; and
- in a game environment that enables play or pretending.

Figure 3-04.

Not just for fun, playing with toys such as this yo-yo helps your body learn to react in rhythm with an event. This increases your ability to coordinate movement.

Shutterstock.com

The yo-yo does not have a set of rules, a goal, or a game environment, but it sure is fun to play with. In this case, **play** is defined as the participation in an entertaining activity. Our earliest ancestors had to learn to play and have time to play. Remember, there were no grocery stores then. Basic survival was still the objective of the day. For that reason, most toys and play for children helped develop skills needed for survival. In the past, young girls played with dolls to learn basic child care. Young boys played with sticks, balls, and targets to develop physical hunting skills. So, toys like dolls or sling shots, like that shown in **Figure 3-5,** helped entertain and educate.

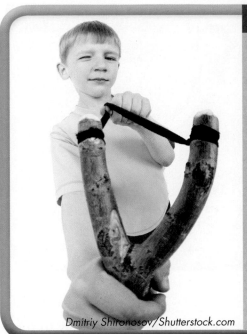

Figure 3-5.

Playing with a toy sling shot can be fun and entertaining to a child. However, for early humans, flinging rocks at tree stumps and targets refined skills needed to hit moving prey, which fed the family.

Dmitriy Shironosov/Shutterstock.com

LEVEL UP! 3.1

Think about a task that you are really good at performing. It might be shooting a basketball, doing a math problem, or anything else. Chances are you were not a superstar on your first attempt at doing this task. How did practice make you better?

Physical Competition

The enjoyment of toys eventually led to the natural desire to **compete** to see who was the best. Rules were invented to turn simple toys into game objects. **Physical trials** such as long jumps, sprinting races, boxing, and sparring were some of humankind's first competitive events. These are the simplest games invented.

Green Gamer

Saving money is at the top of the list for many schools as well as consumers. Up to 25 percent of energy costs can be saved by simply turning off equipment when not in use. Turn off all computers and game consoles each evening to save energy. Make sure the lights are off whenever you leave a room or if there is enough natural light to brighten the room.

Figure 3-6.

Jogging for entertainment is not a game. Without a victory condition or rules, it lacks the structure found in competitive event games.

According to the definition of a game, a simple competitive event such as the 100-yard dash may fit into the category of a game. The 100-yard dash has rules, such as a starting line, a marked distance, and contestants all starting at the same time. It also has a victory condition: the first runner to cross the finish line wins. The game environment of a structured running course layout establishes this competitive sport as a game. However, simply running for enjoyment, shown in **Figure 3-6,** is not a game.

By adding some simple toys to the environment, such as a discus, shot put, javelin, hurdles, and other obstacles, more game elements come into play. This starts the process of creating more-structured game environments for individual competition. Later, formal competitions involving these physical activities became known as the Olympic Games.

Sports eventually developed more-structured rules. Game environments began to develop involving team sports. Games such as baseball and soccer are good examples of how sports have designed a game environment. **Figure 3-7** shows the game environment for baseball. A big, grass-covered field with standing goal posts and fixed dimensions of length and width establish the game environment for a soccer game.

The *game environment* is a setting altered or designed to play a specific activity. In the example of a soccer field, the physical environment is

Figure 3-7.

The game of baseball is a good example of how a sport designed a game environment. The shape and size of the infield is set by the rules, as is the height of the pitcher's mound. Many rules govern gameplay. The victory condition is the team who scores the most runs after nine innings. If the game is tied after nine innings, additional innings are played.

significantly altered by clearing trees and obstacles, creating a flat playing surface, and constructing goals. Notice how this differs from the environment needed to run a 100-yard dash race. For a foot race, any stretch of more-or-less flat land may be the setting for the race. A soccer, baseball, or football field is a fully designed environment that specifically enables play for the particular game.

Intellectual Competition

Just as the concept of games was established for physical events, **mental acuity** games were developed. These games were accessible to most people as they did not require athletic skill. Games that involve intellectual competition include puzzles (puzzle games), board games, and card games.

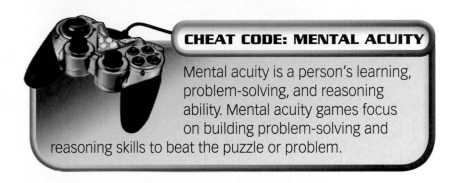

CHEAT CODE: MENTAL ACUITY

Mental acuity is a person's learning, problem-solving, and reasoning ability. Mental acuity games focus on building problem-solving and reasoning skills to beat the puzzle or problem.

Puzzles

Puzzles require the player to mentally analyze and solve a problem. They were easy to make and play. Examples of puzzles include the wooden peg games that require a player to jump other pegs to obtain the fewest remaining pegs, as shown in **Figure 3-8.** These games had rules such as game setup, how to begin, and moves permitted or not permitted. Additionally, these puzzles had a victory condition, which was the solution to the puzzle. Lastly, these puzzles created a game environment specific to enable play: the construction of a game board for the pegs. Puzzles are played by a single player to achieve a victory condition. In other words, the competition was with oneself.

Figure 3-8.

This is a simple puzzle played with wooden pegs and small stones. Puzzles similar to this have been played throughout human history.

Ethical Gamer

Most schools establish a set of ethics that outlines acceptable behavior when interacting with other students and school personnel. As a student, it is important to know the code of ethics for your school so you can behave in a correct manner.

Early Board Games

Board games soon followed the first puzzle games. **Board games** require two or more players to engage in mental competition. These games may have more elaborate game pieces than puzzles. Games similar to chess that had rules for the specific movement of individual game pieces were commonly used to play an artificial war game between the two opponents. One of the earliest known board games is the ***Royal Game of Ur,*** shown in **Figure 3-9.** It dates to around 3000 BC. This game was played similar to the modern game of backgammon. It relied on strategy and chance to determine a winner.

The *Royal Game of Ur* and others of its time used irregularly shaped dice to randomly generate a number for the player movement. Technology and game design grew over time. Around 700 BC, the first know cubical dice were fashioned. This gave competitive board games a better random-number generator to determine movement.

A **random-number generator** is any device used to fairly and without bias create a number at random within a given range of numbers. A wide variety of dice—basic random-number generators—are shown in **Figure 3-10.**

Figure 3-9.

Royal Game of Ur is one of the earliest known board games. This example is shown in a museum.

Figure 3-10.

Dice are used as a random-number generator. Many games make use of dice to vary gameplay or add an element of chance to the game.

Random numbers are important to games. Generating random numbers allow for different results every time the game is played. This keeps the game fresh and playable. Without the random numbers, a game would quickly become stale, as the moves would always be the same. The stale condition was often a problem with the earlier puzzle games. Once the solution was found, you could continue to make the same moves and achieve victory, resulting in no real reason to play the puzzle game again.

Card Games

Not until the technology of paper and printing did card games become available. **Card games** involve using a series of uniquely printed cards within the set rules of a game. They were very popular, as a single deck of cards could be used to play several different games. Each game would have its own set of rules. In the late 1300s, tarot cards, shown in **Figure 3-11,** were invented. Originally, **tarot cards** did not have the mystical overtones as used by psychics of today. Instead, they were the common deck of playing cards of the day. Game rules could be changed to play games with only one player, like solitaire, or many players in competition, like old maid or go-fish. Rules could even be changed to create games of **chance**.

Figure 3-11.

Tarot cards are an early example of playing cards. Originally, they were used for playing card games, not for psychic readings, as is common today.

CHEAT CODE: CHANCE

Using random generators, such as dice, card shuffling, or a wild card, add chance to games. Random chance of getting a lucky number or special card added interest to a standard game by allowing different results each time the game was played. These concepts of chance are still used in games today.

Card games continued to grow in popularity as advances in printing technology made the cards cheaper and easier to produce. Once decks of cards became cheap, all classes of people could afford their own. A purchase of a deck of playing cards could provide entertainment for several years with hundreds of games by simply changing the rules of play. With low cost and multiple uses, playing cards were a great investment for the time.

With mass-produced playing cards readily available at cheap prices, more competitive games became popular. Games like **poker** and bridge emerged as the most popular games. In the 1800s and early 1900s, travelers entertained themselves on long ocean voyages, riverboat rides, and train trips. Many of these games are still very popular. In fact, poker is believed to be the most-played game in the world even today.

CHEAT CODE: POKER

Poker is a game of chance played with cards. The name is thought to be derived from the term *poke*. A poke was a personal money pouch. Poker was a gambling game designed to move money from one man's poke to another. Later, the term poke evolved into the word *pocket* when the pouch was sewn into clothing. Poke was recently used to describe a pocket-monster card game: Pokémon.

Themed Board Games

Continued advances in printing technology made game ideas easier to implement and cheaper to produce. The **themed board game** made its mark in history beginning around 1900. In a themed board game, the players are entertained in an elaborate pretending environment where they become characters traveling on a game board. Typically, there is a random number generator in the form of dice or numbered cards. Players make decisions as they travel the board. Popular themed board games include *Monopoly, Clue,* and *The Game of Life.* The board game *Monopoly* is shown in **Figure 3-12.** Each game has a central theme and lays the foundation for role-playing games.

Figure 3-12.

Monopoly is one of the most popular themed board game of all time. Who has not played some version of the game at least once?

Goodheart-Willcox Publisher

Game Immersion

With the invention of the themed board game, pretending became a major part of gameplay. Players must place themselves within the game environment and interact through their decisions as if they were part of the game world. The level of immersion becomes significant once themed board games enter the picture. Related to gaming, *immersion* is the degree to which the player becomes fully involved with the game world. Immersion, pretending, and interaction will be some of the most important design elements for all future games, including video games.

With their first taste of immersion in a game world, many players became increasingly interested in getting more and more "into" the pretend world. *Dungeons and Dragons* was an early role-playing game, published in 1974. **Role-playing games (RPGs)** allow for a very deep immersion as players assume a character (play a role). Many players even dress as their character and act out their roles as they play their way through a live-action adventure, as seen in **Figure 3-13.** Unfortunately, some players can become so immersed in their role that they lose track of the real world. In some cases, these individuals have a very difficult time trying to relate to the real world.

Figure 3-13.

Role-playing games offer great immersion. Many avid players attend conferences and shows dressed as their characters.

Shutterstock.com

The debate on immersion continues to be a very hot topic. Fear from the example of game immersion set by the *Dungeons and Dragons* craze of the late 1970s and early 1980s fuels the concern over today's video games that contain violence. When the immersion becomes too high for some players, they become **desensitized** to the violence. The play gives the illusion that the violence is not so bad and

CHEAT CODE: DESENSITIZED

You become desensitized by repeatedly being exposed to an event until it no longer results in an emotional reaction to the event. When someone sees something disturbing, they usually react badly. When this same disturbing event occurs over and over, you get used to it and eventually believe it to be normal.

perhaps even fun. "It was fun to play that way on the game, maybe it would be more fun to do the same in the real world." This statement has been the defense of many a confused child who failed to realize the difference between the pretending in the game world and their actions in the real world. In some of the worst cases, children and even adults are not able to tell the difference between the game world and the real world. Unfortunately, the real world does not give you three lives and a reset button. Actions in the real world are permanent.

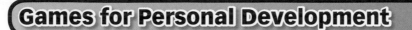

Games for Personal Development

Opinions differ on how video games fit into the historical model of using play to learn and develop. The three areas of focus for this debate are:

- behavioral development;
- cognitive (mental) development; and
- motor skill (physical) development.

Behavioral Development

Behavioral development is learning how to react to situations. In school, the focus of behavioral development is teaching students how to react positively when facing a challenging situation. Some of the main points of contention for behavioral learning through video games stems from the selection of game played. There is no doubt some games reward good behaviors and punish bad behaviors. Consider educational games that use characters such as Dora the Explorer or Carmen San Diego. These games attempt to build teamwork, sharing, positive attitudes, and socially positive behavior. These games have very little controversy and are generally viewed as beneficial.

However, there are so many more games that glorify violent and antisocial behavior. Games such as *Halo, Grand Theft Auto,* and *Resident Evil* fuel the debate over just what behavioral benefits are being learned through video game play. If the line between positive benefits and negative aspects were clear, there would be no debate.

Take a look at the game *Halo.* This is a video game intended for a mature audience. Players can join teams online to do battle in a futuristic military setting. *Halo* has positive behavioral benefits, such as the need for teamwork and communication on missions. It also presents positive social interactions in solving conflicts and obstacles in the game. There are other positive behavioral benefits as well. Unfortunately, there are clearly negative aspects that can offset the positive behavioral growth. The general themes of shooting and war to resolve conflicts limits behavioral growth of communication and compromise to resolve conflicts.

There is also a very serious general concern about video game behavior resulting from cocooning. The term **cocooning** refers to the social phenomenon where people do not play and interact with their physical environment. More simply stated, kids are playing video games alone and inside. They do not play outside and do not play with each other. The cocoon is their home. They seal themselves in and lose interactions that have been typical of past generations of children and adults.

In almost every example, the real test is **balance.** How much good is provided versus how much negative is provided. Too much of anything can be bad for you.

CHEAT CODE: BALANCE

Your life should have balance in the activities you do. There should be a mix of physical activities, mental activities, and entertainment/relaxation activities. Spending too much time on one type of activity means the other types are being neglected.

Cognitive Development

Cognitive development is the building of intelligence through learning, remembering, and problem solving. In cognitive development, the debate is again not focused on educational games, but rather on the mainstream games. Educational games can build mental abilities. Consider a game that uses math problems as obstacles. The player must supply a quick or instant answer to overcome the obstacles. Basic cognitive math skills are enhanced by this gameplay.

On the other hand, a mainstream game like a racecar game may not have much to offer in terms of building mental skill. The car (the game piece) is likely not a representation of anything used in real life. Additionally, the visual displays do not overtly seek to train a mental skill like in the math game. There are some mental skills used to calculate perceived distance to an obstacle or the sharpening of the speed of decision making. For example, in a shooting game with friendly and enemy characters, the brain must quickly decide by shape, color, or other characteristics if the character is a friend or enemy. Shooting the friendly is bad. Hesitation to shoot the enemy may cost you a life. Quicker decisions and the results of those decisions certainly could be a benefit.

Unfortunately, identifying character traits as good or bad carries additional debate. For example, suppose the enemy is always shown in black and friends in white, as illustrated in **Figure 3-14.** In older western movies, the bad guy always wore a black hat and the good guy always wore a white hat. On one hand, a cognitive ability might be enhanced. On the other hand, what does this recognition of friend and enemy do to the behavioral development of the player? More specifically, will this player learn that people who look a certain

Figure 3-14.

Good guy or bad guy? Common traits are programmed into games to help players identify good guys and bad guys. However, in real life, you cannot make assumptions about a person based on how they look or who they are. In a video game, a character with a black shirt may be an adversary, but in real life it means nothing.

Shutterstock.com

CHEAT CODE: STEREOTYPE

A stereotype is a personal opinion that a member of a group of people has the same characteristics as all in the group. Typically, a stereotype is formed when a person has an encounter with someone. Certain characteristics are identified and then the person expects this type of encounter from any person with those same characteristics. Racism is based on negative stereotypes.

way are always a friend or an enemy? Consider seeing a person wearing a black shirt out of the corner of your eye. Is that person immediately identified as a bad person because of what they are wearing? Will the play develop a cognitive recognition of a **stereotype** that sets up racial or social bias? These are good questions that lead to strong opinions on both sides of the discussion.

LEVEL UP! 3.2

Think about your reaction to seeing a character in a game dressed in all black. Now think about the same character dressed in all white. Do you have an opinion as to which one is your friend and which one is your foe? Do you think your first thought of a real person dressed in the same manner would be the same?

Motor Skills Development

The last area of debate regarding games and personal development focuses on motor skills or physical development. **Motor skills development** involves learning to control muscles to perform necessary tasks. This learning to control the muscles in your body is best demonstrated by the process a baby learns to walk. The brain has to coordinate many muscles at the same time to keep standing and shift the body's weight to walk. The baby eventually develops the motor skills needed to walk properly.

Those in favor of video games point out positive possibilities, like improving hand-eye coordination that will benefit typing and computer use. Those on the other side of the discussion will point out statistics linking video game controllers to injuries to the hands and wrists.

Here is where balance enters into the discussion again. Too much use could lead to a serious

LEVEL UP! 3.3

Some people are physically injured while playing video games. Do you think these same people would get hurt playing outdoor sports? Without video games, do you think you would play outside or stay inside and watch television?

Shutterstock.com

condition, such as carpal tunnel syndrome. *Carpal tunnel syndrome* is a condition that causes pain or tingling in the hand. It is caused by something applying pressure on the nerve to the hand and fingers. Often, carpal tunnel syndrome results from repetitive movements. Long hours of game playing while keeping your hands and fingers in the same position may lead to injuries such as carpal tunnel syndrome.

Recently, some have blamed the increasing occurrences of childhood obesity and juvenile diabetes on video games. For example, sitting around playing a basketball video game involves little physical activity. Playing a game of basketball outside on a real basketball court involves intense physical activity. This example illustrates part of the debate over cocooning. Maybe the best solution is once again finding a balance between video game activities and physical activities.

Video Game Beginnings

As early as 1947, video games were being developed. These games were very primitive by today's standards. Early computers were not very impressive and could do very little when compared with today's computers. That did not stop the first computer programmers from looking for fun things to do with these new devices. The first **patent** for a video game was applied for on January 25, 1947 and issued in 1948. Contrary to popular opinion, the game was not *Pong*. It was actually a game for firing a missile at stationary targets drawn by hand on the screen.

CHEAT CODE: PATENT

A patent is issued by the government patent office to protect the rights of designers on their creation. For example, the game *Pong* had no patent when it was released. Since it was making huge profits, many companies copied the game. There was no legal protection for the game inventors to prevent this from happening.

The first *Pong*-style game, named *Tennis for Two*, was made in 1958 and played in the Brookhaven National Laboratory. It only lasted until 1959 before being taken down. Video games in these early times were run on huge computers that cost nearly $100 per hour to operate. Using expensive computers to play games was not considered productive or cost effective.

In 1966, the first television-projection game was invented. Most televisions of that era displayed only in black and white. The player used a light gun to shoot at white targets on a black background. The light gun could detect the location of objects displayed on the television cathode ray tube (CRT). This technology adapted well to shooting games since the programming could tell where the light gun was pointed on the screen. Some video games as recently as the 1990s used the very same technology, similar to that shown in **Figure 3-15.** This technology,

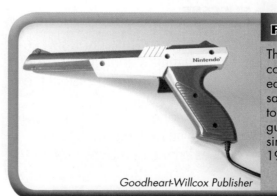

Figure 3-15.

This light gun controller from the early 1990s uses the same basic technology to detect where the gun is aiming as similar controllers in 1966.

Goodheart-Willcox Publisher

however, was almost completely obsolete by the turn of the 21st century as it only works with cathode ray tube (CRT) television sets. It cannot be used on liquid crystal display (LCD), projection, and plasma television sets.

Video game development can be viewed as a progression along a time line. The development is usually broken into generations as outlined in the sections below.

Figure 3-16.

Shown is an original *Computer Space* arcade game. The unique cabinet design helped bring customers in to see the machine. The games were made in several eye-catching colors, including blue, yellow, red, green, and white.

ComputerSpaceFan.com

Generation 1

Generation 1 contains the first series of video games and game systems available to many consumers. Prior to the beginning of generation 1, around 1970, video games were not available to many people. Most people had no idea that computers could be used for entertainment purposes. The computer systems used for games in generation 1 were less powerful than the handheld graphing calculator you use today in math class. The video games in generation 1 are characterized by arcade-style games that had the game built into the computer system.

Again, contrary to popular opinion, the first coin-operated video game was not *Pong!* The first coin-operated video game was only available at Stanford University. It was called *Spacewar!* and operated in 1971. The game required two players to fly spaceships and shoot missiles at each other while avoiding the black hole obstacle.

Nolan Bushnell also built and released a remarkably similar game later that same year as a coin-operated video game, shown in **Figure 3-16.** The game was called *Computer Space*, but it was too complicated for players of that era to play and understand. As a result, it was not a **commercial success.** Learning from his mistake, Bushnell wanted to design a simple game that everyone could play.

CHEAT CODE: COMMERCIAL SUCCESS

A commercial success occurs when something makes enough profit to keep producing it. In the case of the *Computer Space* machines, only 1500 were made. These machines did not earn enough money to keep making the machines. It is reported that Nolan Bushnell made little more than $500 from royalties on the *Computer Space* machines.

The company Atari was founded in June of 1972 by Bushnell and Ted Dabney. Bushnell and designer Al Alcorn set out to design a simple game of "television tennis" similar to the *Tennis for Two* game from 1958. Together they invented *Pong*.

Figure 3-17.

Imagine a game earning $1,000,000 in quarters. That is 4,000,000 quarters.

After only two days of operation, the first *Pong* machine was thought to be broken. It would not play anymore. When Bushnell went to service the machine, he quickly discovered the problem. The machine was so overstuffed with quarters that it could not hold more. With the commercial success of the *Pong* machines, Atari quickly placed thousands of *Pong* machines throughout the United States. The company made a fortune one quarter at a time, **Figure 3-17.** With that success, Atari also created one of the first home video game consoles. The game console only played *Pong,* shown in **Figure 3-18.** Nolan Bushnell sold Atari in 1976, but his love for video games led him to start another company: Chuck E. Cheese.

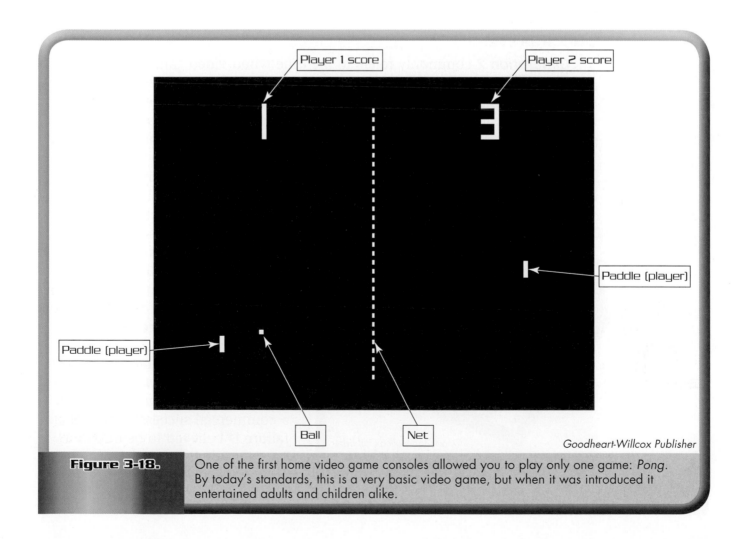

Goodheart-Willcox Publisher

Figure 3-18. One of the first home video game consoles allowed you to play only one game: *Pong.* By today's standards, this is a very basic video game, but when it was introduced it entertained adults and children alike.

In the late 1970s and early 1980s, video games became very popular. The technology to design color graphics and better gameplay made these new games irresistible to the children and adults of that time. Mega hits like *Space Invaders, Pac-Man,* and *Asteroids* were gobbling up quarters at the newest mall hangout: the arcade, as seen in **Figure 3-19.** Entrepreneurs bought stand-up video games and put them all together in a single room to create the ***video game arcade.*** Consumers had their choice of their favorite games. Each play cost the tiny fee of one quarter. Mass production of these stand-up video game consoles made it possible to roll out thousands of these money making machines. This was the golden age of the video game arcade.

Tomasz Trojanowski/Shutterstock.com

Figure 3-19. The video game arcade began to appear in malls during the late 1970s and early 1980s. It offered a variety of video games in one location and became a popular place for young people to gather.

Generation 2

Generation 2 commonly refers to the time when video game computer systems became popular in the home. Beginning in 1972, people could plug a simple computer into their television and begin playing games built into that system. Generally, those games fit best into generation 1. Generation 2 video games are separated as those that could play on a cartridge platform and were built in the mid-1970s.

Part of the commercial success of video games in 1979 and 1980 was due to the popularity of the ***Atari 2600*** video computer system that hit the scene in 1977, which is shown in **Figure 3-20.** This was the first commercially *successful* video game system that allowed the owner to purchase individual game cartridges. The first cartridge-based game system was the Magnavox Odyssey released in 1972. The Odyssey had better technology than the Atari and was the first in the market. However, it was not a commercial success. Part of the failure is believed to be due to a consumer belief that the system only worked on a Magnavox television. Magnavox later included

Goodheart-Willcox Publisher

Figure 3-20. Shown is the Atari 2600. This was the first commercially successful video game cartridge system.

a statement that its systems worked on all models of television, both black and white and color.

The **ROM cartridge** (read-only memory cartridge) made it possible for a single computer game console to play several different games. The game was contained on the cartridge like those shown in **Figure 3-21.** By changing cartridges, the game console could play any number of games. This was a huge benefit and cost savings. The consumer only needed to buy a different game cartridge, not a new game console for each new game release.

The interchangeable game, whether by ROM cartridge or disk, quickly became the way to get games into homes. This technology allowed the home video game market to rapidly develop. Atari, Nintendo, Sony, and Microsoft still pay royalties to Magnavox for using their patented technology for home video game systems.

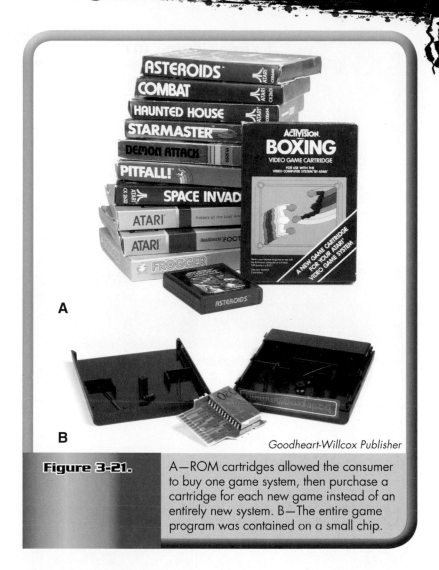

Goodheart-Willcox Publisher

Figure 3-21. A—ROM cartridges allowed the consumer to buy one game system, then purchase a cartridge for each new game instead of an entirely new system. B—The entire game program was contained on a small chip.

Generation 3

Generation 3 began with the computer systems that could process more movement, better graphics, and sounds. Beginning in the mid-1980s, game systems were using 8-bit processors that could handle much more information than the earlier generation 2 systems. In addition to home systems, handheld systems and games were made available.

By the mid-1980s, the home video game system was here to stay. People quickly embraced the idea of buying games to play at home instead of taking quarters to the arcades. In 1985, Nintendo took over the home system market with the **Nintendo Entertainment System,** more commonly known as the NES or just Nintendo, shown in **Figure 3-22.** The now famous *Super Mario Brothers* game came with

Goodheart-Willcox Publisher

Figure 3-22. This is the original Nintendo Entertainment System, or NES.

CHEAT CODE: BIT

A bit is a computer term for a single binary digit (0 or 1). Computers process bits of information to run programs. A processor is measured in how many bits of information it can read at the same time. For example, 8-bit processors read eight bits at a time and 128-bit processors read 128 bits at a time.

1-059360 TOP-059360 2-000000
PLAYER
ENEMY

TIME 0655 -A-

Figure 3-23. Like earlier game systems, the NES had simple, flat graphics.

the system and quickly became the most popular video game character in history. The NES was an 8-**bit** video game console with flat, or two dimensional (2D), graphics, as illustrated in **Figure 3-23.**

Nintendo took the next big step in releasing the handheld Nintendo *Game Boy* in 1989, shown in **Figure 3-24.** It was an 8-bit system with a black and white screen. The handheld system featured interchangeable ROM cartridges and was packaged with *Tetris.* *Tetris* was a popular video puzzle game where the player tried to fit interlocking pieces as they drop from the top of the screen. Shortly after the release of Game Boy, the Game Boy Pocket and Game Boy Color were released. The Game Boy Pocket was slightly smaller and thinner than the original. The Game Boy Color had a color screen. Nintendo sold over 115 million Game Boy systems over the three versions. The third generation of video games was a huge success for Nintendo, with both its home system and handheld system.

Figure 3-24.

The Nintendo Game Boy is a handheld gaming system. It uses ROM cartridges similar to the full-size NES.

Generation 4

Generation 4 began with higher powered computer systems in the late 1980s. Computer systems that were 16 bit led to better game graphics and the beginnings of three-dimensional (3D) game environments.

In 1989, Sega introduced the **Sega Genesis** system. It was the first 16-bit video game console. Graphics, colors, and character movement were greatly improved. However, the graphics were still two dimensional. Nintendo produced the **Super Nintendo** 16-bit system in 1991, shown in **Figure 3-25**. Both

Goodheart-Willcox Publisher

Figure 3-25. The Super Nintendo (Super NES or SNES) was a 16-bit system, where the first NES was an 8-bit system.

systems still used the ROM cartridge system to change games. Nintendo also advanced the design of the Game Boy system with the release of Game Boy Advanced and Game Boy Advanced SP. Competition between manufacturers allowed for more game systems and video games to be designed and available to the in-home video game market.

A major benefit with the Game Boy Advanced systems was backward compatibility. **Backward compatibility** allows old games to play on the new system. The new games were not, however, compatible with the older systems. The new game system was needed to run the new games. The Game Boy Advance also used a 16-bit chip and more internal memory to run games with better graphics and faster gameplay. The 16-bit chip allowed for 3D emulation on a handheld game.

Systems that allowed 3D *emulation* did not provide true 3D graphics. Two-dimensional graphics were layered to create the effect. These graphics would change with player movement to emulate the player moving in a 3D environment. The game *Doom* was a huge success in this generation. It had 3D emulation and was designed as a first person shooter (FPS) game.

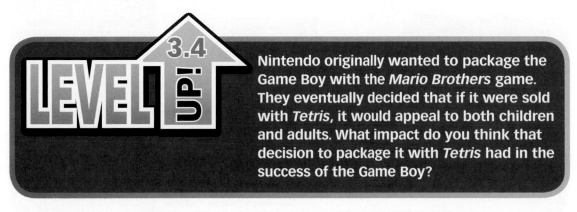

LEVEL UP! 3.4

Nintendo originally wanted to package the Game Boy with the *Mario Brothers* game. They eventually decided that if it were sold with *Tetris*, it would appeal to both children and adults. What impact do you think that decision to package it with *Tetris* had in the success of the Game Boy?

Generation 5

Generation 5 began in the mid-1990s with more technology advancements in computer technology (32- and 64-bit systems) and game storage. Nintendo continued to lead the marketplace until 1994 when it fell victim to a new technology: CD-ROMs. **Compact disc, read-only memory (CD-ROM)** was a replacement technology for ROM cartridges. Nintendo rejected this technology as it was comfortably the market leader. Also, at that time, the ROM cartridge provided better security against copying.

Nintendo rejecting this technology opened the door for Sony. Sony saw a need for games that appealed to an older market segment. It also wanted to capitalize on the inexpensive CD-ROM technology. Sony built a new game system and called it the **PlayStation,** shown in **Figure 3-26.**

Additionally, Sony and the other major competitor to Nintendo, Sega, launched their new systems as 32-bit video game consoles. This technology finally allowed for true 3D graphics. Sony PlayStation quickly became the market leader in system sales. PlayStation had a **competitive advantage** as the games in CD-ROM format were less expensive to produce. This meant lower-cost games for customers.

CHEAT CODE: COMPETITIVE ADVANTAGE

When a company provides a benefit to consumers that other companies cannot provide, it has a competitive advantage. This advantage can be something that reduces cost, provides higher quality, better availability, better selection, more delivery locations, or any number of ways to create a competitive advantage.

In addition to designing and selling its own games, Sony also licensed the game-creation code, known as the **source code,** to many game manufacturers. These manufacturers are called **third-party providers.** Licensing the source code to third-party providers allowed many different game titles to be quickly developed and delivered to stores. Customers for the PlayStation could buy the most technologically advanced system and had access to numerous games at low prices. Sony used marketing strategies to enhance their unique selling point (USP) of CD-ROM technology to become a serious competitor.

Figure 3-26.

The Sony PlayStation was a 32-bit system and made use of inexpensive CD-ROM technology. These features gave it a market advantage.

Goodheart-Willcox Publisher

Gaming technology really started advancing quickly in the mid-1990s. Nintendo released the Nintendo 64 (N64) system as a ROM-cartridge system in 1996. This 64-bit system was the first Nintendo system with 3D graphics. Games looked good and played well, but the ROM cartridges were more expensive to produce. This caused several third-party providers to abandon the N64. Instead, they developed games for the PlayStation, which used the less expensive CD-ROMs. The trademark Mario character and the *Super Mario 64* game kept Nintendo as a major player in the market, but the PlayStation maintained control over the market. This was true even though Sony did not release a 64-bit system.

Generation 6

Generation 6 began in the early 2000s with 128-bit game systems and DVD-ROM technology. With fast computing and large storage available on the DVD, games of this generation began to have realistic 3D movement.

The most anticipated gaming product of the new millennium was the PlayStation 2 (PS2). This was a 128-bit system and numerous games were available from third-party designers. This system was the envy of the game world. Additionally, games would play on DVD-ROM discs. The system would also play movies on DVD. A **digital video disc (DVD)** is similar to a CD-ROM or music CD, but can hold much more information.

In 2001, Nintendo's Game Cube used technology similar to a DVD called an optical disc drive, as shown in **Figure 3-27.** While the discs were cheaper to produce, they were not the same standard size as a DVD and the console could not play a movie or game on DVD. The Game Cube was also considered to be a "kids console" due to the lack of mature game options. Nintendo continued to lose market share and the Game Cube was not a commercial success.

At this time, a new manufacturer entered the game console marketplace. The most powerful company in the technology world was ready to take a bite out of the video game market. Microsoft, the maker of Windows, designed and released the **Xbox** system, shown in **Figure 3-28.** With a tremendous amount

Figure 3-27.

The Nintendo Game Cube used an optical disc, which is similar to DVD technology in a smaller format.

Figure 3-28.

The Microsoft Xbox entered the video game console market later than other systems. It did not make a profit for the first few years, but eventually became a major player in the market.

Goodheart-Willcox Publisher

of cash from the sales of Window and Microsoft Office, Microsoft decided that it could sell the Xbox at a loss to obtain market share. In the first few years, Microsoft tallied heavy losses thought to be more than $10 million. But, the strategy worked and the Xbox quickly overtook Nintendo. Many believed the Xbox to be as good as the PlayStation 2.

The inexpensive DVD-ROM technology made it easy for third-party designers to produce games in both the Xbox and PlayStation 2 formats. Most games could be **ported** to both systems. However, both the Xbox and PS2 had licensing agreements for certain games as well as proprietary games. This meant that these games could only be played on one system and not any other system. By keeping some games on a single platform (system), a unique selling point was provided for each system. For example, the very popular game *Halo* was designed, manufactured, and distributed for only the Xbox. PlayStation 2 owners could not purchase *Halo* for their system. If they wanted to play *Halo,* they had to purchase an Xbox.

CHEAT CODE: PORTING

In the software world, porting is translating a program to work on a different system. Game designers often program their games in a way that makes it easy to translate the programming to work on different game systems, such as the Xbox and PlayStation. The technology of the systems must be similar; otherwise the game cannot be ported and will have to be rebuilt for each platform.

Generation 7

Generation 7 began in the mid-2000s with multicore processor game systems and new user interfaces. This allowed for amazingly fast computing for extremely realistic graphics, immersive gameplay, and online play.

The introduction of the **Wii** system was an attempt by Nintendo to reclaim market share. Many still considered the available games to be suited only for children. But, the Wii set out to change the way video games are played. No more joysticks and game pads. The Wii uses **motion-based controllers,** like those shown in **Figure 3-29.** This allows the player to swing the controller like a bat when playing a baseball game or a tennis racket when playing a tennis game. The game console was constructed from little more than a Game Cube and a Bluetooth interface. Nintendo was banking that the Wii controllers would overshadow the low-resolution graphics and simplistic gameplay. This was a risky marketing strategy, but it clearly established a USP for the Wii.

The PlayStation 3 (PS3) was released in 2006 just before the Nintendo Wii was introduced. The PS3 is shown in **Figure 3-30.** The Xbox 360 was released in 2005, and is shown in **Figure 3-31.** Both the Xbox 360 and PlayStation 3 have very fast processors and can display exceptional graphics. These systems also allow online play. **Online play** is when players connect to games with other players via the Internet. The *Halo* franchise of games has been the most popular online game series to date. Often, players will hold a **LAN party.** This is where players meet at a location and connect their machines to a local area network (LAN) to play an online game together in the same room.

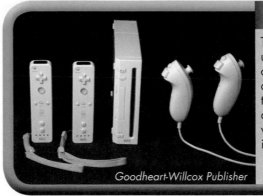

Goodheart-Willcox Publisher

Figure 3-29.

The Nintendo Wii uses motion-based controllers. These allow the player to move with the action in the game, which helps increase immersion.

Goodheart-Willcox Publisher

Figure 3-30.

The PlayStation 3 (PS3) has a very fast processor, can display exceptional graphics, and allows online gameplay.

Goodheart-Willcox Publisher

Figure 3-31.

Like the PS3, the Xbox 360 features a very fast processor, can display exceptional graphics, and allows online gameplay.

The next generation of handheld games also hit the market in the generation 7 era. In 2004, the Nintendo DS (dual screen) and the Sony PSP (PlayStation portable) were launched for the holiday sales season. Nintendo continued to stick with the ROM cartridges on the DS, while Sony chose a small DVD-ROM disc for the games and movies on the PSP. High prices, limited games, and the emergence of cell phones with games and entertainment features made selling these handheld platforms challenging.

Other significant advances for generation 7 included unique, **game-specific controllers.** Games like *Guitar Hero* and *Rock Band* use controllers shaped like musical instruments to enhance the game immersion. Other game-specific controllers, such as dance pads, also came to market. These types of controllers can only be used to play one game.

While the Wii has the most games with unique controllers, PlayStation and Xbox also use them. Sony also invented the six-axis controller to allow greater player movement. The **six-axis controller** allows the player to shake or twist the controller to input some commands. While it does not allow as much interaction as a Wii controller, it can be used in a game like *Call of Duty* to rifle butt an enemy. If you were using a standard controller, this action would require the use of a button.

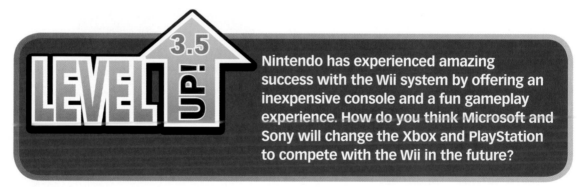

LEVEL UP! 3.5

Nintendo has experienced amazing success with the Wii system by offering an inexpensive console and a fun gameplay experience. How do you think Microsoft and Sony will change the Xbox and PlayStation to compete with the Wii in the future?

Generation 8

www.g-wlearning.com

Level up your know-how with Animated Review 3-1.

Will the future hold greater user interface and a deeper immersion through virtual reality? The prevailing opinion is, yes. Only the cost of technology and imagination limits the adoption of new user interfaces. Consumers seem eager to purchase games and systems that provide challenges and immersion in the game world. Luckily, you will likely be one of the first to see and play generation 8 games.

It can be argued that some generation 8 technology has already made it to the market. The Microsoft Xbox Kinect is a controller that senses the player's movements. These movements are translated into game action. No handheld controller is required. Only time will tell if this will be considered advanced generation 7 technology or the first generation 8 technology to reach the market.

Complete entertainment systems, like the PS3, will see more online content. Games are quickly becoming downloadable content (DLC), as opposed to disc-storage content. Will it become economically viable for games to be made with such detail and complexity to need the storage capacity of the Blu-Ray discs?

Game Licensing

A game produced exclusively for Xbox is not necessarily designed by Microsoft. By the same token, a game produced exclusively for PlayStation may not be designed by Sony. Under a *licensing agreement,* third-party designers can obtain the source code needed to create a game for a specific system. To obtain a licensing agreement, third-party designers typically pay a fee up front and then royalty on each game sold. Without a licensing agreement, a company cannot produce a game for a system that did not issue it a licensing agreement. For many years, Nintendo did not provide a licensing agreement for any games rated M for mature audiences or higher ratings. This aided in creating the notion that Nintendo systems were just for kids.

If a game system developer such as Microsoft or Sony creates a game on their own, it is known as a *proprietary game.* By designing or licensing a game that can only run on a single console, these companies seek to create a competitive advantage that requires a customer to buy a specific console to run that proprietary game. This is another way of ensuring there are video game titles that just work on their system. For several years, Nintendo has enhanced its USP by making the Mario games proprietary. These characters are proprietary to Nintendo as they created them and only made them for the Nintendo system.

This practice of proprietary and exclusively licensed games helps create the specific purpose for buying one particular system over another. Without this practice, video game systems would quickly become generic, much like DVD players. If any system could play every game, then there would be few benefits over each other. In the example of DVD players, every unit can play any movie on DVD. Regardless of the brand, you can watch your movies. Certain quality attributes and special functions attempt to differentiate DVD players in this generic-style marketplace. Manufacturers of game systems want to avoid this situation by maintaining unique selling points.

How Computers Changed the Game

Earlier, this chapter explored the history of games. Examples of games were presented, along with examples that are not classified as games. Video games are modern games made possible by the invention of computers. The popularity of computer-based games stems from the elements a computer brings to the game. Most importantly, a computer allows things to occur in video games that cannot occur in any other type of game. Unique to computer-controlled games are strict enforcement of rules, virtual gameplay, and the presentation of a virtual reality.

With a good user interface and gameplay, a player may lose track of the outside world. As discussed earlier, the degree to which the player becomes involved in the game world is called immersion. Immersion is not unique to games. A good book or movie can make the reader or viewer feel like part of the action, as seen in **Figure 3-32.** A feeling of total immersion can occur when someone becomes so focused on the story that they forget about the outside world.

Shutterstock.com

Figure 3-32. A good book or movie can cause total immersion into the story and the entertainment world. A well-designed video game will also allow for a high level of immersion.

As a result, the player focuses exclusively on the artificial world they are experiencing. With rich 3D graphics, motion-based controllers, online social interaction, and realistically shaped controllers, the level of immersion can feel complete. The computer made this possible.

Video Game Ratings

The *Entertainment Software Rating Board (ESRB)* is the nonprofit, self-regulatory body that assigns age and content ratings for computer and video games, enforces industry-adopted advertising guidelines, and helps ensure responsible online privacy practices for the interactive entertainment software industry. The ESRB ratings provide concise and impartial information about the content and age-appropriateness of computer and video games so consumers, especially parents, can make an informed purchase decision.

ESRB ratings have two equal parts:

- *Rating symbols* are found on the front of virtually every game package available for sale in the United States and Canada. These symbols suggest age appropriateness for the game.
- *Content descriptors* are displayed on the back of the game package. These indicate elements in a game that may have triggered a particular rating and/or may be of interest or concern.

See **Figure 3-33.** These ratings are similar to the MPAA ratings assigned to movies in that both systems provide parents with guidance as to whether content is appropriate for various ages. Just like movie ratings, the ESRB ratings are not legally binding and having a game rated is voluntary.

Titles rated **EC (Early Childhood)** have content that may be suitable for persons ages 3 and older. Titles in this category contain no material that parents would find inappropriate.

 Titles rated **E (Everyone)** have content that may be suitable for persons ages 6 and older. Titles in this category may contain minimal cartoon, fantasy, or mild violence and/or infrequent use of mild language.

 Titles rated **E10+ (Everyone 10 and older)** have content that may be suitable for persons ages 10 and older. Titles in this category may contain more cartoon, fantasy, or mild violence, mild language, and/or minimal suggestive themes.

 Titles rated **T (Teen)** have content that may be suitable for ages 13 and older. Titles in this category may contain violence, suggestive themes, crude humor, minimal blood, simulated gambling, and/or infrequent use of strong language.

 Titles rated **M (Mature)** have content that may be suitable for persons 17 years and older. Titles in this category may contain intense violence, blood and gore, sexual content, and/or strong language.

 Titles rated **AO (Adults Only)** have content that should only be played by persons 18 years and older. Titles in this category may include prolonged scenes of intense violence and/or graphic sexual content and nudity.

ESRB Content Descriptors

- **Alcohol Reference:** Reference to and/or images of alcoholic beverages.
- **Animated Blood:** Discolored and/or unrealistic depictions of blood.
- **Blood:** Depictions of blood.
- **Blood and Gore:** Depictions of blood or the mutilation of body parts.
- **Cartoon Violence:** Violent actions involving cartoon-like situations and characters. May include violence where a character is unharmed after the action has been inflicted.
- **Comic Mischief:** Depictions or dialogue involving slapstick or suggestive humor.
- **Crude Humor:** Depictions or dialogue involving vulgar antics, including "bathroom" humor.
- **Drug Reference:** Reference to and/or images of illegal drugs.
- **Fantasy Violence:** Violent actions of a fantasy nature, involving human or non-human characters in situations easily distinguishable from real life.
- **Intense Violence:** Graphic and realistic-looking depictions of physical conflict. May involve extreme and/or realistic blood, gore, weapons, and depictions of human injury and death.
- **Language:** Mild to moderate use of profanity.
- **Lyrics:** Mild references to profanity, sexuality, violence, alcohol, or drug use in music.
- **Mature Humor:** Depictions or dialogue involving "adult" humor, including sexual references.
- **Nudity:** Graphic or prolonged depictions of nudity.
- **Partial Nudity:** Brief and/or mild depictions of nudity.
- **Real Gambling:** Player can gamble, including betting or wagering real cash or currency.
- **Sexual Content:** Non-explicit depictions of sexual behavior, possibly including partial nudity.
- **Sexual Themes:** References to sex or sexuality.
- **Sexual Violence:** Depictions of rape or other violent sexual acts.
- **Simulated Gambling:** Player can gamble without betting or wagering real cash or currency.
- **Strong Language:** Explicit and/or frequent use of profanity.
- **Strong Lyrics:** Explicit and/or frequent references to profanity, sex, violence, alcohol, or drug use in music.
- **Strong Sexual Content:** Explicit and/or frequent depictions of sexual behavior, possibly including nudity.
- **Suggestive Themes:** Mild provocative references or materials.
- **Tobacco Reference:** Reference to and/or images of tobacco products.
- **Use of Drugs:** The consumption or use of illegal drugs.
- **Use of Alcohol:** The consumption of alcoholic beverages.
- **Use of Tobacco:** The consumption of tobacco products.
- **Violence:** Scenes involving aggressive conflict. May contain bloodless dismemberment.
- **Violent References:** References to violent acts.

When a content descriptor is preceded by the term *Mild*, it conveys low frequency, intensity, or severity of the content it modifies.

Online Rating Notice

Online-enabled games carry the notice "Online Interactions Not Rated by the ESRB." This notice warns those who intend to play the game online about possible exposure to chat (text, audio, video) or other types of content created by other players (e.g., maps, skins) that have not been considered in the ESRB rating assignment.

For the most up to date list of content descriptors and definitions, go to http://www.esrb.org

Entertainment Software Association

Figure 3-33. The ESRB is the game industry's self-regulating organization. These logos appear on video games to indicate the appropriate age group for players. The ESRB rating icons are registered trademarks of the Entertainment Software Association and are used with permission.

Even with ratings, it is still up to parents and players to choose appropriate games. Some parents choose to purchase M-rated games for their children, who may be under the age of 17. Instances where parents choose not to abide the age recommendation provided by the ESRB ratings may be used by certain groups to argue that video games depicting violence and mature themes should not be made. Contrary to a censorship approach, however, the ratings empower parents with the ability to make informed decisions about the games they themselves deem suitable for their children and families. There have been attempts by various state and local governments to enact laws prohibiting the sale of M-rated video games to those under age 17. However, these attempts have been consistently struck down on constitutional grounds.

LEVEL UP! 3.6

Young children are still able to play violent video games that the regulators have marked as unacceptable for young children. What steps would you take to keep these games out of their hands?

Chapter Summary

- Non-electronic games date back to early humans who used them as a means of building strength and agility needed to survive.
- Electronic games began being developed as early as 1947 and continue through today.
- Beginning in the mid-1990s, technological advances in computers have allowed video game systems to make dramatic increases in speed, resolution, and complexity.
- The next generation of video games will likely enable deeper immersion through virtual reality as well as more online content.
- Play has been important in developing societies and cultures in that it enhances coordination, motor skills, and socializing.
- Play helps children and adults gain knowledge by challenging the player to analyze and solve a problem.
- Violence in video games can affect children and adults if they become desensitized to the violence or lose sight of the difference between game play and reality.
- Video games can affect behavior development if players learn how to react to situations, cognitive development in the case of educational games, and motor skills if the game involves learning to perform certain tasks.
- Video game content is self-regulated by the industry, including the Entertainment Software Rating Board, which assigns age and content ratings, enforces industry-adopted advertising guidelines, and helps ensure responsible online privacy practices.
- Video game designers need to be well-versed in the terminology used to communicate in the video game industry.
- Video game designers need to be well-versed in the terminology used by gamers and online gaming communities.
- Player immersion is the degree to which the player becomes involved in the game world.
- A good user interface and gameplay may cause a player to become so focused on the story that they forget about the outside world and focus exclusively on the artificial world they are experiencing.
- With rich 3D graphics, motion-based controllers, online social interaction, and realistically shaped controllers, the level of player immersion can feel complete.

Check Your Video Game IQ

Now that you have finished this chapter, see what you know about video game design by taking the chapter posttest.

www.m.g-wlearning.com

www.g-wlearning.com

Review Your Knowledge

On a separate sheet of paper or in a word processing document, match the following terms with the definition that fits best.

A. generation 1
B. Game Boy
C. behavioral development
D. Nintendo Entertainment System (NES)
E. physical dexterity

F. cognitive development
G. game environment
H. Atari 2600
I. motor skills development
J. mental acuity

1. Learning to control muscles to perform necessary tasks.
2. Began selling in 1985 and dominated the home system market at that time.
3. Person's learning, problem-solving, and reasoning ability.
4. First series of video games and systems; available to consumers in the early 1970s.
5. Skill or ability at performing physical tasks.
6. Handheld device released by Nintendo in 1989 with 8-bit processor and interchangeable ROM cartridges.
7. Learning how to react to situations.
8. First commercially successful video game system (1977) for homes; allowed the owner to purchase individual game cartridges.
9. Setting altered or designed to play a specific activity.
10. Building of intelligence through learning, remembering, and problem solving.

On a separate sheet of paper or in a word processing document, answer each of the following questions.

11. List four physical conditions that can be developed through physical play.
12. Define *socializing*.
13. Describe a *mental acuity game*.
14. How do board games differ from puzzles?
15. Place the following developments in the proper chronological order.
    A. Sporting games.
    B. Card games.
    C. Simple toys.
    D. Video games.
    E. Board games.
    F. Puzzles.
    G. Themed board games.

16. What is *immersion,* as related to video games?
17. Define *desensitization.*
18. What are the three areas of debate concerning learning and development?
19. Describe the phenomenon of *cocooning.*
20. What is a *cognitive skill?*
21. Define *stereotype.*
22. Of the three areas of debate concerning learning and development, in which area is hand-eye coordination?
23. What is one physical injury that can result from video game play?
24. In what year was the first video game patent issued?
25. In what year was the first television-projection game invented?
26. What was the first coin-operated video game and where was it located?
27. The first commercially successful video computer system that used interchangeable cartridges was the _____ system.
28. Which generation saw the introduction of the Nintendo Game Boy?
29. DVD technology was introduced in generation 6 by which two manufacturers?
30. Define *backward compatibility,* as related to video games.
31. What is a *third-party provider,* as related to video games?
32. A(n) _____ controller allows the player to swing the controller like a bat when playing a baseball game or a tennis racket when playing a tennis game.
33. Describe *online play.*
34. When is a *licensing agreement* used for video game development?
35. What is a *proprietary game?*
36. What is the most important thing computers have brought to the world of gaming?
37. List four things that help create a nearly complete level of immersion in today's video games.
38. What is the game industry's self-regulating organization?
39. How are the six different ratings for games categorized?
40. Who has the ultimate responsibility to choose appropriate games?

Apply Your STEM Knowledge

Science

1. Moths, butterflies, mosquitoes and other holometabolous insects have an interesting life filled with stages and metamorphosis. There are four stages in the life of a moth: egg, (embryo stage), caterpillar (larvae stage), cocoon (pupa stage), and adult (imago stage). Between the caterpillar stage and the adult stage, a metamorphosis occurs transforming a worm-like insect into a winged insect that looks almost nothing like it did earlier. This change occurs while in the cocoon. In the cocoon, a caterpillar wraps itself with silk thread and becomes isolated from the rest of the world as it changes. It remains still as it changes from the inside out. The caterpillar body parts morph into wings, long legs, and a different mouth design, or proboscis. This pupa stage of metamorphic transformation ends when the adult moth emerges from the cocoon.

   A. Examine the life cycle of the moth and describe how these stages of metamorphosis can be applied to the history and evolution of the game.

   B. In explaining how home entertainment media like video games have isolated children, writers coined the term cocooning. Is this use of the word cocooning an accurate description? Explain why or why not.

Mathematics

2. Games evolved to include chance and probability. A pair of cubical dice can be used to generate a random number for a game. A probability chart can be created to indicate the chance of rolling a number:

   As shown, there are 36 combinations possible using two die. To generate the total possible combinations without making a table and counting them, you could simply multiply the number of faces on the die by the number of faces of the other die (six faces × six faces = 36 combinations). Game makers incorporated probability and chance in their games using random-number generators like dice. Changing the number of sides or faces changes the amount of outcomes of a single turn.

   A. What is the most likely total if you use a pair of six-sided cubical dice?

   B. What would be the hardest numbers to roll with a pair of six-sided cubical dice? Why?

   C. If you wanted your game to have 100 possible combinations with only two identical dice, how many faces would each die have?

   D. What is the probability of rolling a total less than seven with a pair of six-sided cubical dice?

   E. What is the probability of rolling a total of two using a pair of dice each with 1,000 faces?

Dice Total	Possible Combinations	Chances of Occurring	Fraction
2	⚀⚀	1 out of 36	1/36
3	⚀⚁ · ⚁⚀	2 out of 36	2/36
4	⚀⚂ · ⚁⚁ · ⚂⚀	3 out of 36	3/36
5	⚀⚃ · ⚁⚂ · ⚂⚁ · ⚃⚀	4 out of 36	4/36
6	⚀⚄ · ⚁⚃ · ⚂⚂ · ⚃⚁ · ⚄⚀	5 out of 36	5/36
7	⚀⚅ · ⚁⚄ · ⚂⚃ · ⚃⚂ · ⚄⚁ · ⚅⚀	6 out of 36	6/36
8	⚁⚅ · ⚂⚄ · ⚃⚃ · ⚄⚂ · ⚅⚁	5 out of 36	5/36
9	⚂⚅ · ⚃⚄ · ⚄⚃ · ⚅⚂	4 out of 36	4/36
10	⚃⚅ · ⚄⚄ · ⚅⚃	3 out of 36	3/36
11	⚄⚅ · ⚅⚄	2 out of 36	2/36
12	⚅⚅	1 out of 36	1/36

Goodheart-Willcox Publisher

Science

3. Based on the trend and advancements in the past 20 years of video game design, list ten features that you believe would likely be new or improved features in the next generation of video games and systems. Consider trends in graphics, displays, user interface, gameplay, story development, as well as trends in popular games and current technology advancements. Then, create a ten- to 15-slides presentation to present your findings on the future generation of video games.

Language Arts

4. Form into groups of two or three. Research, debate, and form a group opinion on each of the Level Up! activities in this chapter. Prepare a PowerPoint presentation of ten slides (five to seven minutes) to present to the class explaining the group's opinions for each Level Up! activity. Include text, pictures, video, animations, and slide transitions as appropriate to help explain your positions.

Social Studies

5. The history of manufacturing for a brand of video game consoles, like those of Nintendo, can be traced back through the generations. A family tree for Nintendo would include the NES, Super Nintendo, Game Boy, Game Boy Advance, Nintendo 64, Game Cube, Nintendo DS, Nintendo Wii, and some other related products in that family of products. Conduct research on your own ancestral family history by speaking with parents, grandparents, aunts, and uncles. You can also conduct Internet research. Then, create a family tree that lists your relatives from each generation of your family. Go back three generations (for example, parents, grandparents, and great grandparents).

Working in Teams

Working with a team, brainstorm ideas on how a video game can be created and marketed as environmentally friendly. Divide the workload by having one person record the ideas, another create a drawing that portrays the idea for the game, and a third person to create the written narrative. Present the team's ideas to the class.

Gamer Portfolio

As you collect items for your portfolio, you will need a method to keep the items clean, safe, and organized for assembly at the appropriate time. A large manila envelope works well to keep hard copies of your documents, photos, game screen shots, awards, and other items. Three-ring binders with sleeves are another good way to store your information. Plan to keep like items together and label the categories. For example, store sample documents that illustrate your writing or artistic skills together. Use notes clipped to the documents to identify each item and state why it is included in the portfolio.

1. Select a method for storing hard copy items you will be collecting for your portfolio.

2. Write a paragraph that describes your plan for storing and labeling the items. Refer to this plan each time you add items to the portfolio.

G-W Learning Mobile Site

Visit the G-W Learning mobile site to complete the chapter pretest and posttest and to practice vocabulary using e-flash cards. If you do not have a smartphone, visit the G-W Learning companion website to access these features.

G-W Learning mobile site: www.m.g-wlearning.com

G-W Learning companion website: www.g-wlearning.com

Common Core

College and Career Readiness

CTE Career Ready Practices. Maintaining a healthy lifestyle has an impact on how you function physically and mentally. What unhealthy behaviors could have an effect on how well you do your job? How do you think employers should deal with behaviors that affect the personal health of their employees?

Speaking and Listening. Perform an Internet search on the use of video games for personal development. Look for opinions regarding how video games fit into the historical model of using play to learn and develop. Focus on games for behavioral development, cognitive development, or motor skill development. After reading a few expert opinions on this topic, use this information to form your own opinion. Discuss your findings and reasoning with the class. Respond to any questions you are asked. As you listen to your classmates' stances on this topic, take notes and ask questions about positions or terms you do not understand. Evaluate your own position. How does their reasoning contribute to your understanding of the role of video games in personal development? Does your opinion change or is it strengthened?

Reading. Consider how the author uses the term *game* throughout this chapter. How did your understanding of this term change as you were reading? Look up the word *game* in the dictionary. As needed, derive meaning of the environmental print and use visual and contextual support to confirm understanding. Use support from classmates and your teacher as needed to help in comprehension of the material. How did the author shape this definition to fit the subject matter in this chapter? Write a few paragraphs about what the term *game* means to you after reading this chapter.

Event Prep: Computer Game Performance

Creating a computer game is a competitive event that may be offered by your Career and Technical Student Organization (CTSO). This may be an individual or team event. There may be two parts to this event: the prejudged program and the performance portion. To prepare for the performance portion of a presentation:

1. Read the guidelines provided by your organization. Make certain that you ask any questions about points you do not understand. It is important you follow each specific item that is outlined in the competition rules.
2. On your CTSO's website, locate a rubric or scoring sheet for the event.
3. Confirm the use of equipment or other visual aids that may be used in the presentation of the game and amount of setup time permitted.
4. Review the rules to confirm if questions will be asked or if the team will need to defend a case or business plan.
5. Make notes on index cards about important points to remember. Use these notes to study. You may also be able to use these notes during the event, depending on event rules.
6. Practice the presentation. Each team member should introduce himself or herself, review the game being presented, defend the game construction, and conclude with a summary.
7. After the presentation is complete, ask for feedback from your teacher. You may also consider having a student audience listen and give feedback.

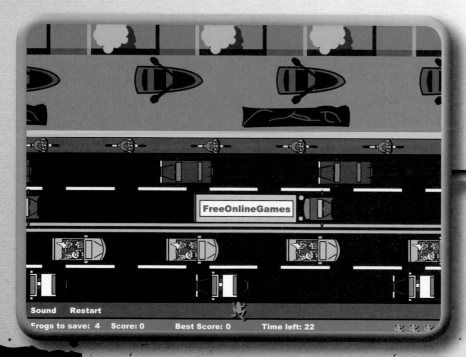

Objectives

After completing this chapter, you will be able to:

- Explain game perspectives.
- Describe the elements of a scene.
- Identify elements used to convey mood and theme.
- Explain issues of clarity for scaled computer-generated images.

Chapter 4
Perspective, Scene Design, and Basic Animation

art of designing video games involves creating amazing images and realistic game worlds. To create these features, a designer must decide how to present the view to the player and how to make everything move in a realistic fashion. In this chapter, you will become familiar with the differences between first-, second-, and third-person perspectives. You will also see how character and scene designs are completed in both two-dimensional and three-dimensional game worlds. Lastly, you will explore how the player moves in the game world and how realistic movements are created with characters and background objects.

Check Your Video Game IQ

Before you begin this chapter, see what you already know about video game design by taking the chapter pretest.

www.m.g-wlearning.com

www.g-wlearning.com

Reading Prep. Before reading the chapter, skim the photos and their captions. As you are reading, summarize the chapter content and determine how these concepts contribute to the ideas presented in the text.

College and Career Readiness

- Compare and contrast bitmap and vector images.
- Explain how blitting and double buffering can reduce CPU usage.
- Describe how to construct 3D models.
- Contrast static and active animation.
- Define terminology used in artistic creations and computer-generated images.
- Create artistic assets for a video game.
- Summarize how pixel and vertex shading are used to create the illusion of depth.

Perspective

The gameplay is how the game is presented to the player. The perspective of a video game is the view that the player has during gameplay. There are three different modes of perspective: first person, second person, and third person. The **perspective** describes how the gameplay is displayed on the screen and the position of the player within the game.

First-Person Perspective

First-person perspective is a view of gameplay where the player sees the game through the eyes of the character, as shown in **Figure 4-1.** First person is often used for driving and shooting games. For a game to be in first person, the player would not be able to see the character being controlled, but can see everything the character sees. This is the closest a player comes to "being the character."

Imagine a racecar game where the view of the gameplay is that of looking through the windshield. You can see all of the turns and cars in front of you, maybe even some in the rear view mirror. You can also see the dash displays and even "your" hands on the steering wheel. It looks just like you are sitting in the driver's seat. This view is from the first-person perspective of the driver. It is as if your character has a head-mounted camera and you only see exactly what your character sees.

A substantial amount of programming is required to create first-person games. The reason for this is that the player view remains nearly centered in the screen.

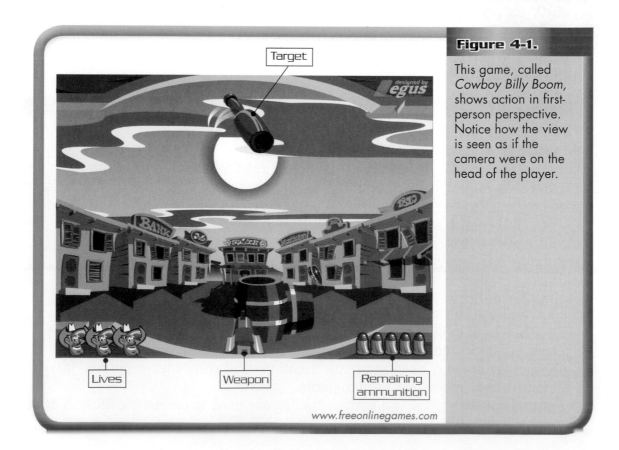

Figure 4-1.

This game, called *Cowboy Billy Boom,* shows action in first-person perspective. Notice how the view is seen as if the camera were on the head of the player.

www.freeonlinegames.com

All movements of the character require the entire scene to move. Instead of seeing your character take a step forward from an overhead view, in first-person perspective the entire background scene moves one step closer to the **camera.**

CHEAT CODE: CAMERA

Camera refers to the viewpoint of the game. The camera records the action of the game and displays it on your screen. The camera should follow the player wherever the character goes.

LEVEL UP! 4.1

Second-person perspective is the least-used view in video game design. Other than an example of baseball, when do you think it is appropriate to use second-person perspective?

Second-Person Perspective

Second-person perspective is extremely rare in video games. In **second-person perspective,** the player sees the game as if the player were the opponent or an intermediary, as illustrated in **Figure 4-2.** Some sports games use second-person perspective. Imagine a baseball game where your character is at bat and the view, or perspective, is from the pitcher throwing the ball. See **Figure 4-3.** The pitcher is the second person involved in the action, making this a second-person perspective. This perspective does not work very well in shooter and combat games. The player would be given a view of their character from the point of view of the person the player is attacking.

Directions to player

Action takes place on this screen, which the player cannot see

Action is seen from this person's perspective

Okay, um... you're in a room, facing north. There's a hallway in front of you.

CONTROLS   RESET

www.kongregate.com

Figure 4-2.

This is a unique concept for a second-person shooter game from kongregate. com. The person in the chair tells you where you are and what you are doing. You have to shoot the monster without seeing the screen. Here is an implementation of second-person dialog (speaks directly to you) in gaming.

Figure 4-3.

Happy Land Homerun Derby is a second-person perspective game. You see your character from the view of the pitcher. This game can be played from the perspective of either the pitcher (first person) or the batter (second person).

Goodheart-Willcox Publisher

Third-Person Perspective

Often called a *spectator view,* third-person perspective is the most versatile view in video game design. In **third-person perspective,** the play is viewed by a person who is not the player's character or the player's opponent, but rather a neutral third person. This view shows both the player and the opponent. This perspective also allows for multiple viewing angles. The player could be viewed from overhead, behind, or any angle left, right, or forward of the player. Most two-dimensional games use either the overhead or platform view. **Platform view** shows the character in profile and a side view of all obstacles, as illustrated by the two examples **Figure 4-4. Overhead view** shows the character and surroundings from a perspective high overhead, as seen in **Figure 4-5.**

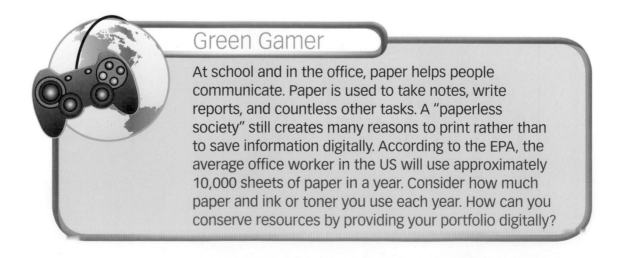

Green Gamer

At school and in the office, paper helps people communicate. Paper is used to take notes, write reports, and countless other tasks. A "paperless society" still creates many reasons to print rather than to save information digitally. According to the EPA, the average office worker in the US will use approximately 10,000 sheets of paper in a year. Consider how much paper and ink or toner you use each year. How can you conserve resources by providing your portfolio digitally?

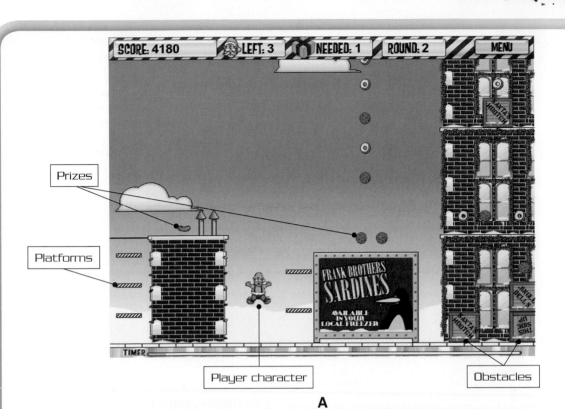

Prizes

Platforms

Player character

Obstacles

A

MENU   "P" for pause   01 : 05

Obstacles (Platforms)

Player character

B

Figure 4-4. A—This game, called *Adventure Elf*, uses a classic platform view. Your elf avatar must collect the cookies, navigate the platforms, and capture the penguins. B—This game also uses a classic platform view. In this game, called *Dirt Bike*, you must navigate the motorcycle avatar across the obstacles.

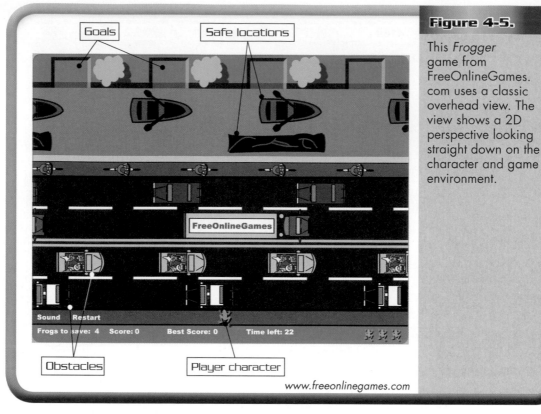

Figure 4-5.

This *Frogger* game from FreeOnlineGames. com uses a classic overhead view. The view shows a 2D perspective looking straight down on the character and game environment.

Goals

Safe locations

FreeOnlineGames

Sound   Restart

Frogs to save: 4   Score: 0   Best Score: 0   Time left: 22

Obstacles

Player character

www.freeonlinegames.com

Changeable Perspective

Some games allow the player to set the camera perspective. Many driving games allow the player to switch from first person (behind the steering wheel) to third person (overhead view that shows your car and the cars near you), as shown in **Figure 4-6.**

A first-person shooter game may show action from a third-person perspective when moving through the battlefield. When the player gets to the

Figure 4-6.

This arcade racing game allows the player to change perspective by pressing the View button. On the right-hand side of the steering wheel is a button that allows the player to look behind their car when the current view is a first-person perspective.

Allows a change in perspective

Goodheart-Willcox Publisher

correct location, the perspective changes to first person. The player then looks down the sight of the weapon.

Scenes

A *scene* is the placement of objects on a game frame to create an attractive layout, obstacles, and objectives that convey the story and mood. An essential part of designing a video game is creating the background images to enhance the gameplay experience. The background can be composed of many different objects to create the environment—the feel and mood of a scene. **Figure 4-7** illustrates an environment in which mixed messages are being sent about the mood; the designer did not pay careful attention to the desired mood of the scene. The choice of trees, buildings, sky, clouds, lighting, and general **color palette** are put in place as boundaries and simple scenery for the gameplay.

CHEAT CODE: COLOR PALETTE

A color palette is the set of colors used consistently throughout a scene to maintain mood. Generally, the desired mood sets the color palette that will be dominated by one of four general colors to maintain the mood: red, yellow, blue, or gray. In general, red is used for passion, yellow for cheerful, blue for peaceful, and gray for gloomy. The rest of the color palette is selected using contrasting and complementary colors from the color wheel.

Some background objects can have active characteristics. Other background objects are simply there to act as scenery or to set the mood of the scene. An *active object* is one with which the player can interact. A *background object* is one with which the player cannot interact. Most scenery is a background object. However, some scenery, such as platforms, can be active objects if they provide some interaction. In the case of a platform, the player must be able to walk on it, like the platforms shown in **Figure 4-8.** Most active scenery

Figure 4-7.

Notice how this scene has dark colors for the sky and ground. It even has a dark, scary tree and a ghost character. Yet, the building is a gingerbread house, there is a holiday tree out front, and an elf character is carrying presents. These items are created with bright, cheery colors. This is a mismatched scene. The dark, scary parts do not go with the bright cheery parts.

Goodheart-Willcox Publisher

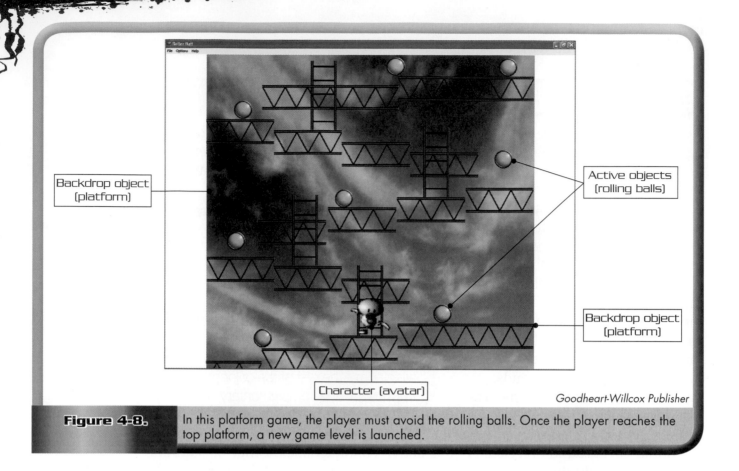

Backdrop object
(platform)

Active objects
(rolling balls)

Backdrop object
(platform)

Character (avatar)

Goodheart-Willcox Publisher

Figure 4-8.   In this platform game, the player must avoid the rolling balls. Once the player reaches the top platform, a new game level is launched.

objects restrict the player's movement or damage or reward the player. In a game, a ***backdrop*** may include buildings, trees, and other objects that do not damage or reward the player. These are active objects as they present obstacles for the player to avoid. A backdrop object differs from a background object because it is an element of the scenery that the player can touch or walk behind.

Think of a background object like the sky. It adds artistic design to the scene, but does not move or interact with the player. This is like when you get your picture taken. The photographer pulls down a background screen of a beach at sunset. It is just there to make the scene look better. You are not actually at the beach, it just looks that way.

The photographer might also use some backdrop objects to help it look like you are at the beach. Here, the photographer places some stairs on one side of the scene leading to an imaginary dock. The stairs are part of the scenery, but you can walk on them. Therefore, they are considered a backdrop object. The combination of the background object (sky) and the backdrop object (stairs) really helps sell the idea that you are at the beach.

In video game design, a designer must set a mood for a scene to help add emotion and anticipation to the gameplay. Two very different moods are conveyed in **Figure 4-9.** The choice of an object, its color, and shape help set the mood of the frame. The choice of a backdrop color could determine if it is a blue sky, a sunny day, or a dark night.

CASE STUDY

Composing a Scene

A game scene starts with a background object, like a blue sky with a few white puffy clouds painted in. The background object prevents the character from passing through it. It is always behind all other objects in the scene.

Goodheart-Willcox Publisher

The sky is a background object. It is always behind all other objects.

You then add backdrop objects like a road, trees, bushes, light poles, and buildings. Backdrop objects, like the tree, will not let the character pass through it. The character might be able to walk in front of or behind a tree, but should not be able to walk *through* a tree.

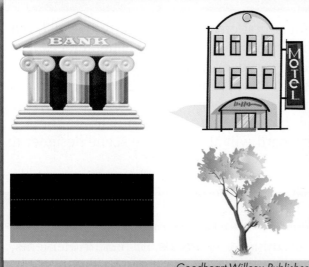

Goodheart-Willcox Publisher

These are backdrop objects. The character may pass in front or behind these objects, but may not pass through them.

The tree also does not move on its own. As a backdrop, the tree will move with the scene, but it does not approach the player, harm the player, or add points for the player.

Goodheart-Willcox Publisher

These are the active objects for the game.

If a tree is supposed to fall and become an obstacle, it must be programmed as an active object instead of a backdrop object. Active objects can be the player, obstacles, objectives, tokens, or anything programmed to move or interact with the player.

Goodheart-Willcox Publisher

The background object, backdrop objects, and active objects are assembled to create the scene.

The background, backdrop, and active objects are assembled to create a game scene. With these objects in place, the character can be programmed to collect the healthy food items to build strength points and subtract points for eating junk food like a cupcake.

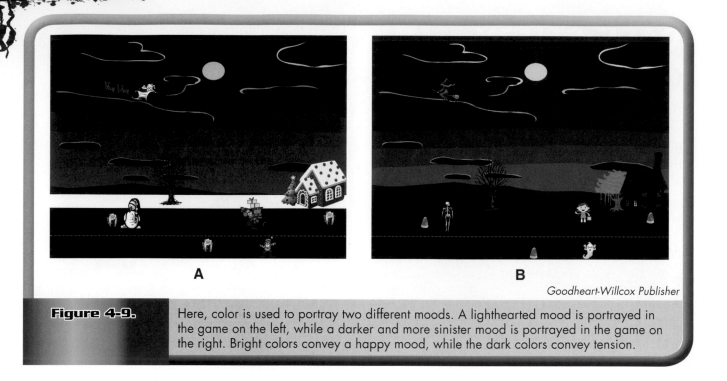

A

B

Goodheart-Willcox Publisher

Figure 4-9. Here, color is used to portray two different moods. A lighthearted mood is portrayed in the game on the left, while a darker and more sinister mood is portrayed in the game on the right. Bright colors convey a happy mood, while the dark colors convey tension.

If the designer is setting a scary scene, the use of dark colors, a gray or muted palette, and sharp-edged shapes will help set the mood. As players enter this scene, they would anticipate seeing characters and traps related to this type of setting. Opponents would be dimly colored and might be ghosts and skeletons. Anything brightly colored, like a shiny coin, would likely be a reward. In general, dark colors identify opponents and bright colors identify rewards or friends.

Storyboards

Before you design a scene you must first create a storyboard to sketch out the design. A sketch of the important frames, each with the general ideas for motion, traps, and rewards, is called a storyboard, as shown in **Figure 4-10.** Storyboards have been used for years in the motion picture industry. They help organize and plan what will happen in a video game or movie. Your storyboard does not need to present great detail, but it should serve as a guide to the digital design of the scene. The storyboard will also help the scene designer to set the dimensions of the frame.

Image Properties

The scene dimensions are measured in pixels. *Pixels,* or picture elements, are the smallest points or dots of color a computer screen can generate. A pixel can only be one color at any given time. All objects displayed onscreen are created with pixels. The computer uses these points to create an image.

Date _____   Sheet _____   of ___
Project _____   Artist _____

Frame/Time _____

_____
_____
_____
_____
_____
_____
_____
_____
_____
_____
_____
_____
_____
_____
_____
_____
_____

Frame/Time _____

_____
_____
_____
_____
_____
_____
_____
_____
_____
_____
_____
_____
_____
_____
_____
_____
_____
_____
_____
_____

Goodheart-Willcox Publisher

Figure 4-10. A storyboard is used to plan an animation or video game. The key frames or events are shown on the storyboard. Then, once the plan is set, the work needed to complete the game can begin.

While pixels are only used in reference to video displays, this same concept has many applications. Think of drawing a picture by only tapping the point of a pencil on the paper. Each dot represents one pixel used by a video display to show the line. You might have to tap 50 dots to make a line one inch long. The resolution of this line is said to be 50 ***dots per inch (dpi).*** The higher the dpi, the higher the resolution.

CHEAT CODE: CLARITY

When designing digital images, clarity refers to how clearly images are defined with either line or pixel density. Blurry, faded, too light, too dark, or pixelated images are not clear or have poor clarity.

A fax machine prints at 300 dpi. A standard laser printer prints at 600 dpi. A photographic or fine-quality printer might print as high as 1200 dpi or higher. The **clarity** of an image is directionally proportional to the dpi. The smaller the pixel point, the more dots per inch can be generated and the clearer the picture. However, the image being printed must have a corresponding dpi.

You cannot simply take a low-resolution image and make it bigger. If you do, the image will become blurry, or ***pixelated,*** as illustrated in **Figure 4-11.** The reason pixelation occurs is the process of interpolation that the computer performs. By breaking apart the word *interpolation,* you can construct the correct meaning: *inter* is the space between and *polation* is a polishing or finishing. Therefore, the definition of ***interpolation*** is a refining of the spaces between the points or pixels of an object.

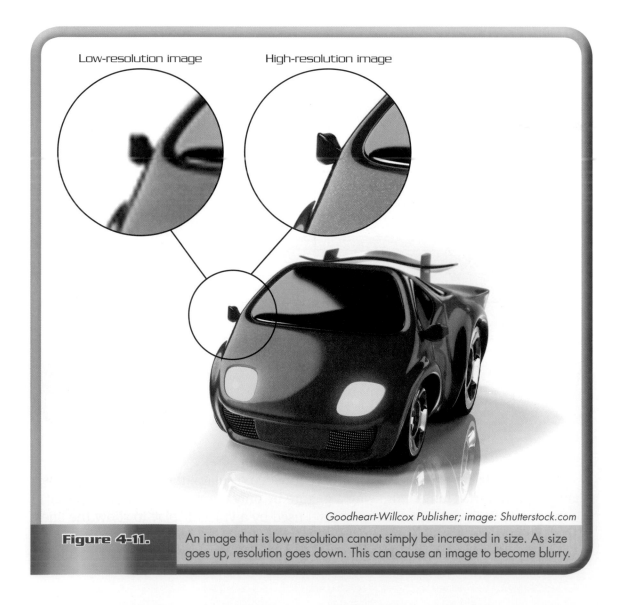

Goodheart-Willcox Publisher; image: Shutterstock.com

Figure 4-11. An image that is low resolution cannot simply be increased in size. As size goes up, resolution goes down. This can cause an image to become blurry.

When a computer makes an object larger, it needs to fill in the spaces between each pixel. This effect is called *dithering*. If it does not fill in that space, the object would look really funny as it would separate into little dots. The computer uses interpolation to dither an image when it is resized.

When dithering an image, the computer chooses a blended color to fill in between the pixels that moved. This process repeats every time the object is enlarged by more than one pixel spacing. As more blended pixels are inserted, the object develops a blurry look as the color between the two **native poles** or pixels continues to distort.

CHEAT CODE: NATIVE POLES

Native poles or native pixels are the original pixels of an object before it was modified. The computer creates an interpolated pixel between two native pixels when an object is resized.

In **Figure 4-12,** green pixels touch red pixels in certain locations. If this picture is enlarged, the computer must interpolate a new pixel between these two native pixels. The figure shows what an interpolated pixel might look like. The computer adds a pixel and colors it based on information from the surrounding pixels. The red-green-blue (RGB) color of the red pixel is 222,0,0 (222 density of red, 0 green, and 0 blue). The RGB color of the green pixel is 0,128,0 (0 density of red, 128 green, and 0 blue). The interpolated pixel has an RGB color of 222,128,0. As you can see, that color is nothing like either of the original colors. This causes the picture to get fuzzy, distorted, and discolored as the size increases.

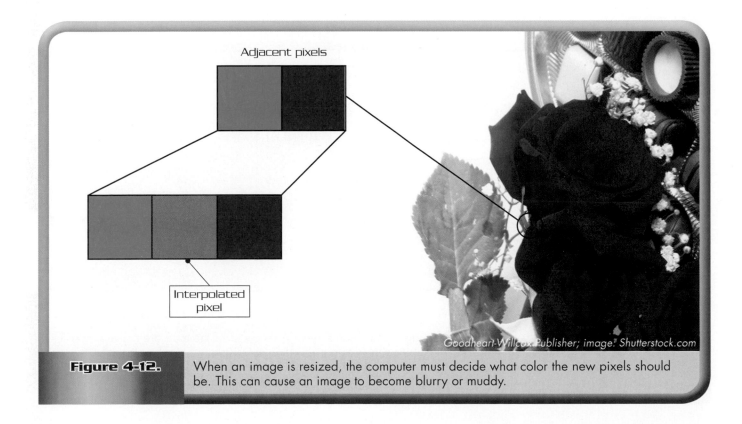

Adjacent pixels

Interpolated pixel

Goodheart-Willcox Publisher; image: Shutterstock.com

Figure 4-12. When an image is resized, the computer must decide what color the new pixels should be. This can cause an image to become blurry or muddy.

Designers of digital scenes need to make the images clear enough to look like the item being shown. However, making images too fine will take more computer memory to generate items due to the greater number of pixels. The designer will also have to know on what type of computer system the game will be played. That determines the total background frame size in pixels. For example, if the computer monitor setting is set to 1280 × 780 resolution, a designer must create a frame that is 1280 pixels wide and 780 pixels high to fill the screen. If a game frame is set larger than the screen size, some images may not show. If that happens, a designer might need to modify the screen settings to fit or allow the game frame to scroll. If the frame scrolls, it moves with respect to the character, as illustrated in **Figure 4-13.**

After determining the screen dimensions, the designer needs to determine the gameplay dimensions. The gameplay can be designed as 2D, 2.5D, or 3D.

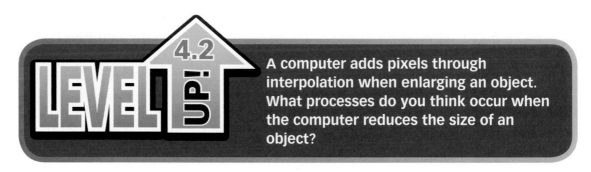

A computer adds pixels through interpolation when enlarging an object. What processes do you think occur when the computer reduces the size of an object?

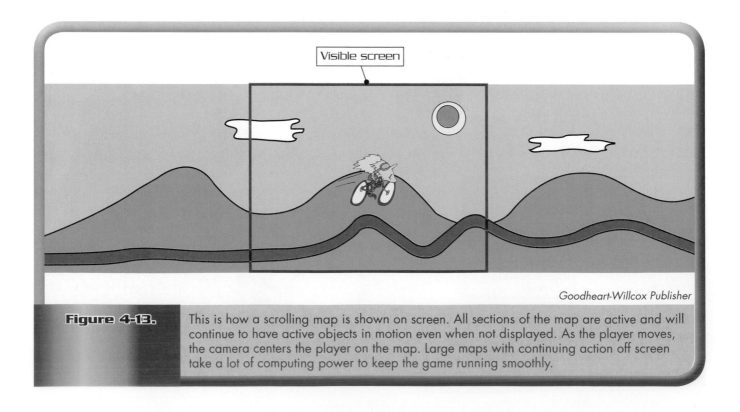

Visible screen

Goodheart-Willcox Publisher

Figure 4-13. This is how a scrolling map is shown on screen. All sections of the map are active and will continue to have active objects in motion even when not displayed. As the player moves, the camera centers the player on the map. Large maps with continuing action off screen take a lot of computing power to keep the game running smoothly.

CASE STUDY

Digital Color Models

To create the millions of colors we see in real life, computers need to mix basic colors. In Chapter 1, you saw how the color wheel allows you to mix the three primary colors (red, blue, and yellow) to create the complementary and contrasting colors. Digital color models are similar, but slightly different. Two common digital color models are RGB and HLS.

The RGB, or red, green, blue, model combines three colors in different densities to create different colors. The RGB color model is used on most personal computers, television sets, LCDs, and handheld devices. These display screens can easily blend the three color components to create white, black, and millions of colors in between. The bit depth of the color (8 bit, 16 bit, 32 bit, etc.) determines the number of colors that can be created.

In the RGB model, a color value of 0,0,0 (red = 0, green = 0, blue = 0) is black, as shown in the figure. This makes black the base

color for the RGB model. So starting with black, when you add red, blue, or green in different densities (values), new colors are created. If you add a maximum amount of red, green, and blue (255,255,255), the color is white. The maximum amount of color that can be added is 255. Every digital color can be written in RGB format.

The HSL model uses hue, saturation, and luminescence values to create colors. The hue value determines which color in the spectrum shown is the basis, from red to purple. The saturation level is the amount of hue. In other words, it is the density of the color. The higher the saturation, the more of the base color used.

Together the hue and saturation work like the X and Y coordinates of a number line. Notice in the figure the target site that is created on the palette by entering a value for the hue and saturation below. This technique chooses a color from the palette.

The luminescence setting is how bright or dark the color appears. The average color brightness is 112. If luminescence is set to 0, the color has no luminescence and is black. If luminescence is set to 255, the color is white. Values in between result in varying degrees of the darkness/lightness of the base color.

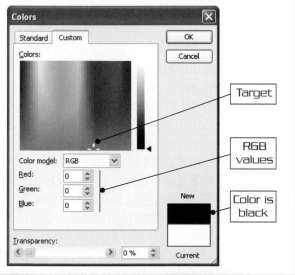

Goodheart-Willcox Publisher

This is the **Colors** dialog box from a Microsoft Office application. In this example, the RGB color model is used to define black.

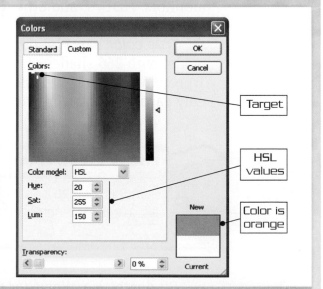

Goodheart-Willcox Publisher

In this example, the HSL color model is used to define orange.

Images

Video games are a visual media. Much of the experience of playing a video game involves the images the player sees on screen. There are two basic types of images: raster and vector. In addition, images may be compressed to save storage space.

Raster Images

The most common type of images used in 2D video games are raster images. **Raster images** are images that are made of dots or pixels. Each pixel in the image has a specific color and location to construct the final image. A raster image is called a **bitmap** because the location and color of each pixel is mapped. The computer reads a bitmap image by creating a coordinate grid with the origin at the top-left corner and increasing the X value moving right and the Y value moving down. In each space of the coordinate grid is a single pixel. A pixel can only be one color. To determine the color of a pixel at a particular coordinate location, the color value of a pixel is read by the computer and displayed.

Originally, bitmaps were only made at a bit depth of 1. **Bit depth** is a binary measurement for color. Binary allows for only two values, either a 1 or a 0. A bit depth of 1 describes the exponent value of the binary digit. A bit depth of 1 means 2^1. A bitmap value of 1 would, therefore, assign a white pixel on the coordinate grid where required. This produces a black and white image with no gray.

Eventually, computers were able to read bitmaps to a bit depth of 4. A bit depth of 4 allowed for a total of 16 colors, as 2^4 equals 16. The modern minimum standard for computer-displayed color is a bit depth of 8 or higher. A bit depth of 8, or 2^8, allows for 256 colors. Two hundred fifty-six–color devices are typically handheld devices where graphic quality is not needed. Computer monitors, HDTVs, and other devices that require quality graphics try to achieve true color or deep color.

True color has a bit depth of 24. True color uses the familiar RGB color model with 256 shades of red, 256 shades of green, and 256 shades of blue. True color produces 2^{24} colors, or 16,777,216 colors. Since the human eye is only capable of discriminating a little more than 10 million colors, 24-bit color can result in more colors than the human eye can see. Other color depths above 24 bit fall into the deep color range. **Deep color** is supported by Windows 7 up to a 48-bit depth. This provides more intense colors and shadow. Deep color can produce a **gamut** of over 1 billion.

CHEAT CODE: GAMUT

Gamut is a range or series. A gamut of color is the entire range of colors.

Bit depth also allows for transparency. With a large gamut of color, an alpha channel can be allocated. Alpha channel varies the opacity of the color. The **alpha channel** can support from full transparency all the way to full opacity. A 16-bit alpha channel can support 65,536 values of transparency.

Ethical Gamer

It is important to be respectful in your use of computer equipment. It is unethical to use the computer, without permission, for personal means such as playing games, shopping, or other activities that are outside of your assignments. It is also unethical to access confidential information, download copyrighted material, or harass others. Many organizations monitor users to make certain that the computer activity is ethical and legal.

Alpha channels can also allow for a masking color. A **masking color** is a single shade of a color that can be set to be transparent. If you have ever seen a weather report on TV, you have likely seen them using a masking color. Using a green or blue screen, called a chroma screen, will allow a background of the weather map to digitally replace the blank screen. In image creation, mask colors are typically chosen so they will not interfere with natural colors. Using a masking color such as white would be a very bad choice. If white was made to be transparent, then the whites in a person's eyes and other white items would be transparent.

Vector Images

Another popular type of image is a vector image. **Vector images** are images composed of lines, curves, and fills. Vector images do not store the color value and location of each pixel. Rather, the image is displayed based on the mathematical definition of each element in the image. In other words, in a raster image a line is composed of dots, while in a vector image the line is defined by a mathematical equation. For a vector image to be displayed, the software must rasterize the image before it is sent to the display device.

A vector image can be a very small file size because the image is drawn by the computer using a mathematical formula. Since the formula draws the image, the image can be resized infinitely smaller or larger without loss of clarity. This is one of the biggest advantages of a vector image.

However, raster images offer an advantage over vector images because a vector image requires the CPU to work hard to draw the image. In the world of handheld devices with small CPUs and low memory, a vector image may have the benefit of small file size, but may take up a large amount of CPU ability. Bitmaps do not take up a large amount of CPU ability, but have higher file size. The designer will need to understand the limits and capabilities of each device on which the image will be rendered to correctly match the file size and CPU usage to prevent lag and crashing the device.

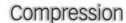

Compression

Raster images are often compressed from their original raw format to reduce file size, save computer memory, and decrease download time. *Compression* uses mathematical formulas to approximate the location and color of each pixel and thereby reduce the total file size.

A computer algorithm is used to record the pixel data in a smaller file size and then uncompress the image when it is opened in image-editing software. Almost all compression formats seek to eliminate the color values stored in the image that are beyond the capability of the human eye. The two most popular image-compression algorithms are lossy and lossless. The *lossy compression algorithm* compresses the image, but does not keep perfect image clarity. The image generally will have an acceptable appearance, but it will not be as clear when uncompressed as the original image. The *lossless compression algorithm,* or losslessly compression algorithm, compresses the image and keeps perfect clarity when uncompressed. There is a tradeoff between clarity and file size. To reduce the file size to run on a handheld device, the clarity may need to be reduced to fit the memory needs of the device and program.

File formats are needed for each type compression so the computer will understand how to read the compressed image. **Figure 4-14** lists several popular image file formats and the compression model needed to expand the image.

Image Format	Name	Compression	Benefit
GIF	Graphic Interface Format	Lossless	Popular for use on websites; 256 colors and can be animated
PNG-8	Portable Network Graphic, 8-bit depth	Lossless	Same as GIF, but cannot be animated
PNG-24	Portable Network Graphic, 24-bit depth	Lossless	Same as PNG-8, but more colors and transparency options
JPEG	Joint Photographic Expert Group	Lossy	Generally offers the smallest file size
BMP	Bitmap	Run length encoded (RLE)	Device independent
RAW or CIFF	Camera Image File Format	None	Raw data at full uncompressed value
CGM	Computer Graphics Metafile	Vector	Can be used with many vector-imaging programs
AI	Adobe Illustrator	Vector	For use with Adobe Illustrator
EPS	Encapsulated PostScript	Vector	Generic vector format that can be used in any PostScript-enabled software

Figure 4-14. This table shows image file formats and the compression model needed to expand the image as well as the benefit of the format.

Goodheart-Willcox Publisher

Reducing CPU Usage

One solution to a device with low CPU power is to use blitting or double buffering with bitmaps. The basic premise of blitting or double buffering a bitmap is to significantly reduce the amount of CPU usage. Imagine running the same scrolling image in one case where 90 percent of the CPU is used and another that uses only 10 percent of the CPU—without loss of quality. This can be achieved using blitting and double buffering.

Blitting

Blitting is a computer operation that takes one or more bitmap images from a memory block and displaying it on a display device or copying it into another bitmap image. Blit stands for bit block transfer. When video games are designed and programmed, several different images and objects must be displayed on the screen. The computer tracks all of these images independently, combines them, and displays them all as a single screen image. Blitting takes out all the individual images and only sends a single rasterized image to the CPU to display. The CPU has less work to do because only the pixels that change from one screen to the next must be generated. The unchanged pixels remain illuminated from the previous screen image.

Blitting works because the display refreshes very quickly. The *refresh rate* is how often the screen is redrawn. Refresh rates are measured in Hertz (Hz), which is how many times per second something occurs. A refresh rate of 1 Hz refreshes the screen once every second. Refresh rate is different from frame rate. *Frame rate* is the speed at which frames are played, while refresh rate is the frequency that a displayed frame is redrawn. Video displays have a refresh rate higher than the frame rate. For example, a computer typically has a frame rate of 30 frames per second, but most monitors have a refresh rate of at least 60 Hz. This combination means each frame is redrawn twice and there are 60 calls to draw per second ($30 \times 2 = 60$).

For digital video displays, each pixel must be drawn in at a refresh rate of 60 Hz or higher. Because some television, movie, and HD monitors have substantially higher refresh rates—as high as 600 Hz or more—blitting is not needed for equipment with these high-end specifications.

Double Buffering

Blitting uses double buffering to combine the individual game objects into a single bitmap that is rendered on the screen. *Buffering* is preloading data into a section of memory called the buffer. Everyone who has downloaded a song, game, movie, or other streaming video or audio has seen a playback bar at the bottom of his or her screen, as shown in **Figure 4-15.** The data bar typically shows the current position of the video and also the downloaded amount in the buffer. The video display is reading the information directly from the buffer memory location. If the playback rate is faster than the download rate, the audio or video will stop, lag, pause, or even display an hourglass with a message stating "Buffering…".

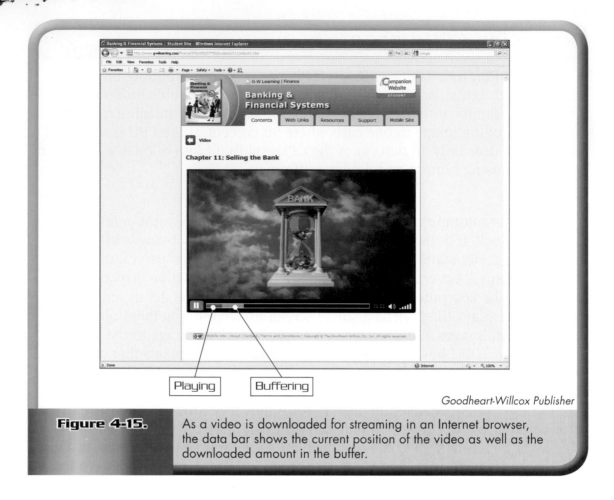

Playing　　Buffering

Goodheart-Willcox Publisher

Figure 4-15. As a video is downloaded for streaming in an Internet browser, the data bar shows the current position of the video as well as the downloaded amount in the buffer.

When the refresh rate is too low, the human eye will see flickering on the screen. *Flickering* occurs because portions of the screen are not being illuminated quickly enough and black from nonilluminated pixels shows. This differs from tearing. Video *tearing* occurs when frames are out of sync or are only partially refreshed. When the packets of video data are sent to the monitor, some of them do not get to the monitor and the image is only partially refreshed. The solution to tearing is using a multiple buffering system, such as double buffering, to assure that the image displayed on the screen is complete.

Double buffering requires two buffers, called the front buffer and the back buffer. The front buffer contains the composite image being displayed on the screen. The back buffer feeds to the front buffer only the segments of the composite image that have changed. Instead of having to rewrite the entire front buffer data, only the changed pixels are uploaded to the front buffer. This keeps the computer only reading front buffer data. The back buffer contains all preloaded data that can be changed on the screen.

To understand this, think about a game like *Pong*. Most of the screen remains the same throughout the game. CPU load will decrease if the back buffer only sends information to change the front buffer, for example to add white pixels where the ball moved, black pixels where the ball was before, new pixels for the score, and new pixels for paddles.

Tile-Based Games

Tile-based video games that use a grid map, like checkers, would also work well for blitting and double buffering. Only the tiles that contain a moved checker or the tile where the checker was would need to be redrawn for each turn. Tile-based games can be very complex and use standard sized tiles to represent a portion of the game map, actor, or asset.

Tile-based games use standard-size tile images to make a composite game map and other objects within the game. To save computer memory, the computer only draws in the tiles that are composited as the display image that the player sees. The other tiles are stored in the back buffer so they can be quickly drawn into the next frame to be displayed.

Traditional tile based games, like *Scrabble,* use a square tile that is placed on a grid game board. Tile-based video games work the same way by adding square tiles to create a composite image of the game map. Characters, vehicles, game pieces, and more are drawn as tiles on a layer above the game map to move with the action of the game, as shown in **Figure 4-16.**

The video games *SimCity* and *Civilization* are examples of tile-based games. If you use the map editor functions of these games, the tile-based aspect is clear. *Civilization 5* introduced hexagonal tiles to that series of video games. Previously, the *Civilization* games had rectangular tiles.

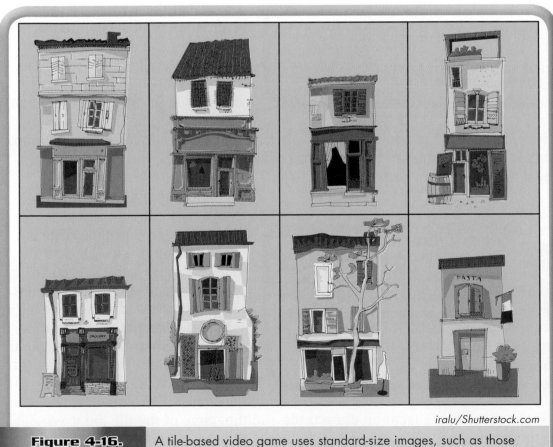

iralu/Shutterstock.com

Figure 4-16.   A tile-based video game uses standard-size images, such as those shown here, for the characters and objects within the game. The chroma green marks areas of transparency.

Loading the tile-based game map involves having the computer arrange each bitmap image of a tile from the back buffer into the correct order in the front buffer. The graphics processing unit reads the front buffer and displays the game map on the output device. As the player moves, the map may scroll to keep the player avatar on the *stage,* which is the visible portion of the game map. When that occurs, the game map in the front buffer is replaced with a new map that is drawn using new tiles from the back buffer.

The idea of breaking a game into tiles is that the back buffer does not need to store large bitmaps. Since many tiles are the same bitmap image laid side by side, only one instance of that tile needs to be stored in the back buffer. This way the front buffer can store the tiles in current use on the stage and the back buffer can store tiles surrounding the stage.

An infinitely large tile-based game can be constructed using only a few tiles. Imagine a grass tile, a road tile, and a river tile. Using just these three tiles, a large game map with several roads and rivers could be constructed. To **draw** the tile-based map, the computer need only place the correct tile in the correct location to keep building the map in any direction. Instead of having a massively large single bitmap for the game map, only a few small bitmap tiles need to be stored. This makes tile-based games ideal for low-memory devices.

Rendering a tile map is very similar to rendering a single bitmap image. Since the stage is a coordinate grid, each tile acts like one large pixel to fill in each cell in the coordinate grid. Imagine a tile map that uses a standard-size tile of 32 pixels high and 32 pixels wide. If the stage dimensions are 480 pixels tall and 640 pixels wide, the map is 15 tiles tall and 20 tiles wide, as illustrated in **Figure 4-17.**

The coordinate location of each tile and the name of the tile are used to render the map. The computer aligns each tile to make, or blit, a single composite image. When that composite enters the front buffer, the pixels are all aligned to make one large bitmap display that the player sees.

Figure 4-17.
This is a tile map that is 15 tiles tall and 20 tiles wide. The location of each tile is a coordinate on the grid and a specific tile is associated with that location.

Goodheart-Willcox Publisher; image: Matthew Cole/Shutterstock.com

To make tile-based games easier to construct, many designers create and share tile sets and sprite sheets. **Tile sets** are standard-size tiles arranged next to each other on a single sheet as a single bitmap image. **Sprite sheets** are similar to tile sets, except the sprite sheet is a single bitmap image of all the frames of animation for a sprite movement, as shown in **Figure 4-18.** Only the portion of the sprite sheet for the current animation frame is displayed at any given time. A single sprite character may have several movements and thereby have several **movement sets** included on a single sprite sheet. The tiles from a sprite movement set are played to create frame-based animation.

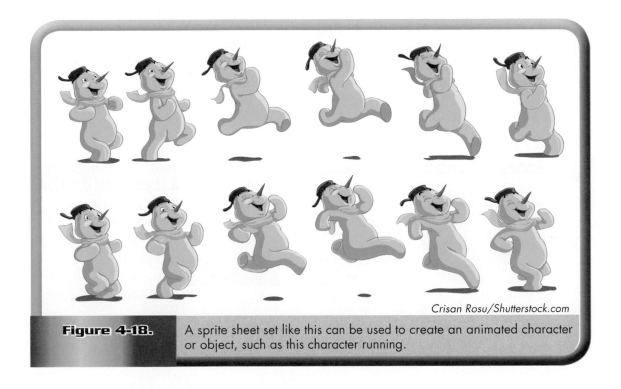

Crisan Rosu/Shutterstock.com

Figure 4-18.   A sprite sheet set like this can be used to create an animated character or object, such as this character running.

Two-Dimensional Games

Two-dimensional (2D) games have characters and backgrounds that play in only two dimensions: length and width, as illustrated in **Figure 4-19.** A character in a 2D game can only move up, down, left, or right to the limit of the length and width of the game frame. This style of game has flat characters on a flat background.

There are two terms commonly used to describe the presentation of a 2D game on the screen: game frame and visible play area. A *game frame* includes all of the items programmed for a complete scene or level of a game. The game frame is the entire game world for that scene. This includes items visible on screen and all items that exist off screen. The part of a game frame that is displayed on the video screen is called the *visible play area*, *stage*, or *scope.*

In addition to tracking off screen objects, the computer may also have to scroll the game frame as the player moves. *Scrolling* is where the game frame is moved so the position of the player is always in the visible play area. It is important to remember that all objects on the game frame remain, even though they are not visible. Refer to **Figure 4-13.**

Scrolling can easily be demonstrated using your hand and a textbook. The textbook is the game frame and your hand is the visible play area. Lay your hand on the textbook and move the book without moving your hand. That is how the computer scrolls the larger game frame to present a moving view in the visible play area.

A 2D character can be made into multiple poses to create a sprite character set to display the movement animations used in the game. Recall from Chapter 1 that a sprite is a 2D asset. A *sprite character set,* then, is a collection of 2D assets, such as different poses, for a single character. As discussed earlier, a sprite sheet contains the sprite character set. A sample sprite character set from RPG Maker XP is shown in **Figure 4-20.** RPG Maker XP is a game engine for developers creating role-playing games. Direction of travel for sprites is typically defined by compass directions: North, South, East, and West. Some sprite character sets can have 16 directions of motion just for walking on a flat surface.

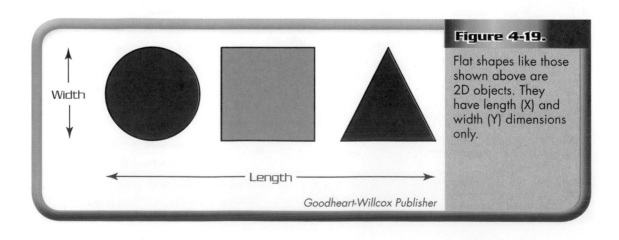

Figure 4-19.

Flat shapes like those shown above are 2D objects. They have length (X) and width (Y) dimensions only.

Width

Length

Goodheart-Willcox Publisher

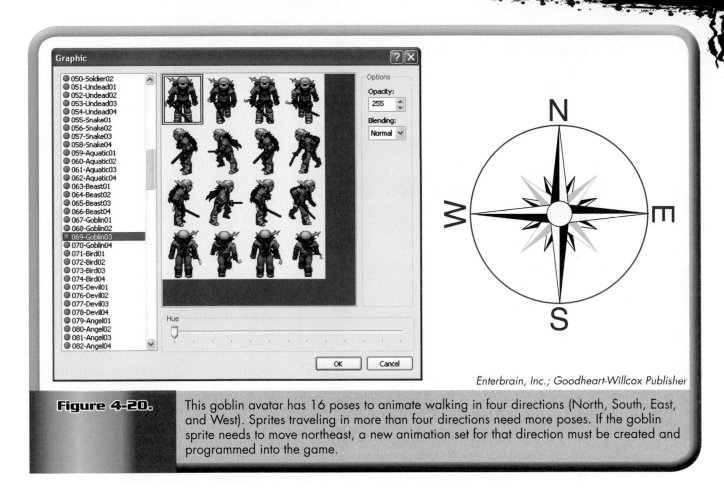

Enterbrain, Inc.; Goodheart-Willcox Publisher

Figure 4-20.
This goblin avatar has 16 poses to animate walking in four directions (North, South, East, and West). Sprites traveling in more than four directions need more poses. If the goblin sprite needs to move northeast, a new animation set for that direction must be created and programmed into the game.

Everything in a game frame is located with a ***coordinate system.*** The coordinate system is very similar to the coordinate graphing you have done in your math and science classes. It involves the X coordinates (left and right, horizontal directions), Y coordinates (up and down, vertical directions) and Z coordinates (depth or closer and farther directions). In 2D games the Z value is always 0.

If you remember Cartesian coordinates from your math class, moving to the right of the origin, the value of X changes in the positive direction. When you move up from the origin, the value of Y changes in the positive direction. The coordinates of the origin are written as (0,0,0). This means X, Y, and Z all have a value of zero. The X value is always first, followed by the Y value and then the Z value. Since the Z value is always zero in 2D games, it can be removed from the coordinate set. Then, the origin is written (0,0), as illustrated in **Figure 4-21.**

If you move to a different point other than the origin, you need to identify where on the X and Y axis

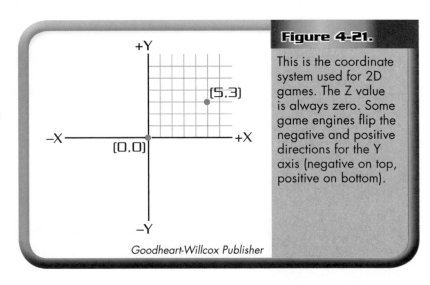

Figure 4-21.

This is the coordinate system used for 2D games. The Z value is always zero. Some game engines flip the negative and positive directions for the Y axis (negative on top, positive on bottom).

Goodheart-Willcox Publisher

that point exists. If you locate the colored dot on the graph in **Figure 4-21,** the coordinates are (5,3) or X = 5 and Y = 3. The same concept of coordinates applies to game design, except the Y axis is flipped in some game engines.

Figure 4-22 shows an image from The Games Factory 2. This shows a 2D frame where the origin of the coordinate system (0,0) for the frame start is the top-left corner. If the pointer moves one pixel to the right along the X axis, the coordinates are 1,0. If the pointer then moves one pixel down along the Y axis,

CHEAT CODE: PARALLAX

Parallax describes how objects in the distance seem to move more slowly than objects in the foreground. This creates a slight change of perspective when the foreground object moves. An easy way to practice this is to hold one finger up as you point at an object in the distance. Close one eye at a time and the object in the distance seems to jump to the other side of your finger.

the coordinates are 1,1. To find the total screen size, the pointer can be moved to the bottom-right corner. Here, the coordinate indicator would read 420,680 as this screen size is 680 pixels wide and 420 pixels tall.

Also included in the concept of 2D depth perception is **parallax** movement. To create depth when a 2D character moves, designers create a background from multiple

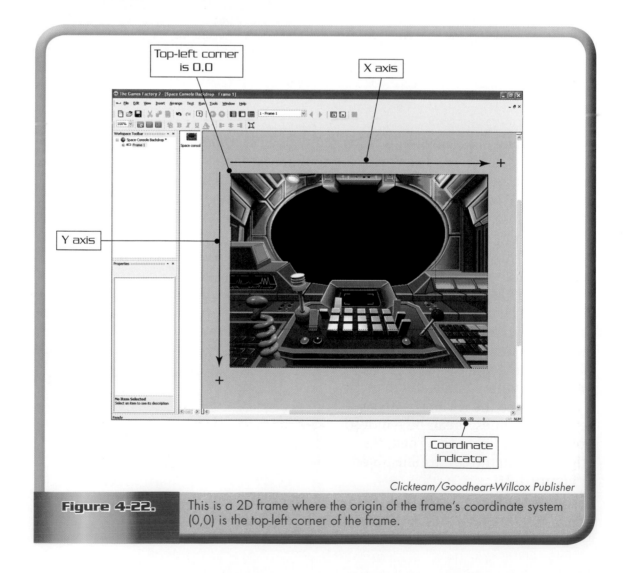

Clickteam/Goodheart-Willcox Publisher

Figure 4-22. This is a 2D frame where the origin of the frame's coordinate system (0,0) is the top-left corner of the frame.

background maps. By layering these maps so closer objects are in front of distant objects, the feeling of depth is created. The designer then programs these layered background maps to move at different rates to simulate the movement you see in nature. The map closest to the player moves fastest. The map farthest from the player moves slowest. Next time you play the classic game *Mario Brothers,* look at how the backgrounds move behind the action. You will build a game with parallax later in this course.

Two and One-Half–Dimensional Games

Two and one-half–dimensional (2.5D) games have two-dimensional background graphics, but uses three-dimensional (3D) characters and obstacles, an example of which is shown in **Figure 4-23.** This type of game is a **hybrid.** The graphics are designed with three dimensions (length, width, and depth), but the gameplay is still defined by only length and width. This style of game has 3D characters and objects on a flat background. In a true 3D game, objects are

CHEAT CODE: HYBRID

A hybrid is created by combining features from two different items. A hybrid car is a combination of an electric car and a car with an internal combustion engine. A 2.5D game is a hybrid because it combines 2D gameplay with 3D objects.

3D obstacle

3D avatar

Gameplay is in a 2D frame even though the graphics appear 3D

Firaxis Games/Goodheart-Willcox Publisher

Figure 4-23. This is a 2.5D game. The game frame is two dimensional, but the characters and obstacles are three dimensional.

programmed to resize, re-shade, and shift view in relation to the camera. In a 2.5D game, however, multiple poses are used. These poses change similar to a 2D character, but each sprite has a 3D appearance.

To create a sprite character set for 2.5D game, the characters and obstacles are all generated with length, width, and depth. Multiple camera angles can be used with a 3D character to produce a character that works. The character will need to be designed so it can be seen from all of these different angles. Most game designers create these simulated 3D characters with a minimum of 26 viewing angles for each pose. Highly defined characters may have more than 100 viewing angles for each pose.

In some 2.5D games, the character set is replaced with actual 3D models with full articulation. *Full articulation* means all of a character's body parts can move through a range of motion in a realistic manner. In these games, the background is still flat and two dimensional, but the characters and interactive objects are true 3D models.

Three-Dimensional Games

Three-dimensional (3D) games have 3D characters and 3D background objects called models. Recall from Chapter 1 that models are different from sprites. Sprites are defined in two dimensions (X and Y). Models are defined in three dimensions (X, Y, and Z), as illustrated in **Figure 4-24.** They are computer generated in real time to show the correct angle and pose. It takes a lot of computer processing to make a 3D model move.

The discussions in the following sections are actually oversimplified explanations of how perspective, pixel shading, vertices, scaling, and depth work within a game. However, these discussions should give you a good idea of these concepts that are used to make a 3D scene in a game.

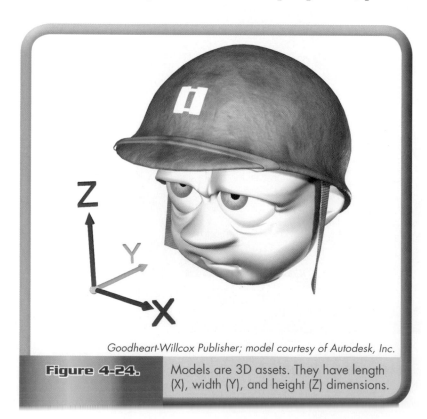

Goodheart-Willcox Publisher; model courtesy of Autodesk, Inc.

Figure 4-24. Models are 3D assets. They have length (X), width (Y), and height (Z) dimensions.

Perspective

Background models on the 3D game map are complex as the computer must generate a game frame that moves in three dimensions. It is really not moving in three dimensions, but rather the computer displays a view that *appears* to move in three dimensions. It does this by using visual perspective. *Visual perspective* creates the sense of depth using shading and narrowing to represent the third dimension of depth on a two-dimensional screen. Important to visual perspective is the concept of a vanishing point.

A ***vanishing point*** is the point in the background where edges of all assets will meet at a single point if extended. A rectangular surface will appear pinched into more of a triangular shape. In other words, parallel lines do not appear parallel. Notice how the road in **Figure 4-25A** appears to narrow and darken as it recedes into the background. In the far distance, the road vanishes to a single point. In **Figure 4-25B,** you can better see the vanishing point. By blocking out the background images, you can see the road appears to form a triangle. The farthest point in the distance—the vanishing point—is the top of the triangle. Of course, the edges of the actual road remain parallel, they just appear to meet in the distance.

If you look more closely at the picture, you will also see that the treetops and all other "north/south" objects vanish to the same point. In **Figure 4-25C,** red lines are added to the trees where the trunk meets the branches and to the road edges. You can clearly see all objects recede to the same vanishing point. In this case, the vanishing point is centered in the middle of the view. This scene is now divided into four triangles of visual perception.

A 3D game engine will create an object using a vanishing point in the center of the screen if the view is first person. If the view is third person, then the vanishing point will be at the midpoint of where the camera is pointed. To achieve a vanishing point, the 3D engine uses the concept of pixel shading and **vertices.**

CHEAT CODE: VERTICES

While some consider the plural of vertex to be vertexes, it is actually vertices (ver-ti-sees). A group of more than one vertex is a group of vertices.

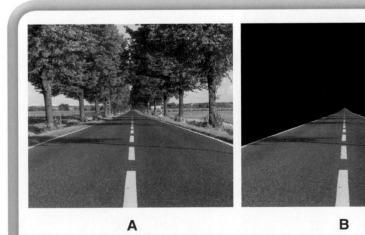

A B C

Goodheart-Willcox Publisher; image: Shutterstock.com

Figure 4-25. A—The vanishing point is clearly visible in this photo. It is in the middle of the image. B—If the trees and sky are blocked out, the point where the edges of the road converge is obvious. C—Red lines are added to show the receding lines on the road and trees. The receding lines converge at the vanishing point.

Think about the phrase, *the light at the end of the tunnel.* Think about how you might draw this concept in a very long straight tunnel. How does the use of a vanishing point work in this drawing?

Pixel Shading

Pixel shading is based on the idea that as you move farther from the light source, things get darker. The game engine shades the pixels of distant objects darker and closer objects lighter. As you move toward a distant object, it will get brighter until it reaches full color when you are next to the object. In addition to distance shading, an object will have different shades of color on different surfaces to give contrast to the object.

Vertices

Pixel shading is useful, but something has to make the objects get bigger and move as though you were seeing them get closer. The 3D engine does this by adjusting the distance between vertices on the model. A **vertex** is a point on a 3D model where the corners of adjacent faces meet.

For example, a cube object has six faces and eight vertices. See **Figure 4-26.** The maximum number of vertices visible on a cube in a given shaded view is seven. This means from one to four vertices are hidden from view, depending on where the camera is located. Also, notice the pixel shading of the cube shown in **Figure 4-27.**

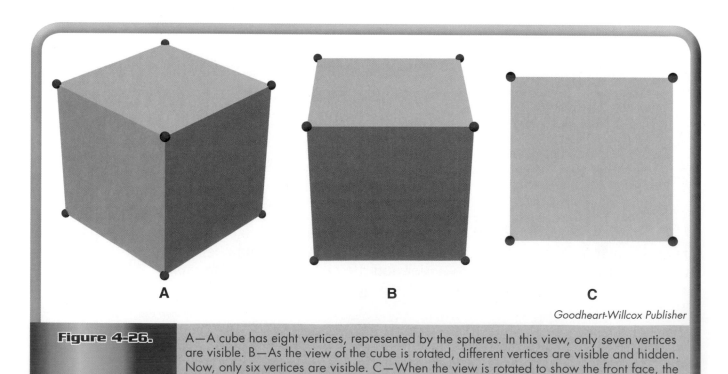

A   B   C

Goodheart-Willcox Publisher

Figure 4-26. A—A cube has eight vertices, represented by the spheres. In this view, only seven vertices are visible. B—As the view of the cube is rotated, different vertices are visible and hidden. Now, only six vertices are visible. C—When the view is rotated to show the front face, the cube looks like a square and only four vertices are visible.

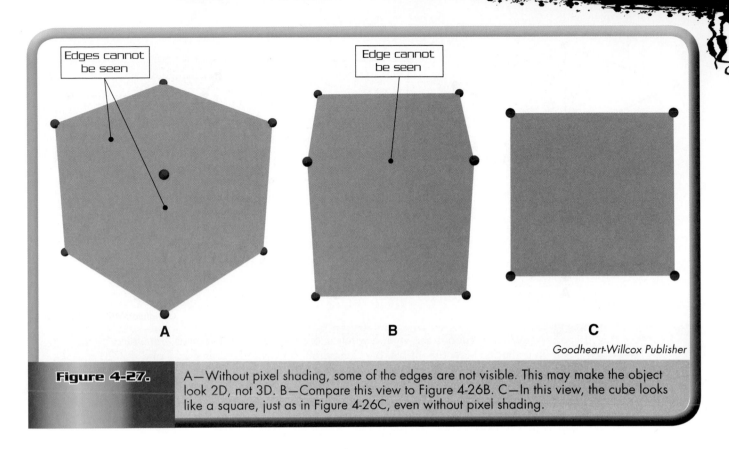

Edges cannot
be seen

Edge cannot
be seen

A

B

C

Goodheart-Willcox Publisher

Figure 4-27. A—Without pixel shading, some of the edges are not visible. This may make the object look 2D, not 3D. B—Compare this view to Figure 4-26B. C—In this view, the cube looks like a square, just as in Figure 4-26C, even without pixel shading.

To give depth, a shading effect must be added to differentiate between the flat surfaces on the cube. These flat surfaces are known as *faces*. Without this shading effect or contrast, the object would not be seen as a 3D object. Instead, it would appear as an irregular 2D shape. The same cube in a **wireframe** view shows the hidden edges and vertices. See **Figure 4-28.**

CHEAT CODE: WIREFRAME

Wireframe is a view showing objects as if they are built with wire, not opaque faces. In a wireframe view, 3D objects have visible lines on the edges, but the faces are invisible. A view with opaque faces is called a shaded view.

Scaling

The 3D engine has more work to do than just render the object on the screen. It must also move the object in a realistic manner. Remember how an object in the distance appears smaller and darker? The 3D engine must make the object larger and brighter as it gets closer to the viewer (the player).

To make an object larger as the player approaches it, the 3D engine must scale the object. To *scale* an object, its dimensions are changed in a way such that the object remains proportional. This is done by moving the vertices of the object farther apart or closer together at the same rate.

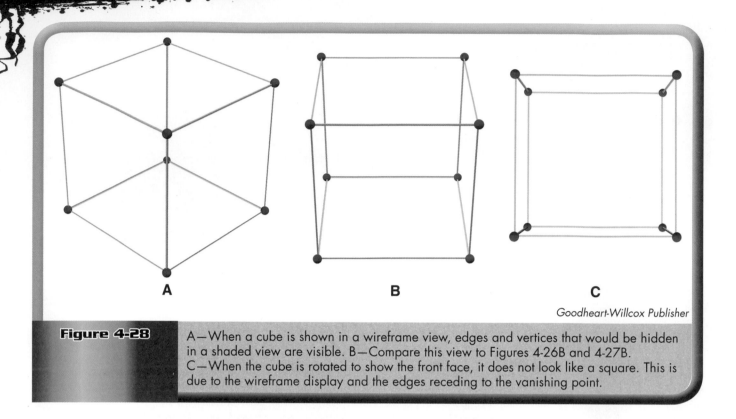

A B C

Goodheart-Willcox Publisher

Figure 4-28 A—When a cube is shown in a wireframe view, edges and vertices that would be hidden in a shaded view are visible. B—Compare this view to Figures 4-26B and 4-27B. C—When the cube is rotated to show the front face, it does not look like a square. This is due to the wireframe display and the edges receding to the vanishing point.

In the example in **Figure 4-29**, the front (and back) face of each original cube has been scaled to twice its original size (200 percent). The orange-black cube is proportionally scaled. This means that all sides of the cube also doubled in size. Notice how each side of the new cube has four checkerboard squares on each edge. The original cube has two checkerboard squares on each edge.

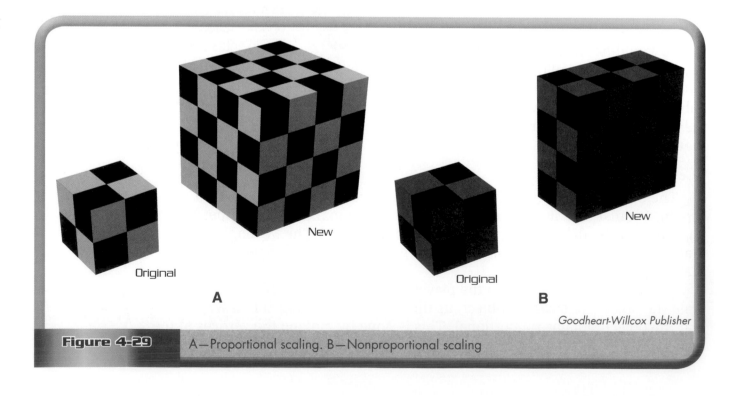

Original New A Original New B

Goodheart-Willcox Publisher

Figure 4-29 A—Proportional scaling. B—Nonproportional scaling

Now examine the blue-black cube in **Figure 4-29B.** This original cube is not proportionally scaled. The front and back faces of the new cube have four checkerboard squares on each edge. This means these faces are scaled by 200 percent. However, the other faces still have two checkerboard squares on each edge. These edges have not been scaled. Therefore, the original cube was nonproportionally scaled to create the new object. Also, it is no longer a cube, but a rectangular box. As such, the new object in **Figure 4-29B** cannot be the original object moved closer to the viewer.

Think of the original cube as a building in a game. In the distance, the cube (building) is small. It must be scaled up to make the building appear closer as the player's character walks closer. With every step of the character, the 3D engine proportionally increases the distance between the vertices and interpolates the object.

Depth

To reduce the amount of programming needed by early computer game systems, the reading edge was developed. This allowed the computer to read a single edge in each direction instead of trying to read all vertices of a 3D object. The *reading edge* is a programmed line between two vertices. When the reading edge changed, the entire object would be scaled to the reading edge dimension. Early game designers used only two reading edges on perpendicular, horizontal surfaces. All vertical height changes on 3D objects were handled by scaling to the size of the horizontal reading edge line changes.

The benefit to programming a reading edge was to reduce programming load. The computer no longer needed to interpret all of the vertices of all objects at the same time. It could change only the reading edge lines. A subroutine controlled the sizing of each object's vertices based on the reading edge change.

The 3D engine, therefore, measured the depth from the front vertex to the rear vertex along the angle to the vanishing point. On the cube shown in **Figure 4-30,** the reading edge is colored blue. As this reading edge changes in size, the cube will be proportionally resized.

In newer, more powerful game engines, 3D objects are surrounded by a bounding box. A *bounding box* is an invisible cube inside of which the 3D object completely fits. The computer resizes the bounding box with the main graphics processing module. Then, a subprocessing module scales the vertices of the actual object inside of the bounding box. Essentially, all of the edges of the bounding box are reading edges.

Goodheart-Willcox Publisher

Figure 4-30. The reading edge on this cube is shown in blue.

In **Figure 4-31,** two rectangular buildings are placed next to the road in the scene discussed earlier. If the building is moved closer to the viewer, the reading edge is longer. The building must be proportionally increased in size. The 3D engine increases the distance between the vertices to stretch the object.

Additionally, when the player moves around the scene, the vertices on objects must move to show a change of direction. **Figure 4-32** shows two cubes. Notice the position of the character and vertices in **Figure 4-32A.** In **Figure 4-32B,** the character has moved in the scene. The cube is exactly the same, just viewed from a different angle. Notice the new positions for the vertices.

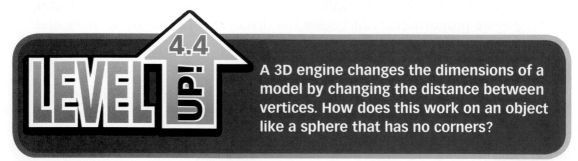

A 3D engine changes the dimensions of a model by changing the distance between vertices. How does this work on an object like a sphere that has no corners?

Round Objects

Rounded objects like spheres can be a challenge for a 3D engine. A sphere has no corners. Different engines may use different solutions to this problem. In most cases, the sphere is made up of several flat, rectangular or triangular faces that make the object look round. Where these faces connect is a vertex. With these vertices,

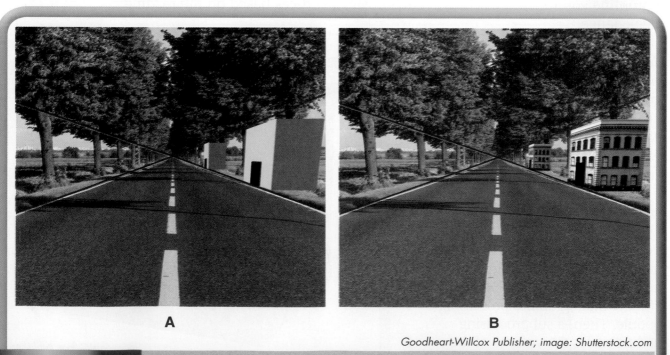

A   B

Goodheart-Willcox Publisher; image: Shutterstock.com

Figure 4-31. A—Two buildings have been added to the scene. The building closest to the viewer appears proportionally larger than the building farthest from the viewer. In reality, the models are the same size. B—Textures have been added to the building models.

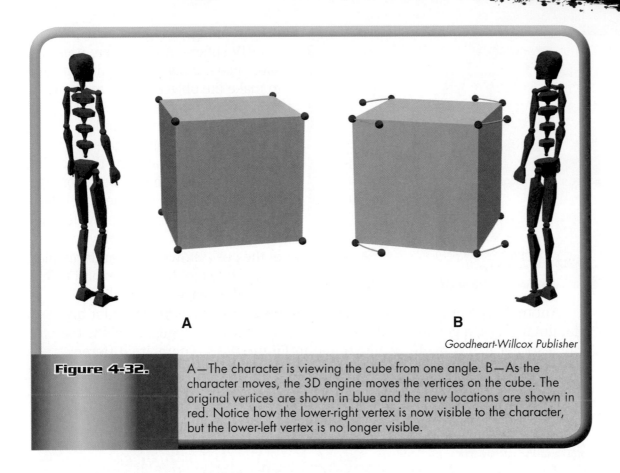

A

B

Goodheart-Willcox Publisher

Figure 4-32.   A—The character is viewing the cube from one angle. B—As the character moves, the 3D engine moves the vertices on the cube. The original vertices are shown in blue and the new locations are shown in red. Notice how the lower-right vertex is now visible to the character, but the lower-left vertex is no longer visible.

the 3D engine can resize the sphere by changing the distance between the vertices. This is also how facial features and other rounded character assets are resized.

The type of sphere described above is called a **UV sphere.** The name comes from the process needed to wrap a texture map around the object. A 2D image is stretched around the sphere, as illustrated in **Figure 4-33.** U is the same as X and V is the same as Y. In some applications, a third element (W) is added for the Z dimension.

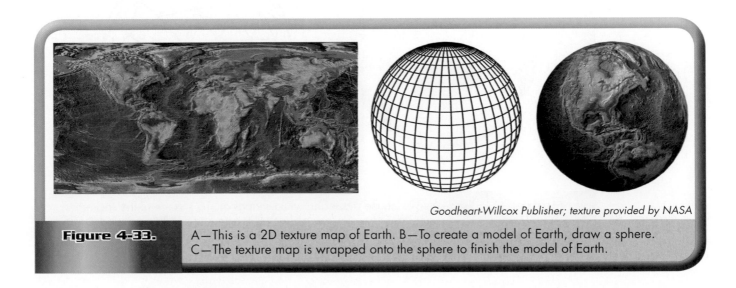

Goodheart-Willcox Publisher; texture provided by NASA

Figure 4-33.   A—This is a 2D texture map of Earth. B—To create a model of Earth, draw a sphere. C—The texture map is wrapped onto the sphere to finish the model of Earth.

Figure 4-34. The segments of an orange are fit together to approximate a round shape. Notice how the segments relate to the sphere shown in Figure 4-33B.

An orange is a good example of a UV sphere. A UV sphere uses slices like the segments of an orange to make the object round, as shown in **Figure 4-34.** The more slices (segments), the more rounded the sphere appears. Imagine the segments of the orange as the faces of the UV sphere. The peel of the orange is the texture map stretched over the sphere. The texture map provides the orange color and the wrinkly quality of the peel. Brown spots and irregular flaws added to the texture map will make the image more realistic.

Another type of sphere is a *geodesic sphere.* Instead of rectangular and triangular faces, a geodesic sphere has faces of regular polygons. This is the way a soccer ball is made, as illustrated in **Figure 4-35.** There are different types of geodesic spheres. For example, an icosphere is based on a 20-sided object. Its faces are equilateral triangles.

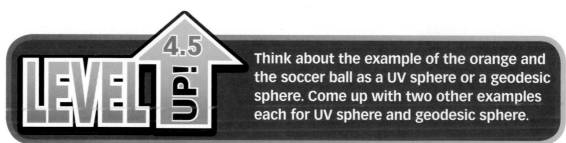

Think about the example of the orange and the soccer ball as a UV sphere or a geodesic sphere. Come up with two other examples each for UV sphere and geodesic sphere.

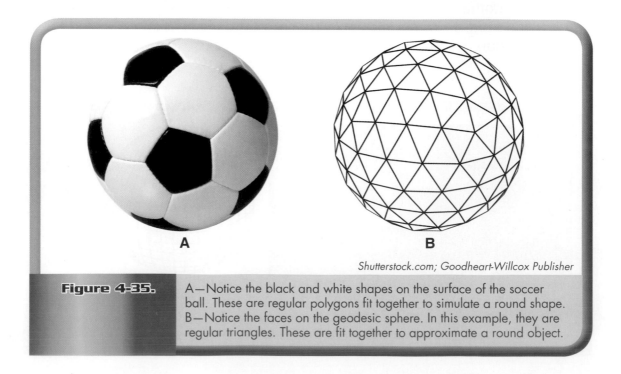

A   B

Figure 4-35. A—Notice the black and white shapes on the surface of the soccer ball. These are regular polygons fit together to simulate a round shape. B—Notice the faces on the geodesic sphere. In this example, they are regular triangles. These are fit together to approximate a round object.

What Is a Mesh?

All 3D objects are made from interconnected polygons stuck together to form a shape. These polygons, or *polys,* stick together along their edges and vertices in what is referred to as a ***mesh.*** Creating a mesh is like gluing all of the pieces together to make one object. However, the computer does the "gluing" based on the size you give the object.

The mesh provides the shape for an object, as illustrated in **Figure 4-36A.** After the mesh is complete, textures, called materials, need to be applied, as is done in **Figure 4-36B.** Often, a single 2D texture map contains more than one image, like those shown in **Figure 4-36C.** Once the texture map is wrapped onto an object, the images are aligned to create the finished object, illustrated in **Figure 4-36D.**

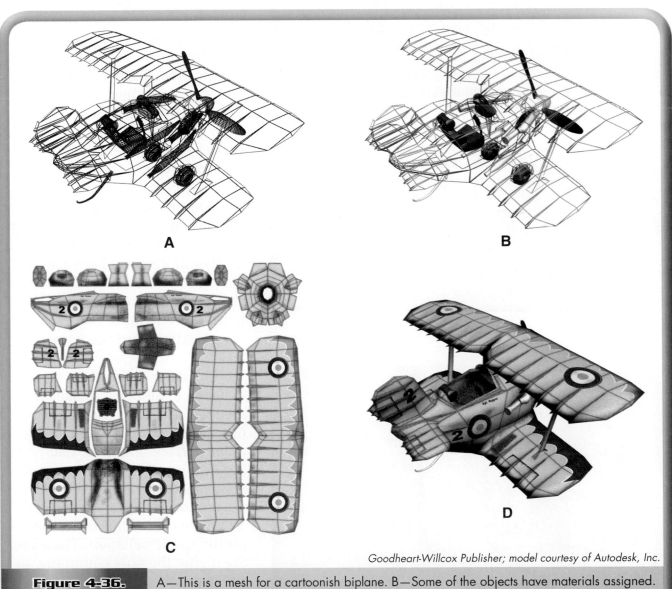

A

B

C

D

Goodheart-Willcox Publisher; model courtesy of Autodesk, Inc.

Figure 4-36.   A—This is a mesh for a cartoonish biplane. B—Some of the objects have materials assigned. C—This is the 2D texture map that will be assigned to the remaining parts of the biplane. D—The fully textured biplane. Notice how the 2D texture map has been applied to the mesh.

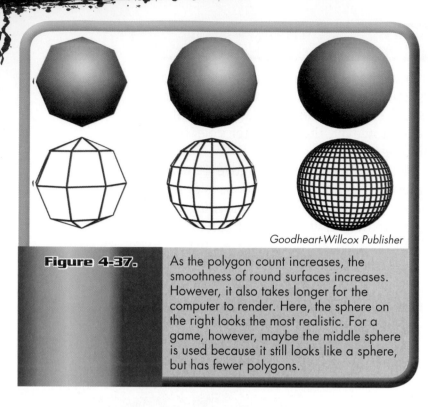

Goodheart-Willcox Publisher

Figure 4-37. As the polygon count increases, the smoothness of round surfaces increases. However, it also takes longer for the computer to render. Here, the sphere on the right looks the most realistic. For a game, however, maybe the middle sphere is used because it still looks like a sphere, but has fewer polygons.

CHEAT CODE: MOSAIC

A mosaic is a design created by placing colored tiles, stones, or glass in a pattern to make a picture. This relates to 3D models because the model uses colored polygons to create an image just like the mosaic picture.

Figure 4-38.

Notice how these tiles fit together to make the image. If you think of each tile in the mosaic as a polygon, you can see how a texture would be mapped to the polys on a 3D game object.

Shutterstock.com

The ***poly count*** is the number of polygons used to make a 3D object. This number is a critical measurement. The more polys, the more lifelike the object becomes, as illustrated in **Figure 4-37.** So, why not make all objects with a high poly count? Simple; every polygon needs to be morphed as the object is moved. The computer needs to calculate the change in distance between each vertex of the polygon as the object gets bigger, smaller, and moves to a different view. If every object has a high poly count, it would take an enormous amount of time for the computer to render the objects as they move. Some processors would not be able to keep up with the calculations. On these systems, the view may skip, play slowly, or appear to have glitches.

Look at the example of an expanding-ball toy. Imagine how long it would take to calculate the change in distance between every vertex each time the ball changes shape. The computer must do just that. The more polygons, the more vertices and the harder the task.

The color and texture maps assigned to an object ***tessellate*** around the object. Each poly has a piece of the texture image on its surface, like a **mosaic.** See **Figure 4-38.** The amount of tessellation is controlled by the number of polys on the object. The higher the poly count, the greater the tessellation. Therefore, the higher the poly count, the smaller each slice of the color or texture map.

Animation

When a character or object moves on the screen, it is said to be animated. An **animation** is a series of frames played in sequence with small differences between each frame. The brain interprets these small differences as motion. Think of the flip cartoons you may have sketched on the corners of notebook pages. This is a very basic animation.

Static animation is where the object retains its original pose while moving. An example is a stick figure with arms, legs, and head kept in the original position, but the figure moves across the computer screen, as shown in **Figure 4-39.** Since the arms and legs do not move, the figure appears to slide across the screen. You can try static animation at your desk. Pick up a pencil or pen and hold it in front of you. Move the pencil up and down while holding it in the original position. Hurray! Static animation in practice.

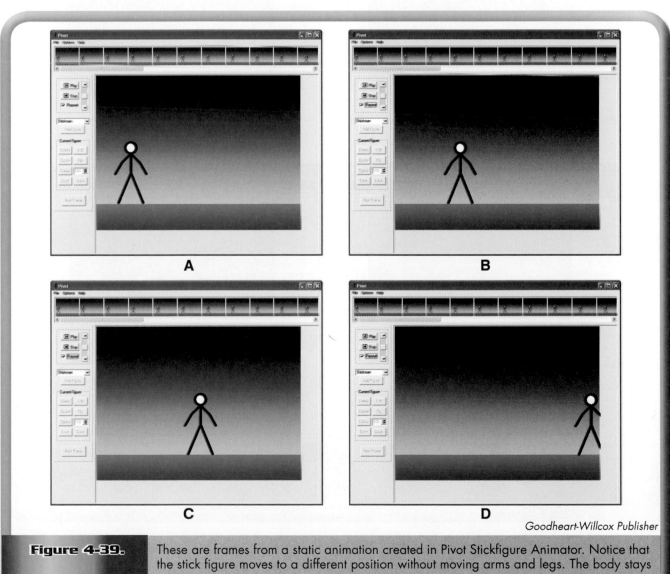

A

B

C

D

Goodheart-Willcox Publisher

Figure 4-39. These are frames from a static animation created in Pivot Stickfigure Animator. Notice that the stick figure moves to a different position without moving arms and legs. The body stays static as it moves.

In *active animation,* an object changes pose while moving on the screen. An example of this is a stick figure with legs that move in a walking motion to take steps as the figure moves across the screen, illustrated in **Figure 4-40.** A real world example might be flipping your pencil in the air. The top and bottom of the pencil change position as it moves up and down. Hurray! Active animation in practice.

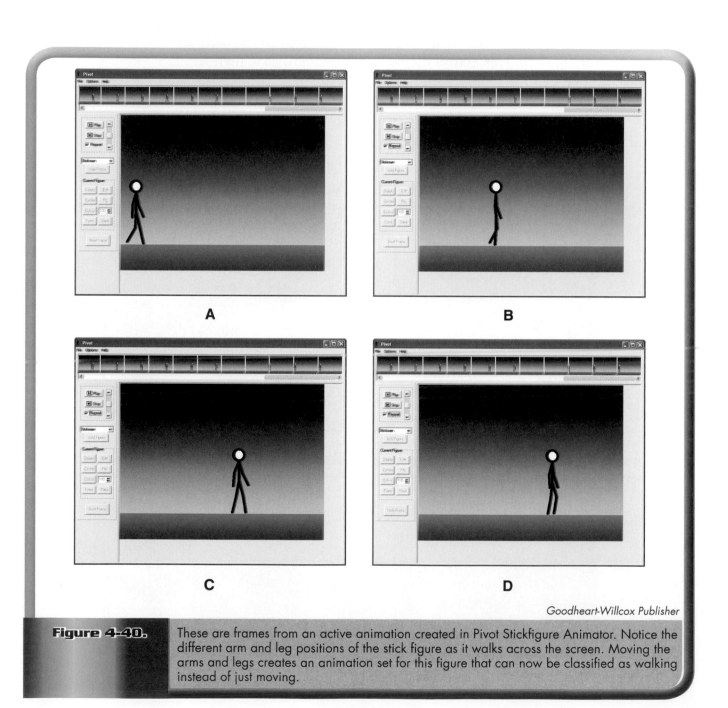

A

B

C

D

Goodheart-Willcox Publisher

Figure 4-40. These are frames from an active animation created in Pivot Stickfigure Animator. Notice the different arm and leg positions of the stick figure as it walks across the screen. Moving the arms and legs creates an animation set for this figure that can now be classified as walking instead of just moving.

CASE STUDY

Disney Animation

Frank Thomas and Ollie Johnson recorded the 12 Principles of Animation in their book *Disney Animation: The Illusion of Life* in 1981. The authors were two of Walt Disney's Nine Old Men that were the core group of animators that began working at Disney from 1927 through 1935.

The book contained a huge collection of animations and became known as the Bible of Animation. The book details the physics involved in simulating real life through animation. By applying the first 11 of the 12 principles of animation, an artist could create realist movement for characters.

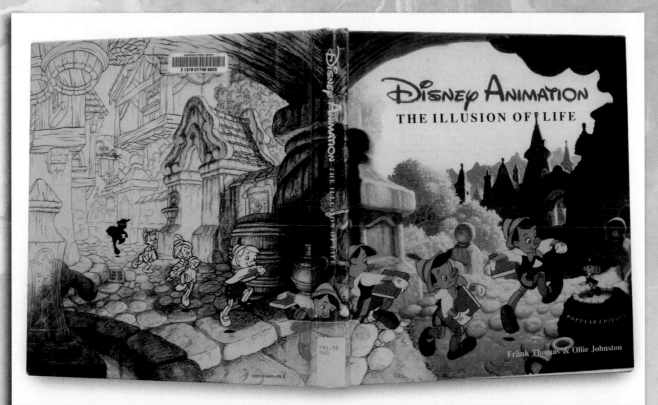

Goodheart-Willcox Publisher

Disney animators laid the groundwork for animation in the early to mid-twentieth century. The principles they developed are still valid in today's video game animation.

(Continued)

CASE STUDY   (Continued)

#	Principle	Description	Animation Example
1	Squash and Stretch	Gives a sense of weight and flexibility to an object; volume remains the same, but shape flexes due to the strain of movement forces.	A bouncing ball will compress as it hits the ground and stretch as it springs upward.
2	Timing and Motion	Timing is how long a given action lasts. *Physical timing:* correct timing makes objects appear to abide the laws of physics. *Theatrical timing:* less technical in nature; is developed mostly through experience and can also be a device to communicate aspects of a character's personality.	Synchronization of translation and articulation; objects behave as real-world objects.
3	Anticipation	Prepares the audience for an action; a visual hint that an action is about to happen.	Bend knees before a jump. Baseball pitcher winding up before throwing the ball.
4	Staging	Direct audience attention to an area of greatest importance.	Use light and shadow such as a dark scene and a character holding a candle.
5	Follow Through and Overlapping Action	Objects have inertia; separate parts of an object will follow the movement of the main object.	A person jumps and their hair extends backward to show motion; when landing, the hair continues moving forward.
6	Straight Ahead Action and Pose-to-Pose Action	Drawing each frame of animation as it would occur from beginning to end; pose-to-pose uses keyframes or major action frames and then fill in-between frames later.	Draw a walk animation with each step (straight ahead). Drawing a crash animation by drawing a car moving and skipping to impact scene. Fill in crash details to match in-between action (pose-to-pose).
7	Slow In and Slow Out	Due to inertia, objects take more time to speed up and slow down than traveling at sustained speed; adding more frames at the beginning allows action to start slowly, adding more frames at the end allows action to stop slowly.	Swing of a hammer is slow at first, is fastest just before it hits a nail, and slows or remains still for several frames after it hits the nail.
8	Arcs	Movements in nature are rarely straight lines; an arc forms when an object rotates around a pivot point.	Arcs define the natural movement of a rotating joint or an object thrown at a level trajectory. Cars turn around a corner in an arc not a 90° angle.
9	Exaggeration	Artistic license taken to divert from reality; a nonrealistic item made larger, brighter, noisier, etc., to provide higher contrast or interest in the object.	Caricature drawings with larger heads on small bodies. Big tires on the back of fast cars. Coins or other collecting tokens in video games.
10	Secondary Action	Action of the main object causes smaller secondary actions that are affected by the primary action.	Walking person swings arms as a secondary action.
11	Solid Drawing	Applying artistic skill using knowledge of the elements of art, principles of design, anatomy, and three-dimensional space.	The hero character is drawn sharply with good color contrast from enemies.
12	Appeal	Having attributes that viewers can relate to and like; using symbolism and color to convey meaning; having actions consistent with the archetype of the character; character unity and charisma.	A hero who looks like a hero and behaves like a hero. A villain who looks and acts evil. Consistent characters design attributes applied.

This table provides a brief overview of the 12 Principles of Animation.

Chapter Summary

- Perspective describes how gameplay is displayed on the screen; choices include first-person, second-person, third-person, and changeable perspective.
- The scene is the placement of objects on a game frame to convey the story and mood.
- Elements used to convey mood and theme include the color, layout, obstacles, and objectives.
- Clarity refers to how clearly images are defined; a high-resolution image will maintain clarity as it is scaled larger whereas a low-resolution image will not retain clarity as it is scaled larger.
- A bitmap is a raster image file format that digitally maps the location and color of each pixel whereas a vector is an image composed of lines, curves and fills; vector image does not store color value and location of each pixel—each pixel is assigned a color as the vector image is drawn.
- To reduce CPU usage when drawing images they can be blitted, which combines two or more bitmaps into a single bitmap, and double buffered, which combines individual game objects into a single bitmap that is rendered on the screen.
- Three-dimensional models are defined by X, Y, and Z coordinates taking into account perspective, pixel shading, vertices, scaling, and depth.
- In static animation the object retains its original pose while moving within the frame; in active animation, in contrast, the object changes pose while moving on the screen.
- Video game designers need to be well-versed in the terminology in artistic creations and computer-generated images.
- Artistic assets for a video game include two-dimensional, two and one-half-dimensional, and three-dimensional objects placed within a scene that sets the mood and theme.
- The game engine shades the pixels of distant objects darker and closer objects lighter and it adds shading effects to distinguish between the different faces created by vertices on a shape to create the illusion of depth.

Check Your Video Game IQ

Now that you have finished this chapter, see what you know about video game design by taking the chapter posttest.

www.m.g-wlearning.com

www.g-wlearning.com

Review Your Knowledge

On a separate sheet of paper or in a word processing document, match the following terms with the definitions that fit best.

A. active animation

F. static animation

B. backdrop

G. background object

C. first-person perspective

H. third-person perspective

D. geodesic sphere

I. active object

E. second-person perspective

J. mesh

1. Object in the game frame with which the player cannot interact.
2. Player sees the game as if the player were an opponent or intermediary; rarely used in video games.
3. An object retains its original pose while moving.
4. A 3D shape created with interconnecting polygons stuck together along their edges.
5. Object in the game frame with which the player can interact; can be programmed.
6. Gameplay is viewed by a person who is not the player's character or opponent, rather a neutral third person; spectator view.
7. An object changes poses while moving on the screen.
8. Objects in a game frame that the player can touch or walk behind, but do not damage or reward the player.
9. A 3D model created with faces of regular polygons, like a soccer ball.
10. Gameplay view where the player sees through the eyes of the character.

On a separate sheet of paper or in a word processing document, answer each of the following questions.

11. What is the view that the player has during gameplay?
12. Which type of game is shown through the player's eyes?
13. Overhead view and platform view are examples of _____ perspective games.
14. Define *scene* as it relates to video games.
15. What is the difference between an active object and a background object?
16. Briefly describe the purpose of a *storyboard*.
17. What is a *pixel?*
18. What is the resolution of an image?
19. Define *interpolation.*
20. If a video display can support only 256 colors, what is the highest bit depth the computer graphics card can read?
21. Describe the basic difference between a raster and vector image.

22. What is video display flicker?
23. Describe how the front buffer and back buffer work together in *double buffering.*
24. How does a double-buffered computer load a tile map?
25. How is drawing a tile map similar to drawing a bitmap?
26. How can a tiled background reduce the file size of a large map?
27. What is the typical minimum refresh rate of a computer monitor?
28. Describe the difference between *frame rate* and *refresh rate.*
29. Describe how a *sprite sheet* is used to create a tile based animation.
30. What characterizes a 2D game?
31. Describe how a 2.5D game is a hybrid of a 2D game and a 3D game.
32. _____ creates the sense of depth using shading and narrowing to represent the third dimension of depth on a two dimensional screen.
33. What is the point called where edges of all assets will meet if extended?
34. How does pixel shading simulate depth?
35. Define *vertex.*
36. If a sphere is proportionally scaled by 200 percent from an original diameter of 1″, what is the new diameter?
37. Briefly describe a *mesh.*
38. What is a *poly count?*
39. What term describes using geometric pieces of tile or glass on the surface of an object to create a decorative surface?
40. Define *animation.*

Apply Your STEM Knowledge

Mathematics

1. The boxes shown below are proportionally sized. Analyze the figure and determine the correct dimensions for the larger object. The large box is 2.5 times the size of the small box.

   A. Large object X dimension _____
   B. Large object Y dimension _____
   C. Large object Z dimension _____
   D. In terms of percentage, how much larger is the blue object compared to the orange object? _____
   E. In terms of percentage, how much smaller is the orange object compared to the blue object? _____

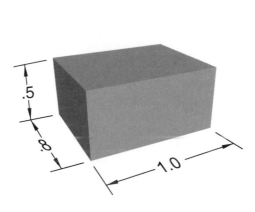
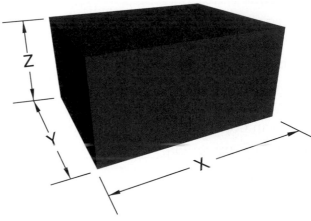

Social Studies

2. Compass directions such as North, South, East, and West are used in defining the movement of a sprite. Look at the map below. Use map navigation skills and interpret the compass map key to create a path that will lead the pirate to the treasure. Create a script to indicate each step this character would take with N,S,E or W. For example, NNNSSWWSSEEWWN.

Movement = _____

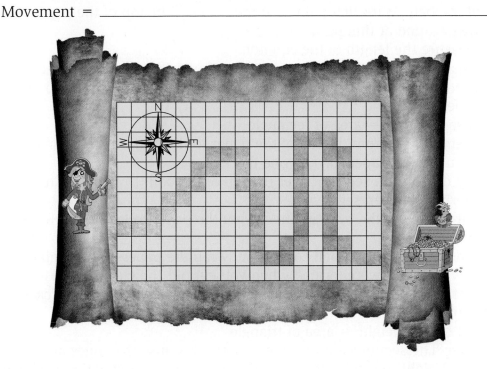

 ## Science

3. To fully articulate an animation, the figure must have moving parts and joints. Research how the knee joint in the human body is constructed and functions. Write a one-page paper to describe how the joint works. Include a discussion on the range of motion.

Mathematics

4. To wrap a texture around an object, the image has to be cut or stretched. Use a round object like a tennis ball to represent a UV sphere.

A. Wrap a rectangular piece of paper around the ball. The bottom edge of the paper should follow the equator (middle of the ball).

B. Bend one point on the top of the paper so it just touches the north pole of the ball. Mark that point and then cut off the top of the paper all the way around at that point.

C. Measure the length of the equator.

D. Measure the height of the paper from the north pole to the equator.

E. Use this formula to determine the area of the rectangle formed by the paper:

base × height = area of rectangle

F. Every 1″, cut from the top of the paper to the bottom. Leave about 1/8″ uncut so the paper stays in one piece.

G. Lay down each segment over the top of the ball. Draw a line to show the overlap between segments.

H. Cut out along the overlap lines to get the paper to lay flat without overlapping.

I. When you have the ball covered, unwrap the paper and examine how triangles were formed when you cut out the curves. Measure the triangular sections. Use this formula to determine the area of each triangle.

1/2 base × height = area of triangle

Note: The sections are not true triangles because the edges are curved, not straight, but this formula will provide an approximation of the area.

J. Add the total area of the *removed* triangles. Determine what percentage of the paper was removed in the wrapping.

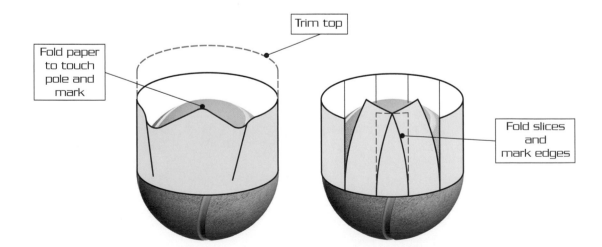

Mathematics

5. Recall from the reading how the computer performs a color interpolation if an object's scale is increased. In this activity, you are the computer and you will average the red, green, and blue amounts shown in the table below to create a blended color for the interpolated pixel.

Open PowerPoint or Word. Create a shape of your choice. Use the "fill custom color" function to create the RGB colors and blend an interpolated pixel.

First Pixel RGB Color	Color Shade	Second Pixel RGB Color	Mixing Color Shade	Interpolated Pixel RGB	Interpolated Pixel Shade
255,0,0	Red	0,255,0	Green	128,128,0	Dark Green
0,0,255		125,125,0			
0,0,0		100,100,100			
125,200,100		75,50,100			
40,0,200		60,50,50			
255,255,255		10,90,25			
	Pink		Yellow		
	Brown		Blue		

Language Arts

6. Create a Venn diagram (overlapping curves or circles) to compare and contrast the first-person perspective and third-person perspective. Write a description of the diagram. Be sure both similarities and differences are discussed.

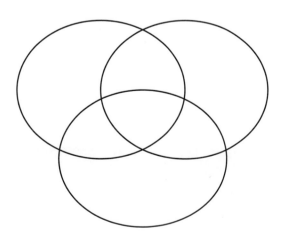

Working in Teams

In teams, research, debate, and form a group opinion on each of the Level Up! activities in this chapter. Prepare a PowerPoint presentation of ten slides (five to seven minutes) to present to the class explaining the team's opinions for each Level Up! activity. Include text, pictures, video, animations, and slide transitions as appropriate to help explain the team's position.

Gamer Portfolio

You will create both a print portfolio and an e-portfolio in this class. You have already decided how to store hard copy items for your print portfolio. Now you need to create a plan for storing and organizing materials for your e-portfolio. Ask your instructor where to save your documents. This could be on the school's network or a flash drive of your own. Think about how to organize related files into categories. For example, school transcripts and diplomas might be one category, awards and certificates might be another category, game builds in another, and so on. Next, consider how you will name the files. The names for folders and files should be descriptive, but not too long. This naming system will be for your use. You will decide in a later activity how to present your electronic files for viewers.

1. Create a folder on the network drive or flash drive in which you will save your files.
2. Write a few sentences to describe how you will name the subfolders and files for your portfolio.
3. Create the subfolders to organize the files using your naming system.

G-W Learning Mobile Site

Visit the G-W Learning mobile site to complete the chapter pretest and posttest and to practice vocabulary using e-flash cards. If you do not have a smartphone, visit the G-W Learning companion website to access these features.

G-W Learning mobile site: www.m.g-wlearning.com

G-W Learning companion website: www.g-wlearning.com

Common Core

College and Career Readiness

CTE Career Ready Practices. Everyone has a stake in protecting the environment. Taking steps as an individual to be more environmentally conscious can help the environment and can also help a company be more profitable. What things can individuals do at the workplace to save energy or other resources?

Reading. Using independent research and the information contained in the text, write a report in which you analyze how different perspectives impact the player's experience in a video game. As needed, derive meaning of the environmental print and use visual and contextual support to confirm understanding. Use support from classmates and your teacher as needed to help in comprehension of the material. What perspective was most often used in early video games? What perspective is most often used now? How could a changeable perspective be used in gameplay? Cite specific evidence from the text and your research to support your understanding of these concepts of player perspective.

Writing. Using the Internet, research the available programs for building three-dimensional objects. Make sure to look at the ways in which they allow the viewing of wireframes and meshes. If possible, work with a trial version of several and explore the ease with which you are able to create basic 3D shapes, scale these objects, and add textures to them. After you have explored the programs on your own, use the Internet to locate reviews of these programs. Make sure to look at, among other sources, newspaper and magazine articles from individuals who work in the video game industry. Write a final research report in which you compare and contrast at least two programs, stating your personal experience with each as well as the opinions of reviewers. Cite your sources and be sure to consider their background and point of view as well as any bias that the reviewers may bring to the discussion.

Event Prep: Working in a Team

Some competitive events for Career and Technical Student Organizations (CTSOs) have a performance portion. If it is a team event, it is important that the team making the presentation prepare to operate as a cohesive unit. To prepare for team activities:

1. Read the guidelines provided by your organization. Make certain that you ask any questions about points you do not understand. It is important to follow each specific item that is outlined in the competition rules.

2. Complete the team activities at the end of each chapter in this text. This will help members learn how to interact with each other and participate effectively as a team.

3. Locate on your CTSO's website a rubric or scoring sheet for the event to see how the team will be judged.

4. Confirm the use of visual aids that may be used in the presentation and amount of set-up time permitted.

5. Review the rules to confirm if questions will be asked or if the team will need to defend a case.

6. Make notes on index cards about important points to remember. Team members should exchange note cards so that each evaluates the other person's notes. Use these notes to study. You may also be able to use these notes during the event.

7. Assign each team member a role for the presentation. Practice performing as a team. Each team member should introduce himself or herself, review the case, make suggestions for the case, and conclude with a summary.

8. Ask your teacher to play the role of competition judge as your team reviews the case. After the presentation is complete, ask for feedback from your teacher. You may also consider having a student audience to listen and give feedback.

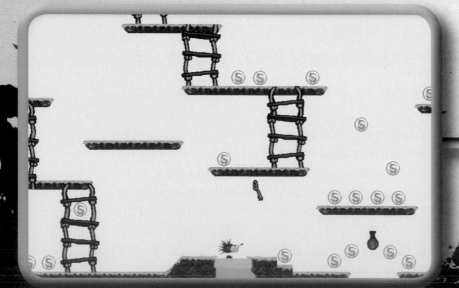

You Must Find:
KEY

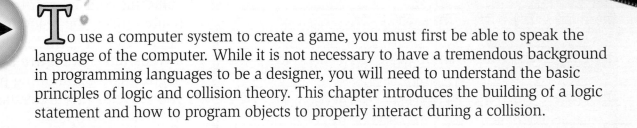

Chapter 5
Collision Theory and Logic

To use a computer system to create a game, you must first be able to speak the language of the computer. While it is not necessary to have a tremendous background in programming languages to be a designer, you will need to understand the basic principles of logic and collision theory. This chapter introduces the building of a logic statement and how to program objects to properly interact during a collision.

Check Your Video Game IQ

Before you begin this chapter, see what you already know about video game design by taking the chapter pretest.

www.m.g-wlearning.com

www.g-wlearning.com

College and Career Readiness

Reading Prep. As you read the chapter, think about the advantages and disadvantages of object-oriented programming. Do you think object-oriented programming is what you would prefer to use? Summarize information from the text and use it to support your opinion.

Objectives

After completing this chapter, you will be able to:

- Use game design software to create a playable video game.
- Integrate animated objects into a video game.
- Create sound and music effects in a video game.
- Describe basic computer logic.
- Build applied mathematics logic statements.
- List features of object-oriented programming.

Logic

The first concept of designing and programming a video game is an action–reaction relationship. To create a game environment that the player can control, the player's actions must cause something to change or react. This is the **action–reaction relationship.** Often, obstacles and challenges are placed within a game to force the player to take action.

Programmers use logic statements to break down these action–reaction relationships. For example, if the action is **colliding** your go-cart into a banana peel, the reaction will be the go-cart spinning out, as illustrated in **Figure 5-1.** To begin this programming process, you will need to understand the five basic operators of a programming language: **IF, THEN, AND, OR,** and **ELSE.**

CHEAT CODE: COLLISION

Collision is the most-used action command in game programming. Often substituted with *hit* or *touch*, a *collision* occurs when an object contacts something. This may be a player contacting an obstacle or other player. It may also be two obstacles contacting each other.

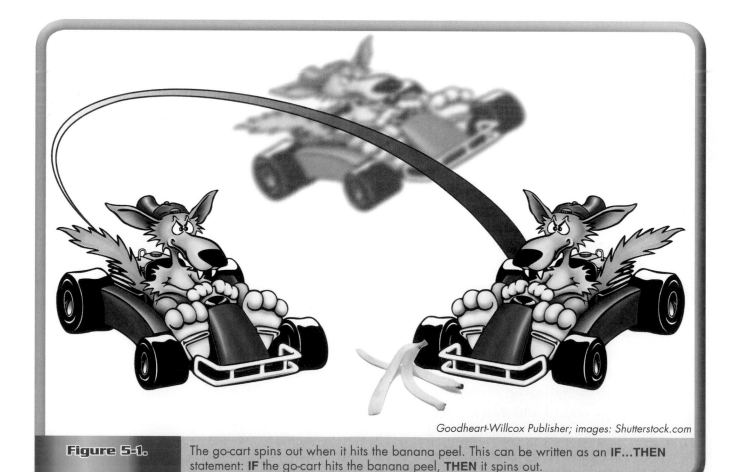

Goodheart-Willcox Publisher; images: Shutterstock.com

Figure 5-1. The go-cart spins out when it hits the banana peel. This can be written as an **IF...THEN** statement: **IF** the go-cart hits the banana peel, **THEN** it spins out.

Basic Logic Statement

Two of the basic operators fit together to make a logic statement. A **logic statement** tests a condition and determines an action based on the result. An **IF...THEN** statement is the most basic example of a logic statement. The operator **IF** is used with the basic statement to test a condition. This is the *action* side of the logic statement. In the go-cart example, the action side of the logic statement is written as:

IF the go-cart collides with the banana peel...

The *reaction* side of the logic statement describes what should happen when the condition is met. The reaction side of the logic statement for the go-cart is:

THEN the go-cart spins out.

Together, the action and reaction sides of the statement form a complete logic statement. The interaction between the go-cart and the banana peel is completely stated as:

IF the go-cart collides with the banana peel, **THEN** the go-cart spins out.

You see that **IF** an *action* occurs, **THEN** a *reaction* takes place. From this basic statement, more complex statements can be created.

Conditions and Events

The action–reaction relationship is everywhere and not just in games. You have several interactions every day. Looking at everyday interactions, they are defined in terms of **cause and effect**. Since cause and effect are exactly the same as action and reaction, the go-cart example can be rewritten in cause-effect language. Here, the *cause* is a banana peel in the road and the *effect* is slipping on the peel. Cause-effect relationships can be written in the same **IF... THEN** logic format. This looks exactly the same:

IF the go-cart collides with the banana peel, **THEN** the go-cart spins out.

The table in **Figure 5-2** shows some everyday cause and effect relationship you might encounter.

When programming a video game, the formal term for an action is a **condition**. The computer checks to see if a condition is met. When it finds a condition has been met, it executes the programmed events. An **event** is a change that occurs when a condition is met. In other words, it is a reaction to the condition.

Operator	Cause	Operator	Effect
IF	you turn in homework,	THEN	you get a good grade.
IF	you buy a ticket,	THEN	you watch the movie.
IF	you miss the bus,	THEN	you are late to school.

Figure 5-2. This table shows the cause-and-effect relationship for some everyday occurrences.

Goodheart-Willcox Publisher

To program the go-cart example using condition-and-event relationships, the logic statement is only slightly modified to describe the exact action the computer must take to carry out the command. That logic statement would read:

IF the go-cart object collides with the banana peel object, **THEN** the go-cart object will change from a linear animation to a spinning animation.

This is still the same idea, but more specific to help the computer identify the object and how it changes when the collision occurs. The table in **Figure 5-3** shows the relationship between the common terms used in constructing a logic statement.

To design a game, many events are required to get it to work properly. When programming a game, logic is used to do more than just describe what happens on screen. The same logic format is used to program the user interface, increase score, change levels, and perform every other interaction the player encounters. A simple user interface to control a player moving North, South, East, and West requires a logic statement for each controlling motion. Refer to **Figure 5-4.**

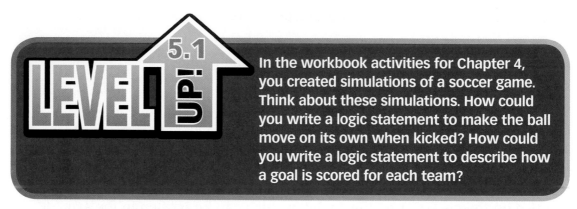

In the workbook activities for Chapter 4, you created simulations of a soccer game. Think about these simulations. How could you write a logic statement to make the ball move on its own when kicked? How could you write a logic statement to describe how a goal is scored for each team?

Programming the user interface shown in **Figure 5-4** uses listeners and triggers. When a program needs input from the game player (computer user) a listener would help the computer understand the input. A *listener* is programming that directs the computer to check or listen for a mouse click, key press, or other input from the user. In the example above, the game listens for an arrow key button press and then triggers the correct game movement. The listener can also be part of an on-screen interface. If the game player has started the game and is on the main page, a "button clicked" listener might be programmed to check if the player clicks the **Start** button.

Operator	Condition	Operator	Event
IF	action	THEN	reaction
IF	cause	THEN	effect
IF	condition	THEN	event

Figure 5-3. This table shows the relationship between the common terms for constructing a logic statement.

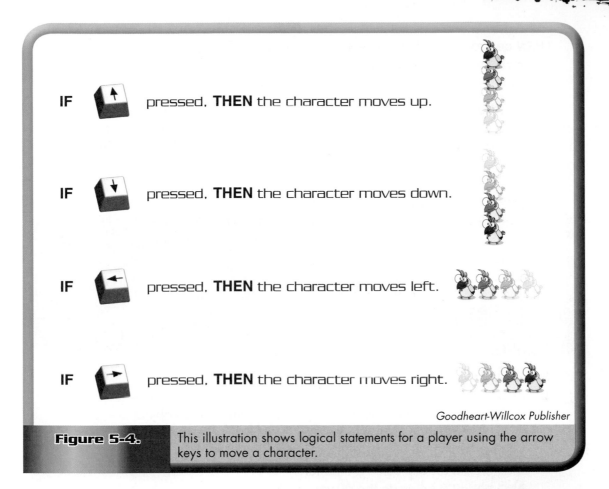

IF [↑] pressed, **THEN** the character moves up.

IF [↓] pressed, **THEN** the character moves down.

IF [←] pressed, **THEN** the character moves left.

IF [→] pressed, **THEN** the character moves right.

Goodheart-Willcox Publisher

Figure 5-4. This illustration shows logical statements for a player using the arrow keys to move a character.

Several game design tools use the term trigger to describe a condition. A ***trigger*** is programming for when a condition is met that a series of actions will begin. In the case of a logic statement, the trigger is the **IF** (condition) and the actions it initiates are the **THEN**. A single condition can act as the trigger for several different actions to begin or end as described in the next section.

Advanced Logic Statements

The next step in basic programming is to add multiple actions or multiple reactions to logic statements. This is done using the **AND** and **OR** operators. These operators work just as they would as conjunctions in any sentence. The **AND** operator will join two or more outcomes for a given condition or action. Refer to **Figure 5-5:**

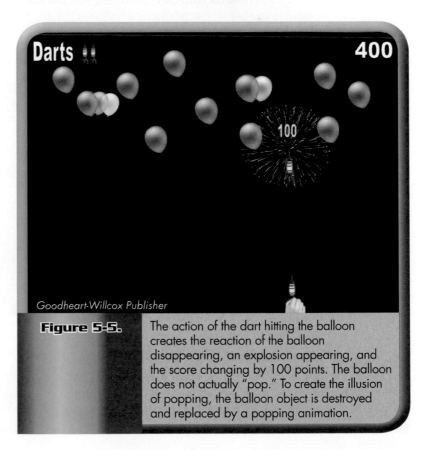

Goodheart-Willcox Publisher

Figure 5-5. The action of the dart hitting the balloon creates the reaction of the balloon disappearing, an explosion appearing, and the score changing by 100 points. The balloon does not actually "pop." To create the illusion of popping, the balloon object is destroyed and replaced by a popping animation.

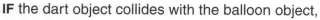

IF the dart object collides with the balloon object,
THEN destroy the balloon object
    AND create an explosion animation object
    AND add 100 points to the player's score.

In this example, the **AND** operator allows three events to occur from a single collision action. The balloon is destroyed (1), an explosion appears (2), and the player scores 100 points (3). An **AND** operator can also be included in a condition statement. Refer to **Figure 5-6.**

LEVEL 5.2 UP!

Look at the dart in Figure 5-6B. When the balloon pops, the dart has not been programmed to stop or be destroyed. How do you think a logic statement should be written to describe what happens to the dart when it hits a balloon?

IF the dart object collides with a yellow balloon object
    AND
    IF the yellow balloon object overlaps any other balloon object,
THEN destroy yellow balloon object
    AND destroy all balloon objects it overlaps
    AND create an explosion animation
    AND add 500 points to the player's score.

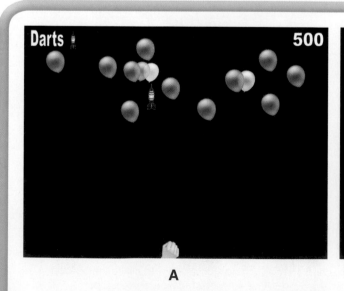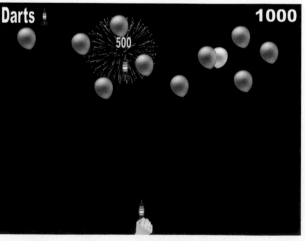

A

B

Goodheart-Willcox Publisher

Figure 5-6. A—The dart is about to hit the yellow balloon. The yellow balloon is overlapped by a blue balloon, which is overlapped by a pink balloon. B—The dart pops the yellow balloon and any overlapping balloons with a single explosion animation; the player scores 500 points.

Just as with the **AND** operator, the **OR** operator works as a conjunction in programming logic. The **OR** operator allows multiple results to take place under a given condition or event. In the balloon pop game, a random balloon begins to deflate during gameplay. When it does, the existing balloon object is replaced with an animation of the deflating balloon and a small balloon underneath the animation. The small balloon is only visible when the deflating animation has finished. In this example, the deflating animation and the small balloon should be treated as if they were only one object. The **OR** operator is perfect for making this happen.

If the dart collides with either the deflating animation or the small balloon, the game should display the same events. The events need to "pop" both the animation and the small balloon underneath. This operation would look something like the example below. Refer to **Figure 5-7.**

> **IF** the dart object collides with a small balloon object
> > **OR**
> > **IF** the dart object collides with a deflating balloon animation,
> **THEN** destroy the small balloon object
> > **AND** destroy the deflating balloon animation
> > **AND** create explosion animation
> > **AND** add 500 points to the player's score.

The last of the basic programming operators is the **ELSE** operator. This operator may also be called the **OTHERWISE** operator. The **ELSE** operator describes what will happen if a certain action or reaction does *not* take place. You have likely seen this many times when trying to beat a level in a video game.

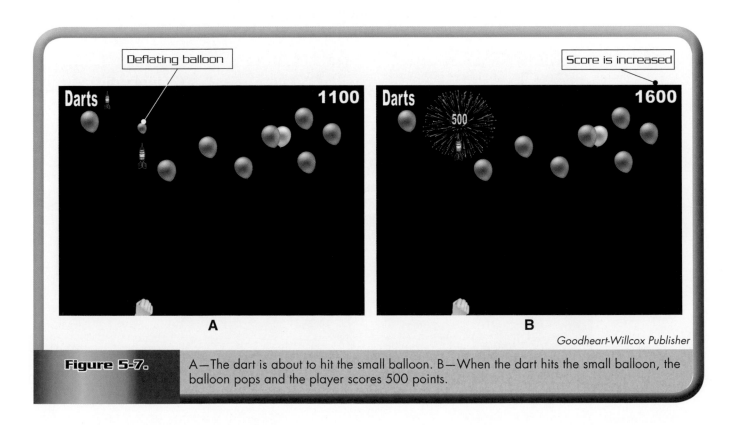

Goodheart-Willcox Publisher

Figure 5-7. A—The dart is about to hit the small balloon. B—When the dart hits the small balloon, the balloon pops and the player scores 500 points.

Think about a game that requires you to collect gold coins and a key. You cannot open the door to the next level without meeting both objectives. The doorway will usually display a message telling you what you are missing, as illustrated in **Figure 5-8.** In the example below, the condition tests if the player has at least 100 gold and one key.

> **IF** gold > = 100
> > **AND**
> > **IF** key = 1,
>
> **THEN** display the message "Well done. You may pass to level 2,"
> **ELSE** display the message "You need 100 gold and the key to pass."

The **ELSE** operator works like a true/false test. If the condition is true, the **THEN** events are initiated. If the condition is false, the **ELSE** events are initiated. In the balloon pop example, the **ELSE** operator helps end the game when the player runs out of darts. Every time a dart is launched, a test needs to be performed to see if there are any more darts. In other words, the question is asked, "is number of darts more than zero?" If the condition is true, then a dart needs to be loaded into the hand (avatar). If the condition is false, the game ends.

The following logic statement can be used to program the end of the balloon pop game.

www.g-wlearning.com
Level up
your know-how
with Animated
Review 5-1.

> **IF** number of darts > 0,
> **THEN** load one dart in the hand,
> **ELSE** display the message "Game Over."

This statement describes what happens each time the player throws a dart. If there is still a dart available, then the player gets to throw another dart. Otherwise, the game is over, as shown in **Figure 5-9.**

Figure 5-8.

A game should tell you what is missing when trying to complete an objective. Here, the game is telling the user the key must be located to open the door and enter the next level.

Goodheart-Willcox Publisher

No darts remain

Darts   1600

Game Over

Goodheart-Willcox Publisher

Figure 5-9.

When a dart is used, the computer looks at the number of darts to see if more than 0 darts are available. Here, the result of the test is **FALSE** since the last dart has been used. The computer then initiates the **ELSE** operation to display the game over screen.

Collision Theory

The most used condition in video game design is *collision.* You may guess the concept of *collision theory* deals with an object running into or hitting another object. It does. However, also included in collision theory is the idea that when objects collide the movements, animations, and events must provide an illusion of reality.

One of the most difficult concepts for beginning designers to grasp is that a picture of an item does not act the same as the real item. When programming a game, the fact that an object *looks* like a wall does not make it *act* like a wall. For it to act like a wall, the object must be programmed with the **properties** of a wall.

CHEAT CODE: PROPERTIES

Images used in video games are programmed to work properly by setting the object's properties. Visibility, interactivity, and movement are some of the properties assigned to an object to make it act like a real item.

A good example of how an image is not a real object can be found in cartoons. The old cartoon trick is to paint a black spot on the ground, as shown in **Figure 5-10.** The black spot looks like a hole, but it is just paint and you should be able to simply walk right over the top of the black spot. The key here is interactivity. *Interactivity* is how one object behaves when it encounters another object. In the cartoon, the interactivity is defined so the black spot actually functions like a hole. When a character walks onto the black spot (interacts with the hole), they fall into the hole.

A B

Shutterstock.com

Figure 5-10. A—The coyote can stand on the black spot because the spot has not been programmed to be a hole. B—The coyote now falls into the hole. The difference is collision programming to make the coyote interact with the hole object.

The black spot is just an image unless you tell the computer to make it act like a hole. To create the properties of a hole, the hole must be programmed so the computer knows how to react when the player comes in contact with the spot. The programming interaction would look something like this:

IF the coyote collides with the black spot,
THEN the coyote falls.

The black spot is still not an actual hole, just an object that triggers a fall event by the coyote. This provides the *illusion* that a black spot is really a hole.

In the cartoon, the coyote falls through the painted hole, while the roadrunner is able to pick up the black spot and run away. Here, the hole reacts differently for two different characters. This would be contrary to collision theory. The hole should act like a hole for all the characters unless one has a magical ability or flight. Anything else would be a glitch.

Collision theory works throughout the game environment. Every object including the background must be programmed to look, feel, and act like it should. Imagine a scene from the *Spiko the Hedgehog* game. During gameplay, you do not expect Spiko to be able to run over the water, rather sink in it, because that is what the game rules state. Instead, Spiko runs across the water, as shown **Figure 5-11.** What is going on here? This common glitch happens when the designer forgets to apply collision theory to the entire scene.

The designer needs to program the platform to act like a solid object. That is to say, **IF** the character collides with the grassy platform, **THEN** Spiko stops falling. The gravity setting makes Spiko fall until he collides with an object programmed to act solid. When an object has no collision statement, it will not alter the character's movement.

A **collision statement** must exist for each object the player touches. If no collision statement exists,

CHEAT CODE: COLLISION STATEMENT

A collision statement is a logic statement that has the condition side of an event beginning with two or more objects colliding.

Figure 5-11.

In this platform game, *Spiko the Hedgehog*, the main character must walk on the grassy platforms to reach the gold. However, notice the glitch in this game. Spiko can walk on the water hole, when he should sink. The collision with the water was incorrectly programmed to act as solid platform.

Spiko does not sink in the water

Goodheart-Willcox Publisher

then the player cannot interact with it. Take the example of a player flying an airplane. There is no collision statement for the sky or the clouds. This allows the airplane to fly through these objects without any reaction. However, if the airplane collides with a bird, then the engine would sputter and the plane would lose altitude. Therefore, birds are programmed to trigger interaction events when touched. In other words, the bird objects have a collision statement.

Remember, just because an object looks like a dart does not mean a balloon will pop if the dart touches it. In the balloon pop game, if an event is not associated with the condition:

IF the dart object collides with the balloon object

then nothing will happen when the dart hits the balloon. No events will occur at all, no balloon pop, no explosion, and no increase in score. The computer has no way of knowing the proper event unless you tell it exactly what to do and how to do it.

This can be a difficult topic to understand. It is easy to think that if an object *looks* like grass, then it should *act* like grass. That is true in real life. A real grassy surface stops you from falling to the center of the earth. But, this real-world logic does not apply in a video game. In a video game, the grass is just an *image* of a grass. The object will only *act* like real grass if the designer programs it to do so. Every interaction with the grass object needs to be programmed to react as though it came in contact with real grass.

Of course, you do not have to program objects to act the way they do in the real world. Some surreal and fantasy games program unusual properties for objects that appear as real-world objects. For example, you may program a road to act as a river. On the other hand, you may have a waterfall act like an elevator.

5.3

Think about a racecar game and how the player's car must interact with the other cars on the track. What do you think will happen if you do not program a collision between the player and the other cars? Would that be fun?

Programming with Collision Theory

Looking at the balloon pop game, a balloon pops when it collides with the dart. This appears to be one event triggered by one condition. However, it is actually a series of events activated when the dart object collides with the balloon object. When the computer recognizes this collision, it sets into action the events programmed by the logic statements. Shown in **Figure 5-12** is an event frame used in The Games Factory 2. This is an object-oriented, game development software. The event frame shows the programming of a collision condition and the resulting events.

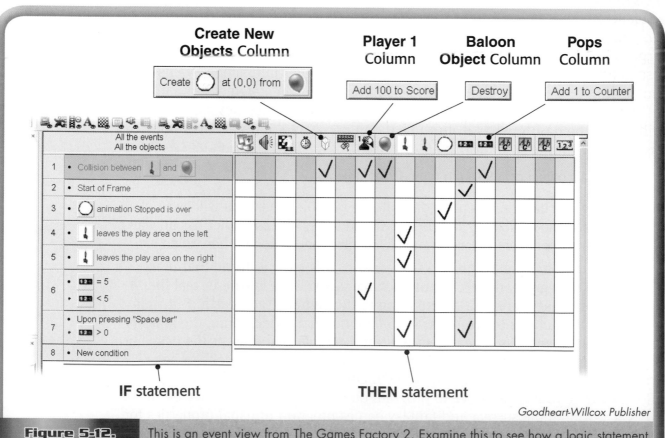

Goodheart-Willcox Publisher

Figure 5-12. This is an event view from The Games Factory 2. Examine this to see how a logic statement is constructed in the software.

Think about creating logic statements for the interactions programmed in Figure 5-12. Examine the conditions programmed on lines 6 and 7. These lines have AND/OR operators between the two conditions on each line. Which conjunction works best in each line?

Look at line 1 in the event frame. The **IF** side of the logic statement is in the first column. The **THEN** side of the logic statement is shown in the remaining columns. The condition on line 1 states "collision between dart object and balloon object." When that condition is met, the computer processes the events in the **THEN** statement.

Notice the four check marks in line 1 in the event frame. The first check mark is in the **Create New Objects** column. This event creates a new explosion animation object at coordinates 0,0 **relative** to the balloon object. The next check mark is in the **Player 1** column. This event adds 100 points to player one's score. The next check mark is in the **Balloon Object** column (the name of this column matches the name assigned to the object). This event is set to destroy the balloon object. The last check mark is in the **Pops** column. This event increases by one the counter keeping track of the number of pops. To see this type of object-oriented programming as a logic statement, add the word **IF** before the condition and the word **THEN** before an event. See **Figure 5-13**.

Remember, collision theory is more than just setting collision events. To make objects appear solid, the programmer needs to add some realistic effects to the collision. Think about what happens when someone walks into a glass door. Do they just stop or do they bounce with their head whipping back and

CHEAT CODE: RELATIVE

The term relative is used when placing or moving an object in a game to describe from where the position is determined. When you place a duck three units to the left of a frog, you are placing it relative to the position of the frog. If something is placed at coordinates 0,0 relative to an original object, it is in the exact same spot as the original.

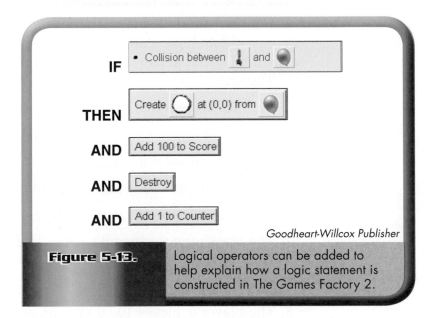

Goodheart-Willcox Publisher

Figure 5-13. Logical operators can be added to help explain how a logic statement is constructed in The Games Factory 2.

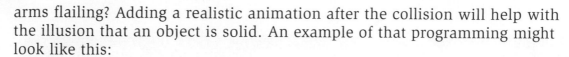

arms flailing? Adding a realistic animation after the collision will help with the illusion that an object is solid. An example of that programming might look like this:

IF the coyote collides with the brick wall,
THEN the coyote will move backward
    AND the animation will change from walking to falling down.

Collision theory controls almost every interaction in video game action. The computer follows the programming of the collision statements that keep objects moving, stopping, exploding, or standing on a platform. Just because it is blue and has waves, does not make it water. The computer does not make these types of visual assumptions; only programmers do! The computer would be just as happy allowing a character to walk on water and sink in land than to do it the way things occur in nature. The game world is yours to create. If you want people to walk upside down or walk on liquids, then program interactions in that way.

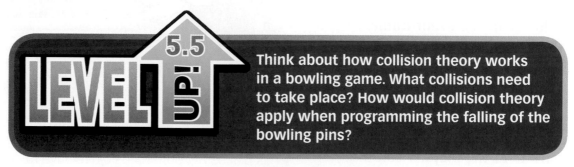

LEVEL UP! 5.5 — Think about how collision theory works in a bowling game. What collisions need to take place? How would collision theory apply when programming the falling of the bowling pins?

Writing a Logic Statement

Consider the following situations. Read the statement and then determine an appropriate logic statement for the situation. On a separate piece of paper, write the logic statements to describe the conditions and events.

1. The grasshopper jumps on a piece of food and the player earns 100 points.

   IF _____ collides with _____, **THEN** add _____ to score.

2. The grasshopper jumps on a lily pad and does not fall into the water.

   IF _____ collides with _____, **THEN** _____ stops.

3. The grasshopper runs into a mushroom, falls into the water, and loses a life.

   IF _____ collides with _____, **THEN** _____ movement falls **AND** _____ loses one life.

4. The grasshopper runs into a four-leaf clover and earns 50 points and an extra life.

   IF _____, **THEN** _____ **AND** _____.

5. The player achieves 10,000 points and receives a bonus extra life.

   IF _____ equals _____, **THEN** add _____ to the number of remaining _____.

Pseudo Code

Writing logic statements is not actual computer code, but is a form of pseudo code. ***Pseudo code*** is similar to, but not actual computer code. It helps by breaking down the interactions into the logical steps that will be converted into the final code statements of a specific computer language. Using the framework of the pseudo code, many programmers can work on the same project at the same time by converting segments of pseudo code into computer language.

Another benefit of pseudo code is that it can be used as the structure for many different computer languages. A program may need to be created for different platforms. The choice of computer language used for each platform may be different. With pseudo code, a team could create the program in Java while another team created the program in Python. A programmer that can write and understand pseudo code only needs to learn the syntax of a specific computer language to program in many different languages.

Syntax

The programming words and symbols and their arrangement is called ***syntax***. Your language arts teachers have been teaching you proper English syntax for years. The first thing your language arts teacher made you learn were definitions of words like the objects around you. Most high-level programming languages use syntax that reads like a regular sentence. A line of programming code contains some words that act like nouns, others that act like verbs, and some numbers and adjectives to help make it all work. Read this line of Ruby code.

```
5.times { print "Hello World!" }
```

This is a command. Just like in language arts class, the word *you* is often omitted from a command. When your mom says, "Wash the dishes!" she is omitting the word *you*. For programmers, the word *you* refers only to the computer, and it takes commands well without having to call it by name.

CHEAT CODE: RUBY

Ruby is one of many computer programming languages. It is a general purpose, object-oriented language.

Reading the **Ruby** command as a sentence states:

Five times print "Hello World!"

Converting this broken English to a working sentence makes it:

Computer, print "Hello World!" five times.

The syntax of the English language is familiar to you and you understand the syntax of this sentence. The computer understands the syntax from the Ruby code better.

The syntax of the Ruby code includes some symbols like a period, quotation marks, and curly brackets. These symbols all mean things in a computer program. Additionally, lowercase and capital letters in front of words often have special meaning. In English, punctuation symbols are part of language syntax. An exclamation point has different meaning than a question mark. Capital letters also have special meaning in English language syntax. Capital letters denote proper nouns or the start of a sentence. Syntax for computer languages use symbols such as punctuation and capital letters just as is done with the syntax for the English language.

Syntax for computer languages creates objects the same way the English language uses nouns. Definition subroutines are called objects. **Objects** are defined by their attributes and properties.

Attributes are characteristics associated with an object. A ball with the attribute red would be a red ball, as shown in **Figure 5-14.** An attribute makes an object unique from others of the same type. Properties define the size, shape, movement, and use of an object. The properties of a ball would be a three-inch diameter sphere, five percent friction decrease, a weight 20 grams, the maximum speed of ten, and so on.

Actions are how an object reacts to input or interacts with other objects. The actions of a ball would be to bounce against walls, accelerate when thrown, arc toward gravity, move left when the left arrow button is pressed, and so on. Attributes and properties are written in the object subroutine and allow the computer to draw the correct object and determine how that object is affected by the game environment.

Other subroutines are called methods. **Methods** are the actions or verbs used in syntax. A **JUMP** method will execute instructions contained in the **JUMP** subroutine. The instructions would tell you how to bend your knees and quickly snap them straight so your feet leave the ground.

Some symbols are used as operational syntax. Most of the mathematical symbols, such as $+, -, <, >$, and parentheses, work just as they do in math class. These symbols will add, subtract, and compare values. In a line of computer code these symbols can also work like words.

Fruit = apples + bananas + grapes

In this example, the words and operational syntax form a sentence. This sentence is also a formula to find the total number of fruit. Each word is also a variable.

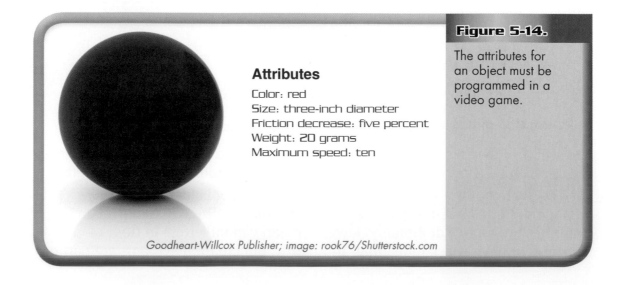

Figure 5-14.

The attributes for an object must be programmed in a video game.

Attributes

Color: red
Size: three-inch diameter
Friction decrease: five percent
Weight: 20 grams
Maximum speed: ten

Goodheart-Willcox Publisher; image: rook76/Shutterstock.com

Variable

Variables are small information storage containers. Programmers give these storage containers names to help them remember what type of information is inside the container. An easy way to think about how a variable works is to think about a cell in a spreadsheet. The cell has a name, like A1. Inside cell A1, different data types can be stored, as illustrated in the table shown in **Figure 5-15A.** Other common data types for most programming languages are shown in the table in **Figure 5-15B.**

Numbers are the most common type of variable. A number can be expressed in many different ways. In real life, numbers can be expressed as money, measurements, amounts, totals, decimals and more. For programming, numbers are most often integers. *Integers* are positive and negative real whole numbers. The numbers 1, –6, 23 and 5000 are all integers. Numbers with decimals are called floats.

Fruit	Apples	Bananas	Grapes			
= Apples + Bananas + Grapes	5	2	3			

A

Name	Data	Range	Description	Example
integer	Whole Number	–2,147,483,648 and 2,147,483,647	Number values up to 4 bytes	X = 543210987
short	Whole Number	–32768 and 32767	Number values up to 2 bytes	X = –12345
long	Whole Number	A very large amount	Number values up to 8 bytes	X = 1234567890111213
string	Character	Any size text amount	Holds text only shown in "quotation". Numbers entered into a string variable are text and not numbers. Meaning those will not be able to be used to calculate.	X = "hello world" X = "4" X = "anything"
Boolean	True/False	On or off state only	Used to check if something is true/active/enabled or not	X = true
single	Decimal Number	Short decimal values	Number with decimal value up to 4 bytes. Single precision floating point	X = 3.14159
double	Decimal Number	Long decimal values	Number with decimal value up to 8 bytes. Double precision floating point	X = 12345.1234567890

B

Figure 5-15. A—Data types such as numbers, strings, formulas and symbols are basic data types. B—Common data types for programming languages include whole numbers, decimal numbers, characters, and Boolean operators.

Floats refer to the floating decimal point that must be accounted for in any decimal computation. The computer has to remember the position of the decimal in the number calculation as well as doing the actual math. Floats can be expressed using decimal notation (1. 0234, –36.7, 15.15, and so on) or scientific notation ($10 \times e^{-16}$, $3.14 \times e^2$, and so on). Scientific notation does not record the non-significant digits of a number. As a decimal number extends past the decimal point the value of those digits become less and less significant. Even extremely exact measurements do not require more than a few digits after the decimal point. Scientific notation includes the significant digits and then tells where to place the decimal. Non-significant digits would be replaced with zero.

Variables can also store text. Text stored in a variable is called a *string*. A string is a series of letters, numbers, or punctuation. The computer will not try to interpret a string. It will only remember the order of the characters of a string. A string is most often identified with quotation marks or quotes. "Hello World", "8746 Main Street", "Applesauce!" or anything else set in quotes would be a string. Strings are often used as labels in spreadsheets and databases or as dialog in a video game.

Variables can contain formulas. In the world of mathematics, variables are common. In the expression:

$$Y = mX + B$$

all of the values have been replaced with variables. The variable Y stores a formula. Inside this formula, the variables m, X, and B can have a value that changes.

At the root of the term variable is the idea a variable is something that can be changed or changes as a result of other information. In a mathematical formula, variables have letters or symbols that can make them hard to remember. In the example $Y = mX + B$, the user would need to remember that m is the slope and B is the Y axis intercept.

In programming, a variable name is not limited to letters and old Greek symbols. Variable names should describe the information stored. These are more like nicknames for the information inside. A variable with the name strGreeting might store the string, "Good morning, how are you today?" A program may contain over 1000 variables. It is therefore important to give each variable a name that is unique and helps describe the contents.

Variables can also contain symbols. Using a symbol to represent a variable is common with mathematics and programming. A symbol can be representational or abstract. A representational symbol might be something like this → or ← (produce by keying -- > or < --) to represent direction or vector.

Vector is a physics term that means direction. An avatar in the game moves at a speed of 10. The vector of right, left, up, down, and so on determines what direction the avatar is moving. Other symbols are abstract such as the pi symbol (π) or dollar sign ($). These symbols have meaning only because they are assigned meaning in a program. A $ in formula in an Excel spreadsheet is used to lock an absolute cell reference and has nothing to do with currency.

Notice how a variable can change an action with the example shown in **Figure 5-16.** Variables here will control the amount or direction of a property that can be changed. In the statement "Jump 10 feet," 10 is a variable.

Statement	Variable	Variable Type
Jump 5 feet	5	Number
Jump left	Left	Vector
Jump left 5 feet	Left, 5	Vector, Number

Figure 5-16.	Variables can be used to change an action. Changing the value of the variable changes the result of the action.

Array

Arrays are a common **data structure** to store and manipulate data. An *array* is a lookup table where the table cells hold variable data, like that shown in **Figure 5-17.** The program can access the array and find the value or string contained in an array cell.

CHEAT CODE: DATA STRUCTURE

A data structure is a way of storing and organizing data. The data can be held in a simple counter, large array, a lookup table or other type of structure. The idea is to use the structure that will most efficiently store and retrieve data for a particular application.

In the array in **Figure 5-17,** the cells contain different data types. To find a value in an array, plot the X and Y locations to identify a cell. In the example for Array_1, the value of X1,Y1 is 24. Also in this array, cell X2,Y3 stores the current value for the experience points, or XP. An array allows values to be easily accessed, recalled, and calculated. An array is also a great way of storing dialogue strings. The possible statements for a character can be inserted into an array and later recalled using a programming statement.

Loops

Programming often requires a loop command. There are four different loop commands common to most languages. These include **LOOP**, **FOR**, **DO WHILE**, and **DO UNTIL**.

Array_1	X1	X2	X3	X4
Y1	24	56	4	0
Y2	Error	Win	Loss	Tie
Y3	HP( )	XP ( )	MP ( )	Gold ( )

Figure 5-17.	Arrays are lookup tables used to store and manipulate data.

The **LOOP** command allows the subroutine to be active for a specific number of iterations. To program a sound effect to repeat three times, a program would include **LOOP (3)** code. This specifies that the activity will only cycle three times and then stop until activated again.

CHEAT CODE: STEPS

When programming, steps refers to how many iterations occur per second. If the steps are set to 20, then the computer will check for interactions every 1/20th of a second. The higher the steps setting, the smoother the game will run. If the steps setting is too high, the program will lag as it tries to test each conditional statement in a fraction of a second.

The **FOR** command allows the subroutine to be active for a specific number of times. To program an avatar to have limited super speed when it collides with a speed fruit object, a programmer would include **FOR (90)** code. The loop will be repeated 90 times. If the program operates at 30 **steps** per second, then the super speed would last for three seconds.

The **DO WHILE** command allows the subroutine to be active only when another condition is active. To program calculating a bonus when using super speed, a **DO WHILE** command would be appropriate. A programmer might write code to have points double when using super speed.

```
DO WHILE (Animation = SuperSpeed)
Bonus = (Points * 2)
```

Note that an asterisk (*) is used for the multiplication symbol. When the super speed animation is over, the bonus stops being calculated.

The **DO UNTIL** command allows the subroutine to be active until another specific interaction takes place. If a programmer wanted to have the avatar in super-size animation until it collided with a minion, then the code might look similar to:

```
DO UNTIL (minion_class, collision)
Animation = Super_Size
```

Different loop commands allow programmers to have limits to special conditions within the program. When the loop ends, the condition would need to be reactivated to start over.

Naming Convention

Here comes the tricky part! You get to create all of the names for the objects, actions, methods, variables, and more. You can use common words like **JUMP** when creating the programming to make something leap in the air, but you can also make up a crazy word like **APPLE** to do the same thing. Remember, you are creating the definitions for the computer to understand. If you make the word **APPLE** have the same definition that most of us use for **JUMP**, the computer will remember **APPLE** means to leap in the air. Doing this "junk" programming makes it very difficult for you to remember what a method is trying to do and impossible for other programmers to figure out the programming. If you program **Character APPLE 5**, then other programmers think your character will find five apples. Instead your character jumps five feet. This can cause confusion because people have memory and definition persistence.

Green Gamer

Paper manufactures are always looking for renewable resources and new ideas to produce environmentally friendly paper products. One ecofriendly paper is made from byproducts of sugarcane with no wood involved in its production. Sugarcane products actually biodegrade faster than wood products and sugarcane paper is cleaner to make than wood-based paper. When purchasing video games, look for companies that use sugarcane paper in the packaging materials.

Persistence means that something continues to exist after the event that caused it has ended. If you have your picture taken with a flash and see spots, you have persistence of vision from the flash. Likewise, you do not have to memorize the definition of each word you use each time you use it. You use the same words every day to mean the same thing. This is not true of a computer. A computer does not remember a definition from one program to another. For a computer, the name of a function, subroutine, variable, and so on, must be declared. **Declared** means that the item is given a name and use in the program you are writing. Therefore, use names that make sense. Use common syntax you already know to easily understand the language you are using.

There is a way for the computer to recall subroutines and variables from one module to another. **Modules** are separate units of programming that perform one function and contain all of the information needed to execute that function. A subroutine or variable can be classified as global or local to a module.

A **global** subroutine or variable works everywhere in the program that you are writing. Global subroutines can be declared by a programmer if the subroutine needs to work inside the current module and also in another module. If you define a global subroutine for level 1 of the game, it can be recalled in level 2. In this way, global subroutines have persistence between modules.

A **local** subroutine or variable does not have persistence outside of the module in which it was declared. If you use a local subroutine on level 1 of the game, the computer will "forget" what it means in level 2. This allows you to use an object called Ball in different levels and have that ball be unique on each level. An example in your class might be using the name Joe for a student in your computer class. Using just the first name of Joe as a local variable works well in the module of your computer class because there is only one student declared with the name Joe. However, Joe does not work well as a global declaration because there are many students with the name Joe at school. A global declaration for the same student might best be done using the first and last name, like Joe Phillips, so he can be identified throughout the school.

Objects should also be named to add information about the use and type. Programmers should avoid just numbering things. It is very difficult to debug a program with 60 objects called Object 1, Object 2, Object 3…Object 60. It is much easier to debug if you have descriptive names such as objCat_Red, objCat_Yellow, objDog_Black,…objWall_Brick. This keeps you from having to read the properties of each object to find out which one is the black dog.

Choice of Language

Computer languages all do one thing, translate syntax into machine code. *Machine code* is a binary language that consists of only two characters: 0 and 1. The programming language used to code the game will do nothing on the computer until it is compiled into machine code.

Some programming languages use fewer words, more symbols, or have more built-in methods. The choice of language used when programming has more to do with a programmer's likes and dislikes than functionality. Some programmers like computer languages that use syntax that is the most natural for them to understand. These languages typically have many built-in methods that they commonly use so they do not have to write custom methods. Others prefer to write custom methods and use many symbols as names for variables and methods so they are faster to type.

Some languages are designed for financial calculations and have many built-in methods like **SUM**, **AVERAGE**, **DEVIATION**, and more. Other languages are designed for physics and have methods for **VELOCITY**, **ACCELERATION**, **TANGENT**, and more. A programming language takes a very long time to create, so it is usually written to a specific audience of users. The memory and speed of computers has greatly increased the ability of computer languages to hold more methods and calculate them quickly. This allows for a language to grow and include more specialty components. This makes the language more appealing to more people because they can write more types of programs easily with the same language.

CHEAT CODE: COMPATIBILITY

When things or people work well together, they are said to be compatible. This applies to computers and computer languages as well.

Other issues with the choice of computer language have to do with **compatibility**. A language may not compile properly for a specific type of computer. A computer that could run BASIC language well might not be able to compile C + + or Java. Fortunately, most computers today have the ability to compile in many different formats. Modern game engines and design software also have the ability to save in different language formats so the game can play on multiple devices. Consequently, the compatibility issues are quickly going away as programs come out that translate one computer language to another quickly and accurately. Today, an efficient game engine may allow the design team to make the game once and compile it to work on many different platforms.

Flowchart

To create a module within a game, it is important to plan all of the parts of the operation using a flowchart or other organizational tool. *Flowcharts* have different text box shapes and connectors to add visual detail to a decision process, as shown in **Figure 5-18**. A flowchart begins with a start/terminal shape and the name of the problem. At an endpoint of a flowchart would be an end/terminal shape and a solution to the problem, as illustrated in **Figure 5-19**. A flowchart works well to map out a process, system, and module.

Flowchart Symbols

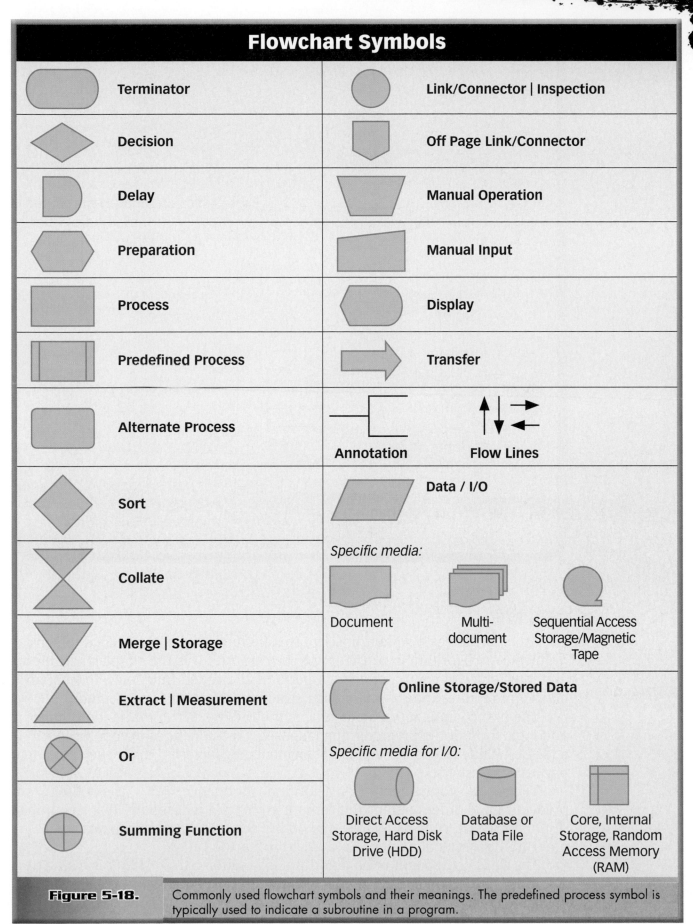

Terminator		Link/Connector | Inspection	
Decision		Off Page Link/Connector	
Delay		Manual Operation	
Preparation		Manual Input	
Process		Display	
Predefined Process		Transfer	
Alternate Process		Annotation Flow Lines	
Sort		Data / I/O	
Collate		*Specific media:* Document Multi-document Sequential Access Storage/Magnetic Tape	
Merge | Storage			
Extract | Measurement		Online Storage/Stored Data	
Or		*Specific media for I/O:*	
Summing Function		Direct Access Storage, Hard Disk Drive (HDD) Database or Data File Core, Internal Storage, Random Access Memory (RAM)	

Figure 5-18. Commonly used flowchart symbols and their meanings. The predefined process symbol is typically used to indicate a subroutine in a program.

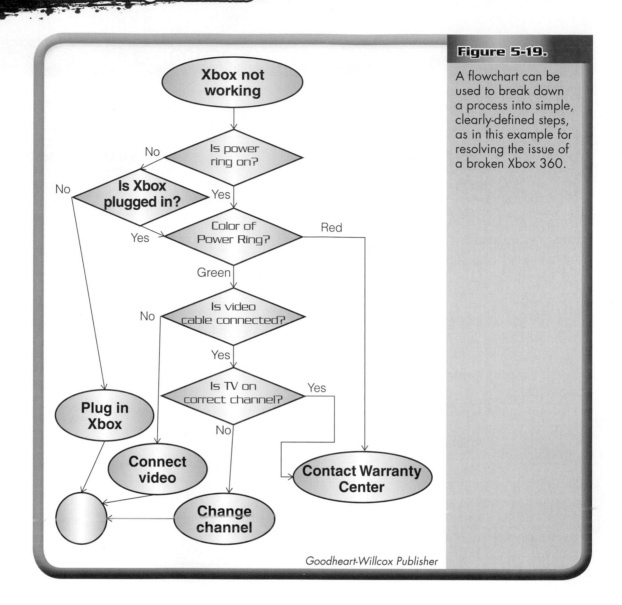

Goodheart-Willcox Publisher

Figure 5-19.

A flowchart can be used to break down a process into simple, clearly-defined steps, as in this example for resolving the issue of a broken Xbox 360.

Algorithm

An **algorithm** is a computer script that performs the steps needed to solve a problem. An algorithm is considered to be *elegant* if it is the simplest, smallest, and most efficient computer code to perform all needed functions. To form an algorithm requires three components: structure, sequence, and iteration.

The first component of an algorithm is structure. **Structure** is the syntax and logic form of the programming language. Structure goes beyond pseudo code to include the actual words and symbols organized to make the computer perform as desired.

The second component of an algorithm is sequence. **Sequence** is the predetermined order or steps the computer program will follow. Just as outlined in the flowchart, such as the one shown in **Figure 5-19**, the sequence gives order to the instructions needed to get from start to finish.

The third component of an algorithm is iteration. An **iteration** is a single run through a programming loop. The iteration component controls how long and how often the algorithm will be active.

To better understand what an algorithm is and how these three components combine to create an algorithm, a real-world example of an algorithm might help. Look at the algorithm needed to wash your hair.

> Directions: Wet hair, apply shampoo to hair, lather, rinse, and repeat. After shampooing, apply conditioner to hair, lather, and rinse.
> Computer program to wash hair:
>
> DECLARE variables—objHair, objShampoo, objConditioner
> DEFINE method subroutines—WET, APPLY, LATHER, RINSE
> Predefined methods—LOOP
>
> WET (objHair)
> APPLY (objShampoo, objHair)
> LATHER (objShampoo)
> RINSE (objHair)
> LOOP (1)
> APPLY (objConditioner, objHair)
> LATHER (objConditioner)
> RINSE (objHair)

The algorithm shown to wash hair demonstrates all three components of an algorithm. The structure of the computer program is the declaring of variables, defining methods, and the syntax of how the variables are called by the methods. The sequence is the order required to get the hair shampooed and then conditioned. The steps must be followed in order to get the hair washed. You cannot do the steps out of order or the process will not work. Finally, iteration is demonstrated by the loop command. The instructions required that it be washed twice and conditioned once. The loop was set to 1, which means that the steps above the **LOOP** command will repeat one additional time. There was no **LOOP** command for the set of instructions for the conditioner steps. Without a **LOOP** command, those steps will not repeat and the algorithm ends.

Ethical Gamer

Plagiarism is a form of theft where you copy somebody else's material without permission. Under copyright law, as soon as something is in tangible form, it is automatically copyrighted. A copyright protects the creator from others using the material without permission. Just about everything you see in print, all the music you listen to, any images you see on television or movie screens, and almost all information on the Internet is copyrighted. Even the computer code used to create websites is copyrighted. This means if you copy any of this material without the permission of the copyright holder, you have committed theft.

CASE STUDY

Game Programmer

A game programmer is the person who can talk the language of the computer. Using that language, the programmer asks the computer to perform tasks. This person is the "computer guru" who takes the design ideas and makes them happen in the game.

If you like math and are good in algebra, geometry, calculus, applied mathematics, and computer science, you would probably be a good game programmer. To be a good game programmer, you need to be skilled in math, logic, and problem solving.

Shutterstock.com

A programmer is the person who takes game design ideas and gives the computer the instructions needed to make the game function.

As a game programmer, you will work with three types of programming languages: computer platform-specific languages, scripting languages, and object-oriented programming languages. Computer languages like C, C + +, C#, Java, and assembly are popular for designing games. These languages can "speak" directly to the computer operating system. Scripting languages like Python, Ruby, and Perl are simplified languages. They are easier for a person to use than a computer language. When a script is finished, it is compiled into a computer language so the computer can read it. The last language type is an object-oriented language. These are very simple, user-friendly languages that build in a script language and are compiled into a computer language. This type of programming language is used by The Games Factory 2.

Shutterstock.com

Several programming languages are common in game programming.

Game programmers are very highly recruited by game design companies. These people have important skills that can be used to build games, proprietary software, and other tools outside of gaming. A programmer straight out of school would likely enter a company as a junior programmer. There they would learn how to function best on the programming team and learn how to make programs needed by the company. Later, they would be promoted to a game programmer and have duties to work with the design team and share ideas on what a game could be programmed to do.

Other game programming-related jobs include lead programmer, technical director, AI programmer, software engineer, network engineer, graphics engineer, and engine programmer. All of these higher-level jobs offer more responsibility and leadership in the projects being created.

Most game programming jobs require a college degree in computer science, game programming, or software engineering. In 2012, the average salary of a game programmer was between $71,380 according to the Bureau of Labor Statistics.

The Games Factory 2

The Games Factory 2 (TGF2) is a game engine developed by Clickteam. It is a powerful game engine that uses object-oriented programming to make two-dimensional video games. The games can be large, multilevel, complex games as TGF2 is very powerful. Two extremely beneficial features of TGF2 are the game engine:

- runs very well on a standard PC; and
- is very user friendly.

The next sections take a look at how the user interface of this software is organized, **Figure 5-20.** Understanding the interface is the first step in building some exciting games. Detailed explanations of each tool are given in the workbook lessons.

Menu Bar

The menu bar contains the pull-down menus. Clicking on the name of a pull-down menu displays the menu. You can then select the tool from the menu. The menu bar and pull-down menus function just as they do in other Windows programs, such as Microsoft Office.

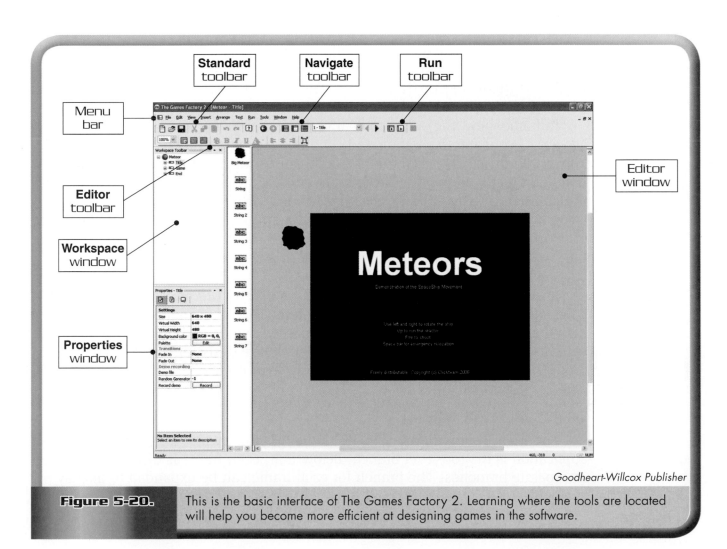

Goodheart-Willcox Publisher

Figure 5-20. This is the basic interface of The Games Factory 2. Learning where the tools are located will help you become more efficient at designing games in the software.

Standard Toolbar

The **Standard** toolbar contains the most common tools found in the pull-down menus, but displayed as buttons for easy access. Basic tools such as **New**, **Open**, **Save**, **Cut**, **Copy**, **Paste**, **Undo**, **Redo**, and **Contents** (help) are located on the **Standard** toolbar. This places the tools just a mouse click away.

Navigate Toolbar

To move quickly from one area of the game programming to another, use the tools on the **Navigate** toolbar. Tools included on this toolbar are **Back**, **Forward**, **Storyboard Editor**, **Frame Editor**, **Event Editor**, **Previous Frame**, and **Next Frame**. Also included on this toolbar is the frame identification and selection drop-down list.

Run Toolbar

To see how your game is working, it is helpful to use the tools on the **Run** toolbar. These tools allow you to test the game to see if everything is working as anticipated. The **Run Application** tool allows you to test play your game from the first frame. The **Run Frame** tool allows you to test play just the current page you are designing. Use the **Stop** button to cancel the **Run Application** or **Run Frame** tool and continue working on your game.

Editor Toolbar

There are two basic **Editor** toolbars. Which toolbar is displayed depends on which mode or view is currently displayed. One version of the **Editor** toolbar is displayed in frame view. The second version is displayed in event view.

In frame view, the editor toolbar contains the tools needed to view all the aspects of your frame creation and conditional programming. The **Zoom** tool allows you to see your work in greater detail by magnifying the view. This can help to properly align your background and character features. The **Zoom** tool is also used to reduce the view. Other options include applying a grid to the editor window and tools for controlling font and style, text color, and alignment of text. The last button is the **Center Frame** tool. This allows you to quickly have the background view centered on any selected object. This is helpful when using a large or scrolling background.

In event view, the **Editor** toolbar displays different tools. The **Zoom** tool is still available, but it appears slightly different. The other tools on the toolbar help the designer to view or exclude from view events and objects. This is very helpful when designing a large game and the designer needs to focus on a single programming element of the game or on a small set of features or objects.

Workspace Window

The **Workspace** window displays the programming tree for the game. The application is the top-level branch. Below that, each frame is displayed in order as separate branches. The branch for each frame can be expanded to display each object used in the frame as branches below the frame.

Think of the tree organization format as you would a real tree. There is a trunk that has branches, twigs (sub branches), and leaves (the final objects). In a program tree, you start with a large file, or trunk folders. From there, the trunk folder has smaller folders, or branches, that contain similar items grouped by categories. Inside each branch folder, there are often more folders that contain even more specific categories. Finally, there will be actual files or applications at the end of the tree, similar to the leaves at the end of a real tree branch.

The **Workspace** window allows the designer to quickly access each part of the game. When an item is selected in the **Workspace** window, its properties are displayed in the **Properties** window (discussed in the next section).

Properties Window

The **Properties** window displays the physical features and properties of any selected object or frame. This window is where the designer sets the size, color, and movement properties. **Figure 5-21** shows the **Properties** window for three different types of objects. **Figure 5-21A** is for a background object, **Figure 5-21B** is for an active object, and **Figure 5-21C** is for a frame. Notice that different tabs are displayed, depending on what is selected. There are many different properties, but not every object has every property.

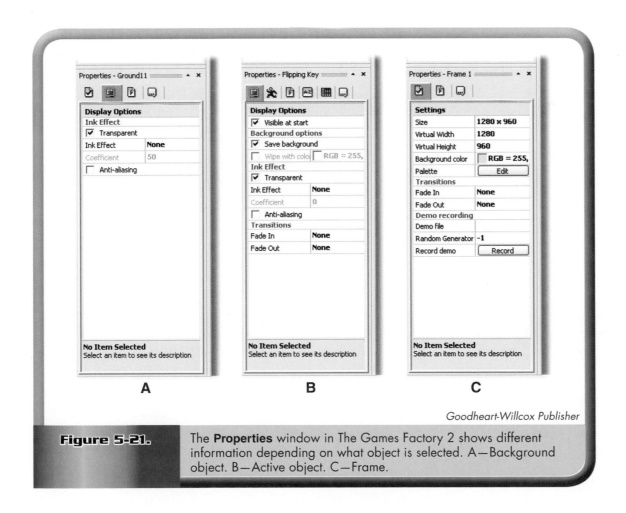

Goodheart-Willcox Publisher

Figure 5-21. The **Properties** window in The Games Factory 2 shows different information depending on what object is selected. A—Background object. B—Active object. C—Frame.

Library Window

Objects preloaded into TGF2 are stored in the *library*. The **Library** window, when displayed, allows you to quickly drag-and-drop objects from the library into the editor window. The items in the library are presented in a standard tree format. In the **Library** window shown in **Figure 5-22,** the branch folder (Games) narrows to a smaller branch folder (Miscellaneous). Inside of the Miscellaneous folder are the leaves (object files).

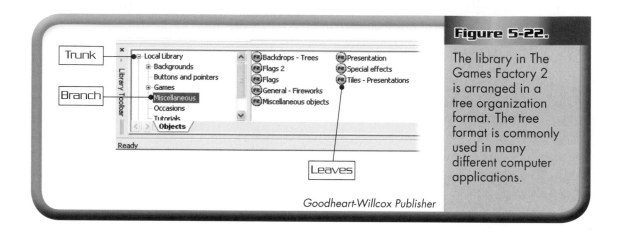

Figure 5-22.

The library in The Games Factory 2 is arranged in a tree organization format. The tree format is commonly used in many different computer applications.

Goodheart-Willcox Publisher

Chapter Summary

- Game design software is used to create a playable video game.
- Animated objects can be integrated into a video game to provide motion.
- Sound and music effects can be created in a video game, which can help increase immersion and the entertainment value of the game.
- Computers use basic logic statements to test conditions and determine actions based on the result.
- Some mathematical symbols, such as $+, -, <, >$, and parentheses, are used as operational syntax and function just as they do in mathematical equations.
- Two features of object-oriented programming are that the game engine runs very well on a standard PC and that the game engine is very user friendly.

Check Your Video Game IQ

Now that you have finished this chapter, see what you know about video game design by taking the chapter posttest.

www.m.g-wlearning.com

www.g-wlearning.com

Review Your Knowledge

On a separate sheet of paper or in a word processing document, match the following terms with the definitions that fit best.

A. floats

B. objects

C. global

D. attributes

E. properties

F. integers

G. collision

H. local

I. algorithm

J. modules

1. Characteristics associated with an object.

2. Condition that occurs when an object touches another object.

3. Positive and negative real whole numbers

4. Definition subroutines that are defined by their attributes and properties.

5. A subroutine or variable that works everywhere in the program.

6. A computer script that performs the steps needed to solve a problem.

7. Separate units of programming that perform one function and contain all the information needed to execute the function.

8. Numbers with decimals.

9. Attributes assigned to an object, such as visibility, interactivity, and movement.

10. A subroutine or variable that does not have persistence outside of the module in which it was declared.

On a separate sheet of paper or in a word processing document, answer each of the following questions.

11. Briefly describe the *action-reaction relationship* in a video game.

12. What is the function of a logic statement?

13. How is a listener used to program the user interface?

14. How are triggers used to program game events?

15. The most basic example of a logic statement is the _____...._____ statement.

16. If a person slips on a banana peel and falls, the banana peel is the _____ and the fall is the _____.

17. In a video game, the formal term for an action is _____.

18. What is an *event?*

19. Which logical operators are used to have multiple conditions or events?

20. Which logical operator is used to initiate an event when a condition is *not* met?

21. What are the two components of *collision theory?*

22. What is a *collision statement?*

23. If object B is placed at 0,0 relative to object A, where is object B?

24. List four different variable data types.

25. Describe how a tree organization format, such as the object library from The Games Factory 2, is arranged.

Apply Your STEM Knowledge

 ## Social Studies

1. Look at the historical events below. Research the cause-and-effect relationship that lead to the end result. Write a logic statement and a half-page summary of each action.

   A. Beginning of World War I.
   B. Sinking of the RMS *Titanic*.
   C. Cuban Missile Crisis.
   D. Emancipation Proclamation.
   E. Development of RADAR.

Mathematics

2. Determine the steps setting for each of the following.

   A. Thirteen interactions occur in one second.
   B. One hundred 48 interactions occur in four seconds.
   C. Four thousand interactions occur in 25 seconds.
   D. One interaction occurs every 1/503 seconds.

Science

3. Real-world attributes like gravity need to be programmed into a game. Research gravity and create a PowerPoint presentation of five to ten slides to describe how different objects are affected by gravity on Earth. Discuss objects that are large, small, light, dense, in liquid form, in solid form, and so on.

Language Arts

4. Consider the simple game of musical chairs. Write the rules and a game script using logic statements for this game. Test the game script with a few friends to make sure you have included all possible interactions.

Mathematics

5. Write the relative coordinate values for each of the following. Remember the layout of the coordinate screen for a video game.

   A. Object X moves three units to the right and four units up.
   B. Object A moves 14 units to the left and one unit up.
   C. Object Y moves five units to the left and ten units down.
   D. Object B moves seven units to the right and six units down.

Working in Teams

In teams, research, debate, and form a group opinion on each of the Level Up! activities in this chapter. Prepare a PowerPoint presentation of ten slides (five to seven minutes) to present to the class explaining the group's opinions for each Level Up! activity. Include text, pictures, video, animations, and slide transitions as appropriate to help explain your positions.

Gamer Portfolio

Your e-portfolio may contain documents you have created. Scanned images of items, such as awards and certificates, may also be included. You need to decide which file formats you will use for electronic documents. You could use the default format to save the documents. For example, you could use Microsoft Word format for letters and essays. You could use Microsoft Excel format for worksheets. Someone reviewing your e-portfolio would need programs that open these formats to view your files. Another option would be to save or scan documents as PDF (portable document format) files. These files can be viewed with Adobe Reader software and some other programs. Having all of the files in the same format can make viewing them easier for others who need to review your portfolio. Also have a plan for providing your game builds to others. In most cases, you will provide game builds as executable files.

1. Search the Internet and read articles to learn more about PDF documents. Download a free program that opens these files, such as Adobe Reader.

2. Practice saving a Microsoft Word document as a PDF file. Note: Use the Save As command. Refer to the Help link, if needed.

3. Create a list of the formats you will use to store your electronic files.

G-W Learning Mobile Site

G-W Mobile

Visit the G-W Learning mobile site to complete the chapter pretest and posttest and to practice vocabulary using e-flash cards. If you do not have a smartphone, visit the G-W Learning companion website to access these features.

G-W Learning mobile site: www.m.g-wlearning.com

G-W Learning companion website: www.g-wlearning.com

Common Core

College and Career Readiness

CTE Career Ready Practices. Whether you see problems as challenges or opportunities, they often require creative thinking to solve them. Many new inventions come about from trying to solve a problem. Describe a situation in your life or in history where a problem led to the creation of a new way of doing things or a new invention.

Writing. Conduct a short research project to answer the question, "How is pseudo code used to allow programming teams to work efficiently and cooperatively?" Using information from multiple sources, write a report on your response to this question.

Speaking and Listening. Research the features of some of the programming languages commonly used in video game design. Compile information about the aspects and features of each type of language that help to make programming easier as well as any other information you find that is applicable. Use this information along with your preference for the types of games you would like to create to select the top three programs you think you would be most likely to use. Using various elements (visual displays, written handouts, technological displays), present your choices to the class. Be sure to use the appropriate vocabulary related to the industry. Explain why you chose the programming languages you did. As you listen to your classmates' presentations, take notes and ask questions about vocabulary you do not understand.

Event Prep: Objective Test

   Some competitive events for Career and Technical Student Organizations (CTSOs) require that entrants complete an objective part of the event. This event will typically be an objective test that includes terminology and concepts related to being a video game designer. Participants are usually allowed one hour to complete the objective part of the event. To prepare for the concepts portion of the entrepreneur objective test:

1. Read the guidelines provided by your organization. Make certain that you ask any questions about points you do not understand. It is important you follow each specific item that is outlined in the competition rules.

2. Visit the organization's website and look for entrepreneurial concepts tests that were used in previous years. Many organizations post these tests for students to use as practice for future competitions.

3. Look for the evaluation criteria or rubric for the event. This will help you determine what the judge will be looking for in your presentation.

4. Review the checkpoint questions at the end of each section of this text.

5. For additional practice, review the end-of-chapter activities.

6. Create flash cards for each vocabulary term with its definition on the other side. Ask a friend to use these cards to review with you.

7. Ask your instructor to give you practice tests for each chapter of this text. It is important that you are familiar with answering multiple choice and true-false questions. Have someone time you as you take a practice test.

Chapter 6
Game Systems, Personal Computers, and Hardware

 Video games are software programs that need special computer hardware to run properly. In this chapter, you will explore the different computer systems typically used to run today's game software. Pay close attention to the advantages and disadvantages of each piece of technology and how it is used to create a unique selling point for that device.

 Check Your Video Game IQ

Before you begin this chapter, see what you already know about video game design by taking the chapter pretest.

www.m.g-wlearning.com

www.g-wlearning.com

College and Career Readiness

Reading Prep. In preparation for this chapter, use the Internet and printed materials to locate advertisements for game systems. Can you find any common themes in these advertisements? What does this tell you about the purposes behind gaming system's advertisements?

Objectives

After completing this chapter, you will be able to:
- Explain features of various game systems.
- Define terms related to gaming systems.
- Contrast major gaming systems.
- Explain successful business models for gaming systems.
- Describe how video games drive and complement new technologies.
- Identify examples of technology transfer from video games to other industries.
- Compare video game systems to personal computers.
- Identify elements of personal computers that limit video game playing.

Dedicated Game System Consoles

The greatest limiting factor for game design is not the imagination or inventiveness of the game designers, it is the hardware systems needed to run a game. Designers are continually imagining games that create deeper immersion. To do this, they need to simulate better virtual environments. This includes using real body movements, without the use of a controller, and 3D glasses to interact in virtual space. Kinect for Xbox 360 is an example of a system that uses the player's body movements without the use of a controller. The real question is not who has a great idea for immersion, but who can get it to run on a system.

The big ideas changing the way games are played will mean game systems need more computing power. As you learned in Chapter 2, today's technology is mainstream and tomorrow's technology is experimental. When designers imagine a new game environment, they have an eye on the experimental technology of the future. To accomplish these innovative dreams, faster computers with more memory combined with new technologies of motion sensing and 3D virtual displays will have to be created.

Today's games push current technology to the cutting edge. A **dedicated** video game console, such as the Xbox 360, PS3, or Wii, can cost more than $500 million in research and development to bring to reality, **Figure 6-1.** All of this money is spent to create a unique selling point (USP) for that console.

CHEAT CODE: DEDICATED

Dedicated is defined as: designed for a particular use or function. A dedicated video game console is engineered for the primary purpose of video game playing.

New parts and technologies will be invented to make the console the best at playing experimental games. Getting to market first with the right system could make the difference between a hot seller and an obsolete box. Each company is trying to get the best and fastest experimental

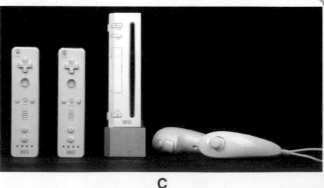

A   B   C

Goodheart-Willcox Publisher

Figure 6-1. Generation 7 video game consoles. A—Sony PlayStation 3. B—Microsoft Xbox 360. C—Nintendo Wii.

component to market before the competition. By doing so, they hope to create a USP for their brand.

Generation 7 Review

Recall from Chapter 3 the discussion on generations of video gaming systems. Generation 7 has been dominated by three big manufacturers in the video game console market: Sony, Microsoft, and Nintendo. The game console from each company incorporated specific experimental technology to give each brand a USP over the other systems. **Figure 6-2** shows a table listing common components used in a generation 7, dedicated video game console. Each company uses different components to build their console. As a result, games designed for a particular system may be able to offer different gameplay.

		Playstation 3	**Xbox 360**	**Wii**
System Component	Manufacturer Release Price Release Date	Sony $599 November 2006	Microsoft $399 November 2005	Nintendo $249 December 2006
CPU	Processor Type Speed Configuration FLOPS	Power PC 3.2 GHz CELL 1.8 TFLOPS	Power PC - Xenon 3.2 GHz Triple Core 1.0 TFLOPS	IBM - Broadway 788 MHz Single 2.9 GFLOPS (0.0029TFLOPS)
Storage	Hard Drive	60 GB	20GB	512 MB Flash Memory
Memory	RAM Memory	768 MB	512 MB	88 MB
Graphics	Graphics Card Graphics Maker Graphics Emulation	RSX Nvidia GeForce Vertex/Pixel Shader	ATI - Xenos ATI Unified Shader	ATI – Hollywood ATI Mapping pixel shader
Disc Reader	Game Reader Game Size Max	Blu-Ray DVD 50 GB	DVD 8.5 GB	Nintendo ODD 4.7GB or double-sided 8.5GB
Online Play	Online Connection Wireless Online Portal Online Cost	Yes 802.11 b/g PlayStation Network Free	Yes 802.11 b/g Xbox Live $5/month and up for multiplayer	Yes Upgradable Wii Internet Channel Varies
User Interface Hardware	Controller Motion - Based	SIXAXIS - Dual Shock 3 Tilt Sensitive Move	Controller S Kinect	Wii Remote Full Motion / Accelerometers
Sales	Units Sold by 8/07 Units Sold by 6/09 Units sold by 10/12	1.75 million 23 million 64 million	6.3 million 30 million 70 million	4.0 million 52 million 97 million

Figure 6-2. This table shows various data related to the three major video game consoles.

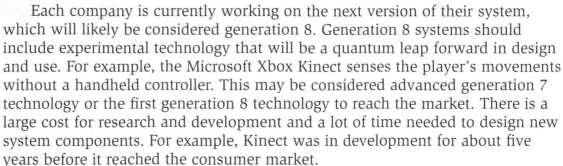

Each company is currently working on the next version of their system, which will likely be considered generation 8. Generation 8 systems should include experimental technology that will be a quantum leap forward in design and use. For example, the Microsoft Xbox Kinect senses the player's movements without a handheld controller. This may be considered advanced generation 7 technology or the first generation 8 technology to reach the market. There is a large cost for research and development and a lot of time needed to design new system components. For example, Kinect was in development for about five years before it reached the consumer market.

CHEAT CODE: BARRIER TO ENTRY

In marketing terms, a barrier to entry is something that prevents competitors from joining. This barrier keeps new companies from competing with the established companies and entering the market. For video game consoles, the barriers to entry are money and technical knowledge.

As mentioned, the amount of money needed to improve a single component and assemble a system is huge. This creates the largest **barrier to entry** of new game systems. It is likely that Microsoft, Nintendo, and Sony will be the only companies with the technical expertise and funding needed to design a generation 8 machine. However, there are always innovative companies looking to break into a lucrative market.

This does not mean these generation 7 systems will remain identical to when they were first released. More efficient and cheaper components are constantly being developed. Some components, like memory, have become much cheaper since these consoles were first produced. The manufacturer can install more memory for less money now than it cost to install less memory when the console was first manufactured. Systems are often upgraded with more memory and better processors. However, the basic design and function of the system remains the same, only with speed and performance enhancements.

Ethical Gamer

When applying for a job, submitting an application for acceptance into a university, or even applying for a position as a volunteer with an organization, it is important to be truthful in your application and résumé. Making up experience or education to gain a position is unethical and could cost you a future opportunity to be a part of that organization.

CASE STUDY

Computer Hardware

The most essential part of the video game console is the computer technology it uses. While technology improved and components have changed over time, the basic parts of a computer game system have remained the same. Inside the case, you will find circuits and wires to route information from several core components: motherboard, central processing unit (CPU), video card, memory, and storage devices.

The motherboard is a printed circuit board (PCB) with tiny wires printed on a piece of plastic wafer board. These wires are smaller than a single hair and connect all the pieces of the computer together. The motherboard also has ports and bays into which components can plug.

The central processing unit (CPU) is the brain of the computer. It is the most important computer chip in the computer. A chip is a separate computer component that performs mathematical calculations and attaches to the motherboard. Other than the CPU, there are many other computer chips, like the math coprocessor, bios, and others. The CPU in a modern computer is always covered with a heat sink and a fan. These are required to remove the heat generated by the processing in the chip.

The clock speed is a setting that determines how long it takes for a transistor in the CPU to switch from a 0 to a 1. In a 32-bit processor, 32 bits of data can enter the CPU at every tick of the clock. If the clock speed is 2 gigahertz, it "ticks" 2,000,000,000 times a second. This chip can receive over 64 billion bits of data per second (32 bits × 2,000,000,000 = 64,000,000,000).

Clock speed is not a standard for how much work is done by the computer in one second. Rather, floating-point operations per second (FLOPS) is a scale to determine the speed of a computer. Most home computers process between 2 GFLOPS and 8 GFLOPS (gigaFLOPS). If you have a fast computer at home, it might process 10 GFLOPS (10 gigaFLOPS or 10,000,000,000 floating-point operations per second). For the mathematicians out there, a FLOPS is like using scientific notation where the decimal point can float depending on the exponent of the multiplier. For the rest of us, it is just a term to indicate how fast a computer is. The greater the number of FLOPS, the faster the computer.

The video card is the set of computer chips that changes the information into a signal readable by the monitor. The video card contains a separate processor and memory to help quickly convert the computer signal into the analog or digital signal needed by the monitor or TV being used. Newer computers and game consoles have an advanced video card that allows 3D graphic movement. These advanced video cards, or graphics processing units (GPUs), have computer chips to allow 3D acceleration.

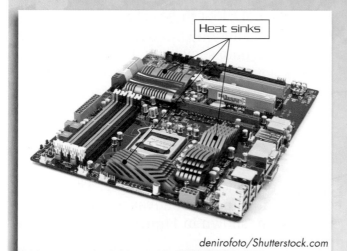

Heat sinks

denirofoto/Shutterstock.com

The CPU is cooled by a fan installed on top of the chip.

(Continued)

Shutterstock.com

In a game console or a computer designed for gaming, the video card is an advanced piece of technology. A fan is usually required to cool the chip.

Shutterstock.com

The hard disk drive has platters (hard disks) on which data are stored. The entire unit is sealed. The cover has been removed here.

Memory holds all of the working information. Random-access memory (RAM) holds information if the computer is on. When the computer is turned off, the RAM clears. RAM is very fast memory storage. RAM chips can be plug-in types or hardwired into the motherboard. A hard disk drive uses magnetic media to store data long term or permanently. The hard disk drive stores the operating system (OS). The OS is a complex program, like Windows or Mac OS, that tells the computer how to work. Without an OS, the computer would not know how to function.

Other than the OS, the hard disk drive stores programs and information that will need to be saved even when the computer is turned off. When you download a game or save a document, the hard disk drive writes the information on the surface of the disk so it can be read later.

Some storage media, such as DVD, CD, or Blu-Ray, are read by a laser. These are optical discs because the laser light is read or "seen" by the optical reader in the computer drive. The main purpose of optical discs is to input a program into a computer. For the most part, these are read-only memory (ROM) discs. For reading and writing data onto something that can be carried around, a removable media such as a RAM flash drive, or "thumb drive," is used.

PlayStation 3

PlayStation 3 (PS3) is Sony's generation 7 video game console. The PS3 designers focused on creating a console that is the most advanced piece of consumer technology hardware ever created, shown in **Figure 6-3.** In so doing, they created a personal supercomputer.

PS3 Hardware

The advanced computer processor used in the PS3 has a unique design called the *CELL processor architecture.* The idea of the CELL design is to allow for multitasking. See **Figure 6-4.** The main central processing unit (CPU)

Figure 6-3.

The PlayStation 3 is Sony's entry into the generation 7 video game console market. This machine has a very powerful processor and can produce high-end graphics.

Goodheart-Willcox Publisher

512 KB Cache Memory (for main processor)	3.2 GHz Triple-Core Processor (main processor)
SPE (128 bit vector processor)	SPE (128 bit vector processor)
256 KB	256 KB
SPE (128 bit vector processor)	SPE (128 bit vector processor)
256 KB	256 KB
SPE (128 bit vector processor)	SPE (128 bit vector processor)
256 KB	256 KB
SPE (128 bit vector processor)	SPE (128 bit vector processor)
256 KB	256 KB

Goodheart-Willcox Publisher

Figure 6-4. The CELL processor architecture used in the PS3 allows for fast, parallel processing.

is a 3.2 GHz clock speed, triple-core processor. This manages all activity on the chip. In addition to the main CPU, there are eight **synergistic processing elements (SPE).**

Each SPE is a 128-bit vector processor. To speed up data handling, each SPE also has 256 kilobytes (KB) of memory attached to it. This is called **cache memory** (pronounced "cash"). Having some memory printed on the processor chip allows for the processor to store, or cache, some instructions close by. This reduces the need to send information to the main memory storage some distance away.

Each SPE handles a section of the processing load. For example, one SPE could be used for graphics, one for sound, one for the user interface, one for the physics engine, and so on. This allows for extremely fast processing of many applications at once. Only six of the eight SPEs are assigned by the game programmer. One of the other two SPEs is used to run the operating system. The other SPE is a backup.

The PS3 is capable of calculating 1.8 trillion FLOPS (1.8 TFLOPS or 1.8 teraFLOPS). That is 1,800,000,000,000 floating point operations per second! Wow! To give you an idea of what a huge accomplishment 1.8 teraFLOPS is on a PS3, look back in time. The PS3 costs around $300, depending on when and where you purchase it. In the year 2000, it cost about $1000 to achieve each gigaFLOPS. That means 1.8 teraFLOPS in the year 2000 cost about $1,800,000, as shown in **Figure 6-5.**

So how did Sony get all that experimental technology down to the low price you see today? Simple—they lost a lot of money on every PS3 sold. Adding up just the cost of components, the PS3 contained nearly $900 in parts. Sony sold the units for almost half that amount and reportedly lost nearly $2 billion on the units in 2007. Today, the component costs have come down in price and it is reported that Sony is no longer losing money on each PS3.

Why build so much power into the PS3? The two biggest loads on the CPU are system operations and graphics processing. The increases in computing power are needed to handle these loads, as well as other loads.

FLOPS 1,800,000,000,000.
kiloFLOPS 1,800,000,000.
megaFLOPS 1,800,000.
gigaFLOPS 1,800.
teraFLOPS 1.8

Decimal point moves

Benchmark	Year	Cost per gigaFLOP
Cray X-MP	1983	$15,000,000
Bunyip Beowulf	2000	$1,000
KASYO	2003	$100
PS3 @ $599	2006	$0.34
PS3 @ $300	2012	$0.17

Goodheart-Willcox Publisher

Figure 6-5. To change from FLOPS to kiloFLOPS, megaFLOPS, gigaFLOPS, or teraFLOPS, simply move the decimal point. The table shows how the cost per FLOPS has dramatically decreased in recent years.

System operations controls the traffic of information from the user interface, to the game system, to the system memory, to the processor comparing the event and action, back to the memory, back to the system, and out to the display. Simple, right? No. That is why it takes a huge amount of processing to control a game today.

The other major drain on CPU power is the video graphics. *Graphics* are the visual images you see on the screen. Three-dimensional graphics require a lot of processing power to render.

High-end graphics also require a *3D accelerator graphics card* to interpret the information from the CPU core onto the screen. A 3D accelerator graphics card allows the 3D objects to move realistically on screen. Without the 3D accelerator, the 3D graphics would appear jerky and slow. Smooth running 3D graphic rendering is the main purpose for designing a video card with its own processor and memory.

In the PS3, an NVIDIA GeForce RSX 3D graphics card processes graphical information. This advanced graphics card is referred to as a GPU. It allows the PS3 to have the cleanest and most advanced 3D graphics on the market. In fact, the GPU of the PS3 contributes about 1.6 teraFLOPS to the total processing power of the console.

To render the graphics, the RSX card uses both vertex shading and pixel shading technology. Vertex shading is how the computer recognizes the coordinates of where a vertex exists and compares it to the position of the player's character. Pixel shading refers to the use of color and shading of each pixel or point of color on an object. Pixel shading must render objects to account for the direction of the **virtual light source** or **lamp**. The GPU on the PS3 has a dedicated portion to perform the vertex shading tasks. Another section is dedicated to performing the pixel shading tasks. This **parallel processing** of vertex and pixel shading gives images a very clean, high-definition look.

CHEAT CODE: LAMP

Designers program a virtual light source called a lamp onto the game map. This causes light/dark shades on objects and can also cast shadows for the illusion of depth.

Green Gamer

The next time your home printer needs ink or toner cartridges, take the empty cartridge to a local office supply and see if they will refill it. Recycling printer ink cartridges instead of buying new ones is a way to save money and help the environment. This can save money and landfill space.

CASE STUDY

Vertex and Pixel Shading

Vertex shading involves a very complex mathematical formula to draw objects. In vertex shading, the computer identifies the coordinates of a vertex and compares that location to the position of the player's character. The computer determines the object's position on the 3D map and then aligns it on the sight angle for the character. The sight angle is the angle from the "eye" of the character to the vanishing point. When the sight angle changes as the player moves left/right or up/down, the computer moves the vertices to match the angle. This shows movement. When the character moves closer to an object without changing the sight angle, the object remains stationary, but increases in size.

The alignment to a sight angle allows morphing. Morphing is a change in physical dimension. The vertex shading changes the size and distance between vertices. Items in the distance appear smaller in scale than objects close to the viewer.

Goodheart-Willcox Publisher

When the player changes position, the vertex shader moves the distance between vertices to a new sight angle. When the player moves straight forward or backward, the sight angle does not change. The vertex shader maintains the sight angle to resize the image, larger or smaller, along the sight angle.

If you look down a street, you could stretch out a finger to cover up a car in the distance. As the car gets closer,

PS3 Multimedia Gaming Platform

To go with this awesome graphics power, PlayStation 3 installed a Blu-Ray DVD reader. **Blu-Ray** is the technology for storing high-definition video on a disc for playback. By including the Blu-Ray feature, the PS3 can play the most advanced DVD format with the clearest high-definition video imaging. This also allows game designers to build very large games. A Blu-Ray disc will hold almost six times as much information as a standard DVD disc. However, Blu-Ray discs are the same physical size as a standard DVD, as seen in **Figure 6-6.** The difference is how compactly the data are written on the disc. Data lines, known as *pits,* are thinner on a Blu-Ray disc. This allows the data lines to be placed closer together.

The data lines on a DVD are read with a laser. The laser on a Blu-Ray reader is 405 **nanometers** (nm) in width

CHEAT CODE: NANOMETERS

A nanometer is incredibly small. The smallest metric measurement used in school is usually one millimeter. There are 1,000,000 nanometers in every millimeter. The point of a needle is about 750 nanometers wide.

the car appears to get bigger and bigger until it reaches you at its actual size. This information is used to change the distance between the vertices or corners of an object.

Goodheart-Willcox Publisher

You can cover the image of the car in the distance with your finger. As the car moves closer, its size appears to change. In reality, the car does not change size, but the computer must make it look different sizes to simulate distance.

Pixel shading refers to the use of color and shading of each pixel or point of color on an object. This effect uses the principle that things in the distance are typically darker and objects closer to the viewer are brighter. In the 3D game world, each object must have a light direction designation. Think of

this as standing next to a tree in the shade or on the other side in the sunlight. There are millions of pixels on the screen and the computer must continuously tell the screen the exact color of each pixel. This process takes a huge amount of CPU power. If the CPU or GPU does not keep up, the game will play with jerky movement or freeze up.

Shutterstock.com

As an object moves through a scene, pixel shading is used to change the perspective of the object. Imagine an object moving from the bright sunlight into the shade of the fence. Also, notice how the shadows are not black, rather have a blue tint. Why is this?

Figure 6-6.

A Blu-Ray DVD (left) is exactly the same physical size as the standard DVD, but it can hold significantly more data.

Goodheart-Willcox Publisher

That compares to the 650 nm width of a laser on a standard DVD reader. A nanometer is one billionth of a meter (0.000000001 meters). A human hair is about one million nanometers in diameter, as illustrated in **Figure 6-7.** The 405 nm laser is a blue-violet color. The 650 nm laser used on a DVD is a red color. The blue-violet color of light emitted by the laser is literally the "blue ray" for which the device is named.

While designed to play the most advanced games, the PS3 also doubles as a great multimedia platform. It appeals to many non-gamers who want to watch Blu-Ray movies and connect to the Internet through their TV. In addition to playing Blu-Ray discs and DVD movies, the PS3 offers a complete multimedia experience through the online portal. With a quick connection of a standard USB keyboard or use of a PS3 remote control, a PS3 user can download movies, shop online, surf the Internet, and download music, all in addition to online gameplay and game downloads.

PS3 Cost and USP

As mentioned earlier, Sony initially lost money on each PS3 console sold. Why would Sony do this? It was all about creating a USP. Looking at **Figure 6-2** you can see that the PS3 was built to have more power than the other systems. The console was designed with a USP of being the fastest system with the best graphics. A game designed to take advantage of all the computing power of a PS3 could *only* play on a PS3. Sony thought that they would eliminate Microsoft and Nintendo as competitors when the game designers ran to create incredible games for the PS3. The PS3 was seeking a USP based on the ability

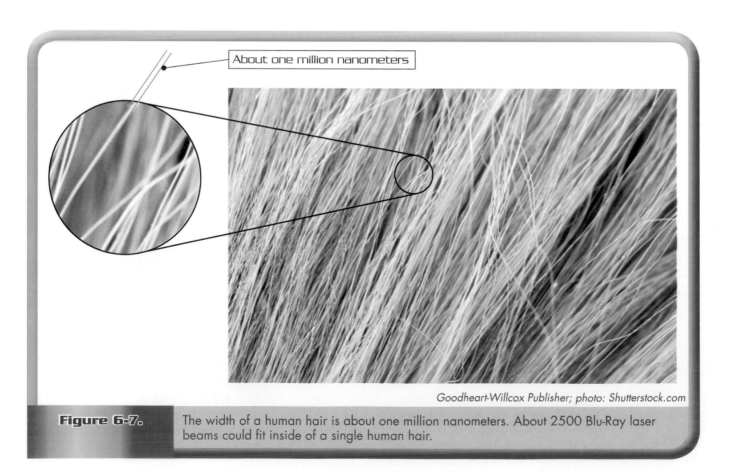

About one million nanometers

Goodheart-Willcox Publisher; photo: Shutterstock.com

Figure 6-7.   The width of a human hair is about one million nanometers. About 2500 Blu-Ray laser beams could fit inside of a single human hair.

of games to have the most visually stunning graphics and fastest 3D gameplay. Unfortunately, the PS3 was released almost a year after the Xbox 360 and for almost twice the price. The price of the PS3 game console was more than many people wanted to pay. Recently, however, the PS3 is pulling nearly even with the Xbox in the battle for market share.

The **market share** is the percentage of the total market or sales for which a single company or product is responsible. If there were ten million game systems sold and one million of those systems were PS3s, the PS3 would have a 10 percent market share. In the first two years of generation 7, the PS3 had less than 15 percent market share. The PS3 was released too late to get the major share of the market based on first-to-market sales. The Xbox 360 was the first generation 7 console available. Being the first to market, it captured most of the market share before the Wii and PS3 even made it to the store shelves. While the PS3 had a clear USP, it was not effective. It did not separate itself from the marketplace as something new that consumers *had* to have.

Sony decided to lose money on the console to try profiting from licensing the games. However, game designers did not want to invest in the technology needed to build a video game that takes advantage of the computing power of the PS3. So, no third-party video games hit the market that would only play on the PS3 system. It was more cost effective for video game developers to make video games that played on the Xbox 360 and then port those games to the PS3.

Porting is converting the computer code from one system to work on a different system. Porting from Xbox 360 to PS3 usually does not require much effort as all the graphics and programming will transfer. However, porting from a PS3 game to an Xbox 360 game would have been very difficult. Also, game features that made use of the extra "power" of the PS3 would need to be removed. Game designers did not want to rebuild a game that would be considered "weaker" to play on the Xbox 360. As a result, Sony's USP did not turn out to be profitable.

Adding to the problem was the fact that only 1.75 million PS3s were sold by August 2007. By the same time, 6.3 million Xbox 360 consoles had been sold. Why build a game for a potential market of under two million users when you could make a game for a market of over six million users? Additionally, you could port the game to the PS3 and increase the potential market by two million users, like the game shown in **Figure 6-8.** A potential market of two million or a potential market of eight million? It was not hard for most game developers to decide on the Xbox format.

Goodheart-Willcox Publisher

Figure 6-8. This game, *G-Force* based on the Disney movie, has been ported to both Xbox 360 and the PSP. Porting means the game program has been altered to function on a different platform.

Another problem presented itself. Sony priced the PS3 low to attract buyers to their game system. However, some savvy buyers realized the consoles were more valuable as pieces. They bought PS3s, took them apart, and resold the parts. Other innovators bought the PS3, changed the operating system to Linux, and made superfast personal computers, like the one shown in **Figure 6-9.** Some even linked three or more PS3s together to make a small, superfast mainframe computer or server. The components offered in the package of the PS3 made the PS3 too good of a deal for these high-tech users to pass. They made innovative use of the high-priced experimental technology developed by Sony. Sony not only lost money on the console bought by these innovators, but also lost because those individuals never bought a video game to play on the system. They just wanted the expensive hardware at the low price.

Early in generation 7, the PS3 could not really be considered a success:

- It was the last to hit the market.
- The console had the highest price.
- There was no strong proprietary game.
- The USP was not viewed as valuable by the market.

Some advances in sales were achieved by 2009 when Sony lowered the price of the PS3 to a suggested price of $299. This was about half of the original price. By mid 2009, game developers were beginning to take advantage of the computing power offered by the PS3. There are now numerous games designed to make use of the PS3 power. Combined with the lower price and games designed for enhanced gameplay on the PS3, Sony has a working USP.

Xbox 360

Xbox 360 is Microsoft's generation 7 video game console, shown in **Figure 6-10.** It was the first generation 7 system released. This caused a buying frenzy in late 2005, one year before Nintendo's Wii and Sony's PlayStation 3 were available.

Microsoft also makes the Windows operating system and the Microsoft Office software. These are two of the best selling software products of all time.

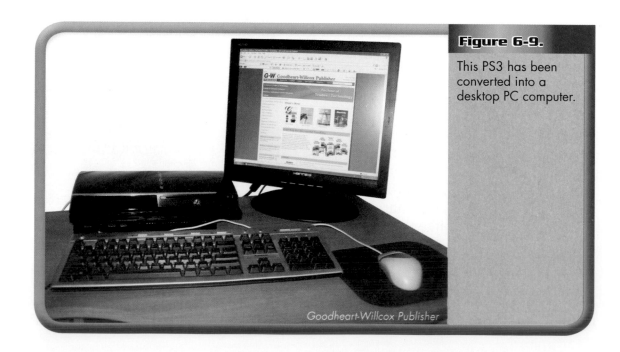

Figure 6-9.

This PS3 has been converted into a desktop PC computer.

Goodheart-Willcox Publisher

As a result, Microsoft had billions in cash to put into research and development. That is exactly what it did to create the Xbox 360. Microsoft spent more money than its competitors and was able to get its system out first.

Being first in the generation, the Xbox set the standard for new game designs. This standard would be hard to dethrone. By 2007, the Xbox had an over 50 percent market share of the generation 7 systems. Only time will tell who will win the battle for generation 7. However, **Figure 6-2** shows that by 2012, the PS3 had essentially caught up with the Xbox. Unfortunately for both manufacturers, the Nintendo Wii still outsells the PS3 and Xbox.

Figure 6-10.

The Xbox 360 is Microsoft's entry into the generation 7 video game console market. This machine contains a powerful processor and can produce high-quality graphics.

Goodheart-Willcox Publisher

Xbox 360 Hardware

Inside, the Xbox 360 is a very good computer. The CPU in this system is not quite as good as the CELL configuration of the PS3, but almost. The CPU has a 3.2 GHz clock speed and uses multicore processing. This allows the Xbox 360 to very quickly process huge amounts of data, just like the PS3. The difference is the PS3 allows for better parallel processing. The CPU in the PS3 can do more things at the same time and that makes it faster. The GPU for the Xbox is also very good, but not quite as good as the one in the PS3.

The GPU in the Xbox is the ATI-Xenos GPU. This is a unified shader device. With a **unified shader** format, the GPU attempts to move the vertices and shade pixels at the same time. Remember, the GPU in the PS3 uses parallel processing for vertex shading and pixel shading. This makes the PS3 faster because it splits the job of calculating the graphics into two parts.

Xbox 360 Drawbacks

By combining a great CPU with a powerful GPU the Xbox 360 is an incredibly powerful console. The total computing power of the Xbox 360 is 1.0 teraFLOPS. A console that powerful means the system moves a large volume of data in a very short time. That movement consumes a lot of power and creates a lot of heat. Early on, the largest drawback to the Xbox was the amount of heat it generated. This led to the rise of a phenomenon known as the **red ring of death**. Heat is also a concern on the PS3,

CHEAT CODE: RED RING OF DEATH

A major recall of the Xbox was for a problem known as the *red ring of death*. Heat has been listed as the most likely cause of this recall. The phrase *red ring of death* spawned from the LED color ring around the on/off button on the Xbox. A green ring means the system is turned on and everything is good. A red ring means it is not operating properly.

but so far no problems have been identified that required a product recall.

Electrical conductors have some resistance. Each time an electron moves in an electrical conductor, heat is produced, as illustrated in **Figure 6-11.** In fact, if not properly cooled, the Xbox 360 can heat up enough to melt the computer chips and ruin them. Players have a hard time keeping these systems cool. Many companies sell cooling stations with extra fans to move more air in and out of the console to keep them cool.

Microsoft accelerated work to bring their system to market one year ahead of the PS3. As a result, it had a design problem with the heat dissipation of the chipset and seating of the DVD discs. DVD discs can experience "laser burn" and ruin the game discs. **Laser burn** occurs when the disc gets too close to the laser or the disc stops spinning and the laser burns the same place for too long. PS3 does not have the same type of problems because Sony spent a year longer in testing and development.

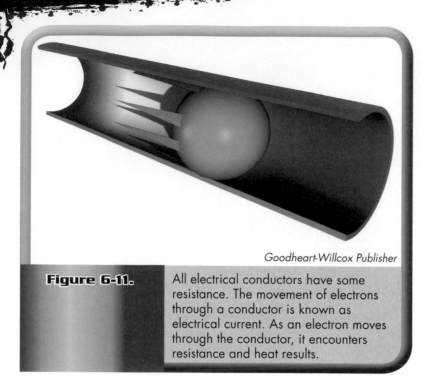

Goodheart-Willcox Publisher

Figure 6-11. All electrical conductors have some resistance. The movement of electrons through a conductor is known as electrical current. As an electron moves through the conductor, it encounters resistance and heat results.

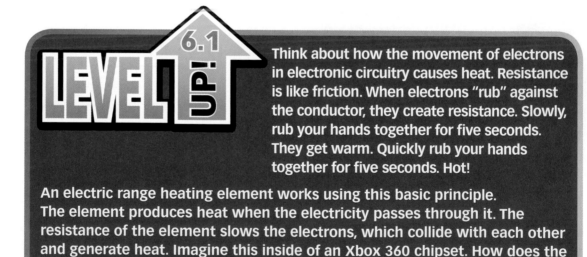

6.1 LEVEL UP!

Think about how the movement of electrons in electronic circuitry causes heat. Resistance is like friction. When electrons "rub" against the conductor, they create resistance. Slowly, rub your hands together for five seconds. They get warm. Quickly rub your hands together for five seconds. Hot!

An electric range heating element works using this basic principle. The element produces heat when the electricity passes through it. The resistance of the element slows the electrons, which collide with each other and generate heat. Imagine this inside of an Xbox 360 chipset. How does the speed of moving data in the Xbox 360 cause the chipset to melt?

Xbox 360 Costs

Microsoft spent a lot of cash to bring the Xbox into the marketplace. Not only did it spend millions of dollars to design the system, but it then sold the console for less than the cost to make. Just as with the PS3, the parts cost more than the price of the console. However, unlike the PS3, the cost of the parts was not twice as much as the retail price of the unit.

It is widely thought that the initial cost to make an Xbox 360 was about $470. The console was sold for $399. That resulted in a $71 loss for each console sold. Microsoft assumed that the cost of production would quickly come down and these losses would not exist for long. It was right. Within a year, the cost to make an Xbox 360 reportedly dropped to about $375. Not much profit, but better than a loss.

Microsoft took company profits, from selling the Windows and Office software, and spent it to cover the losses on the Xbox 360. It assumed some financial loss to bring the system into reality and then offered consumers a deal on the price.

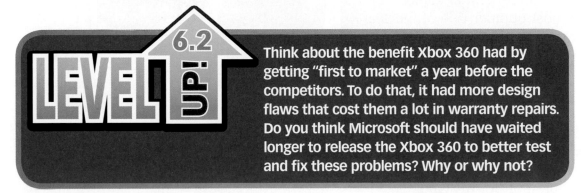

LEVEL UP! 6.2

Think about the benefit Xbox 360 had by getting "first to market" a year before the competitors. To do that, it had more design flaws that cost them a lot in warranty repairs. Do you think Microsoft should have waited longer to release the Xbox 360 to better test and fix these problems? Why or why not?

Xbox 360 USP

In addition to having a great system, the most popular generation 7 game is a proprietary game for the Xbox. Recall from earlier chapters that a proprietary game, or exclusive game, is available for only one system. Microsoft makes up some of the financial losses from the sales of the game system by selling a large number of *Halo* games, shown in **Figure 6-12**. *Halo* and its successors were designed by Bungie Studios. Microsoft put its cash to work again and bought Bungie Studios. This ensured *Halo* would not be ported to other systems; it can only be played on the Xbox. This makes it impossible for *Halo* gamers to switch to the PS3 because their favorite game will not work on the PS3 system. This presents a huge hurdle for PS3 to overcome, referred to as The Halo Effect, and provides an outstanding USP for Xbox 360.

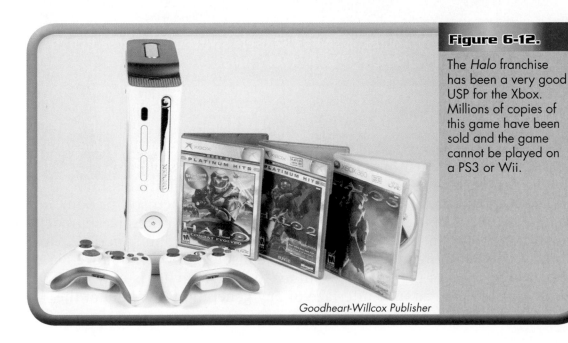

Figure 6-12.

The *Halo* franchise has been a very good USP for the Xbox. Millions of copies of this game have been sold and the game cannot be played on a PS3 or Wii.

222 Video Game Design Foundations

CASE STUDY

The Halo Effect

How strong is The Halo Effect? Microsoft released *Halo 3* on September 25, 2007. In only 12 days it:

- sold more than three million copies;
- outsold the most popular title of the year to that point, *Wii Play*;
- caused the Xbox 360 to outsell the Nintendo Wii in October (the first month it outsold the Wii since its release); and
- is thought to have caused a 27 percent reduction in movie ticket sales in October 2007.

It would seem that Microsoft knew how to build an unbeatable USP for the Xbox 360—something it continues to exploit with new releases of games in the *Halo* series.

Goodheart-Willcox Publisher

The *Halo* series of games has been a big unique selling point for the Xbox. Millions of copies of these games have been sold.

6.3

Halo 3 sold three million copies in the first 12 days of its release and over eight million copies over the next year. *Halo 4* was released in November of 2012 and sold 3.1 million copies in the first 24 hours of its release. PS3 users cannot play *Halo* on the PS3 console. Do you think some PS3 users switched or will switch to Xbox 360 during the *Halo* frenzy? Why or Why not?

Nintendo Wii

Nintendo spent most of generation 6 losing market share and struggling to survive as a player in the gaming market. Entering into generation 7, Nintendo was too late to compete with Microsoft or Sony in research and development on the systems. So, it took a different approach: it used a basic system and made the controllers unique and superior. The Wii is Nintendo's generation 7 video game console, shown in **Figure 6-13**. Wii is pronounced as the English word *we* to describe who is playing. It had the most advanced user interface of any generation 7 system at the time of its release.

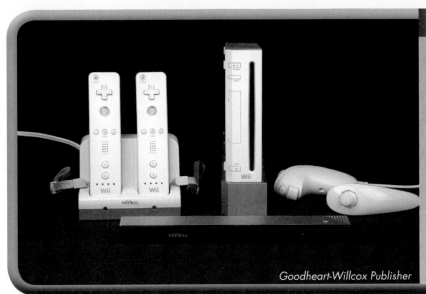

Figure 6-13.
The Wii is Nintendo's entry into the generation 7 video game console market. While the computing power is behind that of the PS3 and Xbox, the Wii is unique in its motion-based controllers.

Goodheart-Willcox Publisher

Wii Costs

To create the Wii, Nintendo essentially took apart a Game Cube; added some updated, but standard, electronic parts; created advanced controllers; and turned the Game Cube into the Wii. This strategy was completely different from that used in developing the Xbox 360 and PS3. Both of these consoles had cutting-edge, experimental technology. Both Microsoft and Sony lost money selling these consoles, at least initially. By contrast, the Wii used little experimental technology and was inexpensive to build.

Additionally, Nintendo made a profit on every Wii it sold. With a low selling price of $249, the Wii flew from the store shelves and into the living room. Estimates place the profit of each Wii console sold between $80 and $130. Multiply that by 97 million consoles sold and you have a phenomenal profit for a company that had been struggling.

Wii Hardware

If you look at the table in **Figure 6-2,** you can see that the Nintendo Wii is far behind the PS3 and Xbox in terms of processing power and video graphics. The Wii is so far behind the others that it really does not look like a generation 7 system. The GPU in the Wii is nearly the same as the one used in the generation 6 Game Cube. The **optical disk drive (ODD)** is proprietary to Nintendo. The games are delivered on optical disks instead of CD-ROM or DVD-ROM like the Xbox and PS3. Other than the ODD, the core components of the Wii are off-the-shelf electronics readily available at most computer repair shops or electronics stores. Nothing fancy or experimental involved!

The Wii rates poor for processing power and graphics in comparison to the Xbox and PS3. So how did Nintendo sell over four million systems—more than twice as many as the PS3—in the first year? And how did it outsell both Xbox 360 and PS3 to top 97 million sold by the end of 2012? The answer is in the USP.

Wii USP

Instead of looking inside of the system to create a better game world, Nintendo looked outside. The USP created by Nintendo is greater player immersion through the use of a superior user interface. The Wii uses motion-based controllers, some of which are shown in **Figure 6-14.** The controllers are called **Wii remotes,** but have been nicknamed *Wiimotes* by users.

The Wii remote senses movement and acceleration along three axes, or directions. In the 3D space of your living room that is up/down, left/right, forward/backward. The ***accelerometer*** part of the controller reads how fast the remote moves from one point to another. The actual speed and distance the controller moves is interpreted by the controller and then input into the system using **Bluetooth** wireless technology. The Bluetooth technology relays the information from the controller via radio frequency signal into the system. Again, in Bluetooth, Nintendo used off-the-shelf technology to save on development cost.

CHEAT CODE: BLUETOOTH

Bluetooth is a wireless protocol capable of transmitting data at up to one megabit per second. Bluetooth is a wireless personal area network (WPAN) technology that uses low-cost transceiver (transmitter/receiver) chips to send and receive radio signals over a short distance. Radio signals do not require a "line of sight" and can even travel through low-density objects (walls, etc.). This is ideal for the Wii where the player's body may get in between the Wii remote and the Wii console.

Some people even use the Wii remote to control other Bluetooth devices. Autodesk, the owner of the software programs 3ds Max, Maya, and AutoCAD, has integrated the Wii remote into its software to move 3D objects and change the view. Others have used the Bluetooth technology to change the radio station on their car radio. You could even use the Wii remote to answer your cell phone. Some unexpected advantages are gained by using off-the-shelf, mainstream technology.

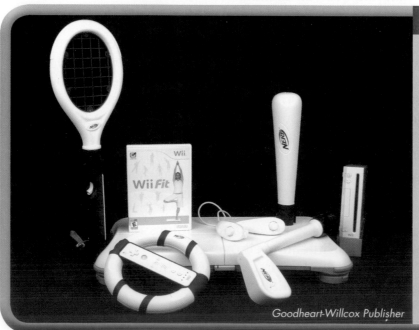

Figure 6-14.

The USP of the Wii is the motion-based controllers. There are many different controllers available. Depending on which game is being played, a different controller may be required.

Goodheart-Willcox Publisher

The Wii continues to gain interest in several different niche markets. A **niche market** is a small or narrow market characterized by potential customers that are very similar in characteristics, needs, and wants. One of these niches is physical fitness. Some say that the Wii gets the couch potato gamer on their feet and moving. While this is no replacement for exercise, it is a more physical interaction.

The other important niche is simulation gamers. With a realistic user interface, those gamers get a greater virtual simulation in real world space. In other words, the Wii is played in real space and displayed in virtual space. This experience is unique to the Wii.

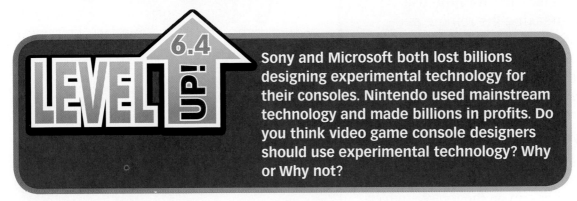

6.4 Sony and Microsoft both lost billions designing experimental technology for their consoles. Nintendo used mainstream technology and made billions in profits. Do you think video game console designers should use experimental technology? Why or Why not?

Wii Drawbacks

Nintendo created a USP of a better user interface and virtual reality simulation. The motion-based controller allows the player to move in real space to affect gameplay. This greatly increases immersion in the game. However, there are some drawbacks to the Wii user interface technology.

The first drawback is that the player needs a cabinet full of accessories to experience the full level of immersion. For example, to be fully immersed in a racing game, the player needs a steering wheel. To be fully immersed in a baseball game, the player needs a bat controller for a baseball game. These controllers are just props. The Wii remote snaps into the toy-like controller and does all the sensing.

The other drawback to the Wii controller is the amount of power needed to read player movement and send it to the system. Since these controllers are wireless, they need batteries to work, **Figure 6-15.** When the batteries get low, the movements on the game get messy and frustrate players. Even worse, when the batteries run out and you do not have extras, you cannot play. In response, Nintendo developed rechargeable remotes, but these are more expensive and need to recharge for several hours when they run down.

Figure 6-15.

The Wii remotes require batteries. As the batteries run low on charge, gameplay can be affected. Some Wii remotes are rechargeable, but they are more costly to purchase and recharging can take several hours.

Shutterstock.com

CASE STUDY

Wii Remote Straps

To keep the $40 Wii remote from flying across the room, each Wii remote has a wrist strap. Nintendo highly recommends using the strap at all times. Without the strap, the remote may fly from the user's hand, possibly breaking the remote and damaging televisions or other breakable items nearby. As long as players use the strap, they and their surroundings are safe. If a player loses his or her grip, the strap will keep the remote attached to the arm.

However, there have been problems with the strap. Initially, a very small cord attached the strap to the remote. This cord could break if the player lost his or her grip on the remote, which allowed the remote to fly across the room.

Because the Wii games are very immersive, players get very involved in the action of the game. They swing the bat and try to hit the home run. They jump around swinging their arms in the motion of the game. Unfortunately, that fast movement is also the one that makes the Wii remote prone to slipping out of players' hands. The original tiny strap could not take the stress of repetitive fast movement.

Goodheart-Willcox Publisher; image: Shutterstock.com

One downside of the user interface for the Wii is the chance that the remote will fly from the player's hand. This vase is a casualty of Wii playing. Breakable items need to be moved to a safe place before you play with the Wii.

Since the original release, Nintendo introduced a thicker strap. But, even that may not be enough for the wild gameplay experienced by Wii game players. All users are cautioned to clear a big space in the play area and to remove all breakable items from the area!

Video Game Consoles Versus a PC

All of the generation 7 video game consoles are computers. So, why the need for these special systems? Why not just use a personal computer (PC)? The PS3 and the Xbox 360 have very specialized, experimental CPUs and GPUs. These are more powerful and faster than those found in a typical home PC. On the other hand, the Wii is likely less powerful than your home computer. Therefore, it must be something more than computing power that makes game consoles preferred to the PC for gaming.

Keep in mind, there is a large market for PC gaming. **PC gaming** is simply playing games on a personal computer instead of a dedicated game console. Many third-party game designers also release their game titles formatted to play on a PC. The PC of today has most of the same characteristics of a game console. However, it is not advanced enough to play many games designed to take advantage of the power offered by an Xbox or PS3.

The generation 7 game consoles are specialists in game playing. They are designed primarily for playing games, where a PC is designed to be very flexible in its use. It would be similar to the difference between a street-legal car and a NASCAR race car. The race car is a specialty car. It is designed to work best in the environment of a racetrack. The street car is designed to work well in all kinds of weather, in traffic, when starting and stopping, and on different road surfaces. The race car does not stop and restart well. It also takes lots of attention by a crew of people just to get it through a race. A street car could drive the same number of miles as is typical of a NASCAR race on a single tank of gas and without stopping for maintenance. This analogy works well in describing the difference between a PC (the street car) and a game console (the race car).

While the typical PC does not play many generation 7 video games well, it can do a really good job of running most generation 5 and 6 games. The 32-bit or 64-bit processor in the PC of today is as powerful or more powerful than those used in generation 5 and 6 video game consoles. Some PCs even use a dual-, triple-, or quad-core 64-bit processor that can run some games designed for a 128-bit game console.

Many of the generation 5 and 6 games can run in an emulation mode on a PC, as shown in **Figure 6-16.** An emulation mode, or an **emulator,** is a method of simulating the original environment. In other words, it creates a "lookalike, play-alike" environment. The mainstream technology of today's PC is so much higher than that of the generation 5 and 6 game systems. Therefore, a newer PC will do a very good job running these games. However, the user interface may still be a problem for gamers used to playing with a controller when they need to switch to using the keyboard. Of course, you could always buy a joystick or controller to plug into your PC to enhance the experience.

The personal computer will always lag in power and speed behind the game systems. The game system manufacturers are pushing current technology and spending hundreds of millions of dollars to outperform the competition. These experimental designs for CPUs and GPUs are proprietary. This is to prevent competing companies from simply buying these new chips and, therefore, negating the USP. But, these new and fast chips are destined to later influence chips designed for PCs. Usually, the manufacturers of the chips will begin producing similar chips for PCs as game systems shift to newer and faster chips. In other words, the PC market gets to use the game console chips when a newer and faster model of game system is released. This always places the PC behind video game consoles in the latest and greatest technology.

The experimental technology that was a USP for a video game system eventually becomes mainstream. Technology developed for video gaming is transferred to many other applications. This is one of the greatest benefits to consumers from the game industry.

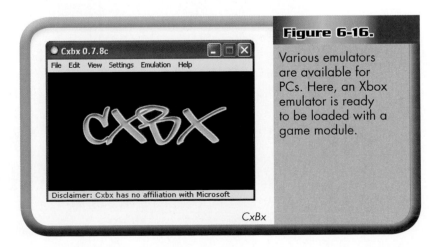

Figure 6-16.

Various emulators are available for PCs. Here, an Xbox emulator is ready to be loaded with a game module.

Technology Transfer

As noted above, the technology from video games has been driving advancements in personal computers. This is not the only area in which **technology transfer** has occurred between game technology and other devices. The technology used in video games has trickled down into most electronic and complementary technologies. The next sections look at a few recent examples.

High-Definition Television

One of the ways manufacturers separate their game consoles from the competition is by creating more advanced displays. To achieve this, game systems have highly advanced GPUs. At the heart of the high-definition television is a very sophisticated GPU, like in the TV shown in **Figure 6-17.** The GPU found in high-definition televisions is inspired by GPU designs developed for video game consoles.

Handheld Consumer Products

Cell phones, smartphones, and music players all benefited from game technology. Most importantly, all of these handheld devices use flash memory. **Flash memory** was the preferred memory-storage device going back to the ROM cartridge of the Atari 2600. Born from that technology, game systems like Nintendo created the first **random-access memory flash** used to store levels and scores for video game systems. You may remember using these memory cards on Nintendo 64 or PlayStation 2. This technology is not too different from that used in today's flash drives, like the one shown in **Figure 6-18.**

In addition to the innovation in data storage, the user interface of handheld devices has benefited from game technology. The interface has buttons, touch-sensitive screens, or navigation wheels. The ergonomic data collected from designing gaming devices helped direct the development of these controls. It may be hard to

Figure 6-17.

High-definition televisions use some technology that originated in game consoles. The heart of an HDTV is the GPU. Advanced GPUs were first available to the mass market in video game consoles.

Shutterstock.com

remember a cell phone without an LCD mini screen. Where did these come from? Most people first saw the LCD mini screen on their Game Boy and their first color LCD mini screen on Game Boy color. Also, do not leave out the first touch screen that appeared on the Nintendo DS years before the iPhone was developed. Now, many touch-screen phones are on the market, like those shown in **Figure 6-19.**

These innovations in video games helped young people become comfortable with the experimental technology. As comfort levels rise, manufacturers of other devices adapt these technologies as a mainstream technology.

Figure 6-18.

The flash memory drives (A) and cards (B) in use today have technology similar to the random-access memory flash used for older Nintendo games.

Shutterstock.com; Goodheart-Willcox Publisher

Look at the handheld devices you carry, like your cell phone. Think about all the parts needed to build that device: small speakers and microphones, wiring, buttons, color screens, touch-sensitive screens, motion controllers, and so on. Think about an example of video game technology that influenced some of these features.

Education

The education field has greatly benefited from technology developed for video games. Students are invited, because of the entertainment value, to play video games. Playing these games builds skills for navigating the user interface; skills which are then put to use in computer applications. The education field also relies on new technology to better engage students, as shown in **Figure 6-20.** By using technology in the classroom, such as smart boards, LCD projectors,

Goodheart-Willcox Publisher

Figure 6-19. The iPhone and other devices have a touch-sensitive screen. This technology appeared much earlier in the gaming world.

Figure 6-20.

Here, a student is using an AirLiner wireless slate from SMART Technologies in a classroom setting.

and computers, students are given tools with which they can excel in learning.

Besides the indirect benefits, students are actually learning directly through educational games. Math, language, and other skills can be refined through the interaction of the student and the game world. Remember your business technology class and the typing game you played to practice and learn keyboarding skills? Games are now a part of the educational process.

Some school districts even integrate test taking systems with games that support the educational needs of the students. If a student does poorly on a specific section of a test, when he or she next goes to play the game, it is geared to challenge the student in those areas where practice is most needed and presents material that is specific to the current level of ability.

Medical

The medical community has also greatly benefited from applying game technology. Surgeons can use custom visual displays that show a 3D rendering of a patient during arthroscopic surgery. Additionally, 3D imaging and simulations help medical students study the human body, as illustrated in **Figure 6-21.** Surgical procedures can also be practiced through gameplay.

In one case, the Wii remote was modified into a laparoscopic surgery tool. This allowed surgeons to practice surgery using an inexpensive and readily available simulator. Before this adaptation of the Wii remote, laparoscopic-surgery simulators cost $300,000 or more. Now, the Wii version costs about $600 and surgeons can practice at home—which also enables them to have countless hours of practice before they ever work on a patient.

Corporate Training

Corporations rely on game technology to provide their employees new or enriched skills. Corporate training is a form of education. One of the products with the heaviest demand in corporate training is foreign-language instruction.

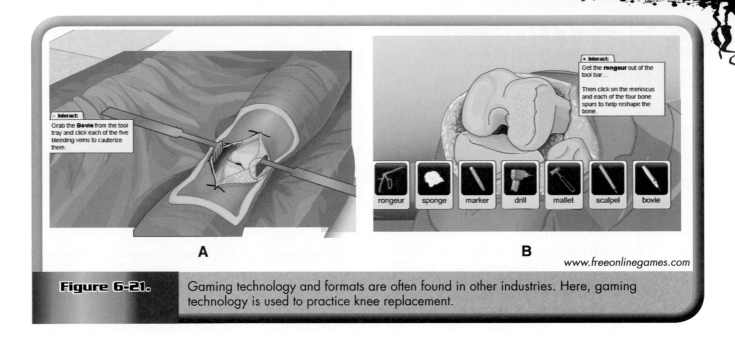

Get the **rongeur** out of the tool bar...

Then click on the meniscus and each of the four bone spurs to help reshape the bone.

Grab the **Bovie** from the tool tray and click each of the five bleeding veins to cauterize them.

A

B

rongeur   sponge   marker   drill   mallet   scalpel   bovie

www.freeonlinegames.com

Figure 6-21. Gaming technology and formats are often found in other industries. Here, gaming technology is used to practice knee replacement.

Consequently, foreign-language training software is in common use in today's corporate training.

This advanced software uses simulated virtual environments with rich graphics and interactive characters. Some gameplay features of foreign-language software include voice or written statements to guide the learner. The learner may get statements like, *Abra la puerta.* The learner interprets the statement as, "open the door" and clicks on the door graphic.

Another example is an interactive character that speaks the foreign language and carries on a simulated conversation in the virtual world. This is not unlike an RPG game in a foreign language. The software checks for accuracy as well. Accurate responses lead to attaining goals, levels, and victory conditions within that virtual environment.

In the game industry, 3D software is used to create worlds and characters. Among the general public, Google SketchUp is an example of 3D software that can be downloaded and used for free. And, as an example of 3D software being used in other specific fields, architects are using 3D software to design simulations of buildings to be constructed, as seen in **Figure 6-22.** Using these models, the client can take a virtual tour of the building before the plans are finalized. The simulation can be complete with furniture, people, and special features like a fountain or fish pond.

LEVEL UP! 6.6

Think about the technology transfer from video games to the military. What military applications of video game technology do you think the military could use? Give examples other than those discussed in the text.

CASE STUDY

Stereoscopic 3D

Have you ever seen a 3D movie where you had to wear special glasses to see images jump off the screen? Advanced computer technology is used to create this stereoscopic 3D effect. Stereoscopic means a view from two independent perspectives to form one solid view.

It is easy to show how each eye sees an object from a different perspective. Look at an object near you. Then, hold your hand over one eye.

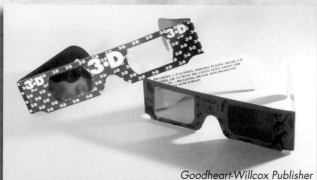

Goodheart-Willcox Publisher

These are two common types of 3D glass: red-blue and polarized.

Make note of how the object appears. Now, cover the other eye. See how the object appears to change?

To create 3D images that project outward from the screen, each object is displayed on two layers. One layer is for the right eye and the other layer is for the left eye. A filter is then used to block part of the image from each eye. The most common example of this is the red-blue 3D glasses. This type of stereoscopic image is called an anaglyph.

Shutterstock.com

To show the change in perspective, look at an object. Cover one eye, and then cover the other eye. Notice how the object appears to change.

Goodheart-Willcox Publisher

This is an anaglyph. If you have a pair of red-blue 3D glasses you can see the 3D effect.

To create an anaglyph, a computer is used to create a red image of the scene and a blue image of the scene, each from a slightly different perspective. The red lens on the glasses blocks the part of the image on the red layer. The blue lens blocks the part of the image on the blue layer. As a result, the brain interprets depth in the scene.

Another type of filter is polarized lenses. This technology uses microscopic lines or circles on the lenses. Only certain parts of the image are visible in each lens of the glasses.

In 2011, Sony released stereoscopic 3D gameplay to the PS3. This allowed players to use 3D gaming glasses to play the newest games like never before. Some of the first games built for stereoscopic 3D include

Batman: Arkham Asylum, Biohazard 5, and *Resident Evil 5.*

A market leader in stereoscopic 3D technology is NVIDIA. Go to their website (www.nvidia.com) and search for *3D*. In addition to games that are designed as stereoscopic, software and programming in the GPU can convert some older games into stereoscopic without reprogramming the original game.

What is the point of stereoscopic games? To increase immersion. Virtual reality is also used to create immersion. There are many applications of stereoscopic display and virtual reality, not only in gaming, but in other areas as well, such as training.

Leah-Anne Thompson/Shutterstock.com; Goodheart-Willcox Publisher

A—This boy is playing a game using a virtual reality headset. B—Virtual reality gear used for gaming.

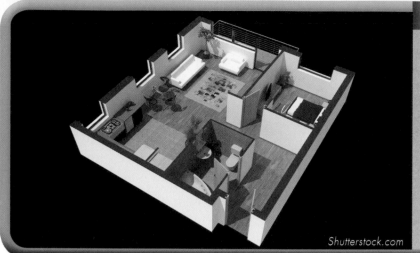

Figure 6-22.

This is an architectural rendering of a house. The similarity between this and many of the assets in a 3D video game is clear.

Military

www.g-wlearning.com

Level up your know-how with Animated Review 6-1.

Maybe the heaviest user of video game technology, outside of the video game industry, is the military. The military has flight simulators, which are nothing more than an ultra-realistic virtual reality game. Additionally, 3D graphics are commonplace on weapons systems and satellite imaging.

The latest use of video game technology can be seen in the ultimate virtual reality machine: the unmanned aerial vehicle (UAV) reconnaissance aircraft. A soldier, airwoman, or airman sits behind a video display watching 3D imaging from the camera mounted on an actual flying plane, as shown in **Figure 6-23.** The soldier is the pilot and flies the unmanned aircraft by remote control using a joystick. How is that for having the game world interacting with the real world? Of course, military activities are not a game; they have real-world consequences.

The United States military has also developed first person shooter (FPS) simulators with realistic rifle controllers and laser guided targeting. It is thought that these simulators help soldiers prepare for war, deal with stress, and build teamwork. Additionally, FPS simulators are used in recruiting efforts to demonstrate the teamwork needed to be successful.

Figure 6-23.

The UAVs used by the military are remotely piloted using a joystick and a video display. The application of gaming technology is obvious in this example.

Chapter Summary

- Each game system has unique features that differentiate it from the others such as the CPU, storage space, memory, graphics used, and the user interface hardware.
- Video game designers need to be well-versed in the terminology related to gaming systems.
- The three major gaming systems are PlayStation 3, Xbox 360, and Wii; each gaming system has unique selling points that allow it to maintain market share.
- There are two successful business models for gaming systems: one is to put a lot of research and experimental technology into the gaming system and sell the system for a loss while making profits on the games; the other is to make a relatively inexpensive gaming system with controllers that offer a USP.
- Video games drive and complement new technologies through technology transfer.
- Some examples of technology transfer from video games to other industries include personal computers, high-definition TVs, handheld devices, education, medical, corporate training, and military.
- Video game systems like PS3 and Xbox 360 are specialized computers; they are more powerful and faster than a typical personal computer but they are specialized for game playing whereas a PC is designed to be very flexible in its use.
- Personal computers lag behind game systems in speed and power and are, therefore, limited for video game playing.

Check Your Video Game IQ

Now that you have finished this chapter, see what you know about video game design by taking the chapter posttest.

www.m.g-wlearning.com

www.g-wlearning.com

Review Your Knowledge

On a separate sheet of paper or in a word processing document, match the following terms with the definitions that fit best.

A. bluetooth	F. Blu-Ray
B. cache memory	G. niche market
C. market share	H. flash memory
D. 3D accelerator card	I. accelerometer
E. technology transfer	J. system operations

1. Hardware in the computer that controls the display and enables 3D graphics to be displayed.

2. How experimental gaming technology is later used in mainstream products.

3. Wireless technology that relays information via radio frequency signal.

4. Memory modules located very close to the processor in the computer.

5. Part of the Wii controller that reads how fast the remote moves.

6. Very small or narrow market segment.

7. Memory chip that retains stored information even when power is turned off.

8. How information is transported between the parts of the user interface, computer system, and video display.

9. High-density data disc that is read by a narrow-beam, blue laser.

10. Percentage of the total market in terms of unit sales held by a single company or product.

On a separate sheet of paper or in a word processing document, answer each of the following questions.

11. List the three major video game consoles and their manufacturers.

12. What is a *dedicated video game console?*

13. What is the largest barrier to entry for new game systems?

Use the table from Figure 6-2 to answer questions 14 through 18.

14. As of October 2012, what was the total market for all generation 7 video game systems in terms of number of units?

15. Market share is the number of units sold by one company divided by the total units sold multiplied by 100 to show a percentage. What is the market share of each generation 7 video game console? Provide the figures for August 2007, June 2009, and October 2012.

   A. PlayStation 3
   B. Xbox 360
   C. Wii

16. Which system had the lowest cost at the time of its release?

17. As of October 2012, which system had the most RAM?

18. As of October 2012, which system uses a standard DVD player to read games?

19. What do CPU and GPU stand for?

20. What are FLOPS?

21. What is the USP for the PlayStation 3?

22. What are the two biggest loads on the CPU?

23. What GPU function requires a virtual light source?

24. What is the process used to make a game playable on other systems?

25. What is the USP for the Xbox 360?

26. Which video game console was the first generation 7 machine on the market?

27. What causes heat in electrical circuits?

28. What was the initial USP for the Wii?

29. What was the underlying market strategy of Nintendo for designing a generation 7 system?

30. On what type of media are Wii games delivered?

31. What is the name of the wireless technology used by the Wii remotes?

32. What is an *emulator?*

33. Describe *technology transfer*.

34. The iPhone uses touch-screen technology. Long before the iPhone was released, this technology appeared in the game world on the _____.

35. Describe one application of the Wii remote to medical technology.

Apply Your STEM Knowledge

Science

1. The PlayStation 3 uses CELL processor architecture. Refer to **Figure 6-4.** The idea of the CELL design is to allow for multitasking.
   A. How does the use of SPEs help produce faster gameplay?
   B. How might the use of cache memory help reduce heat?
   C. What is the total amount of cache memory on the CELL processor in the PS3?
   D. Think about your favorite game. As a game designer, what six main tasks would you assign the SPEs?

Social Studies

2. Developing and manufacturing a game console is a global effort. Research the components used in the PlayStation 3. Using a world map, create a presentation that shows where each of the major components of the PS3 are produced and assembled.

Mathematics

3. Research the current sales of the Xbox 360, PS3, and Wii. Enter these data into a Microsoft Excel spreadsheet. Create a bar graph to display the units sold. Create a pie graph to show the total percentages of market share.

Language Arts

4. Research the use of video games in physical exercise. Prepare a presentation on how video games immerse people in physical activities.

Science

5. Ultra-realistic 3D video games have caused some players to experience motion sickness. Research the cause of motion sickness. Prepare a presentation or display to show how video games can cause a physical response similar to motion sickness.

Working in Teams

In teams, research, debate, and form a group opinion on each of the Level Up! activities in this chapter. Prepare a PowerPoint presentation of ten slides (five to seven minutes) to present to the class explaining the group's opinions for each Level Up! activity. Include text, pictures, video, animations, and slide transitions as appropriate to help explain your positions.

Gamer Portfolio

You have identified the types of items you might place in your portfolio. You will begin adding items in this activity and add other items as you continue this class. Locate certificates you have received. For example, a certificate might show that you have completed a video game design workshop. Another certificate might show that you have passed an exam on a certain programming language. You might have a certificate that you received for taking part in a community project. Include any certificates that show tasks completed or your skills or talents. Also create a document that lists each certificate along with when you received it. Briefly describe your activities, skills, or talents related to each certificate.

1. Scan these documents to include in your e-portfolio. Use the file format you selected earlier.

2. Using the naming convention you created earlier, give each document an appropriate name. Place each certificate and the list in an appropriate subfolder for your e-portfolio.

3. Place the hard-copy certificates and list in the container for your print portfolio.

G-W Learning Mobile Site

Visit the G-W Learning mobile site to complete the chapter pretest and posttest and to practice vocabulary using e-flash cards. If you do not have a smartphone, visit the G-W Learning companion website to access these features.

G-W Learning mobile site: www.m.g-wlearning.com

G-W Learning companion website: www.g-wlearning.com

Common Core

College and Career Readiness

CTE Career Ready Practices. You will have a number of options to consider when thinking about your future plans. Approaching the different options available to you in a logical way, helps in the decision-making process. One simple way is to create a pros and cons chart. Create such a chart showing the pros and cons of pursuing a career that requires additional schooling after high school. Place all of the good or positive things about it on the left under on the "pro" side and all the negative things on the right, or "con" side. Circle the items on your list that you consider the most important when considered rationally. Put a star or asterisk by all those you consider important emotionally. Reflect on the items on the list. Has the list helped you come to a decision? Why or why not?

Speaking and Listening. Perform an Internet search on the three gaming systems described in this chapter. Look for reviews of the systems themselves as well as the games and accessories available for each. Include reviews by consumers as well as reviews by knowledgeable experts in the field of video game design. After reading both lay and expert opinions on the three game systems, use this information to form your own opinion about which system is the best. Discuss your findings and reasoning with the class. Respond to any questions you are asked. Be sure to choose appropriate vocabulary that is routinely used when discussing gaming systems. As you listen to your classmates' opinions on this issue, take notes and ask questions about positions or terms you do not understand. Evaluate your own position. How does their reasoning contribute to your understanding of the pros and cons of each system? Does your opinion change or is it strengthened?

Reading. Read a magazine, newspaper, or online article about the impact of technology on education. Determine the central ideas of the article and review the conclusions made by the author. As needed, derive meaning of the environmental print and use visual and contextual support to confirm understanding. Use support from classmates and your teacher as needed to help in comprehension of the material. Provide an accurate summary of your reading, making sure to incorporate the who, what, when, and how of the situation.

Event Prep: Communication Skills

Competitive events may judge participants' communications skills. Presenters must be able to exchange information with the judges in a clear, concise manner. This requirement is in keeping with the mission of Career and Technical Student Organizations (CTSOs): to prepare students for professional careers. Communication skills will be judged for both the written and oral presentation. The evaluation will include all aspects of effective writing, speaking, and listening skills as applied to the gaming environment. To prepare for the communications portion of the event:

1. Visit the organization's website and determine specific communication skills that will be evaluated.

2. Spend time reviewing the essential principles of communication, such as grammar, spelling, proofreading, capitalization, and punctuation.

3. If you are making a written presentation, ask a teacher to evaluate your writing. Review and apply the feedback so that your writing sample appears professional and correct.

4. If you are making an oral presentation, ask a teacher to review your presentation and listen for errors in grammar or sentence structure. After you have received comments, adjust and make the presentation several times until you are comfortable.

5. Review the reading, writing, speaking, and listening activities that appear at the end of each chapter of this text as a way to practice your skills.

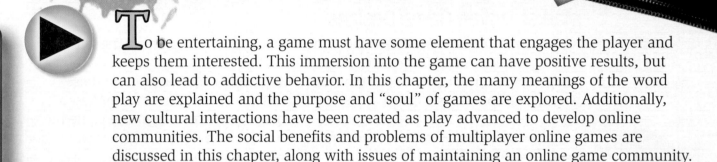

Chapter 7
Play and Game Culture

▶ To be entertaining, a game must have some element that engages the player and keeps them interested. This immersion into the game can have positive results, but can also lead to addictive behavior. In this chapter, the many meanings of the word play are explained and the purpose and "soul" of games are explored. Additionally, new cultural interactions have been created as play advanced to develop online communities. The social benefits and problems of multiplayer online games are discussed in this chapter, along with issues of maintaining an online game community.

Check Your Video Game IQ

Before you begin this chapter, see what you already know about video game design by taking the chapter pretest.

www.m.g-wlearning.com

www.g-wlearning.com

College and Career Readiness

Reading Prep. As you read the chapter, determine and summarize the point of view or purpose of the author. What aspects of the text help to establish the purpose or point of view?

Objectives

After completing this chapter, you will be able to:
- Outline the three driving factors that lead to game design.
- Describe what is meant by the purpose and soul of a game.
- Define the term play.
- Explain the ways in which play is important for people.
- Describe how play provides balance to life.
- List the primary player types.
- Describe online economies and community building offered by video games.
- Define video game addiction.

Driving Design

The main reason to build a game is to have someone play the game. The game is not a picture to be admired. It is an interactive world that begs the player to enter and become immersed in the action. While this premise seems simple, games are not always designed to meet the needs of the market. There are three driving factors that lead to game design:

- market
- designer
- technology

Market-Driven Game Designs

In a **market-driven design,** the game company looks to produce a game that meets the needs of the target customers. The major goal of any market-driven design is to find out what a player wants. Then, design a game to fulfill those wants. The idea here is called player-centric design. Just as the term implies, a **player-centric design** is a game built to focus on what the player wants and experiences in the game.

To help determine what the customers want, market research is done by surveys, focus groups, and sight studies. Collecting data related to what the buying population needs and wants is **market research.** Any activity done by a company to determine what people like or dislike about a product is market research. This may take the form of anything from simple observation to active questioning of paid or unpaid participants. The game developer analyzes the collected data and designs a game based on the result.

CHEAT CODE: SURVEY

A survey is a list of questions about a product. Typically, a survey is a printed or electronic document where someone fills in their answers. Those answers are combined with answers from others to get a clear picture of what the public wants. While written surveys still prevail, online surveys and telephone surveys are also commonly used.

Surveys

When using a **survey,** a game company might include a questionnaire in the packaging for an existing game, offer a discount if the customer completes a survey online, or send representatives to local malls and stores to ask customers the survey questions, as shown in **Figure 7-1.** The collected data are used to determine trends in public opinion. The **public opinion** is a general view shared by a majority of the population.

Goodheart-Willcox Publisher

Figure 7-1. Surveys are one way to collect data about potential customers.

When a survey shows a shift in public opinion, a game company may want to take advantage of this shift. To do so, they will begin designing games to take advantage of the trend. For example, suppose a survey indicates people want to see less violence and greater realism in racing games. A game company might start to design a game with a realistic user interface, but containing less imagery of the crashes and driver injuries.

Focus Groups

The next step after prototyping a game based on public opinion is to test the prototype with a focus group. In a *focus group,* a small group of people are shown scenes from the game, play a portion of the game, and are asked their opinion, as seen in **Figure 7-2.** The goal here is to again determine what the public wants. The opinions of these focus group participants will help refine the game and set a direction for the rest of the game build.

Sight Studies

Another useful market-research tool is a sight study. In game research, a *sight study* is an observation of a person or group of people playing your game. Like the focus group, participants will play an existing or prototype game. However, unlike the focus group, the participants are studied based on their reaction to the game. The activity here is to watch participants play and observe when the player looks bored, quits, gets frustrated, or becomes excited. There is no interaction between the players and the observers. Typically, the activity is recorded with one camera on the player and another showing the gameplay. Later, a split-screen view with the game on one side and the player on the other will be studied to see how the interactions in the game affect the player, as shown in **Figure 7-3.**

Goodheart-Willcox Publisher

Figure 7-2. Focus groups are used to obtain information about what customers want.

www.freeonlinegames.com; Shutterstock.com

Figure 7-3. In a sight study, a split screen is used to show the gameplay and the players reactions at the same time.

Results

All of these marketing research activities are done to build games with features the players want to experience. Too many times, designers do not see the whole picture on their own. Professional game designers are very sophisticated gamers. As a result, they may not be able to relate to novice and recreational gamers. A sophisticated gamer has experienced many games, is proficient at playing games, and is very comfortable with new technology. The general game player might not be a sophisticated gamer.

Think about games for children. All of these kids are new players, or **newbs** (pronounced "new-bz"). They do not know how things work, how to score, and how to survive in the game. They need lots of help and simple controls. A veteran game designer who has designed lots of sophisticated games might not build a game simple enough for newbs to build skill through the levels. Here, market research, like a sight study of kids playing the game, will show where the kids get frustrated and quit. Some changes can be made to the game and the kids might like it much better.

Sometimes, designers build games without the market in mind. Instead, these game builds test the designer's skills or the latest technology. These **designer-centric games** are called designer-driven and technology-driven games.

CHEAT CODE: DESIGNER-CENTRIC GAMES

The focus of designer-centric games is on the design process, not the needs and wants of the player. Designer-centric games often fail as commercial products as the game does not engage the player in meaningful immersion.

Designer-Driven Game Designs

Designer-driven games are those the designer makes to show off artistic and programming skill. It is important to design games with improved graphics, realistic physics engines, and new user interfaces. However, these improvements must be integrated in a way that makes them desirable to the player. Just because you can build it does not mean that you *should* build it!

Imagine a game that has exceptionally clear 3D graphics generated from high-polygon count models. This content requires more computer resources and may slow down the gameplay. As a result, the game may skip and stall. The designer wanted to stuff the most intense graphic environment into the game as possible, but the player just wants a game that plays well and is entertaining.

Technology-Driven Game Designs

Technology-driven games implement new technology, such as hardware, user interfaces, or game platforms. Often, a new technology entices designers to build games that test the new technology just to see how it works. Some recent games tried to implement voice recognition into the gameplay. This has proven very frustrating. Imagine if the computer does not understand what you are trying to say, pauses, and asks you to repeat your commands. Players quickly become frustrated. Early video games, such as in generations 1 and 2, saw many technology-driven games designed to test new video, sound, user interface, and programming technologies.

Look at the examples of the Wii and the PS3 discussed in Chapter 6. Sony loaded the most advanced technology possible into the PS3. The Wii was a simpler machine, but it better met the desires of the players. Since the Wii games do not have high-end graphics, the player focuses on the motion-based interactions, as shown in **Figure 7-4.** Designing a game for the PS3 would provide stunningly realistic graphics, but gameplay may not be any better. These players could not justify the extra cost of the PS3 and its high-end graphic games.

Newer system components like the PlayStation Eye and the Xbox Kinect use great technologies. Only time will tell if the games made for these new technologies are meaningful player-centric games. If the games do not meet the needs of the player, they will likely end up as interesting footnotes of designer-driven and technology-driven games instead of commercial successes.

Today's video games are the highest evolution of the game so far. The rich gaming environment, multiple players, dynamic characters, and virtual reality user interfaces make immersion in the game deeper than ever before. But, the tools of design and technology are meaningless if they are not used to the player's benefit. When designing games, keep the end user in mind and make a game that people want to play, not one that is just fun to build.

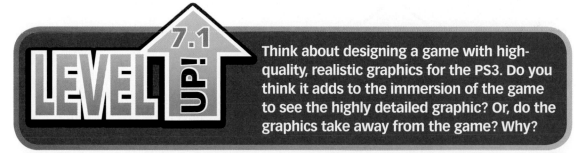

LEVEL UP! 7.1

Think about designing a game with high-quality, realistic graphics for the PS3. Do you think it adds to the immersion of the game to see the highly detailed graphic? Or, do the graphics take away from the game? Why?

Schimd Christophe/Shutterstock.com

Figure 7-4. The motion-based controllers of the Wii turned out to be more desired by players than the high-end graphics that could be generated on the PS3.

Purpose and Soul

CHEAT CODE: PURPOSE OF PLAY

Is there a reason for playing this game or is it just something that wastes time? Market-driven and player-centric games have the best chance of achieving a reasonable purpose for play. This happens because these games are designed to meet some need for players.

In creating richer graphics, cinematic cut-scenes, and amazing advancements in controllers, the technology of the game became more of a focus than the **purpose of play**. Technology can make the game affect more of your senses. Visually, games look real with 3D movement and 3D graphics. Tactilely, a gamer can touch a realistic controller and even get vibration or "rumble" feedback.

Auditory sense is engaged through stereo sounds. Sounds can even cue the gamer to action outside of the visible game frame. All of these sensory stimuli are available in the advanced video games of today.

Think about the classic game of chess. It is a basic board game played by millions of people. It continues to be popular even without fancy graphics and sounds. What about the purpose of play for chess keeps the game popular?

Shutterstock.com

Figure 7-5. Board game designers like those who developed *Chess* created games with rules and mechanics that have purpose hundreds of years after they were invented.

In Chapter 3, you learned that play was important in building skills. Can that same purpose of play be given to the popular video games of today or are they entirely lacking a purpose? Many games have stood the test of time not because of high-end sounds and graphics, but because of the purpose of play, such as the game of chess shown in **Figure 7-5.**

Too many times, a game is created simply to make money. Research and resources are spent to find what people want from a game and give it back to that audience. Since games can cost millions of dollars to create, making money is very important. Face it, everyone wants to make some money to buy the things they want in life. That fact does not mean a designer should focus on creating a game just to make money. There must be something deep inside a game that captures the player's attention and makes them want to keep playing. The central component that makes a game come alive and become important to the player is called the *soul of the game*.

As an aspiring game designer, you need to understand the purpose and soul of the game. The purpose of play lives in the concept. When a game is first conceived, a designer is looking at the reasons why the game is important and others will want to play. Sometimes, a game is conceived to test new technologies, such as *Quadrun,* shown in **Figure 7-6.** While exciting in the moment, these games will rarely survive long as advancing technology makes the games obsolete. The problem is the objective is not the purpose of play, but the purpose of design.

Daniel Brown

Figure 7-6. The build objective for *Quadrun* was purpose of design. *Quadrun* was the first game to use voice for the Atari 2600. It blinked the screen when talking because the voice used too much memory. The game had little purpose of play and mainly tested the voice technology.

Some genres of games have become stale with little advancement in purpose of play. One of these genres is the car-racing game. Many of these games are fun and exciting. However, the purpose for many of the newest games in this genre is only maintaining realistic control of the car as you drive through obstacles. Technology advancements, such as 3D graphics and lifelike steering and braking controls, have made these games more realistic and many have become role-playing games. Still, this genre seems to be stuck with the same idea and focused on creating a more advanced version of what has existed for years: race, crash, checkpoint, finish line, and standings. There is nothing really new in concept or purpose. Why make a new racing game if there is nothing new in design, concept, or purpose?

In addition to creating a greater purpose for play, a designer can create a game with a soul. A game with soul has:
- importance of play; and
- emotional, thought-provoking connection with the game choices.

The soul of the game makes the player think about the game long after play has ended. It generates a need to try again and resolve the internal conflict of the choices in the game. The player must examine possible judgment errors or other mistakes that caused them to lose the game or feel badly about their performance. The soul of the game need not include a negative emotional response. It can have a positive emotion where the player seeks to gain a greater positive emotional response each time the game is played. In the end, a game with a soul hopes to make people think deeply about choices and want to do better.

CHEAT CODE: SOCIAL NETWORKING

A social networking game is a multiplayer game that focuses on having different people interact without a victory condition. An online environment is created where avatars interact with other avatars to talk, trade ideas, and share interests. Here, the goal is meeting new people and doing activities together in the virtual world. A social interactive game is nearly identical except points are awarded when a player adds someone to their friends list or hosts a party, political rally, or other event.

Social Interaction

There is a difference between game immersion and game soul. A game with soul will keep you engaged in thought even when you are not playing. Immersion transports the player into the game and can be a part of a game's soul. Many **social networking** or *social interactive* games use this idea of soul to keep players coming back and playing more. An underlying liking, social consciousness, or empathy for other characters or avatars develops, as illustrated in **Figure 7-7.**

Some avant-garde religious games use this same concept to make the player feel the struggle between good and evil. A situation that places the player in a position to make a hard decision about stealing a loaf of bread to feed their starving family or cancelling a Hawaiian vacation to spend time with a sick friend cause "soul searching" for the best choice. The underlying dilemma of what action you take has an effect on someone else helps the player internally connect to others.

Figure 7-7. Social networking uses avatars. Shown here, many different avatars are gathering for a dance party.

Designing Soul

An example of a game with soul is car-racing game in which the racer is an ambulance driver. The game uses the same general features of a basic car-racing game: start line, finishing destination, crashes, obstacles, and racing. However, the soul, purpose, and emotional connection of this game are very different from a racing game. This driver must make choices on who to take on their next trip from the disaster to the emergency room.

Will you take the injured homeless man or the pregnant woman? A dispatch notice shows you are the only ambulance available for six minutes. You need to make a choice and get them to the hospital as quickly as possible. You still race from the disaster to the hospital with all of the common racing features, but lives are on the line, like those shown in **Figure 7-8.**

If you drive fast enough, you will make it back sooner and be able to help more people. If you crash, your patient must be picked up by the next ambulance. The person you did not choose will not get picked up by the next ambulance and will get sicker as they wait.

Additionally, the game may have real-world annoyances, like cell phone calls from concerned family members who might need your help during this crisis. Other callers might be your boss wanting an update on what you are doing. If you answer the call, the game does not pause. You need to **multitask** when on the phone. Additionally, the driving mechanics work

CHEAT CODE: MULTITASK

Multitasking is doing more than one thing at a time. Each effort is diminished by having some attention focused on the other task. This is one of the reasons talking on a cell phone while driving is discouraged and in some places illegal.

Shutterstock.com

Figure 7-8. When faced with the decision, who do you pick up in your ambulance and take to the hospital first? Is there a correct choice?

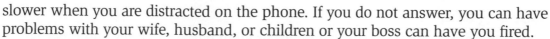

slower when you are distracted on the phone. If you do not answer, you can have problems with your wife, husband, or children or your boss can have you fired.

At the end of the level, the game may have you meet the people you saved and you see a background on that person. It may also show how many people did not make it because you crashed, waited too long, or did not choose them. A biography of these people is also shown.

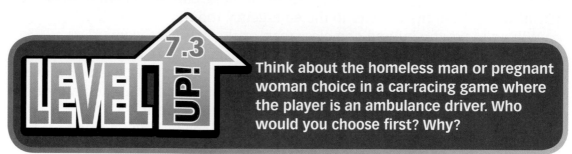

LEVEL UP! 7.3

Think about the homeless man or pregnant woman choice in a car-racing game where the player is an ambulance driver. Who would you choose first? Why?

Reactions to Game Soul

The soul of the car-racing game described in the last section causes many people to have a harsh reaction to the game. These choices are much like those used in simulator trainings. All of the distractions, obstacles, and even forces beyond your control are put in place to make a meaningful experience. The concept may have a perfect solution, but like many things in life, it shows choices and consequences. It makes you think about your motives, your judgment calls, your stereotyping, and your ability to deal with multiple possibilities. After playing, many core gamers find themselves thinking about their choices and how to make better choices in the future.

Is this the future of video games or are all games supposed to be just fun? By changing the rules and the mechanics of a game, you can create a whole new purpose and meaning to a game genre. With the development of strategic and thought-provoking games with soul comes the dilemma of how to define *play*.

Play

The word *play* can be hard to define. Play is a word easily recognized by almost everyone over the age of two. But, this recognition does not mean they know how to define play. Play seems to be redefined as you get older. As a

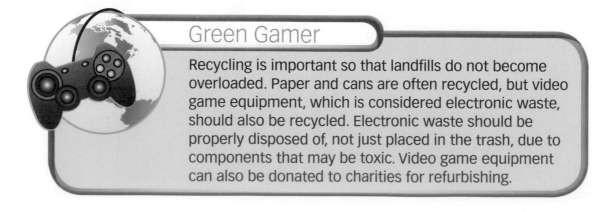

Green Gamer

Recycling is important so that landfills do not become overloaded. Paper and cans are often recycled, but video game equipment, which is considered electronic waste, should also be recycled. Electronic waste should be properly disposed of, not just placed in the trash, due to components that may be toxic. Video game equipment can also be donated to charities for refurbishing.

child, it means anything fun, such as building things with snow as in **Figure 7-9.** Later, as an adult, it means an activity that involves rules and structure to define gameplay.

At the heart of play is the concept of fun or fantasy. Life would simply be all work without play. Play is a break from reality that can take shape as any number of different activities. Some activities may be just fun, while others may be physically demanding.

In looking for a usable synonym for play, no single word would do, as illustrated by the thesaurus shown in **Figure 7-10.** The Microsoft Word thesaurus lists several different synonyms for play. Depending on the context of the sentence and the activities involved, play could mean:

- engage in recreation;
- participate;
- fake;
- a recreational activity;
- fool around;
- pretend;
- theatrical production; or
- perform.

If you look at each of these meanings, you quickly see that each implies an activity outside of the normal routine.

Play to Engage

To engage in recreation is play. Here *play* means to amuse yourself by doing something. As inquisitive beings, humans look for fun and interesting things to do. Different cultures have developed their own idea of what that activity is. But, in general, the point of this engagement is to occupy yourself, amuse yourself, have fun, or simply fool around. An example of this definition would be something like, "I want to play on the slide." There are really no set rules for playing on a slide. Sometimes it

Shutterstock.com

Figure 7-9. For these kids, play means building a snow fort or snowman.

Shutterstock.com

Figure 7-10. The word *play* has many different meanings. Your definition of play may be different from another person's definition.

Figure 7-11.

For children, playing may mean something as simple as having fun on a slide.

Shutterstock.com

is fun to slide down. Other times it is fun to crawl up. The slide is not a game, it is a toy. The activity of playing on the slide is a recreational activity that involves moving around and having fun, as shown in **Figure 7-11.**

Play to Participate

If you ask any small child if they want to play, you might get something unexpected. Children take a broader view of the phrase, "do you want to play," than do adults. A baby interprets play with toys. A school-aged child develops another definition of play as involving participation or cooperation. When asked by another child if they want to play, it means something like, "follow me and we will find something fun to do together." Neither child has any idea what they are going to do, they just want to do something together.

As adults, this idea of play as participation is kept in a context like *playing* the stock market. While the stock market has rules and objectives like many structured video games, an adult does not think of the profits and losses in their account as playing. Here, *play* is really a term used to define participation. Adults are participating in the stock market.

Play Is Fantasy

Remember playing in the backyard or basement as a kid? You did not need much to have fun. You found some toy and used your imagination to create some "non-real" or fantasy use for the toy. This lead to the understanding that non-real objects were **play objects**. A squeaky rubber hammer toy

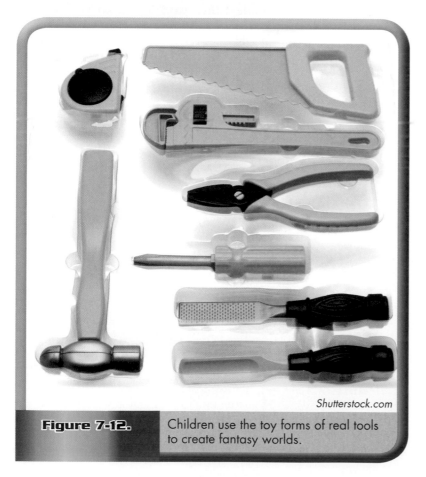

Figure 7-12.   Children use the toy forms of real tools to create fantasy worlds.

Shutterstock.com

became a play hammer and a small clubhouse for kids became a pretend house or fort. **Figure 7-12** shows tool toys that children pretend are real. In these early years, play began to take on the physical form of a fantasy.

Play Is Structure

As you get older, you think of *play* as a structured activity with a goal or purpose. As a recreational activity, you play basketball, football, or other formal recreational activities. The purpose for play changes. Formal rules and a formal ending point or goal of the game provide a structure. This ability to meet an objective helps prepare you for the objectives you will see later in the real world in jobs and family life.

Play Is Being Foolish

When you reach around 10 to 12 years old, you start to imply another definition of *play:* goofing or fooling around. No doubt a teacher or two told you to stop playing and get to work. You were just being a kid that was goofing around, distracted, and not paying attention. This may also be the first time you start to think about play in a negative way. As you mature, there is less play and more work. Playing takes away time from work.

Play Is Pretend

Another action form of *play* means the action is not serious. This adverb form of play can be seen in the phrase, *play fighting.* This is a fake form of fighting, and can be achieved in the real world as well as in video games such as the one shown in **Figure 7-13.**

Play Is Theater

The most literal meaning of the word *play* would come from the world of theater, as illustrated in **Figure 7-14.** In this use, the word means a dramatic performance or show. Many people think of going to see a play as an enjoyable form of entertainment. This adaptation of the word play also implies fake or fantasy. A theatrical play is a fake or fantasy world with characters and costumes.

Figure 7-13. Boxing games, such as this one called *Bully Buster,* are a form of play fighting.

Figure 7-14. In theater, a play is a performance that takes the audience to another place or time.

Shutterstock.com

Play to Perform

www.g-wlearning.com

Level up
your know-how
with Animated
Review 7-1.

Still another version of the word *play* implies the role or part someone undertakes. An example in game design would be your role on the team of those creating a new game. Here you *play* an important role in creating a game world. This adult application of the word *play* refers back to the days when you would play with your friends. It again implies cooperation and participation, but means something serious in adult life when applied to work.

It would take an entire book to explore all of the meanings of *play* that encompass every detail of this seemingly simple word. The reason why this word has developed so many meanings is that the culture and environment of play has evolved throughout history. Each time people learned a new form of entertainment, the definition of play had to change to fit the newest innovation.

Importance of Play

Figure 7-15.

Balance is important in everyday life. Too much play and then not enough work gets done. Too much work and then you do not have time to relax.

Goodheart-Willcox Publisher; images: Shutterstock.com

You should now have some idea of what the structure of play might be. But, why do humans need to play? The old cliché, "all work and no play makes Jack a dull boy," can describe society's opinion for the need to balance work and play, as graphically illustrated in **Figure 7-15.**

Play as Stress Relief

In general, work activities place stress on a person. To balance the amount of stress from work and everyday environments with entertainment, people use play activities. Think about the role a video game plays in this balance. When a player starts a game, they enter a game world. The immersion into the game world allows the player to forget the real-world problems, issues, and concerns causing stress. At least briefly, the environment of the game teleports the player to a fantasy world.

In a video game, a player faces obstacles and challenges, but these challenges do not carry the same kind of stress as found in the real world. The game world allows multiple trials to overcome a set of challenges or obstacles. The real world gives you one try. If you fall off the edge of a cliff in the real world, you are seriously hurt! If you fall off the edge of a cliff in the game world, you can start over. That is a big difference.

In the real world, your body perceives events as life and death trials. Physical reactions and hormones that are triggered by stress cause the body to divert energy to deal with the stress. Since early humans had survival needs to trigger stress, the body still reacts to simple stress as though it is a survival instinct.

For example, a predator animal chasing a prehistoric human would trigger stress hormones in the human. These hormones allowed the body to divert energy to the legs and arms in a fear response known as **fight or flight**. Today's world is not filled with dinosaurs, but the body still interprets flight-or-fight

CHEAT CODE: FIGHT OR FLIGHT

A natural reaction to an attack is to either engage the enemy (fight) or run away from the enemy (flight). Modern reactions to fear and stress still inspire this instinctual reaction.

stresses brought on by the demands in life. That causes some people to act out and pound a desk (fight) and others to run away crying (flight) after getting yelled at by their boss or a teacher, as illustrated by the images in **Figure 7-16.**

Video Games as Stress Relief

Dealing with the challenges in a game may actually cause a calming effect over time. A video game presents challenges that stir up the same fight-or-flight reactions and the release of stress hormones into the body. The difference is that with repeated trials, the body begins to adapt and is slowly trained to

Shutterstock.com

Figure 7-16. Getting mad at a game and hitting your desk is a fight response to a stress. On the other hand, running away from something is a flight response to a stress.

Figure 7-17. The stress of lifting heavier and heavier weights caused this man to develop large muscles to deal with that repeated stress. The same thing happens to your brain. Repeating mental activities helps build stronger memory connections to deal with similar problems.

respond to stress differently. It can be thought of as building up a tolerance to stress, just like you can build up a tolerance for lifting heavy objects. As you lift a weight over and over again, over time your body reacts and slowly builds up muscles in specific areas strained by lifting the weight, as shown in **Figure 7-17.** The same works for stress. Your body builds up stress tolerances that make the burdens of life's challenges easier to handle.

In a real-life example, a pilot must spend hundreds of hours of training in actual flight or a flight simulator, like that shown in **Figure 7-18,** to get a license. The pilot learns to react to situations. The training reduces stress by having the pilot know how to control the plane in almost any situation. Pilot training makes most pilots suppress the fight-or-flight response under normal stressful situations encountered while operating an aircraft.

Figure 7-18. Pilots can use flight simulators to practice various aspects of flying, such as landing in heavy winds. These situations are dangerous in flight and a pilot needs to have mental strength and training to overcome the stress and frustration of the problem.

Imagine what would happen if your pilot became frozen with fear or reacting erratically when there was turbulence. Instead, the pilot remains calm and steady, maintaining stability of the aircraft. Building up a tolerance to the stress of flying an aircraft in bad conditions through the use of simulators allows the pilot to stay calm and land safely.

Game Addiction

Of course, too much play does not pay the bills. There must be a balance of work and play to have a fulfilling life. People who work too much, sometimes called *workaholics,* have some of the highest stress levels in society. Experts agree that stress is bad. But, sometimes people can play too much. Just like the workaholics are out of balance, game addicts are equally out of balance.

Video Game Addiction

Game addicts are people who cannot stop playing games. These players have become physically dependent on the stimulus of gameplay. If this stimulus is removed, they become irritable and depressed. Often, these players need counseling and therapy to help bring their life back in balance.

If someone is addicted to something, they have a compulsive need for it. Students learn about drug addiction in school. You should understand that a drug addict is unable to control the use of drugs. Their body has learned to not only tolerate the drugs, but has become dependent on the drug just to feel normal. This same condition can occur in game addicts. A game addict is someone who cannot stop playing games. For the purpose of this textbook, the focus is on video game addiction, but game addiction can occur in other games as well.

A *video game addiction* is a psychological disorder in which a person feels that they have to play all of the time. This is similar to a gambling addiction. The player's addiction causes them to become isolated from normal social contact. The addict steadily loses track of real-world events and focuses more on game world events. Addiction is a deeper level of isolation than cocooning, which is discussed in Chapter 3. The body becomes used to the stimulus in the game and suffers from withdrawal when it does not receive that stimulus. In video game addiction, the player becomes deeply involved in the game world, and ignores the body's signals for needs such as sleep, as shown in **Figure 7-19.**

Figure 7-19.

Video game addiction can make a player choose the game over friends, family, food, and sleep.

Shutterstock.com

CHEAT CODE: STATUS

The status of an avatar typically increases with level-ups or other features within a game. The level-ups grant the avatar more skills, weapons, and abilities by increasing, for example, from a level 1 mage to a level 2 mage. In some games, the avatar status can change classes when they achieve a high-enough level.

Figure 7-20.

In Pavlov's famous experiment, he would ring a bell whenever he fed his dog. After a while, the dog would salivate whenever the bell was rung, even if there was no food. This is an example of a reward-conditioning behavior.

Shutterstock.com

Fantasy takes over in place of reality. This problem is serious. There are many reports of deaths either directly or indirectly linked to video game addiction.

The reward of achievement is very addictive. Players may feel an intense desire to try to improve the **status** of their avatar. An **avatar** is the representation of a virtual character. If you are receiving rewards for an activity, you will continue to do that activity and become accustomed to the reward.

A good example of the psychology of reward for a specific behavior is Pavlov's dog, as illustrated in **Figure 7-20.** In the experiment of Pavlov's dog, the scientist Ivan Pavlov would ring a bell and then feed his dog. He continued this practice of ringing the bell every time before feeding. The dog's brain began to associate the sound of the bell with eating. At the end of the experiment, Pavlov would ring the bell and the dog would salivate even if no food was present. The dog had physical reactions associated with eating. This **reward-conditioning behavior** can develop with gaming as well.

Massively Multiplayer Online Game Addiction

One of the greatest contributors to the video game addiction phenomenon is the **massively multiplayer online (MMO) games,** such as *RuneScape* shown in **Figure 7-21.** There are four categories of MMO:
- massively multiplayer online role-playing games (MMORPG)
- massively multiplayer online real-time strategy (MMORTS) games
- massively multiplayer online first-person shooter (MMOFPS) games
- massively multiplayer online social games (MMOSG)

These games, like *Second Life, World of Warcraft,* and *RuneScape,* offer a game world with interactions between thousands of people playing at any one time. A player's online persona is represented by the game avatar, like

Figure 7-21.

RuneScape is one example of a massively multiplayer online game.

those shown in **Figure 7-22.** Relationships are formed with other players through their avatars.

Some argue that MMOs are an extended social interaction within a fantasy world. Others feel that MMOs provide no real social interaction because the people and situations are not real. Either way, the effect of becoming too deeply immersed in these games causes loss of reality skills. MMOs, however, are not in and of themselves a problem. There are some really great features about these games that help contribute to online economies and community building. The key to playing MMOs, as with all video games, is to obtain balance.

MMO social games and role playing games rely on having a large number of players to create interaction. Each player creates a custom avatar and assigns character traits of their choice. A player need not create a literal image of themselves. For example, you could be young, but play as an old wizard. You can have any fantasy characteristics allowed by the game world.

Figure 7-22.

In the world of online gaming, you are represented by an avatar. Many games allow you to customize the look of your avatar, such as selecting different hair, eye, or skin color.

Ethical Gamer

Ethics is a set of rules that define what is wrong and right. Ethics helps people make good decisions in both personal and professional lives. Ethics is very important when interacting with other players in online games.

In MMO games, the player character is usually defined by the four dominant actions of MMO games. Each player will seek to select the character class that most closely fits his or her personal tolerance for each of these elements of MMO gameplay. When selecting an MMO class, players consider which type of character fits them best.

The four primary character elements are:

- killer
- talker
- explorer
- achiever

The descriptions of the character elements in the next sections describe extreme characters. Most players are a combination of these elements. A player might be 30 percent killer, 10 percent talker, 30 percent explorer, and 40 percent achiever. The combination of these attributes makes each player interesting and the interactions fun. Additionally, players generally select avatars that match their personalities.

Playing a game as a warrior or hunter might indicate a high percentage of the killer element. Playing the same game as a monk might indicate high percentage of the explorer elements or as a mage might indicate more of the talker element. The combination of elements helps align the player with the character and draw the player into the game. This alignment between the person and the character can, unfortunately, lead to a player's loss of self to the game and the addiction previously discussed.

Killer Character Element

The killer player element measures how much you enjoy being at risk and thrive on the joy of being in danger. If you like the idea of killing other players and taking the risk that your skill will overpower and defeat another, then you are a killer. Most players are not pure killers and enjoy other aspects of the game.

Talker Character Element

The talker is a social character. The talker enjoys chatting and communicating with other players. Even a killer has some talker elements. A killer might join a team to attack a location or enemy stronghold. So a killer need not just be a player versus player, antisocial character. The talker uses the game to extend friendships and develop allies. Talkers also create blogs, articles, walkthroughs, and other social content to help players.

Explorer Character Element

The explorer is excited by the activity of searching and finding. Even if the task is not part of the requirements to complete the level, an explorer might search for Easter eggs or alternate pathways within the level. Explorers often find uses for those often overlooked weapons as well. An explorer might just want to see how something works.

CASE STUDY

Video Game Addiction Treatment

Smith & Jones Addiction Consultants in Amsterdam, Netherlands, is a facility that treats teenagers with video game addictions. Here, patients that cannot stop playing games are given support and training to deal with this problem. The idea is to treat video game addiction in the same way as alcohol or drug addiction in a detox, or detoxifying, model.

Kids and teenagers that are identified with online or video game addiction often exhibit some of these behavioral characteristics:

- Spend more and more time playing games.
- Obsessing about events in the game environment.
- Becoming depressed or angry if they are unable to play.
- Not eating or sleeping to keep playing.
- Preferring their virtual life over their real life.
- Lying to hide the amount of time spent playing games.

With computers and cell phones as part of everyday life, the detox program re-teaches patients how to increase interaction in the real world and to balance computer use for work and play. This may include avoidance of highly addictive RPG games, especially those that are played online by computer and cell phone.

Shutterstock.com

Video game addicts often become depressed when they cannot play games.

If you think you or someone you know might be addicted to games, contact a guidance counselor to get help.

Shutterstock.com

Counseling can help video game addicts recover.

Achiever Character Element

The achiever wants to get to the objectives and move on quickly. Achievers are usually not very good explorers. As an achiever, leveling up and increasing status is the main driving goal. If the level needs 100 coins to advance, an achiever gets the 100 coins and does not spend time looking for any additional coins or exploring the game. The achiever will beat the game and move on to the next.

Player Types

The two basic types of video game player are core gamers and casual gamers. While core gamers attract the most attention, they are not the majority. Most video game players fall into the casual gaming category. Casual gamers make up as much as 90 percent of the total gaming population.

Core Gamers

Core gamers are players that frequently play video games and actively devote time to playing games. This player type will primarily play games that involve action and skill and play those games on a console or PC. Many core gamers purchase and play the newest and most popular game titles immediately on release of the game. If you are a core gamer, you may spend a large portion of your entertainment time playing video games. Most of the issues with addiction come from core gamers.

Casual Gamers

Casual gamers infrequently play video games. They are usually not dedicated to a specific game or genre of games. A casual gamer is looking for an exciting game that will be entertaining until he or she must do something else. If a casual gamer gets bored with a game, he or she will simply switch to another game.

This does not mean that the casual gamer is to be ignored. With the emergence of handheld devices, casual gamers have more access to short-term entertainment. The app market for smartphones and tablets has boomed in recent years. With a few taps of the screen, a casual gamer can play a game demo and buy a new game, most of which sell for under three dollars.

Hits such as *Angry Birds* have demonstrated the market value of casual gamers. *Angry Birds* had a reported $140,000 development and marketing budget. With revenue in excess of $70 million, this simple yet entertaining game has profits that rival large-scale console games. Other top selling casual games, such as *Tetris* and *Bejeweled,* have also raked in large profits by obtaining small per-unit profits from millions of casual gamers.

Online Community

A **community** is considered to be any social structure in which people exchange ideas. The two basic requirements for any community are the ability to communicate and membership in the community. **Communication,** or community interaction, is established through the use of forums, chat rooms, blogs, bulletin boards, instant messaging, and player interactions.

In many MMOs, there are realistic imitations of social and economic dynamics. Socially, players can communicate and exchange ideas, plan strategies, and more. Many online gamers develop virtual friendships and strong virtual interpersonal relationships with the other gamers in the MMO. This is a positive outlet to some people. Since most people who play a game have a similar interest, they can easily communicate on that interest level. This conversation builds as members join until it becomes a community with many members.

Of course, a community needs members. **Members** are the people who contribute to the conversation. If you have too few members or members leave, your community fails. One way to keep members is to regulate use and create rules so members will not alienate others. The **end user license agreement (EULA)** is this set of rules that every member must agree to before they are permitted to join, an example of which is shown in **Figure 7-23.** If a single user posts something that upsets another member, it can be reported and investigated. The comment is typically removed and the posting player is given a warning. If abuses continue, the player can be removed and not allowed back into the community.

Breaking the rules in an MMO can result in the player's status being downgraded, a warning, temporary suspension of play, or termination of the player's membership in the community. Gaming companies that receive fees for joining do not want a single player to cause other paying members to leave. Additionally, negative behavior by members reflects poorly on the gaming company.

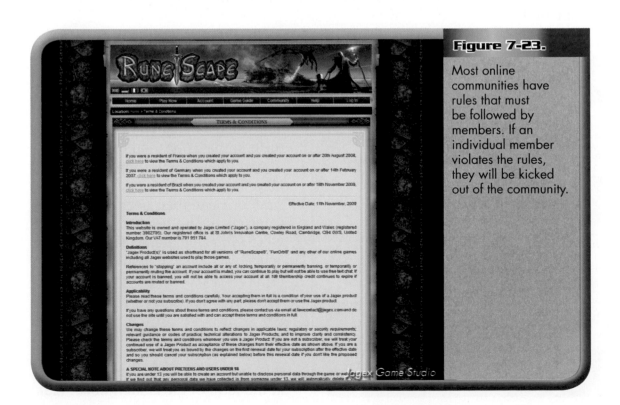

Figure 7-23.

Most online communities have rules that must be followed by members. If an individual member violates the rules, they will be kicked out of the community.

Online Economy

Another positive aspect of an MMO is the online economy. This economy is broken down into the provider economy and the player economy.

The **provider economy** describes how the game manufacturer obtains money for their games and services. Many providers of MMOs use a monthly subscription fee to pay for the maintenance and upkeep of the site. A company might also allow paid advertising to help offset the cost of operation. Sometimes the advertising revenues are enough to pay the bills and no monthly fee is required. When a company advertises on a site, they pay a set amount for each time the advertisement is shown. Many sites call these advertisers **sponsors.** Without sponsors, players must pay fees. Another form of the provider economy comes from the downloading of games, upgrades, and information for a fee.

Most of the transactions by players are handled with credit cards or online accounts. Monthly fees and other products are billed to a player's credit card. Some online communities accept an **online account service,** like PayPal. An online account service is like a bank account that holds money. People can use the money in their accounts to purchase products online or transfer the money back to a regular bank account.

Online account services can also receive monetary credits. Some game companies actually pay players. In these games, fees paid for monthly access are redistributed to establish an economy. This is the **player economy.** Here, players can trade for game weapons, skills, land, or other items. Players can buy or sell with money from an online account service. This takes video games to a whole new level of interaction. An incentive beyond entertainment is created.

Figure 7-24. Shown is the money from real countries. Will a global virtual cash eventually make these currencies obsolete?

In these cases, the game world is interacting with the real world through the purchase of tangible items. Imagine an online game world where you have an avatar. You see lots of leftover items and trash in the game. You then establish a set of rules in the game where players pay you to pick up their trash or clean their pets. You receive game credits from other players, which you can later exchange for actual cash, like that shown in **Figure 7-24.** Games are doing this to gain interest and develop their interactive game world.

The game *Second Life* and the teen version, *Teen Second Life,* use this model. The game issues credits in the form of the **Linden dollar (L$).**

The game creators allow Linden dollars to be exchanged for actual currency. At the time this textbook was published, roughly 205 L$ equal one US dollar. Players with a large amount of L$ will offer those for sale to players who need L$ to purchase items in the game. An example of how the real and game economies can interact is:

1. One player needs virtual cash (like the L$) to buy land in the game.
2. Another player has extra virtual cash and wants some real money to buy a new video game.
3. The two players agree to exchange virtual cash for real cash.
4. The first player has the virtual cash needed to buy land in the game. The second player has real cash to buy a new video game, as illustrated in **Figure 7-25.**

With actual money involved, these online communities face some interesting legal issues. The Internet reaches around the globe, as illustrated in **Figure 7-26.** Issues exist when players from other countries expect that the laws of their country function to govern the use of the site. This is not true. Players must abide by the laws of the country where the game activity is actually occurring. The laws of some countries differ from US law on acceptable online content and money exchanges. Collecting taxes from the money generated from playing the game can also be a tricky legal issue.

The online actions and comments of players can also violate obscenity laws. Additionally, case law has been formed by players suing the manufacturer when they were banned from the game. In one case, a *Second Life* player was banned

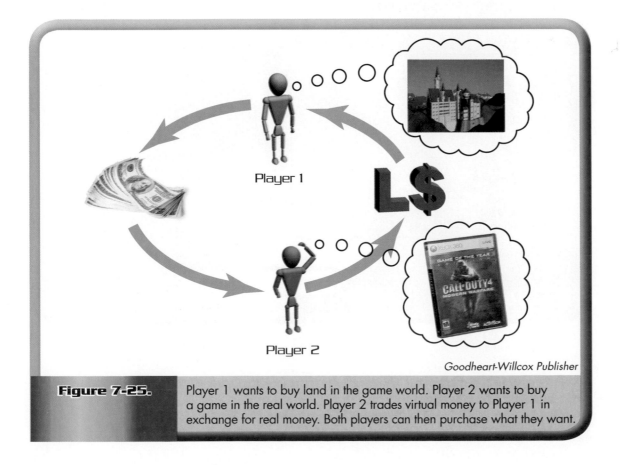

Player 1

L$

Player 2

Goodheart-Willcox Publisher

Figure 7-25. Player 1 wants to buy land in the game world. Player 2 wants to buy a game in the real world. Player 2 trades virtual money to Player 1 in exchange for real money. Both players can then purchase what they want.

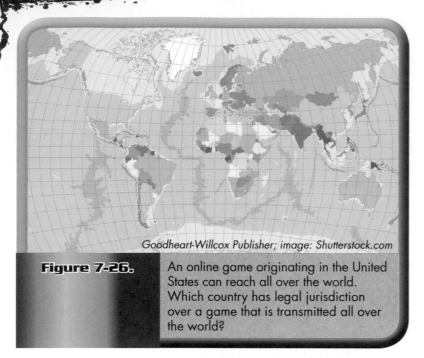

Goodheart-Willcox Publisher; image: Shutterstock.com

Figure 7-26. An online game originating in the United States can reach all over the world. Which country has legal jurisdiction over a game that is transmitted all over the world?

and all of the player's property in the game was deleted. The player sued for real money damages. Since game currency is easily exchanged for real cash, the reasoning was that the manufacturer violated the player's business interests. This case was settled out of court for an undisclosed amount, and the player was reinstated with all property and gaming rights. Without clear legal definitions for the use of new technology like online communities, governments and manufacturers struggle between the enforcement of the EULA and the privacy and other legal rights of the players, **Figure 7-27.**

Figure 7-27.

Laws in other countries are different from US laws. This makes it hard to legally define some rules for a game that may be played all over the world.

Shutterstock.com

Chapter Summary

- The three driving factors in game design are the market, the game designer, and technology.
- The purpose of play in a game is the reason for playing it while the soul of a game is the central component that makes a game come alive and become important to the player.
- The term *play* can mean a variety of things, including: play to engage, play to participate, play as fantasy, play as structure, play is being foolish, play is pretend, a play in a theater, and play to perform (as in a role).
- Play is important for people because it is a break from reality.
- Play, for adults, provides a balance to the stresses of work and other commitments.
- The primary player types are the core gamer and the casual gamer.
- Online communities have realistic imitations of social and economic dynamics, including communicating and exchanging ideas as well as provider economies and player economies.
- Video game addiction is a psychological disorder in which a person feels that they have to play all of the time.

Check Your Video Game IQ

Now that you have finished this chapter, see what you know about video game design by taking the chapter posttest.

www.m.g-wlearning.com

www.g-wlearning.com

Review Your Knowledge

On a separate sheet of paper or in a word processing document, match the following terms with the definitions that fit best.

A. community
B. game addict
C. player-centric design
D. designer-centric games
E. provider economy
F. avatar
G. designer-driven games
H. casual gamer
I. market-drive design
J. core gamer

1. A game build focused on the design process; often a commercial failure.
2. How the game manufacturer obtains money for its games and services.
3. Making a game based on research of what the target market is looking to buy.
4. Player that plays infrequently when he or she has free time.
5. A game build showcasing the artistic and programming skills of the game designer.
6. People who cannot stop playing games.

7. Game built focused on what the player wants to experience in the game.

8. Player that play frequently and actively devotes time to playing games.

9. Social structure in which people share and exchange ideas.

10. Player's online persona represented in a game.

On a separate sheet of paper or in a word processing document, answer each of the following questions.

11. List the three driving factors that lead to game design.

12. Define *player-centric design.*

13. What is *market research?*

14. Describe a *focus group,* as related to game development.

15. How is a *sight study* used in game development?

16. The focus of _____ games centers on the design process, not on the wants and needs of the player.

17. Which type of game is made to take advantage of new hardware, user interface, or game platform?

18. Define *purpose of play.*

19. What is the *soul of the game?*

20. What is lacking from a social networking game to make it a true game?

21. Define *multitasking.*

22. Adults look to play as a competition with rules and structure, while children look to play as anything _____.

23. It is important to achieve a good _____ between work and play.

24. Describe one way in which someone with a flight response to fear may react to being yelled at by a boss or teacher.

25. Describe one way in which someone with a fight response to fear may react to being yelled at by a boss or teacher.

26. Define *video game addiction.*

27. What is the main difference between casual gamer and core gamer player types?

28. What is an MMO?

29. Describe the reward-conditioning behavior of Pavlov's dog.

30. Which character element is dominant in a player who enjoys finding hidden objectives or new uses for game objects?

31. What are the two items needed to build a community?

32. What is an EULA and what is its purpose for online communities?

33. Describe a *provider economy.*

34. List two ways online communities and games pay the expenses of maintaining and upgrading the site.

35. Describe a *player economy.*

Apply Your STEM Knowledge

Science

1. Research the term *stress* and the negative effects of stress on the human body. Prepare a presentation to describe stress and how play is used to relieve stress.

Social Studies

2. Observe some children playing. Write a one-page paper to describe the purpose of play for the group and the social interactions observed.

Mathematics

3. Create a table to show how many hours you spend each day outside of school engaged in:
   ○ working (school work);
   ○ playing video games;
   ○ Internet/mobile activities (research, Facebook, web surfing, texting, etc.); and
   ○ playing without video games.
   Total your hours for each column for the week, and create a bar graph and a pie graph to display the data.

Social Studies

4. *Second Life* currency (Linden dollars) has a trade-in value to real currency like the US dollar. Other world currencies trade on exchanges and have value equal to the US dollar (USD). Conduct research to find the data needed to complete the table below. Identify the currency used in each of the countries and the amount needed to equal $1 from the United States. Use a separate sheet of paper for your answers. If the exchange rate of the Linden dollar is currently different, change those values.

Location	Currency Name	Amount = to 1 USD	Value of 5000 L$
Second Life	Linden Dollar	205	$24
Canada			
England			
Japan			
Mexico			
China			
Brazil			
Switzerland			
Germany			

Mathematics

5. Use the information from the table you completed in #4 to determine how much 5000 Linden dollars (L$) are worth in each country's currency.

Working in Teams

In teams, research, debate, and form a group opinion on each of the Level Up! activities in this chapter. Prepare a PowerPoint presentation of ten slides (five to seven minutes) to present to the class explaining the group's opinions for each Level Up! activity. Include text, pictures, video, animations, and slide transitions as appropriate to help explain your positions.

Gamer Portfolio

Community service is an important quality that interviewers expect in a candidate. Serving the community shows that the candidate is well rounded and socially aware. In this activity, you will create a list of your contributions to nonprofit organizations. Many opportunities are available for young people to serve the community. You might volunteer for a community clean-up project. Perhaps you enjoy reading to residents in a senior-living facility. Maybe raising money for a homeless-animal shelter appeals to you. Whatever your interests, there is sure to be a related service project. Plan to update this list when you have new activities to add.

1. List the service projects or volunteer activities in which you have taken part. Give the organization or person's name, the dates, and the activities that you performed. If you received a certificate or award related to this service, mention it here.

2. Give the document an appropriate name, using the naming system you created earlier. Place the file in your e-portfolio.

3. Place a copy of the list in the container for your print portfolio.

G-W Learning Mobile Site

Visit the G-W Learning mobile site to complete the chapter pretest and posttest and to practice vocabulary using e-flash cards. If you do not have a smartphone, visit the G-W Learning companion website to access these features.

G-W Learning mobile site: www.m.g-wlearning.com

G-W Learning companion website: www.g-wlearning.com

Common Core

College and Career Readiness

CTE Career Ready Practices. Read the Ethical Gamer features presented throughout this book. What role do you think that ethics and integrity have in decision making? Think of a time when you used your ideals and principles to make a decision. What process did you use to make the decision? In retrospect, do you think you made the correct decision? Did your decision have any consequences?

Speaking and Listening. Research the importance of play in cultures around the world. Compile information about the aspects of play in different societies today versus 50 years ago. Use this information to create a timeline of how play has changed within that timeframe. Using various elements (visual displays, written handouts, technological displays), present your timeline to the class. Explain why you chose to highlight the features of play and the specific points in time that you did. Be sure to use the appropriate vocabulary related to the industry. As you listen to your classmates' stances on this topic, take notes and ask questions about positions or terms you do not understand.

Writing. Research the history of social networking. Where did the concept of social networking originate? Write an informative report, consisting of several paragraphs to describe your findings.

Event Prep: Essays

Writing an essay may be a competitive entrepreneurship event offered by your Career and Technical Student Organization (CTSO). This may be an individual or team event with two parts: the written essay and the oral presentation of the essay. The essay may be focused on careers or selected topics. Good writing and communication skills are very important to present the research completed on the assigned topic. Completion of the essay may be required prior to the event or at the event. Written events can be lengthy and take a lot of time to prepare. Therefore, it is important to start early. To prepare for writing an essay:

1. Read the guidelines provided by your organization. There will be specific directions on how the essay should be presented. In addition, all final formatting guidelines will be given, including how to organize and submit the final paper. Make certain that you ask any questions about points that you do not understand.

2. The CTSO may give a topic for you to research. If a topic is not given, select a topic related to video game design that is of interest to you.

3. Do your research early. Research may take days or weeks, and you do not want to rush the process.

4. Visit your CTSO's website and create a checklist of the guidelines for the event.

5. Set a deadline for yourself so that you write at a comfortable pace.

6. After you write your first draft, ask a teacher to review it and give you feedback.

7. Once you have the final version of your essay, review your checklist. Make sure you have addressed all requirements. You will be penalized on your score if a direction is not followed exactly.

Level Up!
You gained 1 Talent Point

Current Level Progress

Chapter 8

Reverse Engineering and Professional Reviews

 **M**any game design companies are hiring people to write critiques of their games and examine the key features and USPs of the competition to identify ways to improve existing games. To determine the overall quality of a game, it must be evaluated to figure out what makes it work. In this chapter, you will explore reviewing and reverse engineering a game. In so doing, you will see how bias can affect a review of the ten key elements of a game and how copyright laws protect intellectual property.

Check Your Video Game IQ

Before you begin this chapter, see what you already know about video game design by taking the chapter pretest.

www.m.g-wlearning.com

www.g-wlearning.com

College and Career Readiness

Reading Prep. In preparation for reading the chapter, consider what the term ethics means to you. Have you ever been confronted with an ethical dilemma? As you read, focus on how ethics influence many of the safeguards against copyright infringement in video game design.

Objectives

After completing this chapter, you will be able to:

- Explain intellectual property as it relates to video game development.
- Analyze various aspects of a game, such as rules, gameplay, and longevity of design.
- Describe techniques used by the video game industry to analyze games.
- Conduct a critical review of a video game.
- Compare the plot, interactivity, and reward system of commercial video games.

Reverse Engineering

As you begin to develop skills for your own video game designs, you will also begin to understand the logic and programming in other games. It becomes easier to understand the collision theory and scrolling in the Mario Brothers games:

IF Mario collides with the coin, **THEN** add points to the score and destroy the coin and play a sound and count the coins.

Once you master the **IF/THEN/ELSE** logic and understand some of the other underlying programming that makes a game work, you can reverse engineer almost any game, like the one shown in **Figure 8-1.**

Reverse Engineering Process

www.g-wlearning.com

Level up
your know-how
with Animated
Review 8-1.

Reverse engineering is the process of deconstructing an existing game to understand how it works. This is kind of like taking apart your computer to see how each part works. When a piece of new technology comes to market, the competitors will purchase the item, take it apart, and see how it works. This reverse engineering is done to quickly understand the unique selling point (USP) of the competition. If a company feels a competitor has a USP that will cut into their sales, it will reverse engineer the technology, then quickly make a version of the same thing.

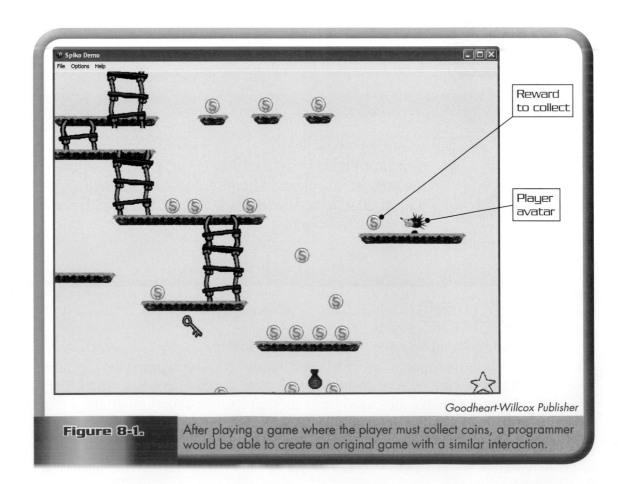

Goodheart-Willcox Publisher

Figure 8-1. After playing a game where the player must collect coins, a programmer would be able to create an original game with a similar interaction.

Video game companies are constantly reverse engineering the games their competitors make. In your own experience, you must have noticed how many copycat games are out there. A *copycat game* is one that has gameplay similar to another game already on the market. In the example of Mario Brothers, there are thousands of copycat side-scrolling games with characters that collect coins or other rewards. Since Mario Brothers was a success, the competition tried to bring a similar product to the marketplace to get some of that business. Nintendo even copied itself with the release of *Wario,* shown in **Figure 8-2.** In this case, any of the copycats was a substitute product for the real version.

Goodheart-Willcox Publisher

Figure 8-2. The character of Wario is a copycat of Mario. Nintendo was capitalizing on the success of their own character when they created the Wario games.

As a **substitute product,** a game would satisfy the same need or want of the original. The substitute game is designed to play and entertain in the same way as the original game. So, a copycat game is always a substitute game, but a substitute game may not be a copycat. A substitute game may simply be a game in the same genre as the popular original.

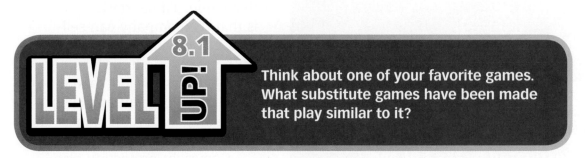

Think about one of your favorite games. What substitute games have been made that play similar to it?

Copyright Issues

Characters within a game are **copyrighted.** This means they cannot be used without permission. The characters used in Mario Brothers are copyrighted and cannot be used without permission from Nintendo. Of course, Nintendo is not going to give you permission to copy their character, so you will still have to design your own characters. Computer code is also copyrighted.

In reverse engineering, you can create a game with the same function, rules, victory condition, and user interface. However, if you copy the game too closely, you will be guilty of copyright infringement. **Copyright infringement** is the unauthorized copying of intellectual property. There are laws to protect against copyright infringement and consequences of breaking those laws, as shown **Figure 8-3.**

Figure 8-3.

Copyright infringement is a serious issue. If you violate copyright laws, you could end up in jail.

Shutterstock.com

CHEAT CODE: ORIGINAL CREATION

An original creation is something of your own design. It can be based on other ideas, but it must be recognizably different from any other original creations.

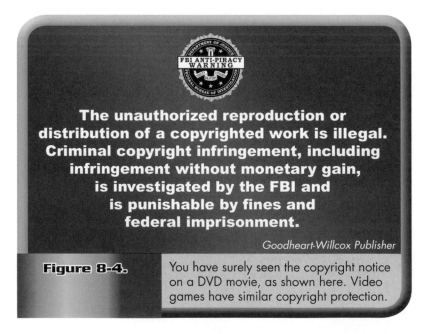

FBI ANTI-PIRACY WARNING

The unauthorized reproduction or distribution of a copyrighted work is illegal. Criminal copyright infringement, including infringement without monetary gain, is investigated by the FBI and is punishable by fines and federal imprisonment.

Goodheart-Willcox Publisher

Figure 8-4.

You have surely seen the copyright notice on a DVD movie, as shown here. Video games have similar copyright protection.

Intellectual property is something original from someone's mind or intellect. In other words, intellectual property is an **original creation**. Intellectual property can be something artistic or creative in nature, like a movie, play, book, character, game, painting, sculpture, and so on. It can also be an engineering design or computer code. For a person to write a book, create a painting, or develop a video game, a certain amount of time and skill are required. The end result is intellectual property and protected by copyright laws.

From a business standpoint, copyrights protect the company, their USP, and their profits. If a company has a copyrighted character like Mario, other companies cannot use Mario or a Mario-like character in their game. This allows the original company to protect their work and marketing effort to promote that game. The underlying benefit is that the company can sell their game and make a profit. Without copyright protection, companies would not take the risk of development and spend the money to develop games or advertise them.

Copyright protection also applies to the game discs as well. It is illegal to copy a game disc, DVD movie, or any other commercial media without permission, as is explained in the familiar FBI Anti-Piracy warning shown in **Figure 8-4.** The punishment for violating a copyright could include a fine, jail, paying damages, and paying the attorney fees for the copyright holder. In the United States, if you copy even one game disc and give it to your friend you are guilty of copyright infringement. This is true even if you do not sell it. International laws also help protect copyrights.

Copyright infringement is a major concern for game companies. When someone copies a game disc and gives it to a friend, the game company losses money, as illustrated in **Figure 8-5.** To prevent copying, the game companies try to make it difficult for the game discs to be copied. Using unusually sized discs, unique disc formats, and embedded copy-resistance codes all help eliminate unauthorized copying. Many games and programs use the Internet to log in and obtain an activation code. Without the activation code, the program will not work. The activation code will only work a set number of times, usually only once. In that way, a game cannot be installed more than the allowed number of times. All of these methods are considered **copy protection**.

CHEAT CODE: COPY PROTECTION

Copy protection is a method used to prevent unauthorized copies from being made. Computer software has used copy protection for decades. In the early days, a user may have been required to enter a word located in a specific location in the user's manual. In other cases, a device called a hardware key had to be installed in one of the computer's serial ports. Now, software keys are the most common form of copy protection.

Player A

Player B

Goodheart-Willcox Publisher

Figure 8-5. This is why copyright protection is important to companies. If player A buys a game from the company and gives a copy to player B, no money goes to the company from player B. However, if player B plays the game at player A's house and then buys a personal copy from the company, the company makes money.

Copyright of intellectual property is a concern for reverse engineering. It is illegal to copy the code used by the original design company. But, it is okay if you design your own code and artwork that achieve the same end result. Ideas cannot be copyrighted. In many cases, it can be hard to determine which parts of a copycat game are original designs and which parts are reverse engineered designs. The burden is on the copycat company to assure that the design is original and not copied from the original program.

When a company reverse engineers a competitor's game, it is looking at the specific techniques, logic, mechanics, and graphics used. If there is a new technology or programming technique, reverse engineering seeks to duplicate the *effect* of that technology. This allows the company to capitalize on the USP created by its competitor. Reverse engineering is one reason why there are several different games with the same theme or in the same genre. Key elements in a new game on the market are analyzed by other companies, and then they develop a substitute game to compete with the existing game.

LEVEL UP! 8.2

Think about a time when you or someone you know watched a copied movie, played a copied game, or downloaded and listened to a copied song. Each of these copies violates a copyright. What would you say to the police if you were caught?

Ownership Rights and Contracts

The most critical legal standing is ownership. When you make a new and original game or piece of artwork, you are the owner…sometimes. Take a look at how this might happen. If you paint a picture and no one has asked you or paid you to do this, you are the owner. However, if someone has paid you to paint the picture, then that person is often the owner, depending on the contract between you and the other person. The difference is the contract.

When you are hired at a game design studio, you will likely be required to sign a contract. That contract will lay out the rules for what the company owns and what you own. The wording of the contract may even give ownership to the company of something you create at home on your own time. This may sound harsh, but think of it like homework. When you do homework, the intent is that the work will be turned over to your teacher. That holds true for most work you do from home for a company that hires you. Your contract will likely state that the company has exclusive rights of ownership of any works you produce on behalf of the company or of a derivative work.

In some cases, you may not be hired as an employee of the company. Instead, you may be a freelancer engaged in a work-for-hire contract. A **work-for-hire contract** states what you are expected to produce, the starting and ending dates of the work, and what you will be paid. The contract should also state the company owns the work you produce and if you may use the work in any way. The work-for-hire contract will state any benefits to be received.

In most cases, a freelancer will not receive any company benefits such as vacation or health insurance. If it is not stated on the contract, you do not receive it.

An **exclusive right** allows the creative work to be used or reproduced only by the person or company who owns the contract, or to whomever they give permission to do so. That means you are not even allowed to use it for yourself. This also includes any derivative works. A **derivative work** is anything based on, or derived, from any part of the original. An example of a derivative work is putting your face on the game character Master Chief. The original character is the original work. You used part of the original work to make a new character. That makes the new character a derivative of the original. So, if you work for a game design company and build a really cool game, you cannot just change the name and sell it on your own.

A good working knowledge of copyrights and other means of protecting your work is important to ensure you keep possession of your creative works or are paid for your work. Make sure you read and understand all parts of a contract before you sign it. If you do not understand something, ask questions and get legal advice from a qualified person. Saying you did not know something was illegal or violated your contract is not a legal defense.

Agreements

A company may require you to sign a confidentiality agreement and noncompete agreement. Both of these agreements are to help keep information secret from other companies with similar products.

A **confidentiality agreement** is a contract that states you cannot share any information about the company or its products with any other company. This protects your employer from developing a game and having the employees leak information to the press or other game companies. A leak might destroy the competitive advantage for the game and make it hard to make a profit.

A **noncompete agreement** is a contract that states you cannot create work that competes with the company while you are employed by it and for a certain period of time after you leave the company. Most noncompete agreements in the game industry are for six months or one year. The company makes a financial investment when they hire you, not only in your salary, but in the potential money it may earn from products on which you work. A noncompete agreement prevents you from taking what you know about the company and its current products and going to a competing company.

Copyrights

The owner of a creative work will want to protect the work from being copied. The United States and most other countries have **copyright laws** to protect the owner of a creative work. Under US copyright laws, as soon as a creative work is in **tangible** form, it is automatically copyrighted.

CHEAT CODE: TANGIBLE

Tangible means capable of being perceived. In this sense, a creative work is tangible as soon as it can be seen or heard.

Misusing or making unauthorized copies of a copyrighted work is called *copyright infringement.* In the United States, copyright infringement carries a heavy penalty. For example, any motion picture you rent or purchase carries a warning similar to the one shown in **Figure 8-5.** Violators can end up in prison or be fined. Some people found this out the hard way when downloading music. Downloading a copyrighted song without permission is an infringement on the copyright of the creative work (music), regardless of whether or not money exchanged hands. Many people were found guilty of copyright infringement and were ordered to pay a penalty of between $750 and $30,000 per download. Some ended up having to pay millions of dollars in fines and penalties.

Copyright laws are both statutory and case. *Statutory laws* have been passed by the legislature. Written into the law is a formal definition of how the law is to be interpreted. *Case laws* are enacted when the first lawsuit to deal with the problem has determined the outcome. That case is then cited in other lawsuits as an example of previous judgment (called precedence). Case law is very important because the legislature cannot enact all of the laws needed as society and technology change.

There are some legal ways to copy and use creative works without getting permission from the owner. These concepts include Creative Commons licenses, fair use/fair dealing doctrine, and public domain. A copyright holder may assign a *Creative Commons license* to the work so it can be used for free with or without restrictions, as shown in **Figure 8-6.** Often, a Creative Commons license may require citing authorship and prevent derivative works.

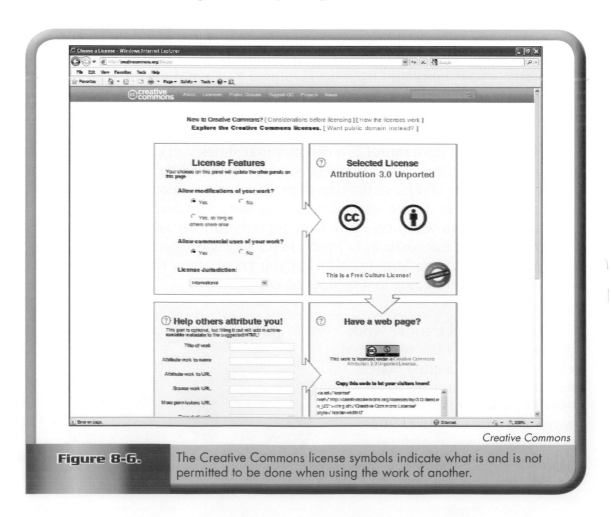

Creative Commons

Figure 8-6. The Creative Commons license symbols indicate what is and is not permitted to be done when using the work of another.

The *fair use/fair dealings doctrine* also allows a creative work to be used without permission, but under very strict guidelines. The fair use/fair dealings doctrine allows someone to reprint or display a copyrighted work without permission for the purpose of describing or reviewing the creative work. That means a student can write a paper about *Halo 3* and include a picture of the game box and the characters. Students, critics, and bloggers often use the fair use/fair dealings doctrine when reproducing pictures or other content. Newspapers and other media also use this doctrine as a tool to report the facts. This doctrine does *not,* however, allow reproducing any copyrighted work outside of the context of describing or reviewing the work nor does it allow claiming the copyrighted work as your own.

When a creative work has been around for a long time, it is placed in the public domain. **Public domain** applies to any work for which the copyright term has expired. It means any and all copyrights on the work have been removed. When the copyright expires, there is no more legal protection preventing duplication and these works are free to use. The concept of public domain assumes that the creative work holds little or no value after a long time. The law establishes different time periods for different types of intellectual property to hold copyright. For example, in the United States the term for work published since 1978 is the life of the creator plus 70 years.

Antipiracy Measures

Piracy is theft. Besides the law, an artist or game designer may want to protect work by making it hard to copy. A game company may use a **software key code** to unlock the game software and allow only one installation. After the game is installed once, it cannot be installed again. To protect works like digital art, tactics such as digital watermarks are used. A **digital watermark** is something that makes the image unusable as final artwork, but allows somebody to review the art for potential use, as shown in **Figure 8-7.** To use the artwork, you must contact the artist or company offering the artwork to obtain a final version without the watermark.

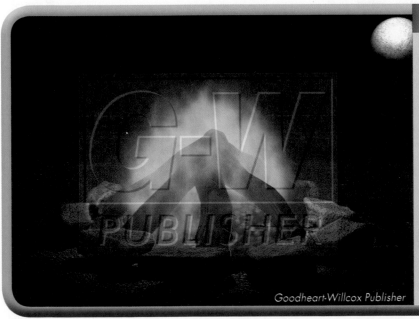

Figure 8-7.

Digital watermarks are commonly placed on images that can be downloaded from the Internet. These images can be viewed and downloaded as samples, but if someone wanted to actually use them, they would need to purchase a copy to obtain one without the watermark.

Goodheart-Willcox Publisher

CASE STUDY

Reverse Engineering the Wii Remote

The Wii remote has two features that allow it to recognize movement. The technologies of accelerometers and infrared triangulation enable the Wii remote to sense speed, direction, and position in space.

The first feature is the accelerometers. These are not unique to the Wii remote. They are used in many electronic devices, even the PS3 six-axis controller. An accelerometer is a device to read the direction and speed of travel of the controller. The technology to accomplish this is actually very simple.

If you place a marble in a box and shake the box, the marble hits the sides, top, and bottom of the box. If a sensor is placed on each side of the box to measure how hard the marble hits that part of the box, you have a simple accelerometer.

The Wii remote uses a similar technology, but much smaller. It involves using a proof mass (like the marble) and tiny silicon springs attached to it. When the Wii remote is tilted in any direction, the springs attached to the proof mass either stretch or compress. The controller reads how much each spring moves and sends that information to the game console to make the movement on screen.

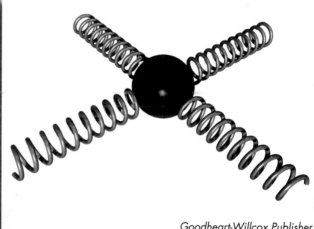

Goodheart-Willcox Publisher

The accelerometer in a Wii remote is a proof mass connected to small springs made of silicon.

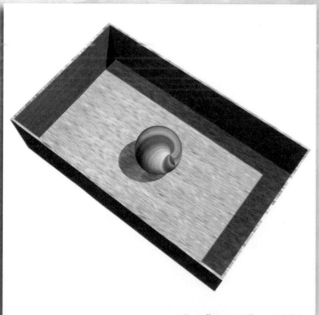

Goodheart-Willcox Publisher

To understand how an accelerometer works, think of a marble in a box. When the box moves, the marble will also move.

The accelerometers only read speed and direction of movement. The console needs to also tell where the remote is located. To do this, it uses infrared triangulation. Infrared is the wavelength of light sent out or emitted by the Wii console. Two LED lights set apart from each other generate the infrared light. The console then measures the distance from each LED to the Wii remote. These measurements are used to triangulate the location of the remote.

The science of triangulation is very simple. In fact, the ancient Greeks solved this type of problem with the Pythagorean theorem ($a^2 + b^2 = c^2$). Although this theorem only works with right triangles, similar math is used to calculate the correct lengths of the triangle legs using angles and trigonometry. To triangulate, you only need to know the length of each leg of the triangle to determine all angles. Since the console knows how far apart the LEDs are, the base length is known. The Wii remote calculates the distance to the LEDs and sends that information back as the length of each leg. This allows the console to triangulate and solve exactly where the remote is located.

When the Wii remote moves, the length of two of the triangle legs changes. The new angles are determined. The computer solves the equation to get the location of the point of the triangle. This process is repeated about 20 times per second to give a real-time location of the remote as it moves.

Test this yourself with a rubber band. Put the rubber band between two fingers on your right hand as the LEDs. Use the pointer finger on your left hand like the Wii remote. Move your left hand to see how the triangle formed by the rubber band changes.

Goodheart-Willcox Publisher

You can demonstrate triangulation with a rubber band and three fingers. As you move one finger, the triangle changes.

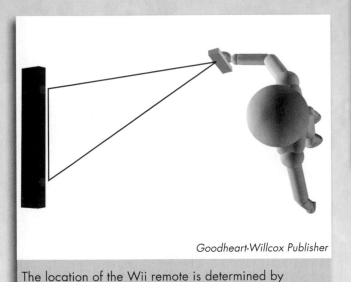

Goodheart-Willcox Publisher

The location of the Wii remote is determined by triangulation.

Critics

Competitors extensively and critically evaluate games to reverse engineer a successful game. However, it is important to understand that the key elements used to develop a USP are also evaluated by gamers and critics.

Critics are people who evaluate a game to provide a summary and opinion of the key elements of the game. This allows potential customers to have more information to make a wise purchase. The purpose of a critic is to evaluate a game and provide information, not to reverse engineer, as illustrated in **Figure 8-8.**

However, a good critic will also have a strong background in gaming and programming to understand the unique differences, new technologies, and USPs of new games. A certain amount of reverse engineering knowledge is required to understand how the new game works. The critic uses this knowledge to know how a new game is significantly different from all other games of the same genre.

CHEAT CODE: CONSUMERS

Consumers are the people who purchase goods and services. When you buy or rent a video game, you are a consumer.

With hundreds of new games released every year, no single person could evaluate each one. **Consumers** often rely on game reviews from critics and friends when deciding whether or not to buy a game.

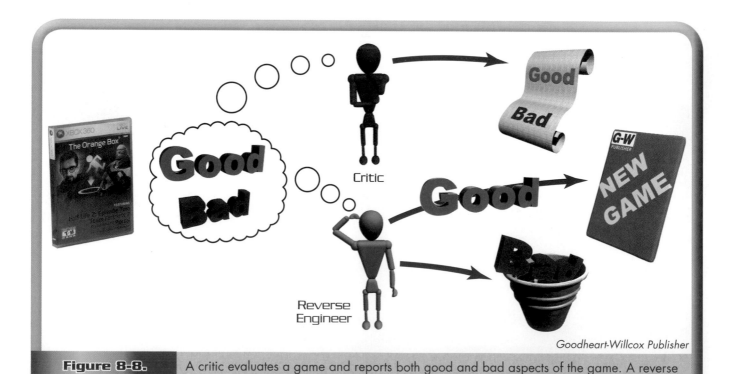

Goodheart-Willcox Publisher

Figure 8-8. A critic evaluates a game and reports both good and bad aspects of the game. A reverse engineer evaluates both good and bad aspects of the game and creates a new game that incorporates the good aspects.

Bias

Having honest and objective critics is important. If the review is from the manufacturer, it will almost always contain some bias in the opinion of the critic. **Bias** is an intentional slant in one direction. With bias, a critic will over-emphasize the positive attributes of the game. Few if any negative attributes of the game are identified. A critic may also have a **negative bias**.

An example of a biased review might be if a critic paid by the game manufacturer says that a game is "awesome," "plays well," and it is "highly recommended." However, the critic fails to point out that the graphics are poorly developed because this would make the game less desirable. This type of bias can typically be found on the back of a video game box or on the game company's website. The bias is created by the motivation to try to get you to buy the game.

An **unbiased** review is one not influenced by outside sources, such as the game manufacturer, as shown in **Figure 8-9.** Your best bet is to look for an opinion from someone who is not trying to sell you the game. The company selling the game wants you to buy it. Of course, the company is going to paint the game in the best light. You may find out later that you should have looked a little harder and found an unbiased source of information.

CHEAT CODE: NEGATIVE BIAS

A negative bias is when a review or comment is intended to poorly portray a game. A critic may be paid by one company to review another company's game. In this case, the critic will have a negative bias.

GameSpot.com

Figure 8-9. There are many sources of unbiased game reviews. This one for *Paper Mario* is from the GameSpot.com website.

Ethical Gamer

Distorting information for your own gain is an unethical practice. Honesty, accuracy, and truthfulness should guide all reviews of games. Do not take credit for ideas that belong to someone else; always credit your sources.

Figure 8-10.
Many different industries often have celebrities promote their products. Here, singer Nicole Scherzinger is photographed with the Ford Escape hybrid at an event. In the eyes of many consumers, association with a celebrity puts the product in a positive light.

Ford

Being biased does *not* mean that the critic is lying. Think about buying a car. You want the best car for the money and something that fits your needs and wants. You look at the manufactures website and it shows a celebrity driving that car with a "thumbs up" signal, similar to what is shown in **Figure 8-10.** You decide to look at an unbiased report from a magazine that does not accept advertising from any manufacturer and thereby maintains an objective opinion. That magazine rates the car eight out of ten and a "consumer's best value." Both sources deliver the message that the car is a good buy, but the manufacturer is biased and the magazine is unbiased.

In forming your own opinions of games, you need to remain unbiased in your assessment of the key elements. Failing to remain objective will not give you the valuable information you are looking for.

Key Game Elements for Evaluation

Each element of a new game is evaluated by the competition and critics to see if it establishes a USP or if it is just a copy of something already on the market. This section identifies ten key elements that are used to compare and contrast games. Keep these elements in mind when reviewing your own work and other games.

Quality of Rules

Games need rules. These rules must be presented to the user in a very clear fashion. The **quality of rules** is how well the rules are explained to the user.

○ Will the players be able to understand the purpose of the game?
○ Will the players understand what they are supposed to do within the game to overcome the obstacles and challenges?

CHEAT CODE: WALKTHROUGHS

A walkthrough is a set of instructions on what needs to be done to complete a game. Sometimes a walkthrough is considered cheating. Other times, a player may refer to a walkthrough when they get to a point in the game where they simply do not understand what needs to be done.

If the quality of rules is poor, the player might need to find documentation on just what they are trying to accomplish. Often, there are several fan sites for a game. These sites may help with **walkthroughs.** If the rules are not well defined, a player will quickly abandon the game, feeling it is pointless or just too hard. There is no fun in that.

User Interface

The user interface is how the player interacts with the game world. This needs to be as simple as possible. The closer the player gets to full immersion in the game world the better. The user interface is a very important part of achieving immersion in a game. Easy-to-handle and intuitive controls are the best.

Intuitive controls are devices that take no explanation of how to use them. These controls are similar to things already used and make sense. An example of an intuitive control is a light gun, as shown in **Figure 8-11**. It is shaped like a pistol and has a trigger. Everyone knows that they aim and pull the trigger. The player knows intuitively how to operate the light gun without instructions. On the other hand, if a player has to press multiple buttons to create a single move, that is difficult to remember and not user friendly. In other words, it is not intuitive.

Navigation

In general, *navigation* is how the player moves in the game world. The player must be able to navigate each level in the game world. In some games, aids are provided to the user, such as the inset map shown in **Figure 8-12**.

- Can the player move well through the level?
- Can the player see the obstacles in time to avoid them?
- Is the player able to return to a reasonable **checkpoint** if damaged?

These are some of the important questions to ask concerning navigation. The answers to these questions will help define if the navigation is appropriate and well designed.

Figure 8-11.

The light gun is an intuitive control. Everybody understands how to use it.

Goodheart-Willcox Publisher

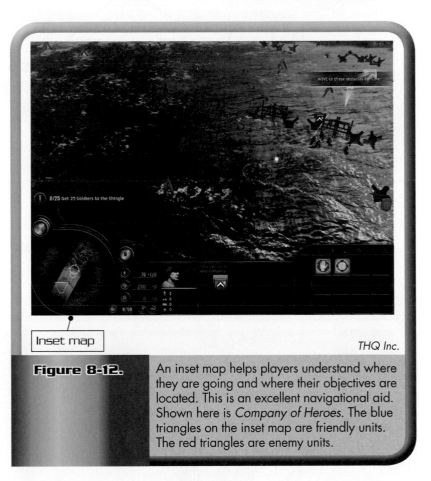

Inset map

THQ Inc.

Figure 8-12.

An inset map helps players understand where they are going and where their objectives are located. This is an excellent navigational aid. Shown here is *Company of Heroes*. The blue triangles on the inset map are friendly units. The red triangles are enemy units.

CHEAT CODE: CHECKPOINT

When the player is respawned, or recreated with a new life, the avatar is placed at a checkpoint. In most games, when a player is destroyed, the player will respawn at the last checkpoint location. This prevents the player from having to replay everything from the beginning point. In some games, the player achieves a time bonus or other status change at each checkpoint.

Performance

The **performance** is how well the game operates on the game system. If the game does not operate well, the player will likely not play the game.

○ Does the game play smoothly or is it glitchy?

○ Do the graphics move properly?

○ Does the player have the movements or abilities as expected or does the game allow unexpected movements?

○ Will the player move when commanded or is there a delay?

The answers to these questions will help define if the game performance is acceptable.

LEVEL UP! 8.3 Think about a game you played that had glitches, flaws, or even froze. Think about how frustrating that was. How likely were you to say good things to your friends about the game?

Gameplay

The gameplay is what the user experiences as the game unfolds. Gameplay is what keeps the player entertained, as illustrated by the games shown in **Figure 8-13.** To help evaluate gameplay, ask the following questions.

○ Is the concept well developed?

○ Can the player perform all of the necessary moves to overcome the obstacles and challenges?

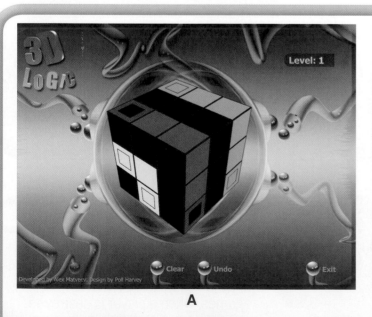

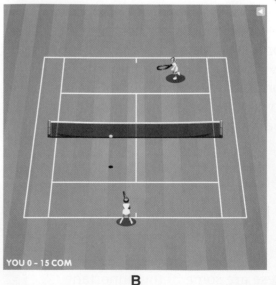

www.freeonlinegames.com

Figure 8-13. A—Puzzle games often have only one solution. The solution may be challenging, making the puzzle fun to solve, such as in this game called *3D Logic*. However, once you find the solution, the replay value of the game is low. B—On the other hand, a sports game where you can play head-to-head with a friend, such as this one called *Tennis Game*, may have great replay value.

- Is the game challenging?
- Does the game have a significant replay value and why?

Artistry

The **artistry** of a game is its visual appeal. Use of complementary colors for unified items is appropriate. Contrasting colors should be used for items that need to be visually distinct. The settings and backgrounds should be artfully created and set the mood for the game and levels.

- Are the characters and avatars visually appealing?
- Are the sounds of the game consistent with what is expected?

All aspects of aesthetics are evaluated. Also, pay attention to the technical aspects of the art. Look for problems such as that illustrated in **Figure 8-14.**

Longevity in Design and Structure

Longevity is the length of time something can continue to be used. For a game, this means the length of time the game is popular and makes money for the game design company. When you evaluate a new game, you need to answer many questions to determine if the game design and structure can be used only once or are easily adaptable for many years.

- Can this type or style of game continue for a long time? Will there be a market for games of this design several years from now?
- Are there already many games of this type on the market?
- Are there any new advances in technology or design of which this game takes advantage? Will these advancements continue?
- Is this a seasonal project or a **fad?**
- Are the design and structure innovative and revolutionary or are they copies of something existing?

CHEAT CODE: FAD

A fad is a product that has a very short product life cycle. It may quickly gain a lot of interest and then die out almost immediately. An example of a fad might be a song that is popular for a couple of weeks and then is never heard again.

Parts become separated

Figure 8-14.

This is an example of poorly designed game art. As the player turns, the avatar's horns separate from the body.

Goodheart-Willcox Publisher; image: Clipart.com

Figure 8-15. The Mario franchise has been very successful for Nintendo. Many different Mario games have been released on every Nintendo game platform, including the Game Cube, as shown here.

The answer to these questions will help determine if you have an idea on which you can build many versions, such as the Mario franchise shown in **Figure 8-15.** For example, a Halloween game is seasonal. Interest in the game is likely to fade after the holiday has past. Therefore, the longevity of the game is limited.

Player Interactions

The **player interactions** are what the player is doing and how the items and characters the player engages respond. When evaluating a game for player interactions, ask the following questions.

- Are the interactions for the player and game objects consistent with the theme?
- What types of interactions are involved (shooting, jumping over, conversing, partnering, battling, etc.)?
- Is the player expected to follow a linear sequence?
- What interactions are expected in the sequence?

A **linear sequence** is a progression of gameplay in a straight line. In other words, the player must do task W first, then task X next, then task Y after, and finally task Z, as shown in **Figure 8-16.** The player cannot do these tasks out of order.

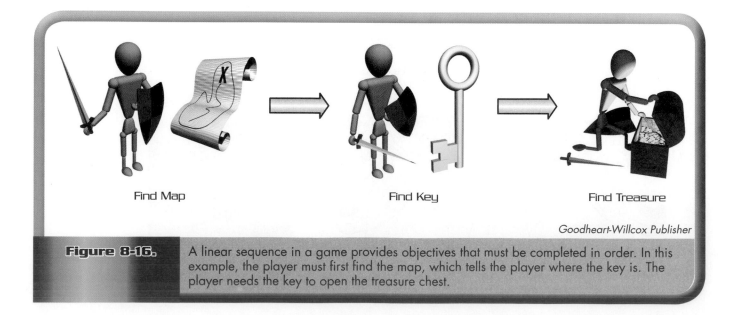

Find Map   Find Key   Find Treasure

Goodheart-Willcox Publisher

Figure 8-16. A linear sequence in a game provides objectives that must be completed in order. In this example, the player must first find the map, which tells the player where the key is. The player needs the key to open the treasure chest.

Plot

Plot is the main storyline of the game. From start to finish, the game should develop a plot and stick to the story until resolution. The story should be well-developed with a proper character backstory. When evaluating the plot, ask these questions.

- Do the actions required by the player fit the game theme and explain why the character is attempting to overcome some obstacle or challenge?
- Will the story conclude at the end of the game or continue?
- Does the player develop relationships whereby he or she cares about other characters in the story of the game?
- Does the storyline help immersion and player involvement in the game?

These questions help identify the quality of the plot. Any gaps in the story will confuse the player. The player must understand the motivation for actions and want to succeed in overcoming all of the obstacles. A plot does not, however, need to be complex for a game to be successful. Some games have a very simple plot, such as the game shown in **Figure 8-17.**

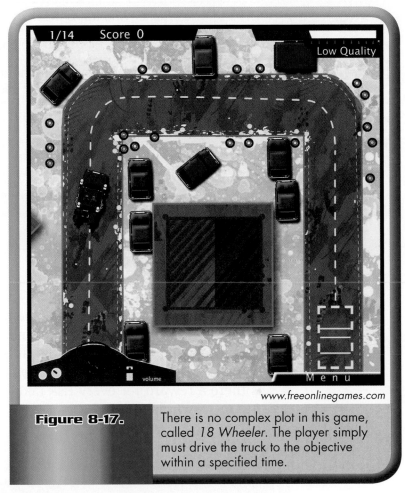

Figure 8-17. There is no complex plot in this game, called *18 Wheeler*. The player simply must drive the truck to the objective within a specified time.

www.freeonlinegames.com

A plot can be enhanced by adding dramatic elements to a scene, which often involves using different player types. Characters are a rich resource of dramatic elements. Since most interaction in the game is done through characters and player avatars, it makes sense to develop rich characters. Rich characters have characteristics that are conveyed to the player through the clothing, costume, behaviors, syntax, motivation, and more. These characters fall into standard categories called *archetypes*. The table in **Figure 8-18** displays many of the most common character archetypes used in video games.

In many games, the player can choose the avatar class to join. In a game like *World of Warcraft,* the player can choose from many different character classes. This aids in player immersion where the player can become an elf, wizard, mage, or other class of character. Each class has different strengths and weaknesses that help change the gameplay and make the player experience unique to each class of avatar.

Archetype Class	Description
Hero	Lead character who faces challenges and drives the story.
Shadow	The villain or enemy of the hero.
Mentor	The teacher who trains the hero.
Herald	Announces vital information to the hero or audience.
Helper	Often sidekicks, companions, or members of a group that supports the hero and helps with special skills or information along the journey.
Guardian	Protects an area. Usually strong, but not very smart.
Trickster	Comedy relief to the story as the trickster likes to play pranks or is just clumsy or inept.

Figure 8-18. These are the most common character archetypes used in video games.

Goodheart-Willcox Publisher

Reward

For every risk taken by the player, a reward must be provided, such as that shown in **Figure 8-19.** A *reward* is something positive provided to the player, such as an increase in score, added lives, or more powerful tools. To help evaluate the quality of the reward in relation to the risks taken, ask the following questions.

○ Is the size of the reward parallel to the risk taken (big risk, big reward)?
○ Is there a reward for every risk taken?
○ Are the rewards unique?

Figure 8-19.

In this game, called *Castle Quest*, you increase levels by building points from eliminating zombies and goblins.

- Are there trivial (meaningless) tasks required of the player?
- Do the rewards fit in a linear sequence to enable the player to overcome a final challenge?

Summarizing the Evaluation

After each of the evaluation criteria is evaluated, critics will typically summarize their findings using the star rating system. The *five-star rating system* is an easy, visual way for potential customers to see what the critic thinks of the game. A rating of five stars means the game is great and all of the key elements rate high. A rating of three stars means the game is average. A rating of less than three stars means the game has little value. The critic considers this game to be below average and you may wish to avoid it.

The stars in the rating system are a lot like the letter grades given for an assignment, as illustrated in **Figure 8-20**. A five-star rating is equal to an A, four stars equal a B, three stars equal a C, two stars equal a D, and one star equals an F. Sometimes, 1/4, 1/2, or 3/4 of a star can be awarded, such as 3 1/2 stars. This is a bit like the difference between an A and an A+.

Green Gamer

Did you know that the batteries in cell phones, iPods, and other handheld devices are composed of hazardous material that will harm the environment if they are disposed of in a landfill? Batteries should always be properly recycled by a reputable organization and never thrown in the regular trash.

Star Rating	Letter Grade
✭✭✭✭✭	A
✭✭✭✭	B
✭✭✭	C
✭✭	D
✭	F

Figure 8-20. The five-star rating system for games is similar to the letter grades you receive in school.

Goodheart-Willcox Publisher

CHEAT CODE: USER REVIEWS

When a user or player of a game posts their comments about a game on a blog, review, or message board, they are creating a user review. For this to be an unbiased user review, the user must not receive any payment for their comments.

Some of the most unbiased critics are consumers like you. Many sites allow you to post **user reviews** for a game, as shown in **Figure 8-21**. The rating is typically only a basic system that covers only a few of the key elements. Most valuable from these reviews are the comments on repeat playability and an opinion on if the game is worth the price. If current players do not enjoy the game or think it was too costly, you might feel the same way.

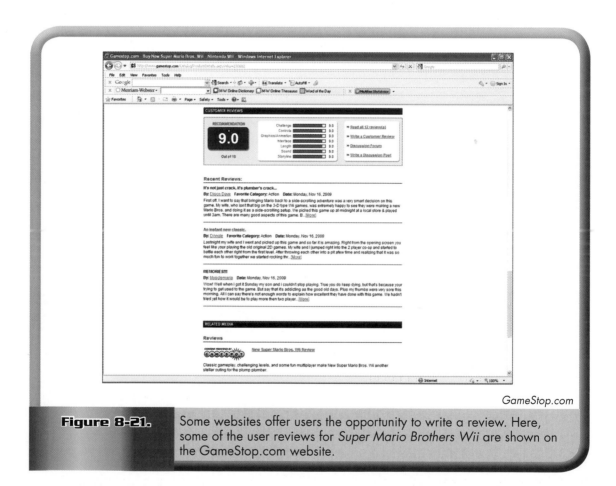

GameStop.com

Figure 8-21. Some websites offer users the opportunity to write a review. Here, some of the user reviews for *Super Mario Brothers Wii* are shown on the GameStop.com website.

Chapter Summary

o Intellectual property is an original creation, such as the development of a video game.

o A critique of a game analyzes various aspects of a game, such as rules, gameplay, and longevity of design.

o The video game industry analyzes games using both biased and unbiased reviews.

o A critical review of a video game includes an assessment of ten key game elements as well as a summary of the evaluation.

o Key components of an evaluation of a commercial video game include the comparison of the plot, interactivity, and reward system.

Check Your Video Game IQ

Now that you have finished this chapter, see what you know about video game design by taking the chapter posttest.

www.m.g-wlearning.com

www.g-wlearning.com

Review Your Knowledge

On a separate sheet of paper or in a word processing document, match the following terms with the definitions that fit best.

A. biased review
B. case law
C. authorship restriction
D. noncompete agreement
E. user review

F. confidentiality agreement
G. creative commons license
H. unbiased review
I. statutory law
J. derivative works restriction

1. Allows the use of the Creative Commons work so long as you give credit to the original author or creator.

2. A contract that states you cannot share any information about the company or its products with any other company.

3. The group of laws that have been passed by legislature.

4. Opinion overemphasizing either the positive or negative attributes.

5. Allows someone to use a creative work for free, with some restrictions.

6. Prohibits the use of the Creative Commons work in any other form than the original.

7. Opinion that fairly evaluates both negative and positive attributes.

8. A contract that states you cannot open your own studio or work for a competing company for a certain period of time.

9. Laws enacted when the first lawsuit to deal with a specific problem has been judged and an outcome determined.

10. Comments about a game from a game player.

On a separate sheet of paper or in a word processing document, answer each of the following questions.

11. Define *reverse engineering.*

12. Why do game design companies reverse engineer a competitor's game?

13. What type of game satisfies the same needs and wants of the original game?

14. What is copyright infringement?

15. Define *intellectual property.*

16. List four ways in which a company may try to prevent illegal copying of game discs.

17. Briefly describe how a game can be designed similar to an existing game without copyright infringement.

18. What is the purpose of an employment contract?

19. Define *exclusive rights.*

20. Define *derivative works.*

21. What is the purpose of a confidentiality agreement?

22. What contract agreements might stop an employee from taking the project he or she is working on and using it to start a new company?

23. Compare and contrast statutory laws and case law.

24. If a teenager downloaded 300 songs illegally from Limewire and was fined $1,500 each, how much would he or she have to pay?

25. How does a Creative Commons license work?

26. How does fair use doctrine help a student use pictures from the Internet without going to jail?

27. Define *public domain.*

28. What is a software key code?

29. What can an artist add to an image to prevent unauthorized use and morphing of the graphic?

30. In general, is the game review on the back of a game case a biased or unbiased review? Why?

31. What is the quality of rules for a video game?

32. Why is the drum set used in a game like *Rock Band* an intuitive controller?

33. Define *navigation* as it relates to the game world.

34. What is the performance of a game?

35. What is gameplay?

36. Regarding the artistry of the game, _____ colors should be used for unified items and _____ colors should be used for distinctly different items.

37. Define *longevity,* as it relates to the game world.

38. What is a fad?

39. What are player interactions?

40. Explain linear sequence, as it relates to gameplay.

41. Define *plot,* as it relates to a game.

42. What is the backstory of a game?

43. How does player type, such as the choice of archetype class, change the way the story affects the player and add dramatic elements to gameplay?

44. Something positive provided to the player, such as an increase in score, for achieving an objective is called a(n) _____.

45. Compare the five-star rating system for game reviews to letter grades used in school.

Apply Your STEM Knowledge

Language Arts

1. Think about your favorite game. Write a one-page, biased review of the game. Be sure to cover all ten key elements discussed in this chapter.

Social Studies

2. Go to the grocery store and look at the cereal aisle. Take notes on how many brands have the same theme. For example, how many different brands are cereal with raisins or chocolate puffed-rice cereal. Create a table listing the five most common themes of cereal, the brand name of each competitor, the price of each, and the size of the packaging (the amount of cereal in the box).

Mathematics

3. Add a column to the table created in #2. Convert the price and amount of cereal to a cost per ounce. Create a bar graph to show the differences in cost per ounce of each cereal brand of the same theme.

Language Arts

4. Choose one cereal from #2 and write a one-page, unbiased review. Highlight any USPs or special features of the product that might make someone choose this brand of cereal instead of others with the same theme.

Science

5. For centuries, people studied birds, insects, bats, and other flying animals. These observations led people to begin trying to figure out how each animal was able to achieve and maintain flight. Testing was done on different ways of building gliders and powered aircraft that mimicked the same flight characteristic seen in nature. Eventually, the process of flight was successfully reverse engineered. Research the characteristics of flying animals and that of a modern airplane. Prepare a reverse engineering presentation of six to ten slides to document the similarities between flying animals and airplanes. Present the slide show to the class.

Working in Teams

In teams, research, debate, and form a group opinion on each of the Level Up! activities in this chapter. Prepare a PowerPoint presentation of ten slides (five to seven minutes) to present to the class explaining the group's opinions for each Level Up! activity. Include text, pictures, video, animations, and slide transitions as appropriate to help explain your positions.

Gamer Portfolio

Your portfolio should contain items related to your school work. These items might include report cards, transcripts, or honor roll reports. Diplomas or certificates that show courses or programs you completed should also be included. At some point, you will likely apply for a particular job or volunteer position. At that time, list the classes you took that helped prepare you for the job or volunteer position. Describe the activities you completed or topics you studied in these classes that relate to the job or volunteer duties. This information will be helpful when you apply for the position by letter or talk with an interviewer.

1. Identify a job or volunteer position for which you could apply. Write a paragraph that gives the classes you took and activities completed that relate to the position. You can use this document as a model when you are actually ready to apply for a position.
2. Scan other documents related to your school work, such as grade reports, transcripts, and diplomas. Place the model paragraph and other documents in your e-portfolio.
3. Place hard copies in the container for your print portfolio.

G-W Learning Mobile Site

Visit the G-W Learning mobile site to complete the chapter pretest and posttest and to practice vocabulary using e-flash cards. If you do not have a smartphone, visit the G-W Learning companion website to access these features.

G-W Learning mobile site: www.m.g-wlearning.com

G-W Learning companion website: www.g-wlearning.com

Common Core

College and Career Readiness

CTE Career Ready Practices. Create an Euler diagram (a kind of multicircle Venn diagram) to show the relationship between your career interests, your preferences, your goals, and requirements of your career choice. Where do the circles overlap? What do you think overlap signifies? What would a diagram with a lot of overlap tell you? What about one with little or no overlap?

Reading. Research information on the five star rating system for video games. What is the history of the rating system? Who compiles and monitors user reviews? How are the ratings obtained? Are the reviews and results available to the public? Is this a good thing? Why or why not? As needed, derive meaning of the environmental print and use visual and contextual support to confirm understanding. Use support from classmates and your teacher as needed to help in comprehension of the material. Write a report in which you analyze the strengths and weakness of the five star rating system, using information from your research and this text. Present your opinions to the class.

Writing. Conduct research on how much money video game designers lost in the last year due to copyright infringement. Write an informative report consisting of several paragraphs to describe your findings and the implications for the video game design companies.

Event Prep: Extemporaneous Speaking

Extemporaneous speaking is a competitive event you might enter with your Career and Technical Student Organization (CTSO). This event allows you to display your communication skills of speaking, organizing, and making an oral presentation. At the competition, you will be given several topics from which to choose. You will also be given a time limit to create and deliver the speech. You will be evaluated on your verbal and nonverbal skills as well as the tone and projection of your voice. To prepare for the extemporaneous speaking event:

1. Read the guidelines provided by your organization. Make certain that you ask any questions about points you do not understand. It is important you follow each specific item that is outlined in the competition rules.

2. Ask your instructor for several topics on video game design so you can practice making impromptu speeches.

3. Once you have an assigned practice topic from your instructor, jot down your ideas and points you want to cover. An important part about making this type of presentation is that you will have only a few minutes to prepare. Being able to write down your main ideas quickly will enable you to focus on what you will actually say in the presentation.

4. Practice the presentation. You should introduce yourself, review the topic that is being presented, defend the topic being presented, and conclude with a summary.

5. Ask your teacher to play the role of competition judge as your team reviews the case. After the presentation is complete, ask for feedback from your teacher. You may consider also having a student audience to listen and give feedback.

6. For the event, bring paper and pencils to record notes. Supplies may or may not be provided.

Chapter 9
Large-Scale Design Process

▶ **A** large game studio works with a lot of structure and documentation. This chapter looks into the formal structure of the three design stages and the governing game design document that guides the designers through the process. Additionally, the process for getting a game from the idea in your head to programming on a disc is discussed. This includes making your sales pitch and choosing the right software for the job.

Check Your Video Game IQ

Before you begin this chapter, see what you already know about video game design by taking the chapter pretest.

www.m.g-wlearning.com

www.g-wlearning.com

College and Career Readiness

Reading Prep. In preparation for the chapter, research one of the game development tools discussed in this chapter. Summarize the developments. Keep in mind the benefits and drawbacks of this tool as you read.

Objectives

After completing this chapter, you will be able to:

- Create a development plan for a video game design.
- Describe the development process for a video game.
- Explain the importance of budget and scheduling on video game design.
- Explain how iterations are used in the design process for video games.
- Create design plans.
- Create character sketches.
- Create storyboards.
- Discuss various game-development tools currently used by the video game industry.
- Describe common video game engines.
- Explain the uses for various tools used for video game development.

Formal Design Structure

To this point, the games you designed have not followed the formal design process. These first few games were small builds. They could be completed on an informal basis to allow for skill building. You now have a foundation of some of the skills needed to program a game. Next, you need to acquire the skills to begin designing games on your own.

CHEAT CODE: BUDGET

A budget is a plan that details how much a project should cost. The cost to complete each task is estimated. All the tasks are listed along with their estimated cost and added up to get a final budget total.

Before you start to program a game's functions, you need to understand the design process. Throughout the design process, ideas are incorporated into the game design until a finished game is ready. Most new games are designed by teams with specialists in several areas to keep the project moving forward.

It is important to understand that delays in production cost money. At the outset of the game's design, the team is given a **budget** and a time schedule. A *delay in production* occurs when the project is not following the projected time schedule.

If the team spends more in development cost than allotted, it is over budget. As a result, the project may be terminated or scaled back. Keep in mind, the overall budget includes the salaries of those employees working on the game.

Say the designers in a game development company get paid $100,000 per year. The company pays each designer about $385 per day in salary. That does not factor in the cost of any benefits. If the design team of ten people is one day off schedule, it costs the company about $3,850 per day. A month late and the company suffers a loss of over $100,000 just in additional salary expenses. The other side of that equation is if the game is completed a month early, the company saves over $100,000. For reasons of budget and scheduling, it becomes very important that projects are ready on time and on budget, as illustrated in **Figure 9-1**.

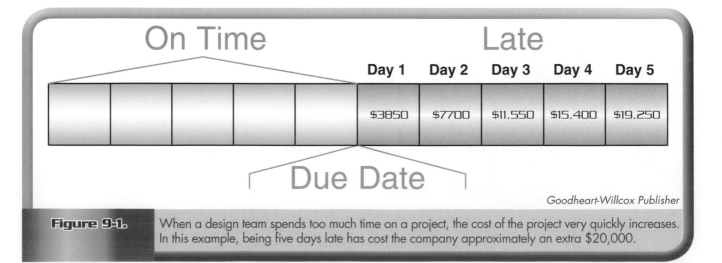

Goodheart-Willcox Publisher

Figure 9-1. When a design team spends too much time on a project, the cost of the project very quickly increases. In this example, being five days late has cost the company approximately an extra $20,000.

In addition to cost issues, there are other reasons why a production schedule cannot be off by even one day. These are called *time-sensitive issues* because timing is critical. When the company sets a production launch date, your team will have to meet this date. If the game is a seasonal or promotional game, such as one based on a new movie, it must be out before the season or promotional activity. After that, the game has little value. Also, a release date might be set to enter the market before a competitor's game has a chance to hit the market. Being first to market can make the difference between a success and a failure.

A major buying time is just before the holiday season, as represented in **Figure 9-2**. If a company wants to get its share of the money spent during the holidays, it must have the game on the shelves so people can

Is this your new game?

Shutterstock.com

Figure 9-2. The holiday season is a big selling time for most game companies. A game that comes out prior to the holidays is better positioned to make money than a game released after the holidays.

buy it. Imagine launching a game at the end of December. Everyone is home playing all of the cool new games they got during the holidays. On the other hand, your game is sitting on the store shelf collecting dust. Most people have already spent their money on gifts and do not have extra cash to go buy your new game release. Missing an October or November release date in the United States might mean your game never gets a chance to make it as a commercial success.

The design team must make the best game possible within the given timeframe and budget. Your design team might come up with several awesome ideas for new levels, characters, and challenges. However, if the time and budget do not exist to properly program these ideas into the game, save them for the next version of the game. As a designer, it can be frustrating seeing your ideas pushed back to another game. However, it is very important that the game release take place on time. It is also important that the game is a polished version without any problems or glitches.

To assure timeliness and quality, game design follows a *three-stage production process.* This allows streamlining of production; makes certain the game will get the best ideas and best build; and meets the demand of time, money, and quality. The three stages of the production cycle are concept, construction, and tuning, as graphically illustrated in **Figure 9-3.**

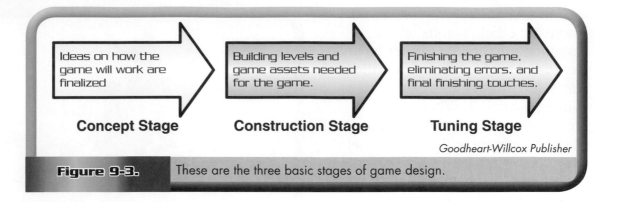

Concept Stage	Construction Stage	Tuning Stage
Ideas on how the game will work are finalized	Building levels and game assets needed for the game.	Finishing the game, eliminating errors, and final finishing touches.

Goodheart-Willcox Publisher

Figure 9-3. These are the three basic stages of game design.

LEVEL UP! 9.1 Think about a game that is released in January and misses the holiday buying season. What events might cause people to buy this game after the holiday season?

Concept Stage

The *concept stage* is the first stage within the production cycle. In the concept stage, you brainstorm ideas, get ideas on paper, form the structure of the game, and prepare for production. In other words, the concept stage begins with an idea about a game and ends with a refined idea about how the game will play.

The concept stage is the foundation on which the entire game will be built, similar to the drawings made before the house is built, as shown in **Figure 9-4.**

Figure 9-4. Every building needs a strong foundation on which it is constructed. In the concept stage of a building, drawings are created that are then used in the construction stage.

shutterstock.com

To build this foundation, a designer must answer the *five essential questions:*

- What is the game going to be about (genre type, basic idea)?
- Who is going to play this game (audience, age, target market, desired ESRB rating)?
- Who is the player (protagonist) going to be in this game (player role, character type)?
- What will the player do in the game (victory condition, obstacles, opponents)?
- What will the world look like in the game (settings, levels, backgrounds, perspective)?

After these five essential questions are answered, the game construction stage can begin.

Think about beginning to build a game and finding out that the technology to make it work does not exist. Would you change the concept, modify the design to existing technology, scrap the project, or do something else? Why?

Construction Stage

The **construction stage** is where the rough idea of the game from the concept stage is refined into something workable. It is important to note that once you answer the five essential questions in the concept stage, you must *not* change the answers during the construction stage. To change any of the concepts after construction begins usually requires a complete rewrite of the game code already created.

During the construction stage, a prototype game is built. A **prototype** is the first **iteration** of a game build. It typically has limited features and structures. As construction continues, more features and structures are added. In other words, the prototype is the first, basic version of the game, as seen in **Figure 9-5.**

A prototype usually contains the basic structure of the game. However, it will not contain detailed character designs, backgrounds, music, or sounds.

CHEAT CODE: ITERATION

An iteration is simply a different version. If you have ten iterations of a game, you have ten different versions of the game. Each iteration is different from the previous iterations, hopefully improving the game.

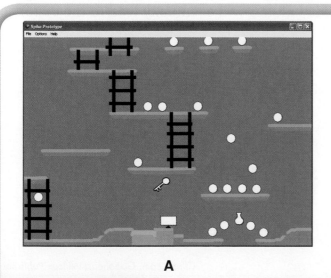

A

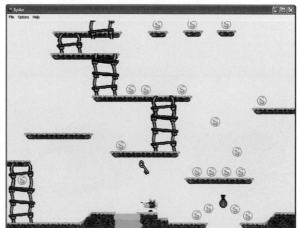

B

Goodheart-Willcox Publisher

Figure 9-5.   A—A prototype game tests the playability of the concept. Basic shapes without animation represent game assets. B—The final game build has the final artwork in place.

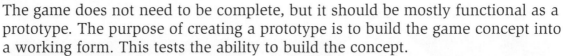

The game does not need to be complete, but it should be mostly functional as a prototype. The purpose of creating a prototype is to build the game concept into a working form. This tests the ability to build the concept.

The entire construction of a video game is an *iterative process,* as shown by the characters in **Figure 9-6.** This process requires several iterations of the game to be constructed with improvements and changes from the previous iterations of the game. With each iteration, the game is refined and polished until a final iteration has full functionality and near-perfect graphics and sound.

This textbook identifies *eight areas of design* that bridge from concept to construction:

- gameplay modes
- protagonist and character development
- game world
- core mechanics
- mode elaboration
- story elaboration
- level design
- testing and debugging

Each of these areas must be defined from the concept and written down in the design documents. Design documents are discussed later in this chapter. The next sections look at how each area must be finalized during the construction stage of design.

Gameplay Modes

During the construction stage, you will need to expand the concept to define each of the gameplay modes. For each game and possibly each level of the game there will be primary and secondary gameplay modes, like those shown in **Figure 9-7.** The *primary gameplay mode* is what the player must achieve as a goal of the game or level. The *secondary gameplay mode* is other objectives or activities the player completes for additional rewards.

A primary gameplay mode for a platform game might be navigation of the platforms to collect coins. A secondary gameplay mode might be collecting a key to open a chest. Both gameplay modes will eventually lead to the victory condition of the game.

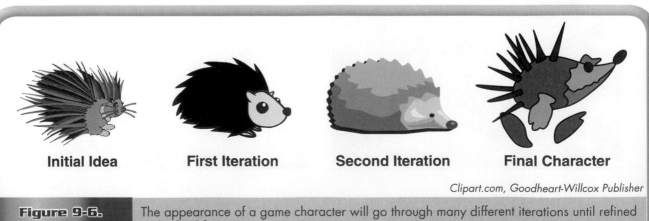

Initial Idea **First Iteration** **Second Iteration** **Final Character**

Clipart.com, Goodheart-Willcox Publisher

Figure 9-6. The appearance of a game character will go through many different iterations until refined to the final form.

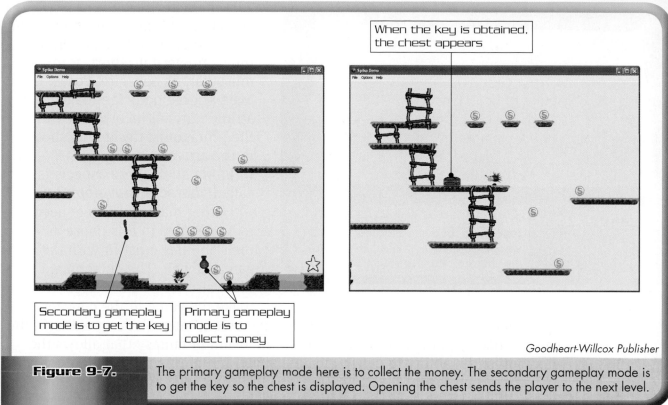

When the key is obtained, the chest appears

Secondary gameplay mode is to get the key

Primary gameplay mode is to collect money

Goodheart-Willcox Publisher

Figure 9-7. The primary gameplay mode here is to collect the money. The secondary gameplay mode is to get the key so the chest is displayed. Opening the chest sends the player to the next level.

Primary and secondary gameplay modes should be defined as to:
- interaction between characters, obstacles, and challenges;
- controls;
- abilities needed to overcome the challenges;
- perspective of the game; and
- movement within the game world.

Of course, any additional aspects of gameplay need to be discussed, decided on, and written down so all designers are working on the same foundation. The iterative process allows for decision making during the construction stage whenever there is a new situation or problem that occurs during the build.

Protagonist and Character Development

With some of the gameplay details in place, the design team can begin working on the **protagonist** of the game. The protagonist needs to be empowered with the abilities and tools needed to overcome the obstacles and challenges defined in the gameplay. After the abilities are defined, physical characteristics of the protagonist need to be designed.

CHEAT CODE: PROTAGONIST

The protagonist is the main character of the game. In a novel, the protagonist is the main character around which the plot revolves. Just as a novel has a plot, a game should have a plot with a protagonist and an antagonist. The antagonist opposes the protagonist.

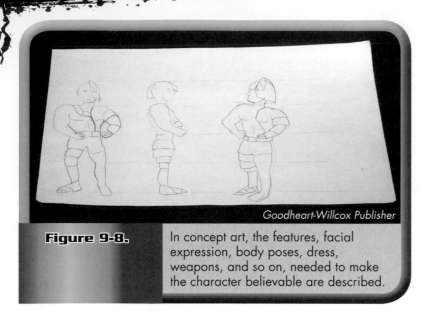

Figure 9-8. In concept art, the features, facial expression, body poses, dress, weapons, and so on, needed to make the character believable are described.

Goodheart-Willcox Publisher

The character abilities must be believable based on the appearance of the character. Is the character tall/short, thin/muscular, or boy/girl? Poses, facial expressions, body language, and attitude are all incorporated into the protagonist design, as shown in the artwork in **Figure 9-8.** Defining all of these aspects is called *character development.*

Other main characters need to be detailed in this phase as their abilities must fit with the game as well. The antagonist must also be well-developed to make the game fit the concept. Character movements, attacks, weapons, and so on, must be designed to fit the game concept. They must also fit within the realm of fantasy that allows the protagonist the ability to defeat the antagonist. In other words, you do not want to make the protagonist a tiny mouse and the antagonist an elephant. However, if you give the mouse some special abilities, powers, or weapons to defeat the elephant, this may fit into the fantasy of the gameplay.

Multiplayer games are even more challenging in character design. In a MMO game, there may be thousands of protagonists. Each one may even be a custom-built character with unique features, moves, or attacks. Custom characters and other user-selected features add to the immersion of the player into the game. However, these are more difficult to add to the game. In multiplayer games, a large amount of time is spent to properly align the classes of characters and the general strengths and weaknesses of each class. All of this must be done before writing code to build the game. If you start coding the game too early, you may have to start over to correct mistakes and omissions.

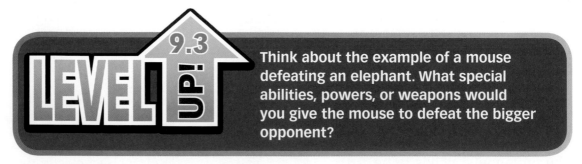

Think about the example of a mouse defeating an elephant. What special abilities, powers, or weapons would you give the mouse to defeat the bigger opponent?

Game World

The game world holds the elements the characters can interact with and conquer. With the main characters in place, you will need to design the entire game world. This means getting out the paper and sketching the buildings, trees, plants, people, cars, pets, and so on, that are going to be in the game.

Think this is easy? Look out a window and start listing all of the objects you can see. Now, give each object physical characteristics (height, width, weight, movement, etc.). Next, add an emotional tone to each element so it can exist in a dark and creepy night scene and change when it is in a bright sunshiny day. A lot of work, right?

Each element of the game world must conform to the concept. The concept dictates how the game world will look and feel. A futuristic space world may look and feel very different from a prehistoric dinosaur world, or maybe they will be combined as in **Figure 9-9.** In most cases, every element must be an original design. Each asset must be drawn and every object made from scratch. Then, every object is redrawn from a different angle or perspective to move with the player.

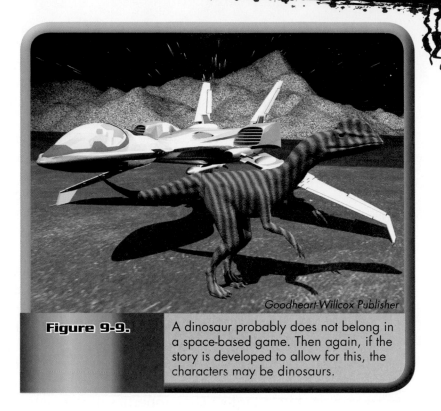

Goodheart-Willcox Publisher

Figure 9-9. A dinosaur probably does not belong in a space-based game. Then again, if the story is developed to allow for this, the characters may be dinosaurs.

Core Mechanics

Earlier chapters discussed how the core mechanics are the programming that enforces the rules of the game. In addition to enforcing the rules of the game, core mechanics also incorporate other "system-shall" commands. A **system-shall command** is a statement that tells what the system is allowed to do.

A system-shall command is simply a statement that begins with the phrase "the system shall . . .". For example, "the system shall total all the points a player receives" or "the system shall switch to the secondary gameplay mode of shopping when the player enters the market." These commands help present challenges and obstacles and regulate the action off screen. This means that the core mechanics works within the game engine to enforce the rules of the game and the system-shall commands.

To see how the core mechanics and game engine function, look at a quick example. Think of the core mechanics as the logic needed to let things function according to the game rules. The game rules state that after launching five water balloons, the player must reload with another five balloons.

Green Gamer

The USB flash drive is a popular storage device. Have you seen the new ecofriendly bamboo USB drives? Bamboo is one of the fastest growing woody plants on the planet, so this renewable resource is a good choice for the case of a USB drive.

If the player presses the launch button a sixth time, the core mechanics attempt to launch a sixth water balloon. The game engine responds to the request of the core mechanics by allowing the first five balloons to launch. But, the game engine enforces the rules and prevents the launch of the sixth balloon. A message is displayed to the player indicating a reload is required, as shown in **Figure 9-10.**

In another example, look at the difference between a racecar and a golf cart. The rules state that the racecar is faster than the golf cart. On the other hand, the core mechanics state that the racecar has a maximum speed of 200 mph and the golf cart has a maximum speed of 60 mph. In this case, the core mechanics quantify the general rule with programming of the actual speeds for each vehicle.

All aspects of the core mechanics must be defined before you can build a single level. Think of the core mechanics as how things are permitted to function. You need to know how everything is going to act and react before you can put it all together in a level. Once all of the objects in the game have their properties, movement, and abilities defined, then a level designer can assemble them to create a game.

In the above example, if the core mechanics fail to define the properties of a water balloon, the balloon might not travel at a realistic speed or pop when it hits a target. The properties of the water balloon must be determined before a level with the water balloons can be built.

Mode Elaboration

Mode elaboration is the adding of secondary gameplay modes for better immersion and storytelling. During the design process, it is common to realize the need for more than just a primary gameplay mode. A single game level may require several different gameplay modes, like those shown in **Figure 9-11.** For example, one level in a role-playing game may have:

- exploration mode;
- quest mode;
- shopping mode; and
- battle mode.

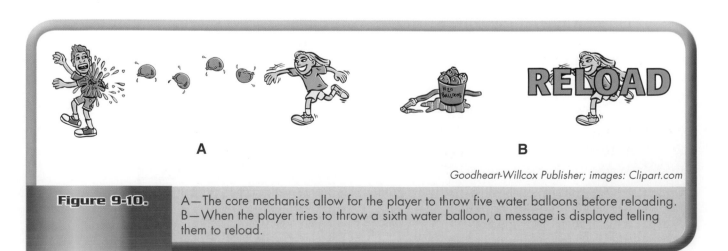

A

B

Goodheart-Willcox Publisher; images: Clipart.com

Figure 9-10. A—The core mechanics allow for the player to throw five water balloons before reloading. B—When the player tries to throw a sixth water balloon, a message is displayed telling them to reload.

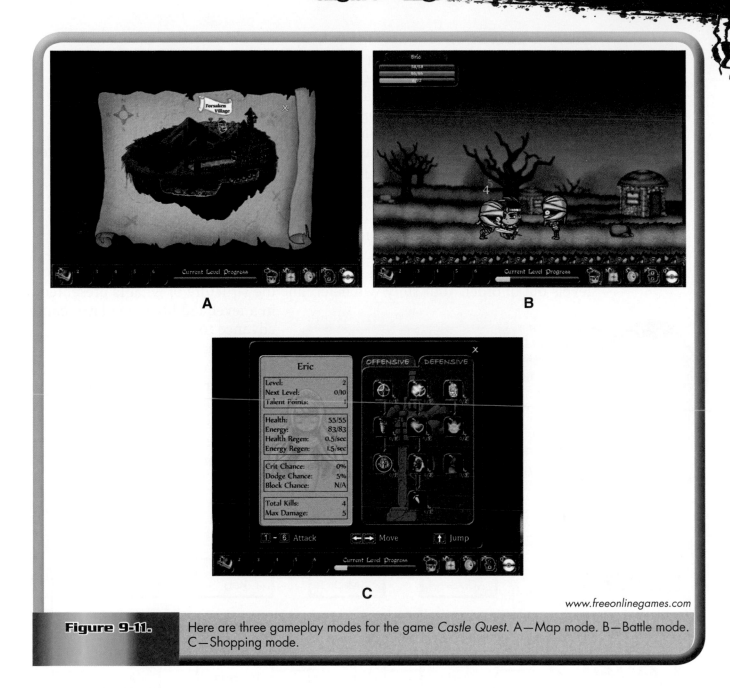

A

B

C

www.freeonlinegames.com

Figure 9-11. Here are three gameplay modes for the game *Castle Quest*. A—Map mode. B—Battle mode. C—Shopping mode.

The addition of each new mode enhances the game experience, but also significantly adds to the programming needs. An example of this extra programming is seen when designing simple triggers or buttons just to switch from one mode to another. Does the player press the X button to reveal a menu to change modes? Or, do they need a toolbar at the bottom of the screen to switch from the quest mode to the shopping/upgrade mode? In another example, a gameplay trigger occurs when the player crosses a bridge guarded by a troll. At this point, the battle mode needs to engage for the player to fight the troll. The quest mode restarts after the player defeats the troll. All of these modes need to be incorporated into the structure of the game.

Story Elaboration

Story elaboration is writing out the concept to put all pieces of the story together. A storyboard must be constructed to allow the designers to fit the game into the story. It must detail:

- what happened to the protagonist before the play level;
- what happens during the play level; and
- what outcome or objective has been achieved at the conclusion of the play level.

Each level will fit into the overall story of the game with a new objective presented after each level until the ultimate victory condition is achieved.

The story usually follows a linear progression. This means a player must complete each level in order to reach the final victory condition, as illustrated by the flowchart in **Figure 9-12.** That is to say the player must complete level 1 before levels 2, 3, 4, and 5. In a nonlinear progression, a player can jump to levels out of order. Your story will determine the structure of what is presented in a level and how the player can advance to other levels.

CHEAT CODE: CUT SCENE

A cut scene is a short video presentation. This is usually placed between levels or at checkpoints within a level. Often, a cut scene is used to occupy the player while the game loads a new portion of the programming.

Any activities needed for the story that do not occur in a level must be created as a **cut scene** between levels to continue the story. Once the storyboard is complete with levels and cut scenes, it is time to begin building the levels to tell the story.

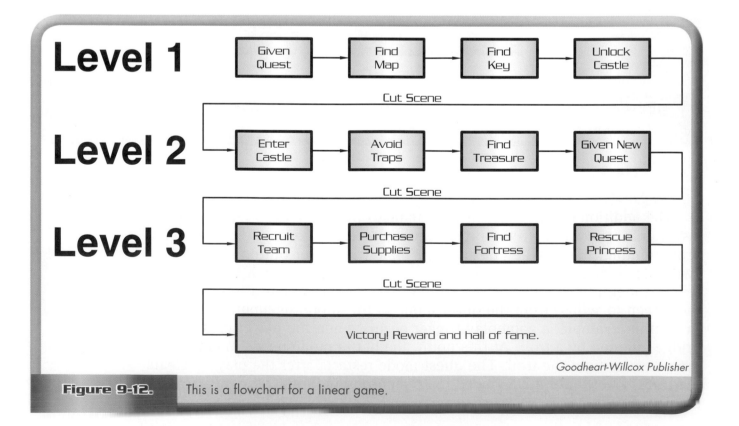

Level 1 | Given Quest → Find Map → Find Key → Unlock Castle

Cut Scene

Level 2 | Enter Castle → Avoid Traps → Find Treasure → Given New Quest

Cut Scene

Level 3 | Recruit Team → Purchase Supplies → Find Fortress → Rescue Princess

Cut Scene

Victory! Reward and hall of fame.

Goodheart-Willcox Publisher

Figure 9-12. This is a flowchart for a linear game.

CASE STUDY

Nonlinear Plot

Some of the more common nonlinear story progressions are hub and spoke, mission-choice sandbox, and simulation sandbox plots.

The hub-and-spoke plot is a story structured like a bicycle rim. You start at the middle of the rim, known as the hub. You can choose any of the spokes attached to the hub to get to the tire. Each spoke is a different mission. On *Lego Star Wars*, the player enters the cantina as the hub. The player chooses a door to exit the cantina and begin a mission. When finished, the player returns to the cantina and can choose the same mission or different mission. Additionally, the cantina allows the player to purchase upgrades in a secondary gameplay mode (shopping). Many car racing games also use the hub-and-spoke structure allowing the player to choose which track they want to race.

Another nonlinear story progression is demonstrated with games like *The Sims*. This game uses a simulation sandbox plot whereby the player can enter any area of the game and create their own story as they play the game. The story is nonlinear as the player does not have to follow a predetermined course. The player has "free will" to make choices that will determine the success of the avatar.

Goodheart-Willcox Publisher

The Sims uses a simulation sandbox storyline.

A game like *Roller Coaster Tycoon* or other "tycoon" simulation games allow the player to make choices and build each level any way they like, or sandbox style.

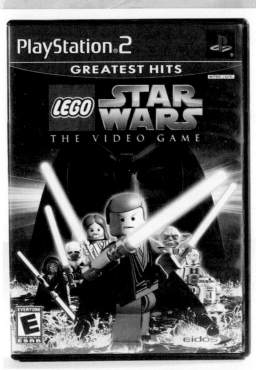
Goodheart-Willcox Publisher

The game *Lego Star Wars* uses a hub-and-spoke storyline.

Microprose

The game *Roller Coaster Tycoon* has a simulation sandbox storyline.

(Continued)

CASE STUDY *(Continued)*

Using a budget, the player can build assets such as roller coasters, food vending kiosks, and bathrooms. They also hire employees to maintain the theme park and keep the customers happy. There are an infinite number of ways to build the theme park to achieve the objectives of the level.

A mission-choice sandbox plot example is found in the game *Assassin's Creed*. In this game, the player is the modern day character of Desmond who is experiencing the historical memories of Altair by using the Animus device. Here, Altair is a member of the Brotherhood of Assassins who are battling the Knights Templar to recover the Piece of Eden artifacts.

The sandbox framework of the plot allows Altair to choose missions and sub missions without following a preset order. Altair travels to the cities of Damascus, Jerusalem, and Acre to perform many different intelligence-gathering submissions to learn more about

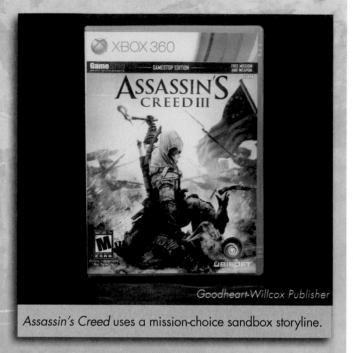

Goodheart-Willcox Publisher

Assassin's Creed uses a mission-choice sandbox storyline.

the mysteries of the Piece of Eden. In addition to the sandbox plot experienced as Altair, the player also follows a more linear plot as the modern day Desmond.

Level Design

In **level design,** the goal is to program all interactions needed to take the protagonist through each level of the story. The first objective of level design is to build a prototype to test the concept and core mechanics. The design team will work to make certain that all elements of the story are technically feasible to build. After prototyping the level elements, the build team focuses efforts on making a complete game level that tells a segment of the story.

The first milestone in design is creating the first playable level. The **first playable level** is the prototype version of the game that actually allows someone to play and test all of the interactions in the game. It is from this first level that most other interactions are defined in all other levels. That is to say, if the protagonist can jump six feet in level 1, this will probably be true in level 2 as well. After the first playable level, most other levels exist to tell the story. Other levels typically do not redefine the rules of the game or the core mechanics.

Equally important in level design is the establishment of the user interface. The controls for moving the protagonist need to be designed and fixed during the first level. This allows the player to become familiar with their use. With practice, it also allows the player to increase speed and accuracy in preparation of completing the harder tasks of higher levels.

Often, the first playable level is extremely difficult to construct when new technologies or innovations are implemented into the game. Not only must the programmers develop the story, they must learn to use a new technology to tell the story.

9.4 Think about how the first playable level needs to have all of the controls and gameplay elements in place. Once the first playable level is built, what structural changes are needed to make a second, third, or fourth level?

Testing and Debugging

Life would be easy if everything worked right the first time. This does not usually happen, does it? Do not get upset when your game has a glitch or something does not work perfectly. That is all part of the process of building a game. When the final level is built, the real work of making a commercial product begins.

Up to this point, the game was built to get the concept into the computer. During the ***testing and debugging*** phase, it is time to focus on finding problems and making the product polished for the customers. **Professional game testers** will play the latest iteration of the game and note every glitch and imperfection, as shown in **Figure 9-13**. Everything from graphics and character movements to gaps in the storyline will be tested. If anything is wrong, this is the time to find out!

CHEAT CODE: PROFESSIONAL GAME TESTERS

Professional game testers are trained on how to push a game to its limits. These people are paid to find the bugs and glitches in the game programming.

Shutterstock.com

Figure 9-13.

Game testers spend a lot of time playing the same part of a game over and over to make sure it works. Many testers will work on one game, each playing only a small part of the game.

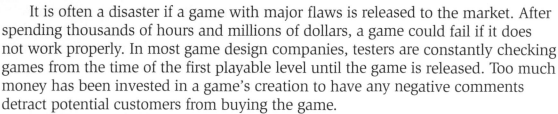

It is often a disaster if a game with major flaws is released to the market. After spending thousands of hours and millions of dollars, a game could fail if it does not work properly. In most game design companies, testers are constantly checking games from the time of the first playable level until the game is released. Too much money has been invested in a game's creation to have any negative comments detract potential customers from buying the game.

Imagine yourself as a game critic. You discover that a game freezes every time you press three buttons on the controller at the same time. You would tell everyone who would listen *not* to buy the game! Your fellow game critics would probably make the same recommendation, as represented in **Figure 9-14.** The company who made the game would likely lose much of the money it invested in the game. People on the design team responsible for the game may lose their jobs. Testing is a very important part of the design process. Every member of a design team should test games as though their job depends on it—because it very well might.

Tuning Stage

When all levels are complete and the story is told, the game enters the tuning stage. The ***tuning stage*** is where the game is tested not just for functionality, but for playability. In the testing and debugging phase, all functions were put through the ringer to make sure they worked. In the tuning stage, the idea is to find the final small adjustments that will make the game a commercial success.

To make the game a commercial success, it must first pass functionality and playability testing. When testing ***functionality,*** the game tester focuses on whether or not the game functions or plays as intended. Here, user interface controls, image renderings, and movements are tested to make sure they all function as intended without glitches and errors.

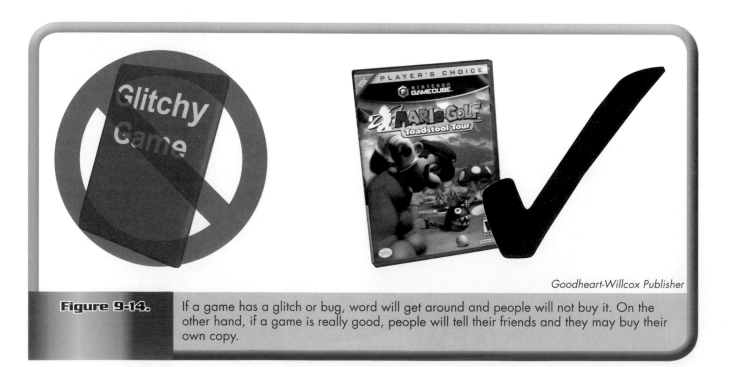

Goodheart-Willcox Publisher

Figure 9-14. If a game has a glitch or bug, word will get around and people will not buy it. On the other hand, if a game is really good, people will tell their friends and they may buy their own copy.

In addition to testing the functionality of the game, the game tester also checks for playability. ***Playability testing*** seeks to find out if the story is completely told, the game holds true to the concept, and if the objectives are obtainable. If there are holes in the story, the tester will note that something is missing between levels or objectives. The designers must fix these errors to make the story flow as intended.

www.g-wlearning.com

Level up
your know-how
with Animated
Review 9-1.

Additionally, the tester will look for anything that does not fit the concept. Seeing a brick road in a jungle or banana tree in the desert may indicate the need for more appropriate assets. A dirt road would be more true to the jungle concept and a cactus would be more appropriate to the desert concept.

Lastly, the tester must assure that the obstacles are appropriate and the objectives are achievable. If the tasks are too difficult on the first level, the player will quit and the game will fail. If the skill level needed to beat the game is beyond human ability, the designers need to make the game more playable. Conversely, the tester also notes if the level is too easy. If the game is not challenging, players will quit or beat the game too quickly.

At some point, a game must be finished. Remember the budget and deadline set at the beginning of the project? In most game builds, there is a point in production where the story is told and the game flows well from beginning to end. Even if more time exists in the production schedule to keep programming features in the construction stage, it is important to move on to the tuning stage when the game has the feel of a completed game.

Your team does not want to be forced to move into the tuning stage without a complete story or with unfinished work. Unfortunately, if the schedule and budget are not flexible, the game must move forward with the best version available. With only weeks remaining before the deadline to begin tuning, **crunch time** sets in. A team may scramble to complete the final storytelling aspects of the game to keep the schedule intact. The most important aspects of the game must be in place before the tuning can begin.

CHEAT CODE: CRUNCH TIME

Crunch time is the end of a project when time begins to run short and decisive action is required. During the crunch time, a game design team will work almost nonstop to finish the game. Many long hours will be put into the work.

In many cases, designers have a hard time with the tuning stage. It often requires removal of some code they spent time to build. Designers are always looking to build more into a game. But, in tuning the game, it becomes an issue of quality. The tuning stage is all about removing any imperfections or problems with the game. Focus on the highest-quality areas. Do not get distracted on a side trail that is cool to play, but does little to carry the story. This focus may make the difference between a commercial success or buggy failure.

As a tuner, the goal is not to add new features, but to polish the game to perfection. No bugs, no glitches, no holes, no pointless activities for the player—these things lead down the road to perfection. Critics and gamers are very suspect of games with bugs. It gives the perception that it is not a quality product and not worth playing. Additionally, every bug or glitch removes the player from the game world. Their attention is no longer focused on the features you programmed to establish and maintain immersion. It is like a red X on a test paper from school. The 99 correct responses are not the first thing you see. Instead, you see that big red X over the one question you got wrong, as illustrated in **Figure 9-15.** Make your game as perfect and playable as possible so there are no "red Xs" for people to focus on.

CASE STUDY

Quality Assurance Team

As a final part of the game design, the game must play properly. The role of assuring the game is a high-quality product falls on the quality assurance team (QA team). The primary objective of the QA team is to play the games and identify bugs. Bugs are errors in the game functionality. When a QA team finds a bug, it sends a message to the design team. The design team must investigate the bug and determine if it is really a bug and, if it is a bug, fix it.

Sometimes, the QA team identifies bugs that are not really bugs. A design team may have designed a component to work in an odd way. An example of "not a bug," or NAB, might be an enemy that fades in and out. If the design team created this enemy to have that power, it is not a bug. The design team then sends an NAB message that the character "works as designed."

Playing games sounds like a great job filled with fun. It can be, but it is also a job. Some pros of being on a QA team is that you do get to play games all day, you are part of an exciting company, and you get a foot in the door to start a career in gaming. Some of the cons of being on a QA team are that you have little to do with creating the game and you may have to play the same level over and over again for several days. The point here is that testing games is not always fun. You have to be a serious employee to be a benefit to the game and the company. Do a great job and you may advance through the company. Basic job requirements for the QA team include:

- Game literacy. You should be familiar with most of the popular game consoles and handheld devices. You need to have played many games in the past to have a good idea of how a high-quality game looks and plays.
- Computer literacy. You must be competent in using a computer. Using a computer to write reports, memos, e-mails, and keep records are all part of daily activities.
- Communication. You must be able to communicate in writing and in person on many issues. Always remember that you are evaluating other people's hard work. You must be polite and professional when explaining the problem. If you report a bug to a designer by saying, "this stinks!", you might be looking for a new job.

Bug reports are prioritized and labeled as A, B, C, or D bugs. This helps the designers identify the most important problems and fix the most important errors first and not simply fix the easiest first.

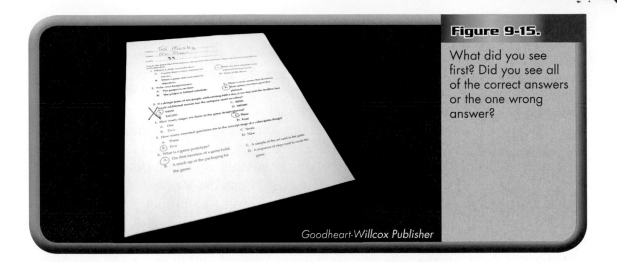

Figure 9-15.
What did you see first? Did you see all of the correct answers or the one wrong answer?

Goodheart-Willcox Publisher

Imagine two bug reports. One report is for a game-crash error when two buttons are pressed at the same time. The other report notes that the avatar has closed eyes when doing the kick animation. Remember, time deadlines and budgets probably will not allow the team to fix all problems. The game-crash error needs to be fixed first as it is very important (level A). In a perfect world all bugs would get fixed. In the real world, often only the bugs that affect the ability to sell the game are fixed.

Bug Type	Meaning	Examples
A	Major problem! The game cannot be released with this bug.	• Game is not fun to play. • Virus in game. • Game crashes. • Game features do not work properly. • Level is too difficult to complete. • Spelling errors. • Legal errors.
B	Big problem! The game can be released with this bug, but it will receive bad reviews for the error.	• Gameplay can typically be maintained. • Some features missing. • Graphic errors to backgrounds or other nonessential areas. • Incomplete menu or menu has options that are never available. • Levels are too easy to complete.
C	Common problem. This should be fixed if time permits, but release of the game will not be delayed by this bug. The easy fixes get done, while the difficult fixes are not done.	• Gameplay is uninterrupted by the error. • A minor problem that may be noted as a glitch by critics. • A problem that is not likely to be experienced by most players. • An error that is hard to duplicate.
D	Suggested feature. This bug will likely not be fixed prior to releasing the game unless there is remaining time.	• Gameplay is uninterrupted, but could be enhanced. • Adding a feature might make the gameplay better. • New technology could be applied. • Two buttons might be hard to press at the same time to activate a weapon.

Goodheart-Willcox Publisher

Design Documents

As a game designer, you will need to create several different types of documents to introduce your game and aid in keeping the design task moving forward. When designing a small or simple game, most designers do not have much of a structured design process. Instead, most simply sit at the computer and start making up the characters and codes as they go. To some extent, they have a good idea of what the final game will look like. Without the need to share this idea with others, they can design it without documentation. While this design process works for a small or individually designed game, it does not work for a large, team-built game.

In a team environment, the same information must be shared with every member of the team. All decisions about the game are written and distributed to all team members. To keep the process moving forward and to ensure all designers on the team are working toward the same goals and objectives, the game industry has adopted written design documents. Having the ideas on paper or electronically helps keep the team on task and helps create a trail of the decisions made on the game. If at any point you need to clarify a decision to remain on task with the game structure, you can refer to the appropriate design document.

The next sections describe the different documents that together make up a complete *governing game design document (GGDD)*. The GGDD is not a single document, but a collection of the different documents used to display information needed for each designer, programmer, or artist working on the project. All companies create a GGDD format that works best for their type of structure. There is no standard model.

Pitch Documents

The *pitch documents* are for presenting the idea to the decision makers that will **green light** the project. There are two basic types of pitch documents: high-concept document and game-treatment document, described in **Figure 9-16.** These documents are typically not included in the GGDD. Independent designers also create these documents to get bigger game companies to buy and make their game.

CHEAT CODE: GREEN LIGHT

Just like in traffic, a green light means go. When a designer is given a green light, the project has been approved and will go forward.

Name	Content Area	Description
High Concept Document	Concept Pitch	Used to introduce the idea or concept of the game and answer the five essential questions.
Game Treatment Document	Presentation and Marketing	This is a colorful document that includes some of the concept, story outline, and artistic concept of the game.

Figure 9-16. This table shows the two types of pitch documents and describes each.

Ethical Gamer

It is unethical to misrepresent data. Do not twist the facts when pitching your idea for a game. Present data and facts as accurately as you can. Let the idea for the game be judged on its own merits, not by an unethical misrepresentation.

High-Concept Document

The **high-concept document** is used as a selling tool to get a company to agree to produce a game. This is usually the first document used in game design. In it, the overall concept of the game is described along with any unique features that would make the game competitive in the current marketplace.

The high-concept document is written in a letter or bulleted format. It should answer *all* of the five essential questions in the concept stage. Ideas are grouped in easy-to-read chunks. If the document is too long or wordy, it probably will not be read. If it is not read, that means the idea will fail to get approved for production.

This document is like a résumé for an idea. The purpose of the document is to share an idea with a design company and get a meeting with a developer to explore possible production of the game. Once you get that meeting, you will have to continue to sell your idea and provide greater detail to convince the company that your idea will work and sell.

Game-Treatment Document

When you get that very important meeting to present your game concept, you need to have a game-treatment document. The **game-treatment document** explains in greater detail the vision of the game. Remember, you are trying to get money from the publisher to get your game produced. That means this document must be very professional and build on your high-concept document as a sales tool. Some things that are included in a game-treatment document are:

- plot overview;
- character features;
- concept art;
- genre;
- possible ESRB rating;
- target audience; and
- any USPs or special features that would make the game stand out from the competition.

The game-treatment document can be a document that you refer to as you go through your presentation. It is often a **leave-behind document** that is left with the publisher for them to look at after you leave. A **brochure** or

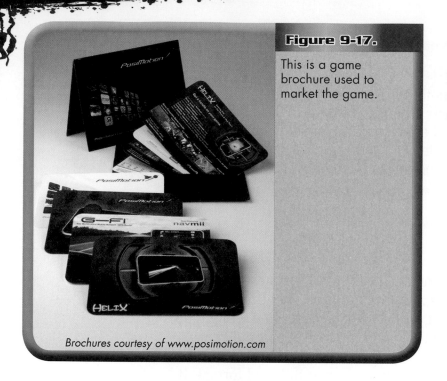

Figure 9-17.

This is a game brochure used to market the game.

Brochures courtesy of www.posimotion.com

presentation folder format will give a polished feel to the presentation and provide a quality example of your work, as shown in **Figure 9-17.** If you are attending a conference or a pitch meeting, you need to have several game-treatment documents available to hand out.

Often overlooked, but highly valuable, is the inclusion of any market analysis, target market identification, or other business statistics that show how releasing your game would make the company money. Remember, a video game design company is a business. All businesses exist to make profits. The closer you are to showing how an idea will make the company more money than it will spend developing and marketing the game, the closer you are to getting your game on the shelf.

Governing Game Design Document

Once your sales pitch is successful, it is time to get a GGDD started. This will formalize all of the design work and decisions from this point forward. Shown in **Figure 9-18** is a sample of documents and topics needed in many game builds. This is not a comprehensive listing of all documents needed, as the GGDD is not standardized. As a student, you will focus on some simplified versions of these documents. This will allow you to create and identify any design document in the design studio.

Market-Analysis Document

The **market-analysis document** details the concept of the game and who the game is targeted to attract. This document includes the formal concept, game overview, game characteristics, target market **demographics,** and gaming platform(s). Most of this information is included in the pitch documents, but may have been changed to get the green light. Once the game is approved, the market-analysis document becomes the master guide for all other decisions regarding the game.

CHEAT CODE: DEMOGRAPHICS

Demographics are measurable characteristics of the potential customers. This may include age, income, race, gender, education level, and many other characteristics. Grouping potential customers by demographics helps form your target markets.

Document Name	Topics	Description
Market Analysis	Concept	Answers the five essential questions.
	Game Overview	Brief synopsis of the game action and how the protagonist will move from the beginning to the end of the story.
	Game Characteristics	A listing of the major element and features, such as worlds, levels, mood, etc.
	Target Market	Demographics on the age, income, maturity, etc., of the gamers. Additionally, a description of the competitors, USPs, and potential popularity of the game, genre, and theme are included.
	Gaming Platform	On what platform is the game built to play: PC, PS3, Xbox 360, Wii, handheld?
World Design	Color Palette	Colors used by all artist throughout the game to create the same mood and feel.
	Scene Drawings	Drawings of scenes from the game with mood, lighting, and contrast noted.
	Scene Notations	Background sounds needed/used and light direction, source, and intensity.
	Storyboard	Structure of the plot within the game showing as linear, mission based, nonlinear (sandbox), hub and spoke, etc.
	Game Controls	User interface, menu systems, in-game information, displays, health/skill database, and other game controls are listed.
Character Design	Concept Art	Basic sketches of characters, major objects.
	Model Sheets	Formal sketches of models, movements, facial expressions and accessories.
Game Script	Decision Tree or Flowchart	Break down the storyline into the decisions and paths a player will take through the game. Levels, skills, and objectives for the player at each point in the story are shown.
	Game Mechanics	How the rules of the game will be applied.
	Game Physics	Gravity, speed, interactions, collision, etc., are defined and set for the game world.
	Animation Sets	Animations and player/nonplayer movements. For character movements, the user interface is indicated.
	Narrative Script	Narrations, voiceovers, and cut scenes.
Character Script	Player Movement	User interface controls that activate each character animation and movement. Nonplayer character (NPC) interactions are set. Active object list is created and interactions are set.
	Player Statistics	Database of attributes, skills, weapons, and health of player character. Checkpoints, storage, and restarting data for selected player are set.
Technical Design	Program Design	Game engine, physics engine, artificial intelligence (AI), etc.
	Poly Rendering	Game map controls and object draw and rendering controls.

Figure 9-18. These are some of the documents that may be found in a governing game design document.

Goodheart-Willcox Publisher

THE SHORT KNIGHT
World Design

- Dragon's cave (dark, dreary).
- Town and building interiors (illuminated by firelight).
- Citizens in town.
- Castle of the king.
- Dragon sounds: snorting, breathing, torch (fire breathing).
- Battle sounds: swords clashing, arrows launching, thumps for shield contact.
- Background music for traveling sequences.

Goodheart-Willcox Publisher

Figure 9-19. The world design game document describes what is needed to create the game world, including graphics and sounds.

World-Design Document

The **world-design document** lists the items that are needed to create the game world, like the example shown in **Figure 9-19.** Emotional descriptors, such as bright and cheery, help in creating this list. If the game is a racing game, the world-design document might include:

- grassy infield;
- stadium seating;
- spectators;
- blue sky at midday;
- cheering sounds;
- engine sounds; and
- announcer sounds.

Notice that the world design is not just shapes and objects, but also sounds and other sensory information in the game world. Small games, puzzle games, video board games, or other games without a narrative element do not require a world-design document.

In this document, a **decision tree** of actions and choices by the protagonist lays out the entire story, as illustrated in **Figure 9-20.** For each of these branches, the programmers need to create a game mode or a cut scene to develop the story. All elements of the plot should be displayed in the decision tree. When complete, the decision tree displays the start of the story, the major choices of the protagonist, levels or cut scenes that each tells part of the story, and the path to the victory condition.

Character-Design Document

A **character-design document** details the look of a character and the abilities of that character. Typically, a character-design document includes concept art. **Concept art** is a sketch that gives basic shape and style, but not overwhelming detail. The concept art usually included in the character-design document is a large sketch of the character along with several smaller sketches of some of the animated poses or movements of the character. Other drawings should include facial expressions, any costume changes, or morphing that the character will perform.

Along with the drawings, the character document includes a name, background story or history, likes/dislikes, strengths/weaknesses, clothing, weapons, class, and so on. Since the drawings are usually a quick pencil draft, a sample color palette is also included for the character to show the colors used in the drawings. The color can be used to help show the emotion or attitude of the character. For example, a cowboy with a white hat is the good guy and the cowboy with a black hat is the bad guy. After approval of the character design, a more detailed **model sheet** is completed to show the actual details and poses of the character, as shown in **Figure 9-21.**

Flowcharts and Storyboards

With the plot laid out in a convenient form, it is time to draft documents to show what happens in a gameplay mode and what the gameplay will look like. Often, flowcharts and storyboards are combined to create a map for the programmers to follow.

In a design studio, the designers write up a flowchart with a few basic instructions. These instructions detail the interactions that will occur in a scene, the user interface, and the entry and exit criteria for the scene. The storyboard shows a brief

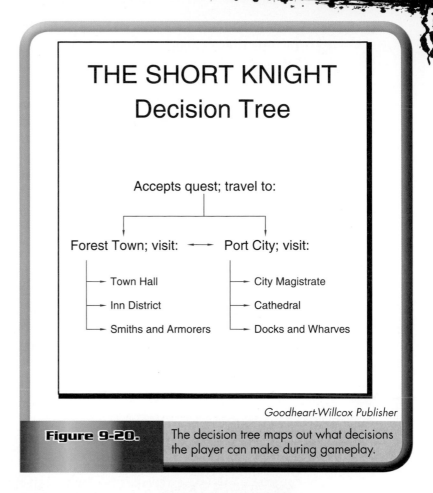

Goodheart-Willcox Publisher

Figure 9-20. The decision tree maps out what decisions the player can make during gameplay.

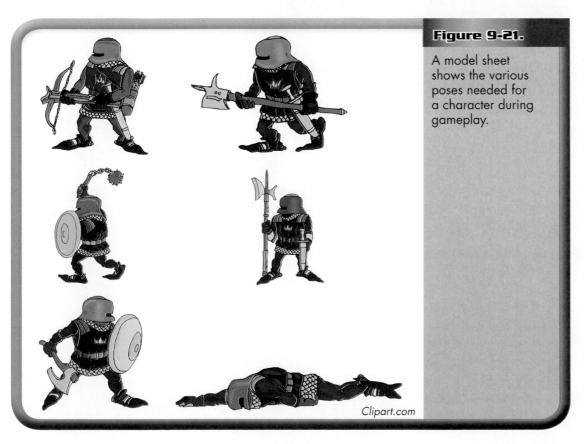

Clipart.com

Figure 9-21.

A model sheet shows the various poses needed for a character during gameplay.

sketch of what everything is supposed to look like. Then, the team literally tapes or pins these sheets to the wall, as shown in **Figure 9-22.** Each page should be labeled with a title so it is easily referred to in discussions.

After these documents are on the wall, they can be easily rearranged to show the structure of the game. Colored string and arrows are used to connect each scene to the next if the game has a nonlinear structure. Revisions and additions are usually written in the margins or on sticky notes and attached to the page.

You can think of the flowcharts and storyboard as a comic strip: a drawing of a scene with a description of the action and then a drawing of a different scene with some additional action are set in order. Together all of the panels tell the story.

The main purpose of these documents is to help create the structure of the game in an easily followed format. Some companies use software to help create these documents and eliminate the stuck-to-the-wall process. This makes sense because they want to share this information. Any changes can be transmitted to the design teams, which may be working remotely all around the country or the world. The software approach, however, has not seen wide acceptance with designers as they like to see the "big picture" for the game. Nothing shows the big picture better than a wall-sized view with all of the important scenes of the game.

Goodheart-Willcox Publisher; image: Shutterstock.com

Figure 9-22.   Posting the storyboard frames and flowchart on the wall allows the designers to see the big picture.

Game-Script Document

The **game-script document** is where the rules and core mechanics are structured. A complete listing of the rules of the game and how the core mechanics will interpret and enforce the rules is the main purpose of the game-script document. This is *not* a document that details how the software for the game will be written. It should *not* contain any of the technical designs or computer coding that makes everything work.

Once the game script is written, a game **mock-up** can be created. With a game mock-up, typically paper or note cards are used to draw a character and act out a game scene, as shown in **Figure 9-23.** The purpose of this is to test the rules and the core mechanics to see if all of the elements will work. It takes a little time to test this with a simple board game or RPG model of the game world, but it may save hundreds of hours later. There is no reason to wait until the very end to see if all of your effort will work. When testing the gameplay against the game script, you should get a good idea of what problems may lie ahead in the programming.

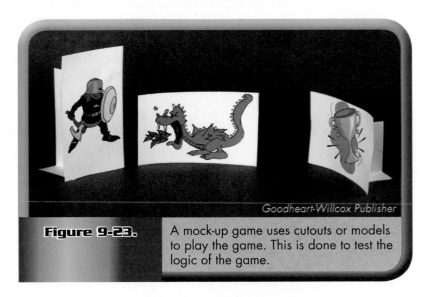

Goodheart-Willcox Publisher

Figure 9-23. A mock-up game uses cutouts or models to play the game. This is done to test the logic of the game.

Technical Design Document

The **technical design document** details the computer codes, event codes, and technical interactions between the user interface and the core mechanics that will be built into the game. It is usually written by the lead programmer. Most game designers use the game engine and other game development tools selected by the lead programmer for the game build.

Game-Development Tools

As a game designer, it is unlikely you will ever get down to the actual computer-code level of programming. Companies use **game-development tools** to streamline and simplify the design process. Game engines and compiler programs take away much of the line-by-line programming required in the early days of video game design. A **compiler program** takes the instructions from a user and restates these commands as computer codes.

CHEAT CODE: GAME-DEVELOPMENT TOOLS

A game-development tool is a software program or hardware device that makes building and programming a game easier. Game engines and 3D modeling tools are examples of software technologies. Motion-capture suits and green screens are examples of hardware technologies.

For example, look at The Games Factory 2 software. It is important to understand the logic needed to create the interactions. However, you do not enter the computer code needed to tell the computer how to perform the interaction. Complex algorithms are reduced down to a simple click of the mouse as you select the type of movement you intend an object to have. In this way, the act of creating is enhanced and the labor of programming is reduced.

Both custom software and COTS software help bring today's video game from concept to the store shelf. These are discussed in the next sections. Without these helpful tools, video games would take much longer to produce, have fewer features, and cost significantly more than they do today.

Custom Software

Video game production companies often create custom software. **Custom software** is applications or tools created for a specific purpose that are not available in existing software. A game development company will attempt to write a more efficient game-development tool or one with enhanced features. The intent is to give the game a competitive edge in either technological superiority or speed of development. Of course, custom software costs both money and time. In a large production company, it is often feasible to create the custom software since the cost can be spread out over several games.

In the **technological superiority** area, the custom software will improve a technical aspect of the game. A tool may be able to render a character with greater detail or movement, yet do so without additional processing power. On the other hand, a custom tool may be able to complete a task that cannot be done with current tools. At one point, pixel shading and vertex shading could only be done with custom software.

In the **speed of development** area, the custom software reduces the time required to create the game. A new development tool may be able to quickly produce an effect or better compile the programming. Remember how much a single day of delay can cost a video game production company? If the team can work more efficiently and complete jobs faster, the same amount of money is saved every day the project is completed before a deadline. Less build time equals less cost and more profits.

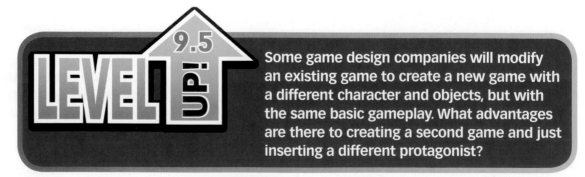

Some game design companies will modify an existing game to create a new game with a different character and objects, but with the same basic gameplay. What advantages are there to creating a second game and just inserting a different protagonist?

COTS

Most people and smaller companies do not have the resources to spend on creating custom software. They must use **consumer off-the-shelf (COTS) software**. COTS means it can be purchased by almost anyone. In other words, it is not custom or proprietary software. COTS software will usually get the job done, though it may not have the technology of custom software. Using COTS software may also take longer to produce a result similar to custom software. A program like The Games Factory 2 is COTS software. It works very well for the games and logic learned in this textbook, as shown in **Figure 9-24.**

Companies use COTS software when they do not have the cash or time to develop custom software. COTS software allows a company to spend less money than for custom software and have a working software product running the same day. An additional benefit to using COTS software is that new employees may already know how to use the software. Since COTS software is available to all companies, it is widely used. If new employees already know how to use the software, they do not need to be trained on the software—which saves time in the short term.

Asset Building

Many COTS software tools are used in the game industry to develop assets. Some of these software programs include Maya, **3ds Max,** Blender, and Photoshop. The benefits to using a game development tool are easy to see. Programs like Maya and 3ds Max are COTS software that help build three-dimensional objects and scenes.

CHEAT CODE: 3DS MAX

The software 3ds Max has been around for many years. Originally, it was called 3D Studio. This was a DOS-based program. It then evolved into 3D Studio MAX for the Windows platform. The current software is called 3ds Max. Many users still refer to this software as 3D Studio or simply max.

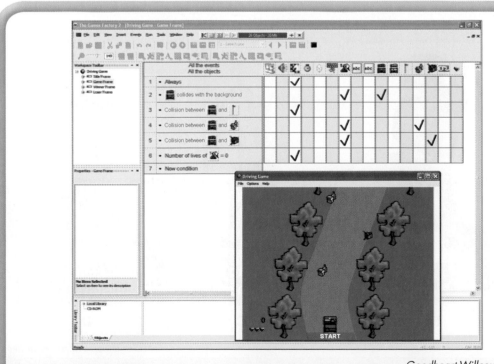

Goodheart-Willcox Publisher

Figure 9-24. The Games Factory 2 is COTS software. This is the software used in the workbook.

A program like Maya is great for making very complex 3D objects. Maya can produce an exceptionally realistic object complete with multiple textures and light refractions. Built into Maya is the ability to create realistic designs with features like moving liquids or hair/fur that blows in the wind. The 3ds Max program does a great job of making 3D characters with easily editable poses, as shown in **Figure 9-25.** These objects can then be exported into other programs to be used as avatars or in cut scene animations. Both products work great for making three-dimensional objects and scenes.

GUI

Common to most COTS software programs is a **_graphical user interface (GUI)._** GUI is pronounced *gooey.* This builds into the program the familiar point-and-click interface that everyone is used to using on their home computers. It also provides the ability to visually see what is being created. Without a GUI, a computer user would have to know programming and type the code into the computer. Gone would be all of the icons and buttons to click with a mouse. Without a GUI, designing a game would be line after line of typed computer code.

The computers you use at home and school have an operating system with a GUI. Windows and Mac OS are both operating systems that have a GUI. Before these graphic-based interfaces, computers operated by showing number, text, and codes that the user would interpret. A simple command to copy something would require a code statement similar to:

COPY A: *.* C:\MY_STUFF

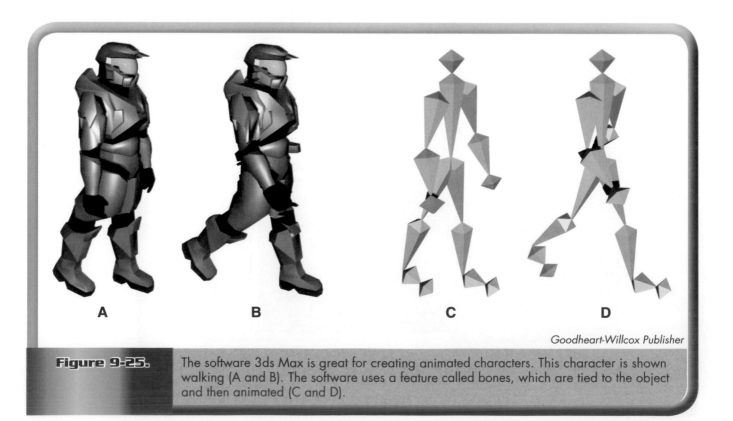

A   B   C   D

Goodheart-Willcox Publisher

Figure 9-25. The software 3ds Max is great for creating animated characters. This character is shown walking (A and B). The software uses a feature called bones, which are tied to the object and then animated (C and D).

Today, you can just drag and drop the file to move or copy it, as shown in **Figure 9-26.** With touch-screen devices, you no longer even need to use a mouse. You just touch the screen and drag the file where you want it.

Visual Programming

A game development tool makes the job of programming much easier. Visual programming languages like Visual Basic, Visual C, Visual C + +, or Visual C# all take clicks of the mouse and turn them into computer codes through compiling. Some programs can compile using only one computer language, while others can compile multiple languages. Some of the most popular computer languages are C, C + +, C#, Python, Ruby, Pearl, Groovy, Fortran, Cobol, PHP, and Java.

Other Tools

Other game development tools such as DirectX, Java, and Flash help to create the game in a playable format. The biggest player in the computer world is Microsoft. With the power of its brand and its money in the bank, this company can produce almost any software product and continuously improve it to perfection. This is the case with DirectX. **DirectX** is an all-inclusive game engine from Microsoft. DirectX reads and interprets the game movements and creates a game environment for use on Windows-based computers and the Xbox game console. DirectX integrates all features from the visual display, sound, media, and user interface into a playable environment.

The latest version of DirectX game programming is XNA. The XNA package is available through the Microsoft Visual Studio for game developers. **XNA** allows game developers the ability to design games for Windows-based computers and the Xbox system. Built into XNA is the source code editor, compiler/interpreter, build automation, and debugger.

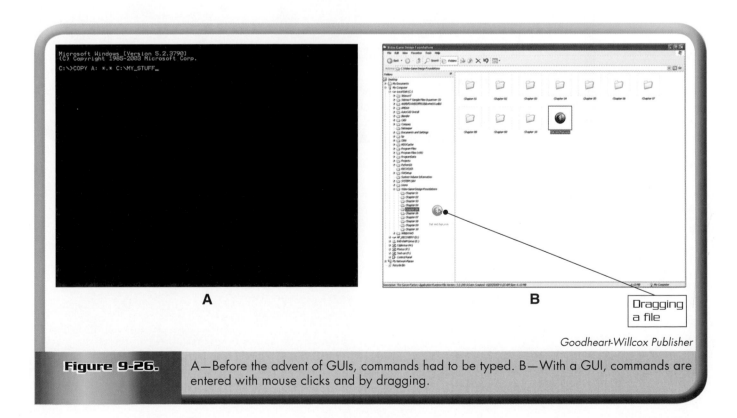

Dragging a file

Goodheart-Willcox Publisher

Figure 9-26. A—Before the advent of GUIs, commands had to be typed. B—With a GUI, commands are entered with mouse clicks and by dragging.

Other free developer tools, like Kodu for the Xbox 360 system, allow developers to create games and post them to the online portal. Subscribers on Xbox Live can download these games for a small fee or even play a free demo, as shown in **Figure 9-27.**

Java- and Flash-based games are also very popular. These games are typically simple games that can be easily played on and downloaded from the Internet. These programming languages allow for fairly easy game creation with low programming needs. Both are a great way for young programmers and video game hobbyists to get started programming and building games.

Microsoft

Figure 9-27. Xbox Live is an Internet site where you can download sample Xbox games. After obtaining 400 points, you can even download Kodu, which you can use to design your own Xbox games.

Chapter Summary

- A video game designer needs to be aware of and able to create a development plan for a video game design.
- The development process for a video game follows a three-stage process: concept, construction, and tuning.
- Budget and scheduling in video game design are critical because game releases are often time sensitive and because the amount of money invested in a product is carefully calculated by the design company to insure that the product can be profitable.
- Iterations are different versions of the game with each version an improvement over the last.
- The design plans include defining the following: gameplay modes, protagonist and character development, the game world, core mechanics, mode elaboration, story elaboration, level design, and testing and debugging.
- Character sketches that include features, facial expressions, body poses, dress, and weapons, among other things, are needed to make the character believable.
- Storyboards are constructed to allow designers to fit the game into the story.
- There are various game-development tools currently used by the video game industry including custom software and consumer off-the-shelf software.
- Video game engines and compiler programs take away much of the line-by-line programming originally required for video game design, enhancing the act of creating and reducing the labor of programming.
- In addition to custom and COTS video game engines, there are asset building tools that aid in the development of video games.

Check Your Video Game IQ

Now that you have finished this chapter, see what you know about video game design by taking the chapter posttest.

www.m.g-wlearning.com

www.g-wlearning.com

Review Your Knowledge

On a separate sheet of paper or in a word processing document, match the following terms with the definitions that fit best.

A. concept stage
B. technical design document
C. prototype
D. tuning stage
E. character-design document

F. game-treatment document
G. construction stage
H. first playable level
I. concept art
J. game-script document

1. Second stage of the three-stage cycle; focuses on building levels and game assets needed for the game.

2. Details core interactions with the game as defined by the general rules and core mechanics instructions.

3. First milestone of the game build whereby an entire level has been programmed in playable fashion.

4. First stage of the three-stage cycle; focuses on formalizing the big idea for the game.

5. Sketch of the basic shape and style of a character or other object.

6. Details the computer codes, event codes, and technical interactions between the user interface and core mechanics.

7. Final stage in game design where the game is tested for functionality and playability.

8. Pitch documents that summarize major game features such as the concept, story outline, character, and art.

9. Basic, first version of a game build used to test the concept.

10. Sketches that detail the appearance, poses, and abilities of a character.

On a separate sheet of paper or in a word processing document, answer each of the following questions.

11. What is a *delay in production?*

12. What does it mean to be *over budget?*

13. If a design team of ten people, each earning $400 a day, is ten days past the deadline, how much additional money has the company spent on salary?

14. Give four examples of why a game's release may be time sensitive.

15. List the stages in the game design process.

16. What is the role of the concept stage?

17. How many essential questions are in the concept stage of a video game design?

18. What is the role of the construction stage?

19. What is a game prototype?

20. List the eight areas of design that bridge the concept to construction.

21. What is the difference between primary gameplay mode and secondary gameplay mode?

22. Define *protagonist.*

23. What is *character development?*

24. Describe what the *game world* encompasses.

25. What are the *core mechanics?*

26. What is *mode elaboration?*

27. Define *story elaboration.*

28. What is the goal of level design?

29. What is the first playable level?

30. In which phase of construction are problems located and the product polished for the customer?

31. How does the tuning stage differ from debugging the game?

32. Describe the *governing game design document.*

33. What are *pitch documents?*

34. Which document is like a résumé for a game idea?

35. List five pieces of information that should be included in the market-analysis document.

36. What is the purpose of the *world-design document?*

37. What is the purpose of a *character-design document?*

38. In which document are the rules and core mechanics of the game structured?

39. Which document details the computer codes, event codes, and technical interactions between the user interface and the core mechanics that will be built into the game?

40. Why do companies use game-development tools?

41. What is custom software?

42. What does COTS stand for?

43. List four commercial software programs that are commonly used to create game assets.

44. List the two all-inclusive game engines available from Microsoft.

45. Which two programming languages are especially suited for young programmers and hobbyists?

Apply Your STEM Knowledge

Language Arts

1. Review the construction stage and the eight areas of design for a video game. Create a Gantt chart to schedule the work flow of the eight areas of design for a 14-day game build.

Science

2. The iterative process of game design means that several improved versions are constructed before making a final version. Research the invention of the electric lightbulb. Write a one-page paper describing the iterative process required to invent the electric lightbulb.

Social Studies

3. Research the typical food eaten in your family's ancestral country. On a single sheet of paper, draw an eight- to 12-frame storyboard on how to make a simple meal from that country.

Mathematics

4. Copy the table below to paper or spreadsheet software.
   A. Construct an expense budget for the following game build.
      Deadline: two weeks (10 days)
      Number of designers: six
      Annual salary of designers: $52,000/year (assume a five-day workweek)
      Consumer off-the-shelf software available: Unity Pro @ $1,200 for each designer
      Proprietary software build: $4,600
   B. How much would the company save if the game build was completed two days before the deadline?
   C. How much overbudget would this project be if the game took three weeks to complete?
   D. The proprietary software can be modified to do its job and the work of the COTS software for $5000 more. Should the company build the COTS software features into their proprietary software? Why or why not?

Item	Cost of Each	Amount Needed	Total
Salary per day	$	days	$
Cost of COTS	$	licenses	$
Cost of Proprietary Software	$	licenses	$
Total Expense Budget			$

Language Arts

5. Form into groups of two or three. Research, debate, and form a group opinion on each of the Level Up! activities in this chapter. Prepare a PowerPoint presentation of ten slides (five to seven minutes) to present to the class explaining the group's opinions for each Level Up! activity. Include text, pictures, video, animations, and slide transitions as appropriate to help explain your positions.

Working in Teams

Working in teams, create a slide show or product demonstration to sell a video game idea to your class. Select an actual game or an idea that the team creates. Use your imagination. Create a brochure, promotional item, or any other item that will help you make this sales presentation. Observe, evaluate, and critique the other class members' sales presentations.

Gamer Portfolio

Your portfolio should contain samples of work that show your skills or talents. Look at past school or work assignments you have completed. Select a book report, essay, poem, or other work that demonstrates your writing talents. Include artwork created for your game builds. Look for projects that show your skills related to critical thinking and problem solving. Have you completed a long or complex project? Write a description of the project and tell how you managed various parts of the assignment to complete it on time. Select completed work from other classes that will help prepare you for a career in the video game design industry.

1. Save the documents that show your skills and talents in your e-portfolio. Remember to place the documents in an appropriate subfolder.
2. Place hard copies in the container for your print portfolio.

G-W Learning Mobile Site

Visit the G-W Learning mobile site to complete the chapter pretest and posttest and to practice vocabulary using e-flash cards. If you do not have a smartphone, visit the G-W Learning companion website to access these features.

G-W Learning mobile site: www.m.g-wlearning.com

G-W Learning companion website: www.g-wlearning.com

Common Core

College and Career Readiness

CTE Career Ready Practices. You may have been taught to treat others how *you* would like to be treated. This is often referred to as *the golden rule.* Productively working with others who have a background different from yours may require that you learn to treat others as *they* wish to be treated. Conduct research on the Internet about cultural differences related to personal space, time, gestures/body language, and relationship toward authority figures. Create a T-chart that show the difference on the left and ways you would adapt your interactions to account for that difference.

Reading. Consider how the author uses the term *budget* throughout this chapter. How did your understanding of this term change as you were reading? Look up the word *budget* in the dictionary. How did the author shape this definition to fit the subject matter in this chapter? As needed, derive meaning of the environmental print and use visual and contextual support to confirm understanding. Use support from classmates and your teacher as needed to help in comprehension of the material. Write a few paragraphs about what the term *budget* means to you after reading this chapter.

Speaking and Listening. Research the features of some of the tools available for creating video games. Compile information about the aspects of several custom software and several consumer off-the-shelf software programs. Include details about features or benefits of the programs that you think you would find most useful as well as anything you think would be a drawback. Use this information, along with what you already know about game development tools, to create a "top five" list of programs. Using various elements (visual displays, written handouts, technological displays), present your choices to the class. Explain why you chose the programs you did. Be sure to use the appropriate vocabulary related to the industry. As you listen to your classmates' stances on this topic, take notes and ask questions about positions or terms you do not understand.

Event Prep: Ethics

Ethics may be a competitive event you might enter with your Career and Technical Student Organization (CTSO). The competitive event may include an objective test that covers multiple topics. However, ethics may be one part of another event that may include objective questions or a presentation. Ethics may also be required as part of your game build presentation. To prepare for an ethics event:

1. Read the guidelines provided by your organization. Make certain that you ask any questions about points you do not understand. It is important you follow each specific item that is outlined in the competition rules.

2. Review the Ethical Gamer features throughout this text. Make notes on index cards about important points to remember. Use these notes to study.

3. Ask someone to practice role playing with you by asking questions or taking the other side of an argument.

4. Use the Internet to find more information about ethics and social responsibility. Find and review ethics cases that involve gamers, video games, or the video game industry.

Chapter 10
Global Economy and Supply Chain

A lot of people are involved in getting a game from an original concept to your hands. This chapter explores how the concept of specialization of labor developed into the modern supply chain. At each phase of the supply chain, value is added to make the product more sellable. In today's global economy, a vast network of providers and suppliers are needed to complete the production and distribution of a video game. As you read this chapter, look at how you fit into the supply chain and how the world economy is changing.

Check Your Video Game IQ

Before you begin this chapter, see what you already know about video game design by taking the chapter pretest.

www.m.g-wlearning.com

www.g-wlearning.com

College and Career Readiness

Reading Prep. In preparation for this chapter, research the employment opportunities globally in the video game design field. Summarize your findings. As you are reading the chapter, keep in mind the global considerations necessary in the video game design field for both designers and the products they design.

Objectives

After completing this chapter, you will be able to:
- Describe how video games are marketed and sold.
- Explain the relationship between video game publishers, developers, distributors, marketers, and retailers.
- Identify how globalization has impacted the design and production of video games.
- Describe how video games affect the economy.
- List various employment opportunities available in the global video game design field.
- Identify the requirements of various jobs in the video game design field.

Early Economy

Throughout history, the way people obtained the things they needed and wanted has evolved. In the past, a farmer might trade a basket of apples to the blacksmith for having shoes put on his horses. This **barter system** of trade occurred before the invention of currency and to some degree still exists today. It allowed some people to specialize in producing additional supply of an item and make it available for barter (sale).

The barter system worked well with some small items that could be easily exchanged. The trouble came in bartering for larger items such as a cow or a house. Just how many baskets of apples is a house worth, one thousand? Who could eat a thousand baskets of apples? Maybe the most famous barter story in history was *Jack and the Beanstalk.* In that story, a cow was worth five magic beans.

Today, currency is almost exclusively used for commerce. Little product-for-product bartering occurs. The invention of **currency** (money) made exchanging goods and services easier, **Figure 10-1.** Precious metals, such as gold and silver, were pressed into standard-size coins and stamped with the value. Eventually, paper money was invented to replace the metal currency. Today, many exchanges are done electronically. The amount of money is stored in an electronic account, but can be exchanged for paper money or coins.

CHEAT CODE: END USER

The end user is the final customer. In other words, the end user is the last person in the supply chain.

In bartering, people simply traded what they had to each other. That was the earliest supply chain. A **supply chain** consists of the links where a product or service is transferred from producer to **end user.**

A

B

Shutterstock.com

Figure 10-1. A—Currency is the standard for business today. Each country has its own currency. An exchange rate is used to determine what each currency is worth, such as 80 yen = 1 dollar. B—Gold is a precious metal that has a lot of value.

For some products, there are many links in a long supply chain to link the product from the original producer to the end user.

Think about the supply chain for the bread you eat with dinner. First, wheat is grown and harvested on a farm, as shown in **Figure 10-2.** Then, it goes into a bulk cargo container for transport by truck. The truck goes to a processing plant. The plant adds value to the wheat by milling it into flour. A bakery buys the flour and adds value by baking loaves of bread. This is called a ***value added*** process because bread has more value than wheat. The bread is then shipped to a grocery store. The grocery store sells the bread to your family. Finally, your family sits down to dinner including the bread.

Video Game Supply Chain

The video game industry also has a supply chain to get your favorite game from the design company into your hands. This chapter focuses on the standard video game industry supply chain. However, it should be noted there are ongoing attempts to reduce the steps in the supply chain.

Farmer ⟺ **Grocer** ⟺ **Family Meal**

Goodheart-Willcox Publisher; images: Shutterstock.com

Figure 10-2. The supply chain for food is clear. It starts with the farmer, goes through the grocer, and ends up with your family.

The links in this supply chain can be divided into five main categories. In order, these are development, production, wholesale distribution, retail distribution, and consumer, as outlined in the flowchart in **Figure 10-3.** There may be many different suppliers at each link in the supply chain. The following sections provide more information on each of these supply chain categories.

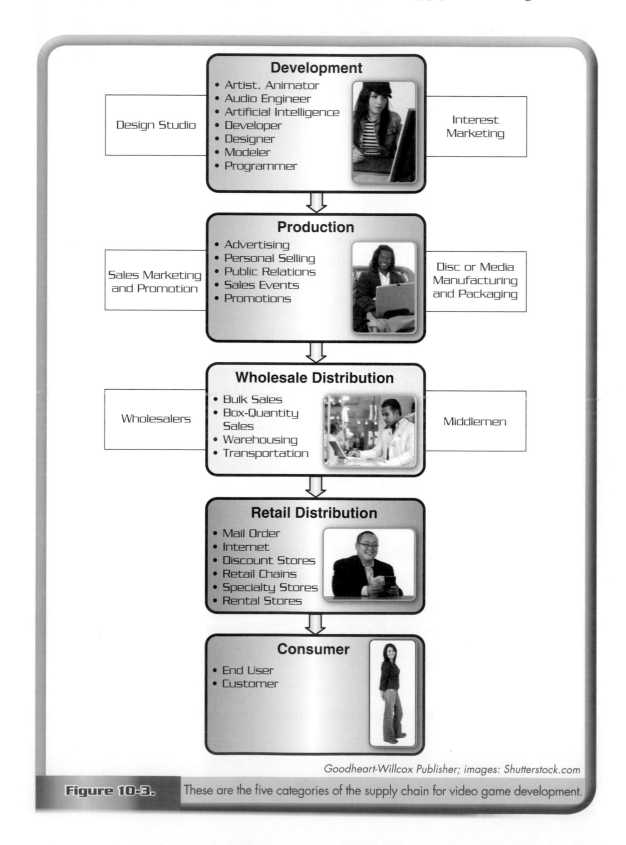

Goodheart-Willcox Publisher; images: Shutterstock.com

Figure 10-3. These are the five categories of the supply chain for video game development.

CASE STUDY

Studio Chief Executive Officer

The chief executive officer (CEO) is the single voice of leadership for a company. This leadership role is responsible for executing the large vision of the company as set by the board of directors. In addition to guiding the firm along the course set by the company vision, the CEO is also the final decision maker. This makes the CEO responsible for all successes and failures of the company.

One such studio CEO is Dustin Clingman of ZeeGee games in Orlando, Florida. With more than a decade of experience in the gaming industry, Mr. Clingman has established himself as both a leader within his company and as director of the Orlando chapter of the International Game Developers Association (IGDA). In 2012, he was named the national chairman of the IGDA.

Recently, Mr. Clingman shared his experiences and the opportunities that took him from a focus tester to a leader in the gaming industry. His love for storytelling helped him progress within the industry and hold many jobs with increasing responsibility. Some of these jobs included: test lead, sound designer, programmer, producer, and external producer. The important thing to learn from his experience is that there are many different paths and opportunities that lead to your dreams. As opportunities or promotions present themselves, evaluate how each will ultimately help you get where you want to be. There is no set path to success in this diverse industry. Some words of advice from Mr. Clingman: focus on the requirements for quality concepts and being a quality employee.

- **Programmers.** Skills of problem solving are most desirable. Experience is a measure of how many opportunities an employee has had to overcome problems. Technical programming skills are important, but the integration of math, science, and technology to create new methods of enhancing gameplay are golden.

- **Designers.** Storytelling, communication, and organizational skills are most desirable. Here, the ability to integrate history, humanities, and mythology combine with knowledge of game history and available technology to develop the stories that only games can tell.

- **Artists.** A proficiency in traditional and electronic platforms is most desirable. Regardless of the implementation of 2D or 3D environments, an understanding of the elements of art and the principles of design will form the foundation of the skills needed to be a successful game artist. The ability to create high-quality sketches, original characters, and game world assets allow game artists to have a huge impact on the final game design. Translating those ideas into artwork using programs like Adobe Illustrator, Maya, or 3ds Max allow artists to see their creations come to life in games.

The future is bright for students willing to learn and adapt. The changing environment of technology and the gaming industry are pushing toward global management. Virtual and collaborative tools are enabling teams to work in diverse locations. Competition forces companies to reduce costs and development time to bring creative games to market. Communication skills within a virtual environment and in person will become increasingly valuable skills. Understanding that, as technology changes, those on the cutting edge of technology must change fastest will be critical to your personal success.

Recent new developments in distribution through portals like Facebook, Xbox Live, and iPhone have revealed how companies will have to change to meet the immediate demands of consumers. Innovation and creativity will open new direct channels to consumers looking for the best stories and best games. Building relationships, enrolling others in your success, and giving back to those that helped you on your journey will light the path to an enriching career in the gaming industry.

Development

The first category of the supply chain is the **development group.** This group actually makes the product. In a video game supply chain, the developer is a design or development company such as EA (Electronic Arts), Acclaim, LucasArts, or Bungie. The development level is easy to identify since the product does not exist until it is created by a developer.

CHEAT CODE: MASTER

A master disc contains the original finished version of the program. All other discs are copied from that master. The master disc is sent to the duplicator by the developer.

At this point, the game is only the programming code. It does not exist in a packaged and sellable condition. The purpose for the developer is to make a game and deliver a gold **master.** The gold master is the perfected final disc used as the original from which all other copies will be made, shown in **Figure 10-4.**

Developer Marketing

In the development stage, the marketing effort done by the developer is typically not geared toward the end user. Rather, marketing is aimed at selling to producers and wholesalers in events such as trade shows and conventions, like that shown in **Figure 10-5.** The developer's sales team will look for a producer for their game. A marketing agreement with the producer will move the game down the supply chain.

Additionally, Internet marketing campaigns may be conducted. Often, developers will release **beta** (trial) versions of the game or video demos to help generate consumer interest in the product. A good beta trial shows a producer good market potential for the game. Sometimes, e-mail blasts are sent to potential users. An **e-mail blast** is a mass electronic mailing targeted at likely customers. Typically, e-mail blasts are only sent to users who have signed up to receive them. E-mail blasts are *not* spam. **Spam** is unwanted and untargeted e-mail.

Gold Master   **Replicated Discs**

Shutterstock.com

Figure 10-4. The gold master contains the final, perfected version of the game. It is used to duplicate all of the discs that will be packaged and sold.

Developer Income

To get paid, a developer typically receives a royalty from the producer. A **royalty** is a percentage of the sale price of the item sold. Sometimes, a flat fee is paid per item sold. Developers typically receive a royalty of about 20 percent to 30 percent of the price the producer receives from a wholesaler, as illustrated in **Figure 10-6.**

Production

The next category is the production group. The **production group** adds value to a product by completing the manufacturing and preparing the product in the final packaged form. If the product were

Barone Firenze/Shutterstock.com

Figure 10-5. The E3 Expo is a large trade show. Many video game developers market their games to wholesalers and retailers at this show.

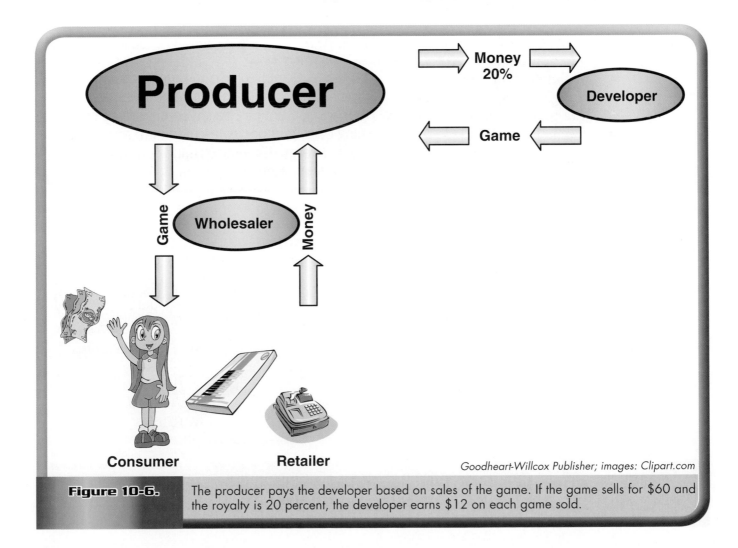

Goodheart-Willcox Publisher; images: Clipart.com

Figure 10-6. The producer pays the developer based on sales of the game. If the game sells for $60 and the royalty is 20 percent, the developer earns $12 on each game sold.

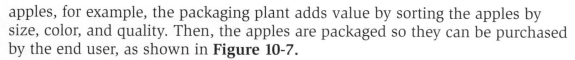

apples, for example, the packaging plant adds value by sorting the apples by size, color, and quality. Then, the apples are packaged so they can be purchased by the end user, as shown in **Figure 10-7.**

CHEAT CODE: PACKAGING

Packaging is how the product is presented to the end user. Most often, this deals with the container in which the product is sold. However, not all products come in a container. The design of packaging is an important part of marketing.

Packaging

Packaging is a very important part of the production group's role. In the apple example, the apples may be packed into a bag of about ten apples. Other apples might be packed in larger containers for restaurants or other end users. The bags have a brand name printed on the front and some marketing information that helps end users differentiate these apples from all other apples. For example, the labels might include where the apples were grown, the type of apple, a quality statement, and a company logo. This helps the person who will buy the apples know more about the product.

Green Gamer

It is a common practice in Europe to unplug equipment that is not in use, including lights, computers, and gaming devices. Up to 25 percent can be saved on energy costs by just turning off and unplugging equipment at the end of the day. Less energy usage also reduces negative effects on the environment.

Shutterstock.com

Figure 10-7. You may not think of apples as being in different packaging, but they may be. Here, apples are shown in bags, individually wrapped, and available loose. Which do you feel has the most value added?

Think about the information included in the labeling information shown in **Figure 10-8.** All of the information on the label helps the end user choose the brand, type, and quality of apple they want. In this example, Red Delicious is the type of apple. The grower is located in Washington state. Grade A and Fresh describe the quality. The brand name is Family Farm. All of this information allows buyers to remember the quality of the product and repurchase that brand again.

In the video game industry, producers take the gold master disc and mass duplicate DVDs or other game media. They also create the packaging for the game including the case, printed insert, and everything you can touch that comes with the game.

Figure 10-8.

This is an example of a product label for apples. What important information about the product can you learn from the label?

Red Delicious
Washington State

Grade A
Fresh Apples
A Family Farm Product

Goodheart-Willcox Publisher; images: Clipart.com

Producer Marketing

In addition to the packaging, producers are responsible for most of the effort of marketing the game to the end user. While the developer works on the game design and programming, the producer creates advertising, sales promotions, sponsorships, public relations, and all other efforts to sell the product, like that shown in **Figure 10-9.** Producers usually spend a large amount of money to generate consumer interest in the game. This is where the **target marketing** pays off. The producer focuses on getting the information about the game to the people who will be most likely to buy it.

Figure 10-9.

This building displays an oversize banner advertising *Assassin's Creed 3*. There is no missing this advertisement.

Barone Firenze/Shutterstock.com

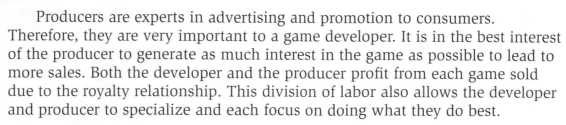

Producers are experts in advertising and promotion to consumers. Therefore, they are very important to a game developer. It is in the best interest of the producer to generate as much interest in the game as possible to lead to more sales. Both the developer and the producer profit from each game sold due to the royalty relationship. This division of labor also allows the developer and producer to specialize and each focus on doing what they do best.

Producer Income

Once the packaging of the product is complete, the producer attempts to sell the product to wholesalers and middlemen. The producer keeps the amount of profit received from a wholesaler and pays the royalty to the developer.

For example, if the producer sells 100 games for $10 each to the wholesaler, the producer receives $1000. The producer pays a royalty of 25 percent to the developer ($250). Suppose the expenses the producer incurred for packaging and printing is $200 for these 100 units. The remaining $550 ($1000 – $250 – $200 = $550) is used to advertise the game, pay overhead expenses, pay salaries, and take profits, as illustrated in **Figure 10-10**. *Overhead expenses* are the costs of being in business, such as electricity, rent, envelopes, paper clips, and so on.

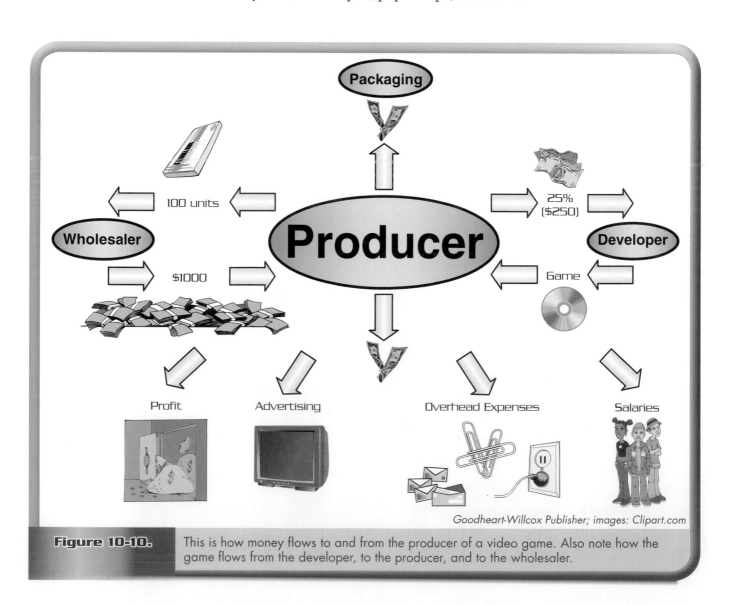

Goodheart-Willcox Publisher; images: Clipart.com

Figure 10-10. This is how money flows to and from the producer of a video game. Also note how the game flows from the developer, to the producer, and to the wholesaler.

Producer Customers

The producer specialized in adding value to the game product through promotional activities and production of the physical discs and packaging. The role of storing and transporting the finished game products after they are packaged and boxed by the producer falls to the next specialists in the supply chain: wholesalers and middlemen. The typical customer in the supply chain for a producer is a *wholesaler* or *middlemen.* Wholesalers and middlemen buy large quantities, known as *bulk.* The producer does not have the warehouses, trucks, and distribution system needed to get the game to the end user, like that shown in **Figure 10-11.** For that reason, the producer sells the games in bulk to a wholesaler at a low cost per unit.

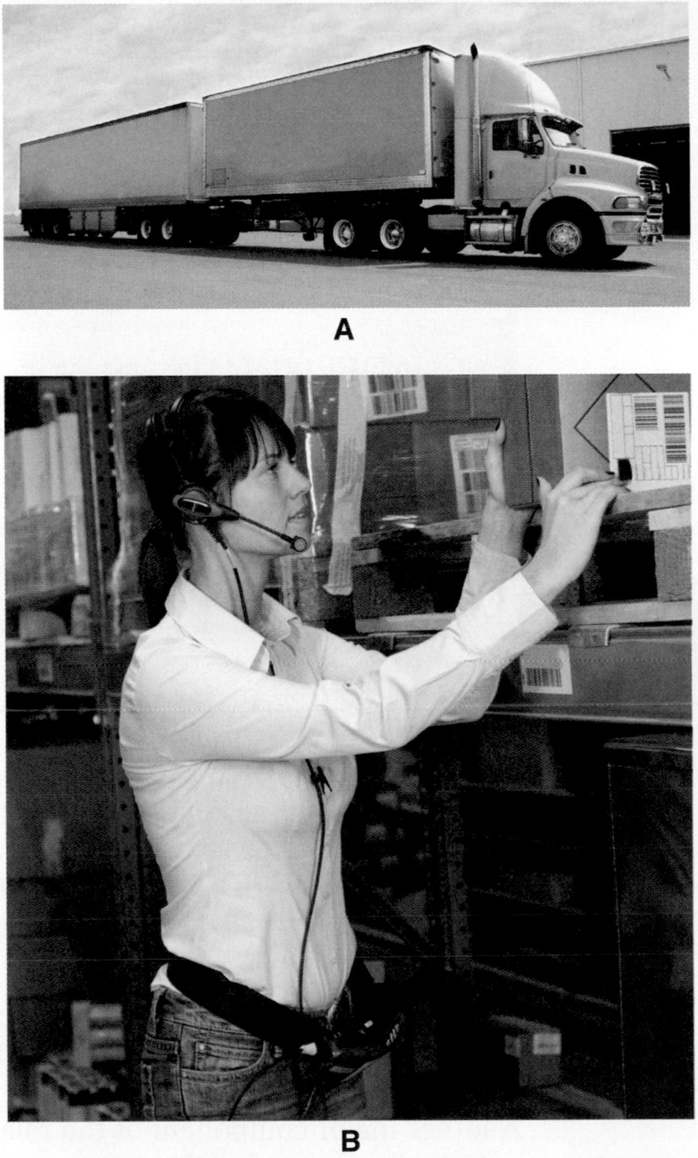

The cost per unit, or *unit cost,* is the average amount each game (unit) costs when purchased in bulk. If a producer sells 100,000 games to a wholesaler for $3,000,000, the unit cost is $30 per game ($3,000,000 ÷ 100,000 = $30). The producer gets a big chunk of cash right away to help cover the money they spent to create the physical product and advertise the game. The developer also gets a nice royalty check to help cover their costs and post profits as well. If the developer has a royalty agreement for 25 percent, the check for the above example is $750,000.

A

B

Shutterstock.com

Figure 10-11. A—A wholesaler buys large quantities and ships them to a warehouse. B—In turn, they sell the product in smaller quantities to other middlemen and retailers.

When selling to wholesalers, the larger the volume they are willing to purchase at a single time, the lower the unit cost. This creates a large incentive for the wholesaler to purchase a very large amount to get the best discounted price per game. An example of wholesale pricing might be something like the table shown in **Figure 10-12.** As you can see, getting the wholesaler to purchase a large amount, like 1,000,000 games all at one time, provides a huge

Number of Games	Cost to Purchase	Unit Cost	Total Savings over 50,000 unit cost
50,000	$1,750,000	$35	$0
100,000	$3,000,000	$30	$500,000
250,000	$6,250,000	$25	$2,500,00
500,000	$10,500,000	$21	$7,000,000
1,000,000	$18,000,000	$18	$17,000,000

Figure 10-12. This table shows how the unit cost decreases as the number of units purchased increases.

Goodheart-Willcox Publisher

CHEAT CODE: DISCOUNT

A discount is a reduction in the cost per unit. The producer sets a price for a game and then offers wholesalers discounts if they purchase more than the minimum amount. The discount gets larger as the number of units purchased increases.

unit cost **discount.** In the example above, the unit cost of $18 is almost half of original cost of $35.

The producers want to make their money as fast as possible. They do not want to spend time and money to sell and ship small numbers of games all over the world. They want the money quickly so they can put it back to work producing the next game.

Wholesale Distribution

When a wholesaler buys a bulk quantity of a game, they perform the next important role in the supply chain. The major value they add to the marketing effort involves the movement of bulk items, warehousing, and distribution. Another major component of the role of a wholesaler is the assumption of risk. For a wholesaler, this means spending a large amount of cash on the assumption that they can sell the product for a profit.

Unlike when you buy a game and later get the same game as a gift from grandma, the wholesaler cannot take the games back. If the wholesaler does not sell all the games, it cannot return them to the producer. It is stuck with them and the producer gets to keep the cash. The wholesaler must find a way to resell all of the units they purchased. Sometimes, this means the games are sold for little or no profit to fix an ordering mistake.

Even if the games are sold for a loss, it makes sense to *liquidate,* or sell out, and get some of the money back. If you ordered 50,000 games and only resold 40,000, you need to liquidate the remaining 10,000 games. If your unit cost is $35, you might have to liquidate and sell the last games for only $10 each. You take a loss, but you still get $100,000 back (10,000 × $10 = $100,000). That is much better than throwing the games in the trash and getting no money. This assumption of risk is the reason why a producer offers discounts to get wholesalers to spend the most money.

Look at the wholesale cost table in Figure 10-12. Think about the decision needed to be a wholesale buyer. Marketing thinks the company can liquidate up to 250,000 games and projects the selling prices needed to liquidate all 250,000 games. They could liquidate 120,000 games at $45 each, 70,000 for $35 each, 50,000 for $25 each, and 10,000 for $10 each. To maximize profits and discounts, how many games should the company purchase? Why?

Wholesale Transportation

When a wholesaler purchases a bulk of games, they have to send a truck to the producer's factory and pick up the games. The wholesaler then takes the truck on a trip to its regional warehouses. A *regional warehouse* is a storage building located in a region or section of the country that stores the product for later distribution to the surrounding area. The concept of a regional warehouse involves delivery time and cost savings.

If the wholesaler has a single warehouse in California, then customers in Texas and New York may have to wait a long time for the product to be delivered. If the wholesaler has three regional warehouses, one each in California, Kansas, and Pennsylvania, then the product can be delivered quickly from the nearest regional warehouse. In this example, the wholesaler divides the United States into thirds so the delivery trucks do not have to travel too far from the source.

In addition to the delivery time, there is also a return route cost to consider. If you drive a truck from California to New York, you still have to drive it back. This time it might be empty. An empty trip is referred to as a *dead head* trip. The company spends money on the driver and fuel, but gets no benefit or product delivered. If a regional warehouse system is used, there is less travel time and lower dead head cost.

Wholesaler Customers

From the regional warehouses, the wholesaler will deliver smaller quantities of the games to middlemen, retailers, and other wholesalers. The wholesaler buys in bulk, stores the product in warehouses and sells smaller amounts to others. A wholesaler might buy 5000 boxes with 24 games in each box. This might be enough product to fill an 18-wheeler semitrailer. The wholesaler warehouses the product and resells it in bulk one box or more at a time. A retail outlet, such as a store at the mall or retail chain store, buys in bulk from these wholesalers to sell to the end user.

Another buyer from the wholesaler is the middleman. Middlemen also buy in bulk directly from the producers or from wholesalers. They typically repackage the bulk products they buy into smaller units or mixed units. A *smaller-unit sale* allows a retail buyer to purchase as few as one unit at a time instead of a box of 24 from a wholesaler, as illustrated in **Figure 10-13.**

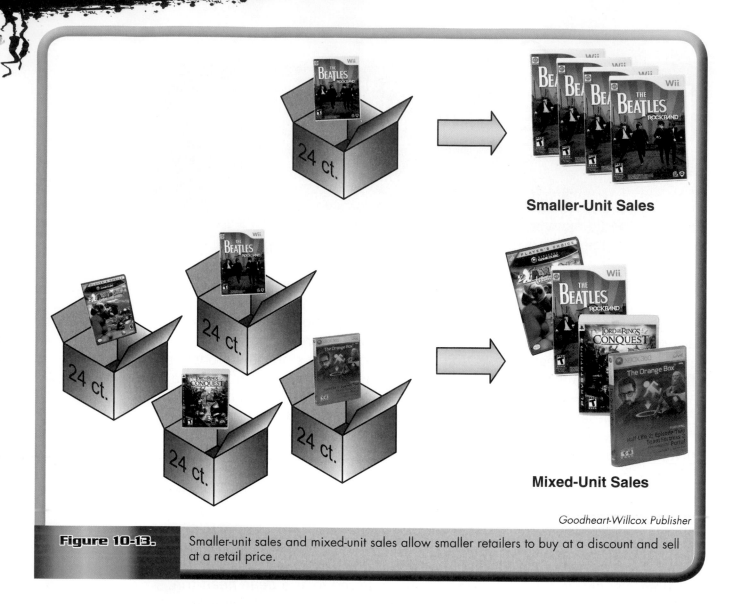

Smaller-Unit Sales

Mixed-Unit Sales

Goodheart-Willcox Publisher

Figure 10-13. Smaller-unit sales and mixed-unit sales allow smaller retailers to buy at a discount and sell at a retail price.

A small store might only need two or three of a product on their shelf. It cannot buy from the wholesaler because the wholesaler only sells this product in boxes of 24. The retailer can purchase from a middleman and still get enough of a price discount to sell at retail price. Additionally, middlemen repackage product into mixed units. A *mixed-unit sale* is a combination pack that contains a few different items. If a small game retail shop wants a few new release games, it could buy a mixed unit that contained three copies of five different games. This 15-pack mixed unit offers the retailer a discount over purchasing the games individually as smaller units.

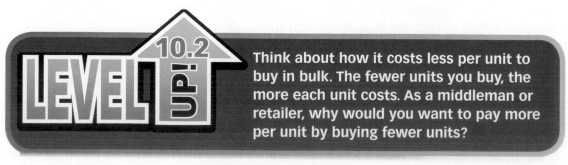

LEVEL UP! 10.2

Think about how it costs less per unit to buy in bulk. The fewer units you buy, the more each unit costs. As a middleman or retailer, why would you want to pay more per unit by buying fewer units?

Wholesale Pricing

Of course, the wholesaler wants to make money. That is why it took the risk to purchase in bulk and resell to others down the supply chain. The assumption is that the wholesalers, middlemen, and retailers it sells to will pay more than the wholesaler did for each unit. To make a profit and cover their costs, the wholesaler must increase the unit price with a **markup.** If the wholesaler pays $30 for a game and resells it for $40, the game has a $10 markup.

CHEAT CODE: MARKUP

A reseller, such as a wholesaler, middleman, or retailer, will add an amount to the unit cost, known as a markup. The unit cost is increased or marked up higher. The markup represents the per-unit potential profit the reseller will receive.

As with the producer, the wholesaler also offers some discounts to encourage higher-volume sales. To do this, the wholesaler lowers their markup to make the unit cost less expensive if the buyer spends more money. If the wholesaler bought 250,000 games from the producer, according to **Figure 10-12** the unit cost would be $25 each. **Figure 10-14** shows a table representing a possible markup a wholesaler might offer its buyers.

Notice that the wholesaler can compete with the producer by offering 50,000 games at the same unit cost (compare **Figure 10-12** to **Figure 10-14**). The reductions in markup encourage buyers to spend more money to maximize savings. This also passes along the same assumption of risk, which is that these buyers will be able to sell the games for more money.

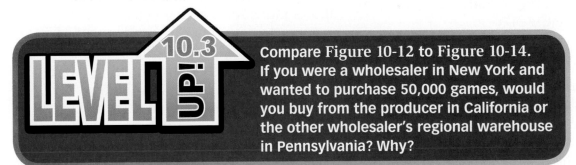

LEVEL 10.3 UP!

Compare Figure 10-12 to Figure 10-14. If you were a wholesaler in New York and wanted to purchase 50,000 games, would you buy from the producer in California or the other wholesaler's regional warehouse in Pennsylvania? Why?

Number of Units	Cost to Purchase	Unit Cost	Wholesale Markup	Customer Savings
1,000	$45,000	$45	$20	$0
5,000	$210,000	$42	$17	$15,000
10,000	$400,000	$40	$15	$50,000
25,000	$950,000	$38	$13	$175,000
50,000	$1,750,000	$35	$10	$500,000

Figure 10-14. This table shows how a wholesaler will reduce its markup as the size of the customer order increases.

Goodheart-Willcox Publisher

CASE STUDY

Middleware Service Solution

In the online supply chain, many game developers and producers use a middleware service solution for both the middleman and retail roles. A small- to medium-size design firm may not have the expertise or resources to launch a game as a stand-alone online product. Additionally, to do the marketing on their own would take away from the job they do best, designing new games. These companies use a middleware service solution to handle the distribution and sale of the online game.

To fulfill the role as a middleman, the middleware service solution bridges the gap between the developer and the consumer. To achieve this, a middleware ad provider, such as Mochi Ad Service (www.mochimedia.com), provides middleware software technology needed to embed advertisements into a game. They also redistribute the game to over 10,000 gaming websites, like hi5.com, MindJolt.com, and AOL.com.

To fulfill the role as a retailer, the middleware service solution provides the online access to the game, known as an end service. To distribute the game, the middleware ad service solution has a gaming website that contains many games from many different developers. By hosting the game on its website, the end service acts like a retail store. People stop by and look at the different products (games) and choose which one they want. This provides a convenient location for the end user (consumer) to shop.

At this type of end-service website, anyone can play games for free! The middleware ad service sells advertising on the website. Each time a person clicks to play one of the free online games, an advertisement plays before the game loads, as shown in the figure. This is sort of like a TV commercial that plays during your favorite TV show. An advertiser or sponsor pays each time its ad plays. The middleware ad service sells the ad space to the advertiser, maintains the website, advertises the website, and pays the game developers. Any money left over after paying the overhead and expenses for the website is the profit the middleware ad service gets to keep.

Mochi Ad Service is a middleware ad provider. In this example, the game *Fashion Star* is sponsored by CandyStand.com, which is another website that offers free games.

The use of a middleware service solution allows individuals and smaller companies to compete with much larger companies. Through expertise and efficient division of labor, the designer and the middleware service solution allow each other to maximize performance and profitability. Everyone benefits from this advertising deal. The developer gets to focus on their specialty—designing games. The middleware service solution makes the game available to a large audience of online gamers. Consumers get to play games for free. The advertiser gets its product seen by thousands of people for a small fee.

Great distribution system, but how does the developer get paid? Each time an ad plays for the developer's game, the middleware service solution pays the developer a royalty. The royalty is very small. In most cases, it can be as little as 50 cents per thousand hits. The way to make a lot of money with an online middleware game is to have a game that millions of people will play over and over again.

Retail Distribution

The fourth category within a supply chain is ***retail distribution.*** Retail is the stage in distribution that sells directly to the consumer, as shown in **Figure 10-15.** Most retailers purchase from wholesalers and middlemen. However, it has become common for massive retailers like Walmart and Target, called big-box stores, to act more like wholesalers. These stores buy in bulk from wholesalers and even directly from a producer. Big-box stores already have regional warehouses to store products and distribute them to their chain stores. That is why you see a semitrailer delivering to Walmart and a small delivery truck delivering to GameStop.

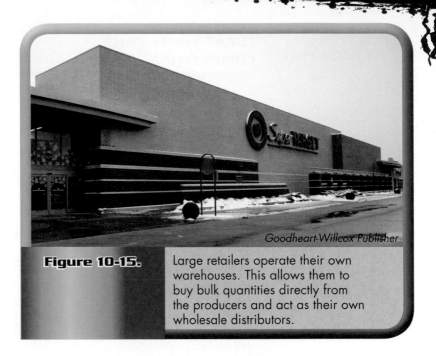

Goodheart-Willcox Publisher

Figure 10-15. Large retailers operate their own warehouses. This allows them to buy bulk quantities directly from the producers and act as their own wholesale distributors.

Retailers function in many roles. This is the store where you find the product on the shelf. A retailer might be a:

- retail chain store;
- department store;
- specialty store;
- discount store;
- mail order service;
- Internet and online distributor; or
- rental store.

10.4

LEVEL UP!

A new release game is sold for the same price at a massive retail store like Walmart and a small retailer. Think about a game that you purchased from a game specialty store like GameStop and a game you purchased from a large retail store like Walmart. As a consumer, why would you buy the game from a massive retail store instead of a smaller game specialty store? Conversely, why would you want to buy from a game specialty store instead of the big-box store?

Retailer Pricing

The selling price for most games is set by the producer. This is the ***manufacturer's suggested retail price (MSRP).*** In the video game industry, retailers are required to sell new-release games at the MSRP. They cannot sell new releases for less than the MSRP.

CHEAT CODE: PRICE COMPETITION

Price competition occurs when retailers set different prices to attract buyers by offering lower prices. For example, if a store is out of the way, it may need to lower its prices to bring customers in.

Video Game Available at 12:01 am
Tuesday, October 13th

Also available at Walmart.com

Walmart
Save money. Live better.

Figure 10-16.

The new release of a game can result in long lines of gamers waiting for the game to be available for sale. Some games have a strong following and gamers will camp out to be near the front of the line. Notice this sign not only provides the release date, but a release time of 12:01 am.

Goodheart-Willcox Publisher

In general, the video game industry does not allow **price competition** on new release games or game consoles. In the video game industry, the new release price will be the same at any retail outlet. This saves the consumer the hassle of searching for a lower price and provides the small retailer protection from the massive retailers that can buy in bulk and offer lower prices. In the retail distribution chain, violators of the MSRP rules may face penalties from the producer. This may range from eliminating future discount pricing, to exclusion from a first-week release (highest sales volume week), to termination of distribution from the wholesaler.

In addition to the MSRP rule, retailers must also abide by the release date rules. If the producer has a specified release date and time, no retailer can distribute the game prior to that, as shown in **Figure 10-16.** The retailer may have the games or systems in stock weeks before this date. In some cases, they can even take preorders or advanced sales on the items. But, the games cannot be distributed before the release date. Similar penalties apply to retailers that violate the release date rules as the MSRP rule.

Direct Marketing

A growing trend in video game sales is direct marketing. In **direct marketing,** the developer or producer sells directly to the end user, cutting out the wholesaler, middleman, and retailer. This marketing is becoming more popular as Internet-based and handheld games are becoming easier to download. If a consumer buys a game directly from the developer, then the developer makes more money than the royalty they would have received from the supply chain.

Here is the sticky part. The producer gets upset that they are losing money. Remember, the producer is spending money to advertise on television, the Internet, or in magazines to generate interest in the game. If the developer sells the game directly to the consumer, the producer gets *no* money.

Eventually the producer may cancel the marketing agreement and stop buying from that developer. The reason a supply chain exists is so a large volume of product can quickly get into the hands of consumers. If they can download the product from the developer, there is a break in the chain, illustrated in **Figure 10-17.**

Direct marketing only works if the developer can add value to their product in the same way that the producer does. In most cases, direct marketing sounds like a good idea, but it may not be. The direct marketing takes away time and other resources from the developer that could be spent making more games.

Applications

A direct marketing media that is very profitable for the developer and individual designer is the ***application (app).*** The iPhone and its app store and the Android Play Store have led to a marketplace where the individual designer can make a game for handheld devices and directly market it as an app, as shown in **Figure 10-18.**

There is *no* supply chain for the production of an app. The designer can make the game and offer it directly to the consumer in the app store on most handheld devices like the iPhone, iPod Touch, Androids, and

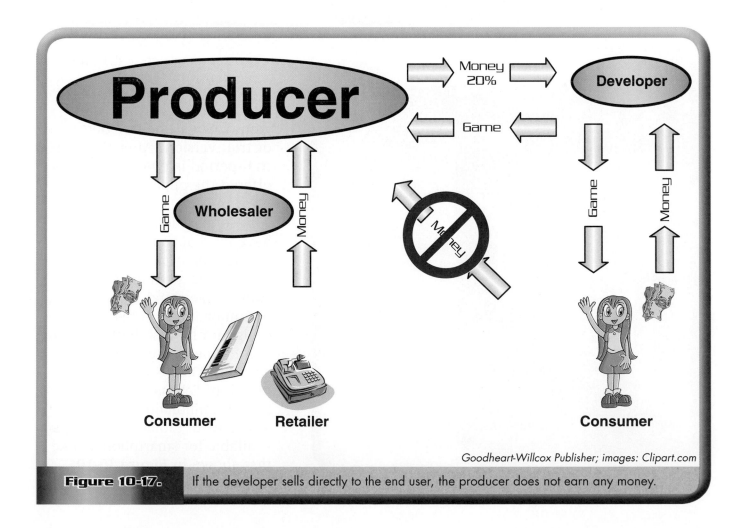

Goodheart-Willcox Publisher; images: Clipart.com

Figure 10-17.   If the developer sells directly to the end user, the producer does not earn any money.

Google

Figure 10-18. The iPhone and other smartphones, such as Android phones, has created a new market for video games: the app.

Figure 10-19.

Many video games are available for handheld devices.

Goodheart-Willcox Publisher

many other smartphones. The typical life cycle of an app game begins as a free demo or trial version. After the free trial period is over, the user is offered the opportunity to buy the app.

Many indie developers have used apps to make money in their spare time. ***Indie developers*** are independent game makers and independent, non-mainstream firms. One designer of a tank battle app for the iPhone sold over 350,000 apps for $3.00 each in the month of February 2009. An instant millionaire! There are now tens of thousands of apps available for smartphones, like that shown in **Figure 10-19.**

CASE STUDY

Money on the Apple Tree

The iPhone app store has become a great way for developers to quickly get games and other applications to an affluent and technology savvy potential customer. Getting started as an iPhone app developer is not difficult and not very expensive. You need to buy three things before you can become an iPhone developer: a design platform computer, developer software, and test platforms.

Many games can be downloaded as apps on the iPhone. Handheld devices are another way to deliver games.

Goodheart-Willcox Publisher

The design platform computer must be a Mac; no PCs here! Many iPhone app developers customize their Macintosh computers to add hardware that makes the job easier, but you can purchase one off the shelf that can do the job.

Next, you need to sign up as a registered iPhone developer. Registering is free and allows you to download the free iPhone software development kit (SDK). The technical requirements of the iPhone SDK software you download will determine the processor and operating system needed for your design computer. While the iPhone SDK is free, you are required to pay an annual subscription fee for the iPhone developer program. Depending on your needs, you can purchase the $99 standard program or the $299 enterprise program. Most independent developers only need the standard program. Check the benefits of each program and purchase the one right for you.

As every good designer knows, the last step is to test the game on the game platform. You will need to have an iPhone and an iPod touch to test your game. You will need to buy one of each to properly test your app for bugs.

Once you have the basic tools for the job, log in to the iPhone developer center and download videos, sample apps, and everything else you need. Of course, you still need to know how to do some programming. Experience programming in Objective-C or the Apple Xcode Cocoa development software will help you code your concept into that playable app.

After you program the game in the Apple Xcode Cocoa software, select **Build and Go** to test in the iPhone simulator. This is where you work out all major bugs. The iPhone simulator is a good debugger tester, but you will still need to test it on a real iPhone and iPod touch.

Then it is time to build your app. You can obtain a "provisioning profile" from the iPhone program portal. The provisioning profile is an app license used for testing. The iPhone program portal is a section in the iPhone developer program. Use the Cocoa Xcode software **Build** command. This allows you to create a testable iPhone app with the null icon (a red circle with a slash) shown to indicate it is not an approved app. You can then download, test, and tune the app before releasing it.

When you have tested your app and are ready for release, go back to the iPhone program portal and create a "distribution provisioning profile" for your game. This is the final version of the game you will be sending in with your app store application information form. Complete your developer keychain profile and information about your app, and then send it all to the Apple review board. The review board checks out each app before releasing it. This process takes approximately a week or two. If you did everything right, you will soon see your game in the iTunes app store or being played on an iPhone.

As a future game designer, you may want to get some specialized training in building iPhone apps. You may also want to check out Android, Blackberry, and Microsoft Marketplace as other supply chains for your handheld game.

Figure 10-20.

The supply chain and all of the associated marketing has one purpose: to get the money in your wallet or pocketbook.

Shutterstock.com

Consumer (End User)

The final link in any supply chain is the end user or consumer. The consumer is also the most important link in the supply chain as this person provides the money to pay for all other links in the supply chain. All of the marketing and distribution of a supply chain is put in place to get the money that is in the consumer's wallet, **Figure 10-20.**

This exchange functions due to the role of currency. A supply chain is difficult, if not impossible, to operate in a barter economy. Each link in the supply chain adds value to the product in either price, promotion, place, or product. These are the four P's of marketing, illustrated in **Figure 10-21.**

The *price* paid by the consumer can be changed to influence more buyers. More people will tend to buy the product if the price is lower. *Promotion* is the advertising and marketing effort used to gain interest in the product. *Place* is the actual location of purchase, such as a store or online. Providing a convenient place for consumers to buy leads to more sales. The *product* is the actual item produced and sold. All of these elements are combined to make a successful product that results in profits throughout the supply chain.

Used Video Game Distribution

A new and profitable retail market is the used video game market. The *used video game market* is one in which consumers make their unwanted video games available for sale to other consumers. This market functions in two ways: direct marketing by the consumer and return marketing to a retailer.

In direct marketing by the consumer, the consumer sells the games directly to other gamers. Marketplaces like ebay, garage sales, and flea markets are good places for people to sell their unwanted games directly to a different end user, as shown in **Figure 10-22.**

Figure 10-21.

The four P's of marketing are price, product, promotion, and place.

Price   Promotion

Marketing

Place   Product

Goodheart-Willcox Publisher

Figure 10-22.

The used video game market offers gamers a way to get rid of games they no longer want. There are many ways to engage in this market, including ebay.

In *return marketing,* a consumer will **trade in** a used game for cash or credit at a retailer, like that shown in **Figure 10-23.** The retailer, such as GameStop or Play N Trade, will clean and recondition the game media and sell it for less than a new game.

Many consumers enjoy buying used games because of the lower price. The real drawback to the used game market is the choices available. Obviously, new releases are hard to find as used games. But, if you are willing to wait a few weeks, you can usually find a deal.

Rental Game Distribution

A popular way to try new games without buying them is the *rental game market,* like that shown in **Figure 10-24.** Rental companies buy directly from wholesalers and rent the games to the end users. Some companies charge a few dollars to rent each

CHEAT CODE: TRADE IN

A consumer can trade in their used games or equipment for cash or store credit to purchase a different game or game hardware. In some ways, this is a form of the barter system.

GameStop Texas Ltd.

Figure 10-23.

Some stores accept used video games for cash or store credit.

GameFly, Inc.

Figure 10-24.
Many video rental stores also rent video games. Additionally, there are online video game rental companies, such as GameFly.

CHEAT CODE: COST EFFECTIVE

Spending money wisely to avoid wasting money is cost effective. Only spending a small amount when renting a bad video game saves you from wasting more money had you bought the bad game.

game for five days. Others offer a membership with unlimited rentals for a monthly membership fee. When the rented games are beginning to lose some of their popularity, they, too, will enter used-game distribution.

Renting is a **cost effective** way of trying new games. Many gamers use rentals to determine what games they will eventually buy. Spending $3 or $4 to rent a game that you find out you do not like is much better than buying it for $50 and selling it used for $25.

Changes in Video Game Supply Chain

Recently, the video game industry began looking for ways to make changes to the supply chain. The first annual GameSupply Conference was held on February 11, 2009. Some of the important topics included:
- combining supply with other electronic media, such as DVD movies;
- downloadable games and media;
- handheld markets;
- avoiding piracy; and
- globalization.

Of great concern is the entire supply chain itself. With new consoles and handhelds allowing for direct downloading of games and upgrades, the entire distribution system may become obsolete in a few years. Developers and producers are in favor of more downloads. The cost of production is lower and there is less chance for piracy. The wholesalers, middlemen, and retailer are *not* in favor of this change. They would be cut out of the supply chain, as illustrated in **Figure 10-25.** This would mean the end of their business life. Despite concerns, downloading will clearly be the way at least some games will be distributed in the near future.

Other winners in a supply chain of downloadable games are the game console companies. These companies offer games for sale on the websites for their game system. Additional revenue is possible in sales commission on each game sold and from the advertising on the company's website or game **uplink** sites. This, however, also has the possibility of limiting consumer choice. A game console could be engineered to prevent game downloads from any portal that is not authorized, **Figure 10-26.**

Current Supply Chain

Goodheart-Willcox Publisher; images: Shutterstock.com

Figure 10-25. Online distribution cuts the normal supply chain for video game development by selling directly to the consumer.

CHEAT CODE: UPLINK

An uplink is the connecting of a small computer network to another larger network. In this case, the computer network of the game player connects to the game provider network via the Internet. In an online or MMO game, players uplink to the game provider site.

Figure 10-26.

The newest game consoles use a computer hard drive to store data. This allows the console to download a game that can only be played on that customer's console.

Shutterstock.com

One limiting factor to downloads is the size of a video game. With intense graphics, sound, and game engines, video games can easily exceed the capacity of a standard DVD. Some games can even exceed 10 gigabytes (GB) of information. The download of a 10 GB game might take 12 or more hours, even with a high speed connection. Until game size decreases or download speeds increase, games will continue to be easier to obtain at a retail store.

Some companies, like OnLive, offer a server-based gaming platform. On this platform, all of the action is controlled on a remote server, instead of on the home system. However, the same limitation is present to render a playable game with impressive graphics. The size of the data packet is just too large to compete with the quality of the current home consoles like PS3 and Xbox 360. Only time will tell if new technology can be implemented to overcome the hurdle of data transmission.

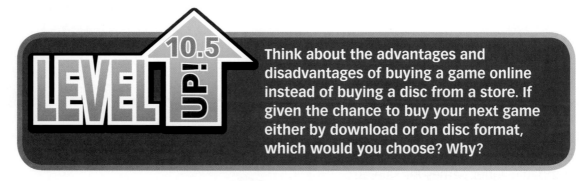

LEVEL 10.5 UP! Think about the advantages and disadvantages of buying a game online instead of buying a disc from a store. If given the chance to buy your next game either by download or on disc format, which would you choose? Why?

Piracy

Another major concern for members of the video game supply chain is piracy. ***Piracy*** is illegal copying and distribution of games, with or without money exchanging hands. Each game that is pirated takes money away from the supply chain, as illustrated in **Figure 10-27.** If a developer does not get the royalties from the games sold, it will go out of business.

It is in the best interest of all members of a supply chain to take steps to eliminate piracy to safeguard profitability. If not curbed, piracy could eventually make it impossible for companies to spend the millions of dollars needed to design and produce games. Then everyone loses as there are no new games.

Globalization

In most computer and technology industries, globalization is an important factor in production and sales. ***Globalization*** means that other countries, in addition to the United States, are involved in production or purchase.

Production of video games and consoles has always been a global process. From the early days, countries like Japan have competed with designers in the United States. Increasingly, these global participants are working together to create content. A design company may have programmers in the United States, graphic artists in Yugoslavia, testers in South Korea, and tuners in India. Thanks to the Internet, all of these people can work on the same project at

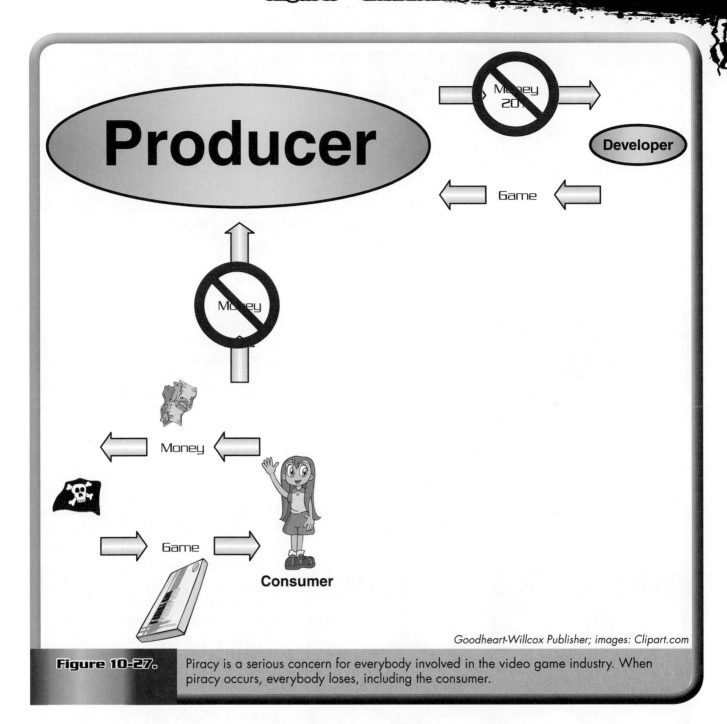

Goodheart-Willcox Publisher; images: Clipart.com

Figure 10-27. Piracy is a serious concern for everybody involved in the video game industry. When piracy occurs, everybody loses, including the consumer.

the same time. Rapid transfer of data and information over the Internet allows people to collaborate—working from different locations all over the world.

Sometimes, a company will use labor in another location because it is lower in cost. This *labor-cost differential* allows a company to produce a game cheaper and lower the cost of production, as shown in **Figure 10-28.** For example, a programmer in India might get paid $10 per hour. On the other hand, a programmer in the United States gets paid $30 per hour to do the same job. Companies use the lower-cost labor to save money. This is called *outsourcing.* However, outsourcing is very controversial because it means people in the United States are not being employed.

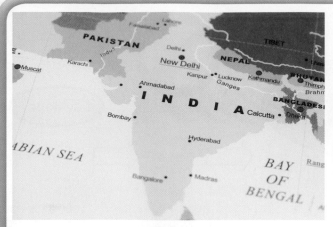

Programmer Labor
Rate $10/hr

Programmer Labor
Rate $30/hr

Shutterstock.com

Figure 10-28. Many companies outsource tasks to save money. For example, suppose a programmer in India is paid $10 an hour and a programmer in the United States is paid $30 an hour. Both programmers do the exact same work in the same amount of time. However, the labor in India is three times less costly than in the United States.

Another reason to use labor in different locations is to design a game faster. If one design team is in the United States and another one is in South Korea, work can be completed in fewer days. It is daytime in South Korea when it is nighttime in the United States, as shown in **Figure 10-29.** So, the programming team in South Korea can work on the game while the team in the United States is sleeping. When the team in the United States gets back to work the next day, the game is further along than when they left. The game is built in almost half the number of days as if it were only worked on in the United States. This is a huge benefit when trying to meet a deadline or beat the competition to an early release date.

Global labor is also used due to the need for specialized skills or a *skill differential.* People with more skills or education in a specialty area will get the work regardless of where they live. A design team might need a specialist in a new 3D program. If the people with that specialty happen to live in Brazil, then a company will hire Brazilian programmers to do the job.

Figure 10-29. By using workers in other countries around the world, companies can have work on a game completed around the clock. The difference in time zones means one team will be at work while another team is asleep.

Shutterstock.com

Technology and currency are the two main reasons why production and sales can exist globally. Production of video games can easily cross national boundaries. Technology allows information to be quickly and securely sent all over the world. Differences in the cost of labor and the skills of other countries mean designers and producers will look around the world for the best prices and skills. Without the function of currency and the ability of currency to be exchanged, these global markets would not be possible.

Globalization exists in sales as well. It is no surprise that people all over the world like playing video games. This opens up the entire world as potential customers. Games are often released worldwide on a single date. Sometimes games have been customized for each different culture or language, as shown in **Figure 10-30.** It is easy to find games in both Japanese and English, like the Pokémon games. Initially, these games were made in Japanese and modified to English to sell in the United States and Europe. These modifications of culture and language also require the hiring of a specialist in that language and culture.

www.g-wlearning.com

Level up your know-how with Animated Review 10-1.

Jobs in the Global Video Game Economy

In recent years, video game companies experienced growth even when the global economy was struggling. With demand for quality video games increasing, the need for software developers, software engineers,

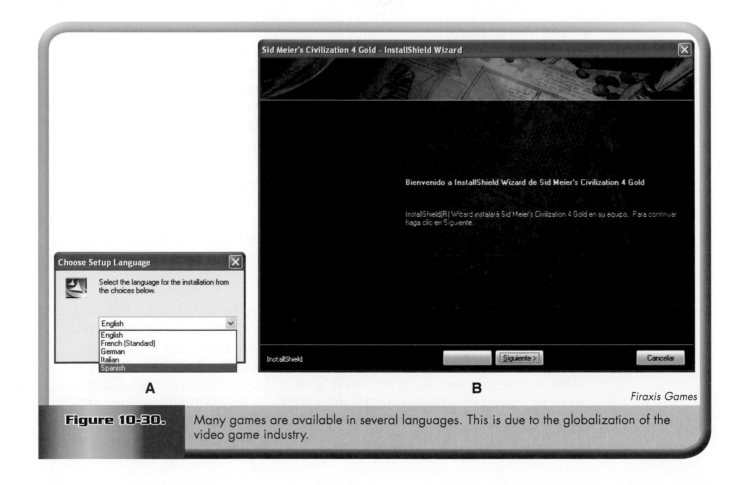

Firaxis Games

Figure 10-30. Many games are available in several languages. This is due to the globalization of the video game industry.

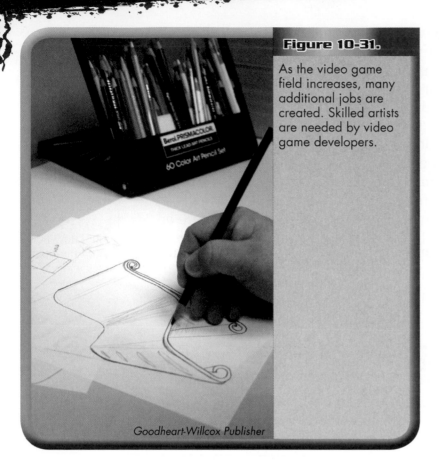

Figure 10-31.

As the video game field increases, many additional jobs are created. Skilled artists are needed by video game developers.

Goodheart-Willcox Publisher

programmers, artists, and testers at the development level is also increasing, as noted in **Figure 10-31.** At the production level, the demand for marketers, artists, graphic design specialist, package design managers, and sales representatives is also increasing.

There has also been a huge increase in critics, marketers, bloggers, magazine writers, event coordinators, and other marketing employment opportunities. In the global economy, these marketing positions must be duplicated in multiple languages and locations.

This has opened the door for many game enthusiasts to be part of the gaming world. With the global demand for video games, there are multiple job openings for almost anyone wanting to participate in expanding the global marketplace for video games.

The idea of being a professional game player goes beyond that of a game tester. One of the newest forms of spectator sport is the ***video game tournament.*** Many game companies sponsor these tournaments as a way to promote their game. EA Sports and Virgin Gaming held the *Madden NFL 13* tournament in Las Vegas with a $140,000 grand prize winner. The tournament drew huge audiences, both present and watching on television. While tournaments with large cash prizes are not new, the televising of these tournaments with high viewership is new. The birth of the professional video game player is emerging with similarities to the growth of the professional poker player tournaments and televised events. However, the growth and potential of a professional video game player may be available to only a few. Just like a career in professional football, soccer, baseball, or basketball, a career in playing video games is equally difficult.

Education

For most people looking to get into a career in the video game industry, it will take schooling, training, and searching. Each career has a set of criteria unique to the position. Those criteria almost always start with the formal training needed in high school and college. Many of the best jobs require a college degree or specialized technical training beyond high school. College-degree programs in video game design, computer programming, computer engineering, information technology, graphic arts, and business management show that you have received specialized training for an entry level position.

After schooling and training, you need to get in the door and get some experience. Everyone wants to work on the high-dollar, AAA projects. *Triple A* projects are major game builds for the most popular game titles. Some AAA game titles include *Halo, Call of Duty, Assassin's Creed, World of Warcraft,* and many more. You do not get to work on one of these AAA projects right out of school. Most firms require you to refine your hard and soft skills and to demonstrate a team mentality before giving you that dream job with the dream paycheck. AAA games pay best and the best people are hired at every position for those games.

Seeking Employment

Regardless of your formal education and on-the-job training, you need to know where to look for your next job. Remember, the job market is a global market. While it is a great idea to begin a job search close to home, you may need to be willing to relocate or travel to work on projects.

Use the guidance counselors at your school or college. They can help get information on internships or other projects related to your field of expertise. These internships and jobs may not be for building a video game, but might be related work such as advertising animations, Flash-based website design, commercial art, or computer programming. All of this on-the-job experience will help you eventually land that video game job.

Many companies advertise on job websites that specialize in video game jobs. These postings typically include a brief description of the job, requirements, location, and salary. Trade magazines are also a good place to look for a job. These magazines focus on one trade, such as video games. Even if the trade magazine does not have a job section, you can learn about companies in the business and whether or not they are expanding and hiring.

You will need to have a résumé and a portfolio available to send to an employer. A *résumé* is a summary of your education and job experiences related to the job you are applying for. Companies use résumés as a first step in screening prospective employees. It is from résumés that a company determines who to bring in for an interview. A *portfolio* is a set of examples of the work you have done in the past, as shown in **Figure 10-32.** Today, many individuals maintain a digital portfolio, or e-portfolio. Whether hard copy or digital, however, it should contain your best work. Together, the résumé and portfolio create a picture of your abilities and the quality of work you can produce.

Start saving your drawings, prototypes, and games. Today is a good day to start building your portfolio and thinking about that job you want.

Goodheart-Willcox Publisher

Figure 10-32. Artists should maintain a portfolio containing their best work. When applying for a job as an artist, you will need to show the employer your portfolio.

Chapter Summary

- Video games are marketed and sold using a supply chain.
- Video game publishers, developers, distributors, marketers, and retailers all make up the supply chain that brings a video game from an idea to a real product for the consumer to purchase.
- Globalization has impacted the design and production of video games in several ways.
- Video game companies have experienced growth even when the global economy was struggling.
- The video game design field employs people throughout the supply chain, from software developers and artists, to marketers and design managers, critics, and event coordinators.
- In order to seek employment in the video game design field, a potential employee needs to meet the education requirements as well as have a résumé and a portfolio representing his or her best work.

Check Your Video Game IQ

Now that you have finished this chapter, see what you know about video game design by taking the chapter posttest.

www.m.g-wlearning.com

www.g-wlearning.com

Review Your Knowledge

On a separate sheet of paper or in a word processing document, match the following terms with the definitions that fit best.

A. supply chain
B. outsourcing
C. used video game market
D. skill differential
E. wholesaler

F. trade in
G. rental game market
H. retail distribution
I. labor-cost differential
J. value added

1. Buys in bulk, warehouses products for convenient delivery, and sells to retailers and others in smaller bulk.
2. Companies that buy games and rent them to the end users.
3. When a consumer takes a used video game to a store in exchange for cash or credit.
4. Stage in the supply chain where a product is sold directly to the consumer via a retail outlet.
5. Specialized skills needed to complete a task or job are present more in one location than another.
6. Benefit in price, product, promotion, or place added to a product as it travels down the supply chain to the end user.

7. How a product moves from raw materials to the end user.

8. Difference in labor rates between different geographic locations.

9. Consumers make their unwanted video games available for resale.

10. Contracting part of the production or marketing to other companies with specific skills or lower cost than the producing company.

On a separate sheet of paper or in a word processing document, answer each of the following questions.

11. Describe the *barter system* of trade.

12. What is *currency?*

13. The _____ consists of the links where a product or service is transferred from producer to the customer.

14. Define *end user.*

15. What does *value added* mean?

16. What is the first category of the video game supply chain?

17. Describe a *gold master.*

18. What is a *beta version* of a game?

19. Define *royalty.*

20. What is the second category of the video game supply chain?

21. What is *packaging?*

22. Who are the two typical customers for the producer?

23. Define *bulk,* as it relates to purchases.

24. Who typically offers *smaller-unit sales?*

25. What is a *mixed-unit sale?*

26. What is the third category of the video game supply chain?

27. What is the fourth category of the video game supply chain?

28. What is the term for the retail selling price set by the manufacturer?

29. Define *price competition.*

30. Describe *direct marketing.*

31. What is an *app?*

32. List the four P's of marketing.

33. Describe *return marketing.*

34. Define *piracy,* as related to video games.

35. Define *globalization.*

36. What is *outsourcing?*

37. The best jobs in the video game industry typically require a(n) _____ or _____ beyond high school.

38. List two places to look for jobs in the video game industry.

39. What is a *résumé?*

40. What is a *portfolio?*

Apply Your STEM Knowledge

 Language Arts

1. Use the Internet to research the most recent facts about video games from the Entertainment Software Association (www.theesa.com). Create a two-minute PowerPoint and oral presentation to summarize the industry facts and statistics for the current year.

 Social Studies

2. Many aspiring game designers go to conventions and conferences to get noticed and pitch their games. Research video game conventions. Plot the location of ten conventions or conferences on a global map. Note: you must include all locations for GDC, E3, and Insert Coin conferences, plus any additional needed to equal ten.

 Mathematics

3. You will travel to all of the gaming conventions and conferences to pitch your game idea. To do so, you will need to plan. Create a timeline for traveling to and from the conventions and conferences. Research the cost of air travel to and from each event from the airport nearest to you. Research the cost of a hotel stay for four days at each location. Create a simple budget including airfare, hotel, meals, rental car, and admission to attend all ten events. Note: convert all prices to United States' dollars.

 Language Arts

4. Use the Internet to research résumé writing. Create a résumé and cover letter for yourself. A cover letter introduces you and why you are contacting the company.

 Language Arts

5. Research a video game job that interests you from a job website like www.gamasutra.com, www.monster.com, or any other appropriate website. Locate a job close to your home. Locate that same job far away or in a different country. Write a one-page report to describe the job. Compare and contrast the job locations and offers. Make a determination as to which job is better for you.

Social Studies

6. For the two job locations you identified in #5, research the cultural activities, city life, population, cost of living, and major industries. Create a two-minute PowerPoint presentation to list the details of your job choice. Showcase each city and your conclusions.

Working in Teams

In teams, research, debate, and form a group opinion on each of the Level Up! activities in this chapter. Prepare a PowerPoint presentation of ten slides (five to seven minutes) to present to the class explaining the group's opinions for each Level Up! activity. Include text, pictures, video, animations, and slide transitions as appropriate to help explain your positions.

Gamer Portfolio

You have collected documents that show your skills and talents. However, some skills and talents are not shown effectively using only documents. Do you have a special talent in an area such as art, music, or design? Have you taken part in volunteer activities? Create a video to showcase your talents and activities. For example, create a video that shows your completed artist works. If you are a musician, create a video with segments from your performances. If you have taken part in a volunteer or service activity, create a video that tells viewers about it. Be sure you have permission from people to include them in your video.

1. Place the video file in an appropriate subfolder for your e-portfolio.

2. Print a few screen shots from the video. Create a document that describes the video. State that the video will be made available on request or provide a link to it online. Place the information in the container for your print portfolio.

G-W Learning Mobile Site

Visit the G-W Learning mobile site to complete the chapter pretest and posttest and to practice vocabulary using e-flash cards. If you do not have a smartphone, visit the G-W Learning companion website to access these features.

G-W Learning mobile site: www.m.g-wlearning.com

G-W Learning companion website: www.g-wlearning.com

Common Core

College and Career Readiness

CTE Career Ready Practices. The ability to read and interpret information is an important workplace skill. Presume you work for a video game design studio. The company is considering a new game on historical simulation of technology advances, but wants you to evaluate and interpret some research on historical technologies. You will need to locate three reliable sources of the latest information on historical technologies. Read and interpret the information. Then write a report summarizing your findings in an organized manner.

Reading. Many argue that piracy of video games is the cause of significant loss of revenue for video game design companies. What do you think? Research the available statistics on piracy. Do you believe that the numbers provided represent a significant problem? What ethical issues does this bring to light? As needed, derive meaning of the environmental print and use visual and contextual support to confirm understanding. Use support from classmates and your teacher as needed to help in comprehension of the material. Write a paper on your stance on these issues. Be sure to include trustworthy sources.

Writing. Using the Internet, research the advice that experts have for video game designers entering the job market. Is the advice different if you intend to work outside of the United States? Make sure to look at, among other sources, newspaper and magazine articles, scholarly reports, and public addresses from prominent figures in the field. Write a report in which you cite the sources that you used and the strengths and weaknesses of each. Be sure to consider the background and point of view of the sources that you find, as well as any bias that the author may bring to the issue.

Event Prep: Community Service Project

Many Career and Technical Student Organizations (CTSOs) competitions offer events that include a community service project. This project is usually carried out by the entire CTSO chapter and will take several months to complete. There will be two parts of the event: written and oral. The chapter will designate several members to represent the team at the competitive event. To prepare for the community service event:

1. Read the guidelines provided by your organization. Make certain that you ask any questions about points you do not understand. It is important you follow each specific item as it is outlined in the competition rules.

2. As a team, select a theme for your chapter's community service project.

3. Decide which roles are needed for the team. There may be one person who is the captain, one person who is the secretary, and other roles that will be necessary to create the plan. Ask your instructor for guidance in assigning roles to team members.

4. Identify your target audience, which may include business, school, and community groups.

5. List the benefits and opportunities of supporting a community service project.

6. This project will probably span the school year. During regular chapter meetings, create a draft of the report based on direction from the CTSO. Write and refine drafts until the final report is finished.

Glossary

3D accelerator graphics card: Hardware in the computer that controls the display and enables 3D graphics to be displayed. (6)

3ds Max: Software used to develop 3D assets. (9)

A

Accelerometer: Part of the Wii controller that reads how fast the remote moves. (6)

Action-reaction relationship: How an action causes something to change or react. (5)

Actions: How an object reacts to input or interacts with other objects. (5)

Active animation: An object changes poses while moving on the screen. (4)

Active listening skill: Allows the person speaking to know that they have been understood. (1)

Active object: Object in the game frame with which the player can interact; can be programmed. (4)

Active sounds: Sound linked to an action. (1)

Aesthetic competence: Ability to determine what is pleasing to the eye. (1)

Algorithm: A computer script that performs the steps needed to solve a problem. (5)

Alpha channel: Varies the opacity of the color from full transparency to full opacity. (4)

Ambient sounds: Sounds not related to the game action. (1)

Animation: Series of frames played in sequence with small differences between each frame that the brain interprets as motion. (4)

Application (app): Program for handheld devices and cell phones. (1)

Archetype: A standardized class of character, such as hero, shadow, mentor, herald, helper, guardian, or trickster. (8)

Array: A look up table that holds variable data. (5)

Art designer: Creates the visual elements and assets of the game. (1)

Artistry: How the visual elements of the game complement each other. (8)

Asset: Characters, objects, sounds, and visual elements of the game. (1)

Atari 2600: First commercially successful video game system (1977) for homes; allowed the owner to purchase individual game cartridges. (3)

Attributes: Characteristics associated with an object. (5)

Audio: Everything you hear. (2)

Audio engineer: Creates all sound assets. (1)

Audio/visual effects: Entertainment that can be seen or heard, but not interacted with by the observer. (2)

Authorship restriction: Allows the use of the Creative Commons work so long as you give credit to the original author or creator. (8)

Avatar: Player's online persona represented in a game. (7)

B

Backdrop: Objects in a game frame that the player can touch or walk behind, but do not damage or reward the player. (4)

Background music: Melody that sets the mood of the level. (1)

Background object: Object in the game frame with which the player cannot interact. (4)

Backstory: History of why and how the protagonist or main player is in the game situation. (1)

Backward compatibility: Older games can be played on newer game consoles. (3)

Balance: Mix of physical, mental, work, and play activities. (3)

Barrier to entry: Resources and technology used by existing firms that are difficult to obtain by others who would want to compete in the market. (6)

Barter system: System of exchanging goods or services without money. (10)

Behavioral development: Learning how to react to situations. (3)

Beta: Trial version. (10)

Bias: Opinion overemphasizing either the positive or negative attributes. (8)

Bit: Computer term for a single binary digit of 0 or 1. (3)

Bit depth: A binary measurement for color. (4)

Bitmap: Raster image file format that digitally maps the location and color of each pixel. (4)

Blitting: Combining two or more bitmaps into a single bitmap. (4)

Bluetooth: Wireless technology that relays information via radio frequency signal. (6)

Blu-Ray: High-density data disc that is read by a narrow-beam, blue laser. (6)

Board game: A portable game environment in which players use imagination to engage in mental or strategic competition. (3)

Bounding box: Invisible cube inside of which a 3D object completely fits; used as a reference to rescale the 3D object. (4)

Brain-extremity pathways: Nerve connection from the brain to movement points throughout the body. (3)

Brochure: Leave-behind document that artistically displays a game concept. (9)

Budget: Plan that details how much a project should cost. (9)

Buffering: Preloading data into a section of memory called the buffer. (4)

Bulk: Large quantities of a product. (10)

C

Cache memory: Memory modules located very close to the processor in the computer. (6)

Camera: Displays the visual play area of the game and follows the player wherever the character goes. (4)

Card games: A series of uniquely printed cards used within set rules of a game. (3)

Carpal tunnel syndrome: Condition that causes pain or tingling in the hand resulting from a pinched nerve in the wrist. (3)

Case law: Laws enacted when the first lawsuit to deal with a specific problem has been judged and an outcome determined. (8)

Casual gamers: Players that play infrequently when they have free time. (5)

Cause and effect: Relationship between what has happened and something changing or reacting. (5)

CELL processor architecture: Advanced computer processor design used in the PS3. (6)

Chance: Adds interest to a game by allowing different random results each time a game is played. (3)

Character design document: Sketches that detail the appearance, poses, and abilities of a character. (9)

Character development: Characteristics and abilities that define the protagonist. (9)

Cheat codes: Programmed shortcuts and ability codes that make the job of the game tester easier. (1)

Checkpoint: Place in a game level where the player receives additional time or other resources or the location where a respawned avatar is placed in a game level. (8)

Cinematic cut scene: Movie-like segment of a game that does not require the player to interact with any game element. (1)

Clarity: How clearly images are displayed with either line or pixel density. (4)

Cocooning: Social phenomenon where people do not interact with their physical environment. (3)

Cognitive development: Building of intelligence through learning, remembering, and problem solving. (3)

Colliding: Action command describing how objects that touch react. (5)

Collision: Condition that occurs when an object touches another object. (5)

Collision statement: Logic statement with a condition of two or more objects colliding. (5)

Collision theory: Idea that when objects collide, the movements, animations, and events must provide an illusion of reality. (5)

Color palette: Set of colors used throughout a scene to maintain mood and continuity. (4)

Commercial success: Product that makes enough of a profit to continue producing it. (3)

Communication: Relaying ideas and opinions to others. (7)

Community: Social structure in which people share and exchange ideas. (7)

Compact disc, read-only memory (CD-ROM): Provides interchangeable video games on an inexpensive plastic disc; replacement technology for the ROM game cartridges. (3)

Compatibility: When programs or languages are able to work together. (5)

Compete: To play against an opponent with a goal or victory condition to determine who is the best. (3)

Competitive advantage: Benefit to consumers that other companies do not provide. (3)

Compiler program: Software that translates simplified script or object-oriented programming into machine-readable code. (9)

Compression: Image file size reduction through the use of mathematical formulas to approximate the location and color of each pixel. (4)

Compromise: Win-win situation when everyone gets some of what they want, but maybe not all of what they want. (1)

Concept art: Sketch of the basic shape and style of a character or other object. (9)

Concept stage: First stage of the three-stage cycle; focuses on formalizing the big idea for the game. (9)

Condition: Term for the IF side of a programming line for a video game. (5)

Confidentiality agreement: A contract that states you cannot share any information about the company or its products with any other company; also referred to as non-disclosure agreement. (8)

Construction stage: Second stage of the three-stage cycle; focuses on building levels and game assets needed for the game. (9)

Constructive criticism: Provides possible improvements or solutions in a positive manner. (1)

Consumer: End user or final link in the supply chain; purchaser of goods and services. (8)

Consumer off-the-shelf (COTS) software: Retail software that can be purchased by anyone. (9)

Content descriptors: Part of a rating system; indicates elements in the game that may have triggered a particular rating. (3)

Coordinate system: Combination of X, Y, and Z values to determine a location in space. (4)

Coordination: How well your hands, feet, and eyes work together to perform a task. (3)

Copy protection: Method used to prevent unauthorized copying of a game. (8)

Copycat game: Has gameplay similar to another game already on the market. (8)

Copyrighted: Legal protection against others copying an original creation. (8)

Copyright infringement: Unauthorized copying of intellectual property. (8)

Copyright laws: Laws to protect owners of creative work. (8)

Core gamers: Players that play frequently and actively devote time to playing games. (7)

Core mechanics: Programming within the game engine to enforce the rules and the system-shall commands. (1)

Cost effective: Money spent wisely; money not wasted. (10)

Creative Commons license: Allows someone to use a creative work for free, with some restrictions. (8)

Creative director: Sets the vision and direction, selects personnel, assigns job roles, and communicates between management and the design team. (1)

Critics: Evaluate a game to provide a summary and opinion of the key elements of the game. (8)

Crunch time: Occurs at the end of a production cycle when time runs short. (9)

Currency: Money. (10)

Current customers: Those who currently own a particular type of game. (2)

Custom software: Computer applications created to perform a specific design purpose. (9)

Cut scene: Movie-like segment of a game that does not require the player to interact with any game element. (9)

D

Data structure: A way of storing and organizing data. (5)

Dead head: Return trip made after delivery when the truck is empty. (10)

Decision tree: Graphic organizer that maps out the decisions available to the player. (9)

Declared: An item is given a name and used in the program. (5)

Dedicated: Performs a special or specific function. (6)

Deep color: A color depth that uses a bit depth of 48, which produces over 1 billion colors. (4)

Delay in production: Occurs when the time schedule is not followed and the project is behind schedule. (9)

Demographics: Measurable characteristics of the potential customers. (9)

Demographic segmentation: Use of characteristics such as age, income, and gender to segment a population. (2)

Dependability: Ability to be relied upon and trusted. (1)

Derivative work: Anything that uses any part of the original. (8)

Derivative works restriction: Prohibits the use of the Creative Commons work in any other form than the original. (8)

Desensitized: Repeated exposure to an unpleasant event until it no longer results in an emotional reaction. (3)

Design documents: Standardized documents used by a design team to record all decisions and the vision of the game. (1)

Designer-centric games: A game build focused on the design process; often a commercial failure. (7)

Designer-driven games: A game build showcasing the artistic and programming skills of the game designer. (7)

Development group: First category of a supply chain; the group that makes the product. (10)

Dialogue: What characters say. (1)

Digital toy: Electronic toy with few structured rules or no clear victory condition. (2)

Digital video disc (DVD): Similar to a CD-ROM or music CD, but can hold much more information. (3)

Digital watermark: Dull spot on the image or words typed over the image that shows up on any unauthorized copy. (8)

Direct marketing: Selling directly to the end user, cutting out the wholesaler, middleman, and retailer. (10)

DirectX: All-inclusive game development tool from Microsoft. (9)

Discount: Reduction in the cost per unit. (10)

Dithering: Computer process of scattering pixels of different colors to approximate a true color. (4)

Division of labor: Each team member does the job that they can do the best and is assigned jobs that favor their strengths. (1)

Dots per inch (dpi): Number of pixels per square inch; the higher the dpi, the clearer the picture. (4)

Draw: The computer displaying images on the screen. (4)

Dynamic: How the strengths and weaknesses of each team member work together to create a balanced team. (1)

E

Eight areas of design: Critical areas of design that are refined through the iterative process. (9)

Elegant: The term for an algorithm that is the simplest, smallest, and most efficient computer code to perform all the functions needed. (5)

E-mail blast: Mass electronic mailing sent to potential customers who want to learn more about a company's products. (10)

Emulator: Simulated game environment that has a look-alike and play-alike feel of the original game environment. (6)

End user: Consumer or last person in a supply chain. (10)

End user license agreement (EULA): Set of rules that every member must agree to before using software. (7)

Entertainment Software Rating Board (ESRB): Nonprofit, self-regulatory body that assigns age and content ratings for computer video games, enforces industry-adopted advertising guidelines, and helps ensure responsible online privacy practices for the interactive entertainment software industry. (3)

Ergonomics: Study of how the body works and how humans interact with tools and environments. (1)

Event: Term for the THEN side of a programming line for a video game. (5)

Exclusive right: Allows the creative work to be used or reproduced by the person purchasing the labor. (8)

Experimental media: Technology and entertainment that is new and cutting edge; used by a small group of people. (2)

F

Faces: Flat surfaces on a 3D model. (4)

Fad: Product with a very short life cycle. (8)

Fair Use/Fair Dealings doctrine: Allows the use of a work without permission from the creator under a very strict guideline; for the purpose of describing or reviewing the creative work. (8)

Fight or flight: Reaction of a person to stress whereby they choose to confront or run away from the problem. (7)

First playable level: First milestone of the game build whereby an entire level has been programmed in playable fashion. (9)

First-person perspective: Gameplay view where the player sees through the eyes of the character. (4)

Five essential questions: Must be answered by a designer to help plan how the concept will be implemented. (9)

Five-star rating system: Visual rating system for the key elements of a game. (8)

Flash memory: Memory chip that retains stored information even when power is turned off. (6)

Flickering: Visible flashes on the screen when the refresh rate is too low and portions of the screen are not being illuminated quickly enough and black (non-illuminated) pixels show. (4)

Floats: Numbers with decimals. (5)

Flowchart: Graphic organizer that displays instructions to be programmed for the game interactions. (5)

Focus group: Small group of people who are shown game scenes or who play a portion of a game and then are asked their opinion. (7)

Frame rate: How many times per second a new frame is displayed. (4)

Full articulation: All of a character's body parts can move through a range of motion in a realistic manner. (4)

Functionality: Testing that focuses on whether the game plays and delivers as intended. (9)

G

Game: Activity defined by rules with an objective, goal, or victory condition; it involves a game environment that enables play or pretending. (2)

Game addicts: People who cannot stop playing games. (7)

Game Boy: Handheld device released by Nintendo in 1989 with 8-bit processor and interchangeable ROM cartridges. (3)

Game build: All effort needed to construct a game from concept to finished product. (1)

Game designer: Establishes the rules of the game, finalizes the design documents, and ensures the game will work as envisioned. (1)

Game-development tools: Hardware and software used to streamline and simplify the game-design process. (9)

Game engine: The programming platform used to create and run a game. (1)

Game environment: Setting altered or designed to play a specific activity. (3)

Game frame: All items programmed for a complete scene or level of a game. (4)

Game script document: Details core interactions with the game as defined by the general rules and core mechanics instructions. (9)

Game tester: Person who tests every part of the game for proper operation. (1)

Game treatment document: Pitch documents that summarize major game features such as the concept, story outline, character, and art. (9)

Game world: Setting in which gameplay takes place. (1)

Game writer: Creates character depth and interaction. (1)

Gameplay: What the player experiences during the game as a result of the core mechanics and structure of the game. (2)

Gameplay modes: Different game segments that change the way the game plays or how the challenges are presented. (2)

Game-specific controllers: Game controllers that can only be used for a specific game, like a guitar controller for *Rock Band*. (3)

Gamut: The portion of all the available colors that can be reproduced by a device. (4)

Gantt chart: Displays the timeline for completion for each task needed by each department and employee. (1)

Generation 1: First series of video games and systems; available to consumers in the early 1970s. (3)

Generation 2: Began in the mid-1970s when home video games became popular and could be played on an interchangeable-cartridge platform. (3)

Generation 3: Began in the mid-1980s and featured home video game computer systems with 8-bit processors that could process better movement, graphics, and sound. (3)

Generation 4: Began in the late 1980s and featured computer game systems with 16-bit processors that led to improved game graphics. (3)

Generation 5: Began in the mid-1990s; introduced 32- and 64-bit game systems with advancements in computer technology and game storage. (3)

Generation 6: Began in the early 2000s; featured 64- and 128-bit game systems, DVD-ROM technology, and realistic 3D movement. (3)

Generation 7: Began in the mid-2000s; introduced multicore processor game systems and new user interfaces; featured immersive gameplay and online play. (3)

Genre: Type or major category of games featuring similar gameplay. (2)

Geodesic sphere: A 3D model created with faces of regular polygons, like a soccer ball. (4)

Geometry: Field of math dealing with shapes. (1)

Glitch: Programming error within a game. (1)

Global: A sub routine or variable that works everywhere in the program. (5)

Globalization: Involving multiple countries in production, distribution, and purchases. (10)

Governing game design document (GGDD): Master collection of design documents used to record information needed for each decision made for the project. (9)

Graphics: Visual images seen on the display screen. (6)

Graphical user interface (GUI): Point-and-click user interface displaying applications and functions as icons. (9)

Green light: Approval to move forward with a project. (9)

H

Hand-eye coordination: Ability to move your hand in response to a viewed object of action. (3)

Hard skills: Technical requirements for a job obtained through training and research. (1)

Hierarchy: Structural organization of a company to streamline decision making. (1)

High concept document: Used to introduce the idea or concept of a game and answer the five essential questions; a résumé for the game. (9)

Hybrid: Created by combining features from two different items. (4)

I

Imagination: Creating a picture in your mind of something that does not exist. (1)

Immersion: Degree to which a player connects to the game world. (1)

Immersion strategies: Game elements that connect the player to the action in the game world. (1)

Indie developer: Independent game makers and independent, non-mainstream firms. (1)

Initiative: Taking on additional responsibilities without being asked. (1)

Integers: Positive and negative real whole numbers. (5)

Intellectual property: Product that is an original creation. (8)

Interactivity: How one object behaves in relation to the objects around it. (5)

Interdisciplinary team: Composed of many members with different hard skill strengths working toward the same goal. (1)

Internal producer (IP): Responsible for ensuring the design objectives required by the production group are achieved by the design group. (1)

Interpolation: When resizing an image, the computer makes a decision to create a blended-color pixel where original pixels are moved. (4)

Intuitive controls: User interface device that requires no explanation of how to use it. (8)

Iteration: A single run through a programming loop. (5)

Iteration: Different version of the same game build with increasingly more refinement. (9)

Iterative process: Process by which a basic prototype game is built and improved through many improved versions until the final version is perfected. (9)

L

Labor-cost differential: Difference in labor rates between different geographic locations. (10)

Lamp: Imaginary bright spot in a game that projects virtual light in a single direction. (6)

LAN party: Players meet at a location and connect their machines to a local area network (LAN) to play an online game. (3)

Laser burn: Burned spot on an optical disc that occurs when the disc gets too close to the laser or the disc stops spinning allowing the laser to stay in the same place for too long. (6)

Lead artist: Manages the art designer and the workflow needed to create all game assets. (1)

Lead designer: Day-to-day leader of the design team. (1)

Leave-behind document: Pitch documents left with the publisher for them to look over after you leave. (9)

Level design: Programming all interactions needed to take a protagonist through each level of the story. (9)

Level designer: Interprets the design documents to create a game world and interactions for a single game level. (1)

Library: Where game objects preloaded into The Games Factory 2 are stored. (5)

Licensing agreement: Provides third-party designers the rights to obtain the game source code for a specific system. (3)

Light gun: User interface that senses the direction the gun is pointed and interacts with objects on a cathode ray tube television.(3)

Linden dollar (L$): Credits issued to online *Second Life* players that can be exchanged for actual currency. (7)

Linear sequence: Story is presented in a straight line whereby the player must complete objectives or levels in a set order. (8)

Liquidate: To sell quickly, even if taking a loss; to recoup some of the money spent on the original purchase. (10)

Listener: Programming that directs the computer to check or listen for a mouse click, key press, or other input from the user. (5)

Listening skills: Understanding the points and opinions spoken by others. (1)

Loading: Transferring data from one location (i.e., the Internet or a CD-ROM) to another. (4)

Local: A subroutine or variable that does not have persistence outside of the module in which it was declared. (5)

Logic statement: **IF** and **THEN** programming to determine an action/reaction relationship in a game. (6)

Longevity: Length of time a game will continue to be popular and produced with new versions. (8)

Lossless: Image compression algorithm that compresses the image and keeps perfect clarity when uncompressed. (4)

Lossy: Image compression algorithm that compresses the image but does not keep perfect clarity when uncompressed. (4)

M

Machine code: A binary language that consists of only two characters, 0 and 1. (5)

Mainstream media: Technology and entertainment that is popular at the time, accepted by most people, and generally a part of everyday life. (2)

Manufacturer's suggested retail price (MSRP): Selling price set by the product manufacturer. (10)

Mark up: Additional amount added to unit cost to represent per-unit profit potential. (10)

Market analysis document: Details the target market and sales projections for a proposed game. (9)

Market-driven design: Making a game based on research of what the target market is looking to buy. (7)

Market research: Activities done to determine the population's likes and dislikes about a product. (7)

Market share: Percentage of the total market in terms of unit sales held by a single company or product. (6)

Marketing effort: Time, energy, and expense undertaken to promote a product. (2)

Marketing tools: Any device or action that draws attention to a product. (2)

Masking color: A single shade of a color that can be set to be transparent. (4)

Massively multiplayer online (MMO) games: Interactive games that involve thousands of people playing the same game, each with an avatar, connecting to the game server over the Internet. (7)

Master: Original, finished version of a program from which all other copies are made. (10)

Medium: Physical object on which information is stored. (2)

Members: People who join and contribute to a community. (7)

Mental acuity: Person's learning, problem-solving, and reasoning ability. (3)

Mesh: A 3D shape created with interconnecting polygons stuck together along their edges. (4)

Methods: The actions or verbs used in syntax; sub routines. (5)

Middleman: Special wholesaler that sells small and mixed lots to retailers. (10)

Mixed-unit sale: Combination pack that contains a few different items. (10)

Mock-up: Simple objects, like paper or note cards, used to act out a scene for testing the rules and designing the core mechanics. (9)

Mode elaboration: Addition of secondary gameplay modes for better immersion and storytelling. (9)

Model: Three-dimensional asset. (1)

Model sheet: Refined detailed sketches that show the character in multiple poses, dress, and emotional expressions. (9)

Modules: Separate units of programming that perform one function and contain all the information needed to execute that function. (5)

Mosaic: Differently shaped and colored geometric pieces assembled to create the illusion of a single image. (4)

Motion-based controllers: User interface that allows the player to move in real space with the action in the game environment. (3)

Motion picture: Movie delivered on film, video, or DVD. (2)

Motor skills: Combination of hand-eye coordination, muscle memory, and brain-extremity pathways to make movements appear smooth. (3)

Motor skills development: Learning to control muscles to perform necessary tasks. (3)

Movement sets: The movements of a single sprite character included on a single sprite sheet. (4)

Multitask: Doing more than one thing at a time. (7)

Muscle memory: How the muscles in the body remember practiced movements. (3)

N

Nanometers: Measurement equal to 1/1,000,000,000th of a meter. (6)

Narrative writing: Creating a story. (1)

Native poles: Original pixels of an object before it was resized. (4)

Navigation: How the player moves in the game world and how the game aids the player in locating objectives and obstacles. (8)

Negative bias: Opinion that emphasizes negative attributes. (8)

Newbs: New players. (7)

Niche market: Very small or narrow market segment. (6)

Nintendo Entertainment System (NES): Began selling in 1985 and dominated the home system market at that time. (3)

Non-Compete Agreement: A contract that states you cannot open your own studio or work for a competing company for a certain period of time—usually six months or a year. (8)

Non-disclosure agreement: A contract that states you cannot share any information about the company or its products with any other company; also referred to as confidentiality agreement. (8)

O

Objects: Definition sub routines that are defined by their attributes and properties. (5)

Obsolete: Something that no longer performs a valuable task. (2)

Online account service: Similar to a bank account that holds money, but which also can trade monetary credits. (7)

Online play: Players connect via the Internet to compete with other players. (3)

Optical disk drive (ODD): Type of optical disc used by Nintendo that is similar to a DVD. (6)

Original creation: Something original from someone's mind or intellect. (8)

Outside producer (OP): Responsible for making game discs and packaging. (1)

Outsourcing: Contracting part of the production or marketing to other companies with specific skills or lower cost than the producing company. (10)

Over budget: Spending more money than has been allocated for a project. (1)

Overhead expenses: General expenses associated with being in business. (10)

Overhead view: Shows the character and surroundings from a perspective high overhead. (4)

P

Packaging: Outer wrapping that protects the product from damage and provides printed information about the product. (10)

Parallax: Describes how objects in the distance seem to move slower than objects in the foreground. (4)

Parallel processing: Performing two or more computer operations at the same time. (6)

Patent: Issued by the government patent office to protect the rights of designers. (3)

PC gaming: Playing games on a personal computer instead of a dedicated game console. (6)

Performance: How well a game operates on the game system. (8)

Persistence: Something that continues to exist after the event that caused it has ended. (5)

Perspective: How the gameplay is displayed on screen and the position of the player within the game. (4)

Physical dexterity: Skill or ability at performing physical tasks. (3)

Physical trials: Competitions featuring athletic abilities as the basis in determining the winner. (3)

Physics: Science of matter and energy. (1)

Physics engine: Uses mathematical formulas to create rules for movement, gravity, speed, flight, path of a projectile, and other game movements. (1)

Piracy: Illegal copying and distribution of video games. (10)

Pitch documents: Documents that present or sell a game idea to the decision makers. (9)

Pits: Grooves that hold data on an optical disc, like a CD, DVD, or Blu-Ray disc. (6)

Pixel: Picture element; the smallest point or dot of color a computer screen can generate (4)

Pixelated: Condition resulting in a blurry image; created by improper resizing. (4)

Pixel shading: Applying the principle of visual perspective such that as you move farther from the light source, things get darker. (4)

Place: Actual location of a purchase, such as a store or online. (10)

Platform view: Shows the character in profile and a side view of all obstacles. (4)

Play: Participation in an entertainment activity. (3)

Playability testing: Type of testing that determines whether the story is completely told, the game holds true to the concept, and the objectives are attainable. (9)

Player-centric design: Game built focused on what the player wants to experience in the game. (7)

Player economy: How players receive money for playing whereby fees paid for monthly access are redistributed back to the players to establish an economy. (7)

Player interactions: What the player is doing and how the items and characters the player engages respond. (8)

Play objects: Non-real or fake objects used in play. (7)

PlayStation: A 32-bit video game system from Sony that used CD-ROM technology. (3)

PlayStation 3 (PS3): Generation 7 video game console manufactured by Sony. (6)

Plot: Main storyline of a game. (8)

Poker: Popular card game with several variations. (3)

Poly count: Number of polygons used to make a 3D object. (4)

Ported: Video game source code translated to work on a different video game system. (3)

Portfolio: Set of high-quality examples of work. (10)

Porting: Converting computer code from one system to work on a different system. (6)

Positive attitude: Outlook on a situation that emphasizes an upbeat outcome. (1)

Potential customer: Anyone willing and able to buy your product. (2)

Presentation folder: Quality example of the designer's work used to present a new game concept. (9)

Price: Amount of money required to purchase a product or service. (10)

Price competition: When retailers offer lower prices to attract buyers. (10)

Primary gameplay mode: What the player must achieve as the main goal of the game or level. (9)

Probability: Math dealing with random numbers and possible outcomes. (1)

Product: Item sold and purchased. (10)

Production group: Second category of a supply chain; adds value to a product by completing the manufacturing and preparing the product in the final packaged form. (10)

Professional dress: Clothing appropriate for the workplace or events. (1)

Professional game testers: Play and test a game and note all glitches and imperfections before it is released to the public. (9)

Project manager: Coordinates all lead managers and ensures all project components are on task and well-managed. (1)

Promotion: Marketing effort used to generate interest in a product. (10)

Properties: Attributes assigned to an object, such as visibility, interactivity, and movement. (5)

Proprietary game: Designed to play only on a single manufacturer's game console. (3)

Protagonist: Main character of the game around whom the plot is designed. (9)

Prototype: Basic, first version of a game build used to test the concept. (9)

Provider economy: How the game manufacturer obtains money for its games and services. (7)

Pseudo code: Logic statements not written in computer code that allow programmers to break down program interactions into logical steps prior to converting the code into a computer language. (5)

Public domain: Removes any and all copyrights on the work as the term covered for copyright has expired. (8)

Public opinion: General view shared by a majority of a population. (7)

Punctuality: Being on time. (1)

Purpose of play: Reason for playing. (7)

Puzzles: Require the player to mentally analyze and solve a problem. (3)

Q

Quality assurance (QA) tester: Game tester; tests every part of the game for proper operation and reports bugs for repair. (1)

Quality of rules: How well the rules are explained to the user and enforced during gameplay. (8)

R

Radio: Wireless audio medium broadcast over distances; entertainment media. (2)

Random-access memory flash: Memory chip that can be written to and read from. (6)

Random-number generator: Any device used to create a number at random within a given range of numbers. (3)

Raster images: Images that are made of pixels. (4)

Rating symbols: Suggest age appropriateness for a game; found on the front of game packages. (3)

Reading edge: Line between two vertices on a 3D object that is used as a reference to rescale the object. (4)

Red ring of death: Colloquial phrase for a broken Xbox 360 that displays a red ring around the power button. (6)

Reflex: Quick, involuntary movement. (3)

Refresh rate: The rate of how many times per second (Hz) the screen is refreshed. (4)

Regional warehouse: Storage building located in a section of the country that stores the product for later distribution to the surrounding local area. (10)

Relative: In relation to the position of an object. (5)

Render: Adding color and shading to represent a solid object. (4)

Rental game market: Companies that buy games and rent them to the end users. (10)

Research: Process of looking for and finding information. (1)

Respect for others: Belief that the opinions and views of others are important. (1)

Respect for self: Belief that you are important. (1)

Responsibility: Ability to make sure an assigned task is successfully completed. (1)

Résumé: Document that summarizes a person's education, job experiences, and skills. (10)

Retail distribution: Stage in the supply chain where a product is sold directly to the consumer via a retail outlet. (10)

Return marketing: Allows a consumer to trade a used game for cash or credit at a retailer. (10)

Reverse engineering: Process of deconstructing an existing game to understand how it works. (8)

Reward: Something positive provided to the player for taking a risk. (8)

Reward-conditioning behavior: Becoming accustomed to receiving rewards for an activity motivates one to continue the activity to continue receiving the rewards. (7)

Role-playing games (RPGs): Allow for very deep immersion as players assume a character and play the role. (3)

ROM cartridge: Read-only memory chip in a plastic case that stored the game program. (3)

Royal Game of Ur: One of the earliest known board games; played similar to backgammon. (3)

Royalty: Percentage of the unit selling price paid to the original developer. (10)

RPG: Role playing game; player takes on the role of the questing hero. (1)

Rules: Constraints that determine what actions can happen in a game. (2)

S

Scale: Proportional change in the dimensions of an object. (4)

Scene: Objects on a game frame that create an attractive layout, obstacles, and objectives to convey story and mood. (4)

Scope: see *Visible Display Area.* (4)

Scrolling: Game frame is moved so the player is always in the visible play area. (4)

Scrum methodology: Tasks are assigned to small teams whereby all team members work toward the same goal. (1)

Secondary gameplay mode: Other objectives or activities the player completes for additional rewards. (9)

Second-person perspective: Player sees the game as if the player were an opponent or intermediary; rarely used in video games. (4)

Sega Genesis: First successful 16-bit video game console (1989); featured improved graphics, colors, and movement in 2D. (3)

Sequence: The predetermined order of steps the computer program will follow. (5)

Sight study: Observing a person playing a game. (7)

Six-axis controller: Interface device for the Sony PlayStation that allows the player to shake or twist the controller to input some commands. (3)

Skill differential: Specialized skills needed to complete a task or job are present more in one location than another. (10)

Smaller-unit sale: Purchasing from a middleman in amounts less than a full box. (10)

Social interactive: Multiplayer online game that focuses on having different people in an online environment where custom avatars are created to talk to each other, trade ideas, and share interests. (7)

Socializing: Interacting in a group environment. (3)

Social networking: Online environment designed to allow people to communicate with each other. (7)

Soft skills: Personal qualities and behaviors that help create better personal and interpersonal relationships. (1)

Software key code: Unlocks game software to allow one, and only one, installation. (8)

Soul of the game: Central component that makes the game come alive and become important to the player. (7)

Source code: Underlying game creation code. (3)

Spam: Unwanted and untargeted e-mail. (10)

Specialist: Possesses strong hard skill attributes and unique strengths, often achieved through special training. (1)

Speed of development: How quickly a game can be built. (9)

Sponsor: Company that pays to advertise on a website. (7)

Spreadsheets: Organization of numbers and data in tables or charts; often computerized. (1)

Sprite: Two-dimensional asset. (1)

Sprite character set: Collection of poses for a single 2D asset. (4)

Sprite sheets: A single bitmap image of all the frames of animation for a sprite movement. (4)

Stage: The visible portion of the game map. (4)

Static animation: Object retains its original pose while moving. (4)

Status: Level or rating of a player's avatar. (7)

Statutory laws: The group of laws that have been passed by legislature. (8)

Steps: How many iterations occur per second. (5)

Stereotype: Opinion that all members of a group of people have the same characteristics; usually considered a negative. (3)

Storyboard: Sketch of the important game frames with general ideas for motion, traps, and rewards. (1)

Story elaboration: Developing the concept to put together all pieces of the story. (9)

String: A series of letters, numbers, or punctuation. (5)

Structure: The syntax and logic structure of the programming language. (5)

Substitute product: Game designed to play and entertain in the same way as another game. (8)

Super Nintendo: A 16-bit game console introduced in 1991 and using a ROM cartridge system. (3)

Supply chain: How a product moves from raw materials to the end user. (10)

Survey: Questions about a product used to get a clear picture of what the public wants. (7)

Synergistic processing elements (SPE): Small processors used in CELL architecture to enable parallel processing. (6)

Syntax: Words and symbols and their arrangement. (5)

System operations: How information is transported between the parts of the user interface, computer system, and video display. (6)

System-shall command: A statement that tells what the system is allowed to do. (9)

T

Target market: Segment of the population determined to be the most likely potential customers. (2)

Target marketing: Advertising to a specific segment of the population. (10)

Tarot cards: Playing cards common in the late 1300s. (3)

Tearing: Occurs when video frames are out of sync or are only getting partially refreshed. (4)

Technical design document: Details the computer codes, event codes, and technical interactions between the user interface and core mechanics. (9)

Technical writing: Creating documents that give directions for the steps and processes needed in design. (1)

Technological superiority: A clear benefit from using higher technology. (9)

Technology competence: Ability to understand and use the current computer/game platforms and programming/script languages. (1)

Technology-driven games: Focus on implementing the newest technology. (7)

Technology transfer: How experimental gaming technology is later used in mainstream products. (6)

Television: Wireless broadcasts of sound and images. (2)

Tessellate: Stretching of a color and texture map to apply a piece of the overall texture to each polygon of a 3D mesh. (4)

Testing and debugging: Stage of construction focusing on finding the problems within a game. (9)

Theater: Performance by actors to tell a story. (2)

Themed board game: Board games with a central theme. (3)

Themes: Subcategory of a genre. (2)

Third-party providers: Manufacturers licensed by the game console manufacturer to make games for that system. (3)

Third-person perspective: Gameplay is viewed by a person who is not the player's character or opponent, rather a neutral third person; spectator view. (4)

Three-dimensional (3D) game: Game with 3D characters and 3D background objects that presents gameplay in a simulated three-dimensional environment. (4)

Three-stage production process: Production cycle with stages of concept, construction, and tuning. (9)

Tile sets: Standard sized tiles arranged next to each other on a single sheet as a single bitmap image. (4)

Time-sensitive issues: Important reasons why the final game must not be delivered late. (9)

Trade-in: When a consumer takes a used video game to a store in exchange for cash or credit. (10)

Trigger: Programming for when a condition is met that a series of actions will begin. (5)

Trigonometry: Field of math dealing with angles and curves. (1)

Triple A: Most popular and well-funded games. (10)

True color: A color depth that uses a bit depth of 24, which produces 16,777,216 colors. (4)

Tuning stage: Final stage in game design where the game is tested for functionality and playability. (9)

Two and one-half–dimensional (2.5D) games: Gameplay with two-dimensional background graphics, but which use three-dimensional characters and obstacles. (4)

Two-dimensional (2D) games: Gameplay with characters and backgrounds that play in only two dimensions: length and width. (4)

U

Unbiased: Opinion that fairly evaluates both negative and positive attributes. (8)

Unified shader: GPU attempts to move the vertices and shade pixels at the same time through the same processor. (6)

Unique selling point (USP): Special feature one product offers that other similar products do not possess. (2)

Unit cost: Value of a single item found by dividing the total cost of the bulk purchase by the number of units purchased. (10)

Uplink: Connecting a single computer or small network to another larger network. (10)

Used video game market: Consumers make their unwanted video games available for resale. (10)

User interface (UI): Controls used by the player to interact within the game. (1)

User interface designer: Creates the controls used by the player to interact with the game. (1)

User reviews: Comments about a game from a game player. (8)

UV sphere: Rounded 3D model created with trapezoidal segments that vary in size to create a round shape that is later wrapped with a 2D image to provide texture. (4)

V

Value added: Benefit in price, product, promotion, or place added to a product as it travels down the supply chain to the end user. (10)

Vanishing point: Point in the background where the edges of all assets will meet at a single point if extended; the faraway point where an object seems to disappear as it becomes smaller. (4)

Variable: Small information storage containers. (5)

Vector: A physics term that means direction. (5)

Vector image: An image composed of lines, curves, and fills; they do not store the color value and location of each pixel—each pixel is assigned a color as the vector image is drawn. (4)

Vertex: Single point on a 3D model where the corners of adjacent faces meet. (4)

Vertices: Plural of vertex. (4)

Victory condition: What is required to successfully complete or win the game. (2)

Video game: Electronic software product that has all the elements of a game; played by combining a computer-generated game environment with a video graphic display and a user interface. (1)

Video game addiction: Psychological disorder in which a person feels that they have to play video games all of the time. (7)

Video game arcade: Variety of coin-operated video games gathered in one location and offered to the public at a price per play. (3)

Video game designer: Possesses a set of physical and mental skills needed to complete design tasks. (1)

Video game tournament: Competition to see who is the best player or team of players for a specific game. (10)

Virtual light source: Imaginary lamp in a scene that projects light in a single direction to cause light/dark shades on objects and cast shadows for the illusion of depth. (6)

Virtual reality: Complex user interface that reads body motion and displays it in the game world. (2)

Virtual world: Imaginary world created by a video game. (1)

Visible play area: The part of the game frame that is displayed on the video screen. (4)

Visual: Able to be seen. (2)

Visual perspective: Sense of depth using shading and narrowing to represent the third dimension of depth on a two-dimensional screen. (4)

Voice-overs: Spoken words used for dialogue and narration during the game. (1)

W

Walkthroughs: Instructions on what needs to be done to complete a game or level. (8)

Wholesaler: Buys in bulk, warehouses products for convenient delivery, and sells to retailers and other wholesalers in smaller bulk. (10)

Wii: Generation 7 game console manufactured by Nintendo; featured the introduction of the motion-based controller. (3)

Wii remotes: Motion-based controllers used by the Nintendo Wii; nicknamed Wiimote. (6)

Win-win solution: Compromise or decision where both parties win. (1)

Wireframe: View showing objects as if they are built with wire with visible edges and invisible faces. (4)

Workaholics: People who work too much and have some of the highest levels of stress. (7)

World design document: Displays and lists the items needed to create the game world. (9)

X

Xbox: First game console produced by Microsoft; became a major player in the market. (6)

Xbox 360: Generation 7 video game console manufactured by Microsoft. (3)

XNA: Game developer tool available through Microsoft Visual Studio for game developers making Xbox 360 or PC games. (9)

Index

DirectX, 331
Dirt Bike, 121
discount, 352
Disney animation, 155
dithering, 129
division of labor, 44
Doom, 99
dots per inch (dpi), 127
double buffering, 135–136
DO UNTIL command, 187
DO WHILE command, 187
draw, 138
Dungeons and Dragons, 89
DVD, 101
dynamic, 19

E

economy,
    early, 342
    globalization, 366–371
Editor toolbar, 196
education, 370–371
eight areas of design, 306
ELSE operator, 170
e-mail blast, 346
employment, seeking, 371
emulation, 99
emulator, 227
end user (consumer), 342,
        362–364
end user license agreement
        (EULA), 263
Entertainment Software Rating
        Board (ESRB), 106
ergonomics, 38
Ethical Gamer, 32, 61, 86, 133,
        193, 208, 260, 285, 321,
        343
evaluation,
    artistry, 289
    gameplay, 288–289
    key game elements, 286–294
    longevity in design and
        structure, 289–290
    navigation, 287
    performance, 288
    player interactions, 290

plot, 291–292
quality of rules, 286
reward, 292–293
summarizing, 293–294
user interface, 287
event, 171
evolution of the game, 79–115
    computers changed the
        game, 105–106
    early play, 80–85
    game immersion, 89
    game licensing, 105
    games for personal
        development, 90–93
    intellectual competition,
        85–88
    video game beginnings,
        93–104
    video game ratings, 106–108
exclusive right, 279
experimental media, 54

F

faces, 147
fad, 289
fair use/fair dealings doctrine,
        281
Fashion Star, 356
fight or flight, 255
first-person perspective, 118
first playable level, 314
five essential questions, 304
five-star rating, 293
Flash-based games, 331
flash memory, 228
flickering, 136
floats, 186
FLOPS, 209
flowchart, 190–192
    and storyboards, 325–326
focus group, 243
FOR command, 187
formal design structure, 302–319
    concept stage, 304–305
    construction stage, 305–316
    tuning stage, 316–319
frame rate, 135

Frogger, 122
full articulation, 144
functionality, 316

G

game, 60–61
    definition, 60
    gameplay modes, 61
    rules, 60
game addiction, 257–262
Game Boy, 63, 98
game build, 35
game design, five basic stages,
        304
game designer, 36
game-development tools,
        327–332
    asset building, 329–332
    COTS, 328–329
    custom software, 328
game engine, 22
game environment, 84
game frame, 140
game immersion, 89
game licensing, 105
gameplay, 61, 288–289
gameplay modes, 61, 306–307
game programmer, 194
games, types of, 64–65
game-script document, 323, 327
game-specific controllers, 104
game tester, 44
game-treatment document,
        321–322
game world, 22, 308–309
game writers, 41
gamut, 132
Gantt chart, 35
generation 1, 94–96
generation 2, 96–97
generation 3, 97–98
generation 4, 99
generation 5, 100–101
generation 6, 101–102
generation 7, 102–104, 206–207
generation 8, 104
genre, 64